Praise for Lessons
FROM THE | Top

"In *Lessons from the Top*, Citrin and Neff have gone right to the source – the CEOs themselves – to determine why successful companies are successful. The writing is crisp. The insights are clear. And managers everywhere can benefit."

– HENRY SCHACHT,
RETIRED CHAIRMAN & CEO,
LUCENT TECHNOLOGIES

"We tend to mystify the reasons for corporate success. Citrin and Neff distill what leads to business mastery to its essence and in the process, identify who the great leaders are. A truly groundbreaking book."

– RAJAT GUPTA,
MANAGING DIRECTOR,
McKINSEY WORLDWIDE

"*Lessons from the Top* is a book full of insights and ideas from our country's top executives. There are numerous lessons to be learned by reading how each CEO operates within their very competitive global ⬚ ⬚ ch should be read by anyone ⬚

– HEN⬚
FOUND⬚
KOHLBERG KRAVIS ROBERTS & CO.

Lessons

FROM THE Top

The 50 Most Successful Business Leaders in America—and What You Can Learn from Them

Lessons
FROM THE
Top

Thomas J. Neff & James M. Citrin

WITH PAUL B. BROWN

CURRENCY ▼ DOUBLEDAY

New York London Toronto Sydney Auckland

A CURRENCY BOOK

PUBLISHED BY DOUBLEDAY
a division of Random House, Inc.
1540 Broadway, New York, New York, 10036

CURRENCY and DOUBLEDAY are
trademarks of Doubleday, a division of Random House, Inc.

Lessons from the Top was originally published in hardcover by Currency in 1999.

Book design by Bonnie Leon-Berman

The Library of Congress has cataloged the hardcover edition as:

Neff, Thomas J.
Lessons from the top: the search for America's best business leaders /
Thomas J. Neff & James M. Citrin.—1st ed.
p.   cm.
Includes index.
1. Leadership.   2. Executive ability.   3. Success in business.
4. Management.   I. Citrin, James.   II. Title.
HD57.7.N44   1999
658.4'092—dc21   99-21724
CIP

ISBN 0-385-49344-4

1   3   5   7   9   10   8   6   4   2

To Sally, David, Mark, Scott, Brooke, and Bailey
—TJN

To Gail, Teddy, Oliver, and Lily—the joys of my life
—JMC

CONTENTS

PART III
Lessons Learned
353

Appendices
389

Introduction to the Paperback Edition

IN APRIL 1997, WE CAME UP WITH AN IDEA. IN NOVEMBER OF that same year, after extensive research and outlining, we formed an agreement with Doubleday to turn our idea into a book. Over the course of 1998, we conducted interviews with the 50 leaders who were the most accomplished and inspiring individuals in American business. In January 1999, we submitted our manuscript, and in August 1999, *Lessons from the Top* became a reality.

From Labor Day to Thanksgiving, 1999, we hit the road to talk about the book. During this period, we were hosted on approximately 50 different radio shows, had over 25 television appearances, were interviewed by over 30 different newspapers and magazines, did a dozen or so Barnes & Noble and other book signings, and led classes at business schools at the University of San Francisco, Harvard, and Wharton. Most important, we joined our Spencer Stuart colleagues in hosting client events to talk about the book in Houston, Dallas, New York, Chicago, Atlanta, San Francisco, Toronto, Montreal, and even Rio de Janeiro, Brazil. What an experience!

We had been hopeful that in *Lessons From the Top*, we had discovered some important findings and tried to package them in a highly readable way. But we were honestly overwhelmed by the positive reaction to our book, both the profiles themselves and principles of leadership and success that we synthesized. Our model, "Doing The Right Things Right," seemed to provide a touchstone for managers at all levels—both inside and outside the business world.

A couple of anecdotes illustrate the range of reactions.

Shortly after the book was released, we received a fax from the office of the Chairman of General Electric. We were copied on one of the famous hand-written notes by Jack Welch. This particular note was addressed to C. Michael Armstrong, the Chairman of AT&T, and it read as follows:

> *Dear Mike,*
> *Your quote on page 36 of* Lessons from the Top *is one of the best I've ever read. I'm going to use it shamelessly! Nice going,*
> *Jack*

This episode showed us several enlightening things. First, that Jack Welch, hailed by *Fortune* magazine as the Manager of the Twentieth Century, is always on the lookout to learn from others—itself a key trait of successful people. Second, it also demonstrates Welch's keen commercial sense. Always customer-focused, Jack Welch looks for every opportunity to strengthen General Electric's corporate relationships. Do you think this little correspondence had a subtle impact on the institutional relationship between GE and AT&T?

In addition to the impact of the book among American corporate titans, we also had rewarding feedback from managers, entrepreneurs, venture capitalists, and even people outside of business. One particular conversation bears mention. One of the Lower School teachers at New Canaan Country School in Connecticut told us that she had purchased a copy of *Lessons from the Top* as a gift for her brother, a businessperson. But after thumbing through it and reading some of the profiles, she became captivated by the fact that the themes, such as leading by example, taking risks, and supporting others, were precisely the same lessons that she had long tried to instill in her youngsters. She ended up keeping the book and never gave it to her brother.

Another unexpected piece of feedback was receiving The Motley Fool's Jester Award, bestowed upon the best business book each month by the popular investment web site. They called the book "the most comprehensive series of insights from the world's most important leaders" and cited "the productive interplay between qualitative and quantitative criteria for what constitutes the best business leaders." Most ambitiously, The Motley Fool picked up on something that we never thought about—considering the book somewhat of a time capsule for the end of the twentieth century. "A fascinating byproduct of *Lessons from the Top* is the creation of a remarkable historical document of the challenges that have faced U.S. and worldwide businesses in the second half of the twentieth century, as well as a record of the strategies employed by those who have prevailed in their respective industries."

So as the hardcover edition has been through nine printings and is now being published in local-language editions in Brazil, Germany, Spain,

China, Japan, Korea, the United Kingdom, and other countries in the works, we are truly grateful for all the time that readers have given to the book.

Transitions

Of course, a lot has changed in the world since the beginning of 1999, when we submitted our original manuscript. Many transitions with companies and their leaders have occurred. And with the passage to the new millennium, the Internet economy has skyrocketed and come back to earth, changing the business landscape forever and raising fascinating questions about the nature of leadership in the new economy. The remainder of this new Introduction will address these two points.

Our list of the best business leaders in America, based on the methodology described in Part I of the book and detailed in the appendices, was a reflection at a point in time. Since the list "closed" in early 1999, there have been a significant number of transitions in the form of landmark corporate events and executive retirements. Here are the major transitions:

- Larry Bossidy (page 61), Chairman of AlliedSignal, retired and was succeeded by Michael Bonsignore, who had been Chief Executive Officer of Honeywell, which AlliedSignal acquired for $13.8 billion. The combined company took the Honeywell name. In October 2000, the new Honeywell agreed to be acquired by General Electric for $45 billion.
- Steve Case (page 73) shocked the world and legitimized the new economy by agreeing to merge with Time Warner in a $350 billion stock merger. He is becoming Chairman of the new company, AOL Time Warner, which will have annual revenues of more than $30 billion.
- Elizabeth Dole (page 91), President and Chief Executive Officer of the American Red Cross until January 1999, became the first serious woman contender for the U.S. presidency and later withdrew her candidacy in October 1999.
- Robert Eaton (page 99), Chairman and Co-Chief Executive Officer of DaimlerChrysler, retired and Jurgen Schremp became sole Chairman and CEO.
- Bernie Ebbers (page 105), President and Chief Executive Officer of MCI WorldCom, continued his bold acquisition strategy with a nearly unthinkable acquisition, agreeing to purchase arch rival Sprint Communications for $129 billion. After many months of integration planning, the deal was called off under regulatory pressure.
- Michael Eisner (page 111), Chairman and Chief Executive Officer of the Walt Disney Company, faced the toughest management and business

challenges of his renowned stewardship, ranging from public pressure to name a successor, to slowing demand in key markets, to accelerating Internet competition. In 2000, the company's fortunes returned once again with strong performance in its key operating units, and the naming of Robert Iger as President and Chief Operating Officer.

- Don Fites (page 123), the longtime Chairman and Chief Executive Officer of Caterpillar, Inc., the maker of construction and earth-moving equipment, was succeeded by Glen Barton, who has been fighting slowing demand for the company's products in North and Latin America.

- Bill Gates (page 129) stepped up to Chairman of Microsoft to focus on the company's long-term product strategy. Longtime partner, friend, and President, Steven Ballmer, was named Chief Executive Officer. Microsoft also was found guilty of antitrust violations and ordered by the court to break the company into two. The company has appealed the ruling.

- Charles Heimbold (page 169), Chairman and Chief Executive Officer of Bristol-Myers Squibb, was asked by the company's board to stay in his position beyond age 65. Peter R. Dolan was appointed as President and presumed successor.

- David Johnson (page 181), Chairman of Campbell Soup, retired but was asked by the company's board to return to the company to lead a search for a new Chief Executive Officer.

- Chuck Knight (page 199), Chairman and CEO of Emerson Electric since 1974, was succeeded by David N. Farr, who now assumes the responsibility to maintain the company's record-breaking run of 42 years of increased earnings per share.

- David Komansky (page 307), Chairman and Chief Executive Officer of Merrill Lynch, led the nation's largest securities firm to overcome a late start and make an aggressive entry into the online brokerage business, with critical acclaim and early success for its Internet offering, ML.com.

- Dennis Kozlowski (page 205), Chairman and Chief Executive Officer of Tyco International, came under enormous pressure from questions about the accounting treatment of the company's aggressive acquisition program, sending the high-flying stock price dramatically lower. Kozlowski and his management team fought the allegations vigorously, helping to restore a substantial portion of the shareholder gains from his 10-year tenure. He and other top company executives put their money where their mouth was by purchasing a significant amount of Tyco shares.

- Lou Noto (page 235), Chairman and Chief Executive Officer of Mobil Corporation, became Vice Chairman of Exxon Mobil, now the world's largest oil company, after Mobil's acquisition by Exxon.

- Paul O'Neill (page 241), Chairman and Chief Executive Officer of Alcoa,

Inc., the world's leading aluminum producer, was succeeded as Chairman and CEO by Alain J. P. Belda.

- John Pepper (page 247), Chairman of Proctor & Gamble, retired and was succeeded by Durk Jager, who tried to aggressively change the United States' largest consumer products company. Having pushed for change too hard and having missed key earnings targets, Mr. Jager was forced from the CEO position and was succeeded by Alan G. Lafley. Mr. Pepper returned to the company as Chairman.
- Howard Schultz (page 259), founder and Chairman of Starbucks, the leading specialty coffee retailer in the United States, was succeeded as CEO by Orin Smith. Mr. Schultz is focusing on long-term strategy and the company's aggressive international expansion plans.
- Charles Schwab (page 265), Chairman and Co-Chief Executive Officer of the company that bears his name, became the dominant online stock brokerage firm and used the company's high-flying market valuation to acquire offline firm U.S. Trust Company.
- Walter Shipley (page 271), Chairman of Chase Manhattan Corporation, the nation's second-largest bank, retired and was succeeded by William B. Harrison. Chase acquired the venerable bank J. P. Morgan, and will become J. P. Morgan Chase when the transaction closes.
- Bill Steere (page 285), Chairman and Chief Executive Officer of Pfizer, succeeded after a bitter corporate fight with American Home Products to acquire Warner Lambert. He announced that he will retire at year-end 2000 as CEO and in April 2001 as Chairman, to be succeeded by Henry McKinnell, formerly President and Chief Operating Officer.
- Alex Trotman (page 299) retired as Chairman and Chief Executive Officer of Ford Motor Company and was succeeded by Jacques A. Nasser as President and CEO and William Clay Ford as Chairman.
- Charles Wang (page 327), Founder and Chairman of software giant Computer Associates, was succeeded as Chief Executive Officer by his longtime President and Chief Operating Officer, Sanjay Kumar. In addition, searching for a way to bolster its stock, the company announced its intention to use spin-offs to tap the value of fast-growing business units that are overshadowed by the company's main businesses.
- Sandy Weill (page 333), Chairman and Chief Executive Officer of Citigroup, took over as sole CEO from former Co-CEO John Reed. He was joined in the office of the Chairman by former U.S. Secretary of the Treasury Robert Rubin. Citigroup acquired Schroders, the British merchant bank, to expand the European position of its Salomon Smith Barney investment banking business.
- Jack Welch (page 339), Chairman and Chief Executive Officer of General Electric, announced his retirement effective at the end of 2001 (a

one-year delay after the acquisition of Honeywell), and will be succeeded
by Jeffrey R. Immelt, who had run GE Medical Systems, in the most
watched CEO succession race in American history. He also went on to
win a $7.1 million advance for the publication of his forthcoming book,
the largest in publishing history.

- Al Zeien (page 347), Chairman of Gillette, retired and was succeeded by
Michael C. Hawley, who was forced to retire amid slowing growth,
launching a search for a successor.

As you can see, exactly half of the 50 business leaders in the book un-
derwent some significant personal or corporate transition over the past
couple of years. As the number and magnitude of these transitions
demonstrate, any list of the best business leaders in America is indeed a
reflection at a moment in time.

Leadership in the New Economy

Much of the discussion in the aftermath of publishing *Lessons from the
Top* has been about how well our findings about leadership work in the
new economy. Based on our research and case work at Spencer Stuart, we
have come to believe that leadership and success in the digitally charged
new economy demand living by the enduring principles that make for
success, and *augmenting* them with additional qualities that enable speed,
flexibility, risk taking, an obsession with the customer, and new intensity
of communications.

It may come as a surprise to some observers that we are not suggesting
throwing out the old to make way for the new. Much has been written
about the "new requirements" for leaders in today's lightning-fast markets, where certain new companies have, with unprecedented speed, successfully challenged long-established market leaders for everything from
customer loyalties and market share to stock market capitalization and
the talent driving these organizations. Clearly, there are new ingredients
that combine for success in the new economy. However, we believe that
the qualities are worthless if a person in a leadership role does not do the
right things right and inspire trust among his or her team, if the strategy
for the enterprise is ill-conceived, if there is a weak management team, or
if employees are apathetic.

How different, then, are the fundamental characteristics of business
leadership in the digital era? What additional qualities are required for
success? There are indeed some major and critical differences between the
old and new economies. But the differences have much more to do with
adapting to the exigencies of the environment rather than establishing

new principles. To be successful on an enduring basis—whether running an e-commerce start-up or a diversified manufacturing concern, successful enterprises must be built upon a rock-solid foundation of classic leadership principles. In fact, we believe the fundamental principles of business leadership are every bit as relevant today as they were in earlier environments. What is different today, however, is the requirement that these principles be tailored to the dizzying pace of competitive, technological, and financial change.

Looking Forward

We feel that the whole subject of leadership in the digital economy deserves much deeper study and attention. Who are the leaders in the digital economy? How does our Business Leadership Wheel framework need to be augmented to be both accurate and complete in describing success in the future? How can managers and employees in traditional companies assess whether they have what it takes from a skill and personal characteristics standpoint to migrate successfully into the digital economy? These are some of the major themes that we are working on.

The Internet is a subject that is taking a more important role in our professional lives at Spencer Stuart as well. Tom has become extremely involved in helping major corporations and venture-capital firms build Internet boards of directors and top management teams, and Jim has moved from running our firm's Communications and Media Practice to heading our global Internet Practice. Spencer Stuart has in fact become one of the dominant firms recruiting CEOs and other top executives to Internet companies and Internet divisions of large corporations.

So digital leadership is a topic very much on our minds these days. But for us, everything having to do with the subject of leadership and success will always be built upon the foundation that we laid in the research and writing of *Lessons from the Top*.

Thomas J. Nef   James M. Citrin
December 2000

Lessons

FROM THE Top

PART I

The Search for the Best Business Leaders in America

CHAPTER 1

What Makes Business
Leaders Great

Our chief want is someone
who will inspire us to be what we know we could be.
—*Ralph Waldo Emerson*

WHO ARE THE BEST BUSINESS LEADERS IN AMERICA? WHAT MAKES them great? What can we learn from them as we try to turn our own aspirations into reality?

These three questions have driven us from the moment that we began this project in April of 1997. They are relatively simple questions to ask. But they are extremely difficult to answer.

We had originally intended to open *Lessons from the Top* with an anecdote describing a real phone call we had received from a corporate board member asking us to launch an executive search for a new chief executive officer.

The board member, someone we had worked with over a period of years, wanted us to develop a list of candidates who could succeed the company's CEO, a man who had just informed the board that he intended to retire at year's end.

Up until that point, the phone call was fairly typical. Recruiting senior executives and board members to build our clients' management teams is what we do at Spencer Stuart. Each year, as one of the world's largest executive search firms, we interview over 40,000 executives around the world, in the course of more than 4,000 assignments that we conduct out of 50 offices located in 25 countries. Our recent assignments have included recruiting new CEOs to lead AT&T, Delta Air Lines, Quaker Oats, Reader's Digest, J. Crew, and Weyerhaeuser.

Spencer Stuart has been recruiting such top talent for more than 40 years. So this particular phone call did not set off any unusual alarms. What was surprising, though, was his next request: Our client asked us to advise the board as well about what they *should be* looking for in their next CEO. Not only what industry background, company size, and geographic breadth, but the more subtle and potentially important characteristics. Who is the right kind of leader? What kind of attributes should he or she have?

The reason this brought us up short was that it was one of a number of similar requests we had recently received from our clients, firms that range from venture capital–backed start-ups, to some of America's largest companies.

Given the growing interest in this question, we decided to forgo opening the book with an elaborate story, and plunge right into the heart of the issue.

What, in fact, makes someone a great business leader? What does it really take to lead an organization successfully in today's ever more competitive and fast-moving world economy?

When we considered this carefully, we realized that it is not surprising that these questions are surfacing more frequently. They are the very things that individuals, whether given the responsibility of running an organization or managing a department, must answer and answer quickly.

As the deposed former chief executives of AT&T, Kmart, and Sunbeam can well attest, managers are being given less and less time to make a difference today.

Operating in what feels like an ever-tightening vise—being squeezed by global competition on one side and a rapidly changing, technology-driven business landscape on the other—it is only natural for managers to look for comfort in what has worked in the past. Unfortunately, as they have learned the hard way, we are no longer operating under the old rules. When a company's board loses confidence in its CEO, it often takes decisive action. And conducting a search for a new leader is often the action it takes. It is often also the point where we come in.

What Spencer Stuart Does

Executive search is a specialized form of management consulting that focuses on defining a company's leadership requirements as a function of its strategy, and then identifies, interviews, and recruits the most appropriate candidate to execute that strategy.

Developing insight into business leaders' careers and lives—what makes them "tick"—is essential for us to fulfill our mandate, as we set out to find the right executive.

To assess a candidate for a top position, we perform an in-depth appraisal of the executive's career accomplishments, management style, obstacles overcome, mistakes made and lessons learned, leadership philosophy, formative life experiences, and personal and professional ambitions. Given that executives are often competing for these high-profile appointments, it is in *their* interest to make certain that we understand their industries, companies, and careers as much as possible.

Meeting with all of these executives, and developing insights into their business successes and what makes leaders great, has provided us with the privilege of learning from many of the top business leaders in the world. We have grown professionally and personally as a result and wanted to share what we have learned. This was one of the principal reasons behind writing this book.

To give these lessons about success and leadership maximum impact, we decided that it was critical to hear from the *very best*. And rather than simply subjectively picking the "best" leaders to study, we felt compelled to apply an objective and rigorous analytical process. This decision was partially the result of the fact-based, analytical approach that was instilled in both of us earlier in our careers as management consultants at McKinsey & Company.

So we undertook to do what no one else has done before. We put together a rigorous methodology aimed at identifying the very best business leaders in America and then interviewed those leaders at length to discover why they have been so successful.

There are, of course, entire libraries of books that analyze key leadership qualities. But most are rather academic in their approach, or are limited by a single author's perspective.

And while there are scores of annual rankings of top business managers, our review suggests that these tabulations have neither the requisite analytical rigor nor the depth to elucidate the stories behind the rankings.

Neither approach seems to bring to life what it takes to be a great leader in a way that can be applied to real life.

In light of this, we set the ambitious dual goals of:

1) Being as analytically sound as possible in constructing our list of business leaders, and
2) Articulating their stories in as personal and approachable a style as possible.

Based on the methodology described below and in Chapter 3, we created the list of business leaders that is as close as we could come to answering our first question, "Who are the best business leaders in America?"

While the list contains a number of CEOs who likely would be on anyone's compilation of America's best business leaders, there are a number of surprises as well—and undoubtedly some CEOs and readers will be disappointed by who is not here.

The guiding principles in assembling the list was to identify:

1) the individuals most well regarded for their leadership traits, and
2) the best-performing organizations over the past five and 10 years and then determine the CEO most responsible for the company's success during that time.

We then reviewed the combined list of CEOs against our criteria of leadership (detailed below) to winnow it down to the final 50.

Are These *the* 50 Best Business Leaders?

Is this the definitive list of the best business leaders in America? We cannot say that. The list is so fluid that in the course of researching and writing this book, a number of companies that made the list completed or announced mergers or acquisitions (i.e., Citicorp and Travelers, Mobil and Exxon); CEOs retired;[1] and even died (e.g., Coca-Cola's Roberto Goizueta). Given how quickly the business world changes, several of the leaders in this book may have changed circumstances between the time we finished writing and publication.

We have tried to make the list as authoritative, comprehensive, and objective as humanly possible, given the constantly shifting ground beneath us. We recognize, however, that any such list, no matter how rigorous the research that went into it, is but a snapshot in time.

Before we discuss the list itself, detail our methodology, and get into the individual profiles in Part II, we feel it is important to put what you are about to read into context, to see if we can explain why more boards of directors, shareholders, managers, and employees themselves are asking, "What does it really take to lead an organization successfully today?"

The Changing Nature of Leadership

Less than three decades ago, successful companies tended to be centrally controlled, financially managed, conglomerates. Alfred Sloan of

---

1. In all, six of the CEOs on our list retired during the course of writing this book. Ford's Alex Trotman, Elizabeth Dole of the American Red Cross, Don Fites of Caterpillar Tractor, John Pepper of Procter & Gamble, Walter Shipley of Chase Manhattan, and Al Zeien of Gillette are included for the obvious reason that they led their respective companies to outstanding performance over the past five years.

General Motors, Harold Geneen of International Telephone and Telegraph (ITT), Reg Jones of General Electric, and Harry Gray of United Technologies stood out among the best-known, and most respected, business leaders of their day. These executives often looked to military leaders like generals Patton and Eisenhower as role models. They led their huge enterprises by exercising stringent financial controls and authoritative discipline.

It made sense. Their workers, after all, were trained in the military or on the assembly line to follow rigorous procedures. These leaders also had another advantage. Because World War II had crippled productive capacity elsewhere around the globe, they had largely unchallenged control over their markets.

By the time the rest of the world started to rebuild from the war and catch up, a new generation of leaders, armed with a new weapon—information technology—transformed American business again. In the 1980s, companies such as Federal Express, Citibank, and Wal-Mart rode the wave of the information revolution and helped restructure the United States' economy.

Leaders of these firms—from Fred Smith of Federal Express to Walter Wriston of Citibank to Wal-Mart's Sam Walton—could operate in a far more decentralized fashion because they knew how to use the new technology to their advantage. They employed their new source of competitive advantage not only to keep track of data but as a means of staying close to the customer. Scanning technology at the checkout counter, for example, let Wal-Mart know minute-by-minute how customers were responding to its latest offerings.

This generation of leaders also understood the new, questioning mentality that employees brought to the workplace, an attitude created in part, perhaps, by the social divisions caused by the Vietnam War.

Today, younger executives such as Michael Dell of Dell Computer and America Online's Steve Case have joined the leadership ranks of IBM's Lou Gerstner, Emerson Electric's Chuck Knight, and AIG's Hank Greenberg, many of whom are a generation or more older. As they look toward one another, these executives are trying to draw leadership lessons from each side of a generational chasm.

And this underscores an important point:

As executives who have embraced everything from total quality management to reengineering have learned the hard way, today, when it comes to leading, one size does not fit all. We need to learn from everyone.

Since there is no single right answer to copy, no one formula to follow, we must create our own solutions. The easiest way to do this is by determining what has worked well for others and then figure out how to apply those lessons to our own unique situation.

This is what we have set out to do with *Lessons from the Top*. Through studying their organizations and speaking at length to the high-achieving leaders profiled in this book (all of whom are CEOs or chairmen), we have tried to discover why they have been so successful.

You will hear directly from the leaders themselves, with the results of our interviews and additional research woven into individual profiles. We have devoted a separate chapter to each of the executives, based, in just about every case, on at least one in-depth interview where the leaders discussed what they believe have been the fundamental reasons for their success.

If you want to learn what makes someone successful, you want to go directly to the source, and that is exactly what we did.[2] Not surprisingly, each of the CEOs and chairmen had his or her own particular take on leadership and business success. Each of the organizations is at a different point of corporate evolution and is operating in a different competitive landscape. Some, like Tyco International and Chase Manhattan, are growing rapidly through acquisitions, while others, like Deere and Dell Computer, are expanding more through internal growth. Some are truly global, such as Gillette and AIG, while others are purely domestic, such as Fannie Mae.

One thing, however, is clear. Different kinds of leaders and leadership styles are appropriate for different circumstances. And predictably, those differences are reflected in our list as well. For example, the last job CEO Al Zeien of Gillette had before assuming the company's presidency was Vice Chairman, International. Five of the CEOs were brought into their companies from outside and a surprisingly large number, 11, have transformed themselves from founder/entrepreneur to major corporate CEO, and/or chairman.[3]

---

2. There were only four instances where we were unable to meet one-on-one with the people profiled. Here is how we handled each one.

  Peter Drucker was kind enough to answer our voluminous questions in writing—using his electric typewriter. Not surprisingly, Microsoft's Bill Gates used a different form of technology. We interviewed him via e-mail. Andy Grove of Intel read our questions and responded by sending us his various writings and speeches on the subject and corrected the couple of instances where we did not capture his precise meaning. IBM's Lou Gerstner took a similar approach.

3. Steve Case of America Online; Michael Dell of Dell Computer; Bernie Ebbers of MCI WorldCom; Donald Fisher of The Gap; Bill Gates of Microsoft; Andy Grove of Intel; Herb Kelleher of Southwest Airlines; Howard Schultz of Starbucks; Charles Schwab of Charles Schwab; Fred Smith of Federal Express; and Charles Wang of Computer Associates. This list of company founders does *not* include either Bill Marriott, who assumed leadership from his father, who founded the company, or Martha Ingram, of Ingram Industries, who took over as CEO of the company following the death of her husband.

The result of these differences is that it is impossible to point to any *one* thing or any *one* characteristic and say: *This* is what it takes to be a great business leader. However, while the stories and circumstances are unique to each of our leaders, there are indeed a series of leadership principles and common traits that are in evidence across these most successful people.

That is why we have devoted Part III to focusing on these lessons learned. By studying the principles of business leadership that derive from the leaders' stories (Chapter 2 of Part III, "Doing the Right Things Right") and the characteristics that they share (Chapter 3 of Part III, "Common Traits: A Prescription for Success in Business") we answer the third question driving this project, "How can we pattern ourselves after these leaders to achieve our own hopes and aspirations?"

Given the nature of our list, we feel it is important to describe our methodology.

In Chapter 2 of Part I, we discuss, in broad terms, how leaders came to be selected for the list. Then in Chapter 3, we review the methodology quantitatively, focusing on what we feel are groundbreaking measures we took to ensure that the people who we selected as among the very best business leaders in America truly are.

CHAPTER 2

Evaluating Today's Business Leaders

NOT SURPRISINGLY, IN CREATING THIS BOOK, WE FOLLOWED THE SAME approach we would use in performing a high-level, high-profile executive search. After all, *the very process of executive recruiting is a search for business leadership.*

While each and every search is unique, Spencer Stuart has, over its 43-year history, developed a disciplined methodology to ensure completeness and the highest level of quality.

A Spencer Stuart executive search normally follows five sequential and interrelated steps. We performed each of them in the course of our research for this book, as we attempted to determine who the best leaders in American business are today.

STEP 1. DEFINING SUCCESS

The first step in any search assignment is to work with the client to understand both its corporate strategy and culture, and the role it expects the person to be recruited will play. Working together, the client and Spencer Stuart define what success will look like. The end product of this step is a document called the position and candidate specification (the "spec").

In this case, our goal was clear: We wanted to identify the "best" business leaders in America.

What would it take for someone to qualify as the best? Certainly quantitative achievements would be important, but this was just one factor. Based upon our extensive research into the literature of business and organizational leadership, coupled with our own professional experience, we concluded that the highest-performing businesspeople achieve strong results when evaluated against 10 quantitative and qualitative measures (which essentially break leadership into its component parts, forming the "spec" for this project).

These individuals should have:

- Produced strong long-term financial results;
- Demonstrated visionary and strategic skills;
- Shown the ability to overcome challenges;
- Developed excellent organizational and people skills;
- Demonstrated consistent strength of character;
- Evidenced entrepreneurship or pioneering spirit;
- Had a demonstrable impact on business, industry, or society;
- Created a track record of innovation;
- Maintained exemplary customer focus; and
- Shown a genuine commitment to diversity and social responsibility.

To be considered for our list, a business leader would have to demonstrate all of these 10 traits to one extent or another.

STEP 2. THE TARGET LIST OF COMPANIES

Developing a target list of companies to examine for potential candidates comprises a core component of any executive search. In traditional searches, we build a target list by selecting the highest-performing companies in relevant industry sectors, or those firms renowned for particular functions such as marketing, finance, or operations.

In the case of *Lessons from the Top*, where candidates could come from any sector—public or private—and from companies of any size, this step required significant analysis. The methodology section described below and detailed in Chapter 3 of Part I and in Appendixes 1 and 2 will explain exactly how we went about incorporating both an ambitious survey by the Gallup Organization and a groundbreaking financial analysis by the investment management firm Lazard Asset Management, a division of the international investment banking firm Lazard Frères, into our research.

STEP 3. RESEARCH TO IDENTIFY PROSPECTIVE CANDIDATES

Complementing the *quantitative* research undertaken to build a target list, the third step in a search process is to perform *qualitative* research to identify the individuals responsible for the success of the companies on the target list.

In traditional search assignments, we extract information from Spencer Stuart's proprietary global database of 637,000 executives and review qualitative information that has been built up on individuals over time based on our contacts with them. In addition, we draw upon our network of industry and company sources for information, insight, and references, and to identify other leaders relevant to our "spec."

We did that in this case as well. And then we added another important step. We commissioned the Gallup Organization to execute an extremely detailed survey to nominate the most successful business leaders in America.

The Gallup team, under the direction of Cal Martin, senior vice president, Deb Christenson, Ph.D., and Bob Tortora, Ph.D., Gallup's chief methodologist and statistician (and the individual who was the lead designer of the 1992, 1996, and year 2000 U.S. Census), developed and executed a survey in which they interviewed 575 businesspeople and leaders, asking respondents to nominate the nation's most outstanding leaders in each of 10 categories.

The list of survey respondents was decided with care. Our objective was to reach a wide cross section of our nation's leaders to ensure that our nominees would be drawn from as broad a group as possible.

The people the members of the Gallup team surveyed included:

- 200 *Fortune* 1,000 CEOs,
- 170 presidents or CEOs of companies on the *Inc. 500* (a ranking of the 500 fastest-growing privately held companies in America),
- 88 leaders of not-for-profit organizations with greater than 100 employees, and
- 117 deans or presidents of major universities.

We asked each of the survey participants to identify leaders of business, industry, and organizations in the United States who they believed are the most outstanding in each of the 10 dimensions of leadership we cited above: long-term performance; visionary and strategic skills; ability to overcome challenges; organizational and people leadership; integrity and strength of character; entrepreneurial or pioneering spirit; demonstrable impact on an industry, business, or society; track record of innovation; exemplary customer focus; and commitment to diversity.

In addition, we asked the respondents to identify the one individual who came to mind who most represented successful leadership overall.

After receiving the results of the Gallup survey, we tallied the number of times the leaders were nominated in each of the 10 individual categories, and how often their peers cited them for being the best overall leader in the United States. We then weighted the results by our assessment of the importance of each leadership criterion. (The weightings we used and mechanics of the analysis of the Gallup survey are demonstrated in Table 1 on page 18.)

The results of the survey were incorporated with our own target list research to help build the "Long List" of executives who had made the first cut, that is, would be among the candidates who we would evaluate further.

As we will discuss later on, we would subsequently winnow that list down, and complement it, by asking Lazard Frères to analyze the financial performance of the companies these nominees led and compare it to the results produced by their peers.

While we will explore all this in detail later, let us make one point here. No matter how high someone scored in the Gallup research, if the performance of that person's company was lacking, they did not make the final list.

STEP 4. CANDIDATE INTERVIEWS AND DOCUMENTATION

In all of our search assignments, based on the completion of an agreed-on list of top-priority candidates, the fourth step is to interview the executives and prepare detailed written candidate presentations for our clients. The purpose of these interviews is to further assess the candidates against the needs and requirements of the position, probe their interest level, and ultimately help make a selection. In *Lessons from the Top*, of course, we used the methodology described here and in Chapter 3 of Part I to determine the list of the best business leaders. We then scheduled one-on-one interviews with each of the leaders on the list to probe the topics of leadership that we wanted to focus on for the book. Candidate presentations typically include two parts:

1) A résumé section, which is a chronological review of the individual's professional experience, responsibilities, and accomplishments, as well as personal data, and

2) An "Analysis and Appraisal," which evaluates the executive against the position and candidate specification discussed in Step 1. The analysis and appraisal is also the place where we detail an executive's early life influences, extracurricular interests and activities, career setbacks and turning points, interpersonal and leadership style, and management philosophies.

In *Lessons from the Top*, both of these components are contained within the individual profiles of the leaders who made our final list.

Because we were looking for common principles of leadership and success, we asked each leader to respond to a common set of questions. The interview guide we created and used can be found in Appendix 3 at the back of the book.

STEP 5. THE CLOSE

Our Spencer Stuart search assignments typically culminate with the selection of a final candidate and a process of negotiating an employment and compensation agreement to recruit the individual.

Obviously, in the case of *Lessons from the Top*, our objective was different. We wanted to find (not hire) the most successful leaders in America—we also wanted to explore why they have been successful.

While all individuals are unique, the lives and careers of successful people follow certain patterns. That is why the latter section of the book—Part III—is devoted to documenting the key factors from which overwhelming success is the natural end result.

Before we go on, we would like to offer readers a more detailed look at the methodology we utilized in creating this list to show how the search played out in practice. We will begin with the Gallup research.

A Word of Warning Before We Begin Our Journey

This is as good a place as any in the book to make an important point. You cannot simply add up all the points someone received in the 10 categories that represent the different dimensions of leadership, and say the person with the highest score is "The Best Leader in America," or that the people with the highest scores should automatically make the final list. Similarly, it would be inaccurate to look solely at the leaders of the companies who were top-ranked when Lazard Asset Management quantified companies' financial performance and define the absolutely best leaders in that way. (We will review those quantitative measures in Chapter 3.)

Different companies require different things from their leaders at different points in their evolution. At some companies, innovation is the most vital requirement. At others, exemplary customer focus is the key. In some industries interest rates, or fuel prices, or some other external factor have an oversized impact on results. And, as we learned, the period of time used to determine the evaluations is a critical consideration.

When it comes to leading, there is no one declarative or best or right answer. But while you cannot look at our list and say this one leader is best, we are confident in saying that these 50 individuals are collectively among the very best—and most successful—business leaders in America.

CHAPTER 3

Methodology:
A Closer Look at the Numbers

THE PURPOSE OF THIS CHAPTER IS TO EXPLAIN IN SOME DETAIL HOW
we analyzed the results of the Gallup survey, and overlaid financial analysis and references to assemble the list of leaders for *Lessons from the Top*,
since clearly this speaks to the authority of the list. Perhaps the easiest way
to do that is to use a few real examples and carry the examples through
the methodology.

We will start with the Gallup results.

Four well-known business leaders who scored among the highest on
the survey are Jack Welch of General Electric, Bill Gates of Microsoft,
Andy Grove of Intel, and Lou Gerstner of IBM. The table on page 18 lays
out the Gallup survey results for these executives.

Along the top of the table we have listed the 10 criteria and have also
included a place for overall leadership. Below there is a criteria weighting
factor that we assigned to each, based on our determination of its importance in the overall leadership equation. Each row lists the number of citations that each of these leaders received by survey respondents (out of a
total of 575). The bottom half of the table lists the weighted "points" by
leader, which is simply the product of the number of citations multiplied
by the weighting factor.

TABLE 1*—RESULTS OF GALLUP SURVEY

GALLUP QUESTION	LT Performance	Visionary/ Strategic	Ability to overcome challenges	Organizational People Leadership	Integrity/Character	Entrepreneurial/ Pioneering	Impact on business/ society	Innovation	Customer Focus	Diversity	Leadership Overall	
WEIGHTING FACTOR	5	3	2	2	2	2	3	2	3	2	10	Total
Total Respondents	575	575	575	575	575	575	575	575	575	575	575	6,325
Jack Welch (GE)	110	56	29	133	66	19	66	53	35	17	110	694
Bill Gates (Microsoft)	66	122	41	22	32	76	149	143	25	12	88	776
Andy Grove (Intel)	52	77	19	54	26	88	76	88	56	15	75	626
Lou Gerstner (IBM)	65	43	85	78	45	19	46	54	98	28	81	642
WEIGHTED POINTS (above responses × weighting)												
Jack Welch (GE)	550	168	58	266	132	38	198	106	105	34	1,100	2,755
Bill Gates (Microsoft)	330	366	82	44	64	152	447	286	75	24	880	2,750
Andy Grove (Intel)	260	231	38	108	52	176	228	176	168	30	750	2,217
Lou Gerstner (IBM)	325	129	170	156	90	38	138	108	294	56	810	2,314

*Gallup Question: As you think about today's leaders of business, industry, and organizations in the United States, who first comes to mind for each of the following areas: 1. Long-term performance; 2. Visionary and strategic skills; 3. Ability to overcome challenges; 4. Organizational and people leadership; 5. Integrity and strength of character; 6. Entrepreneurial or pioneering spirit; 7. Demonstrable impact on an industry, business, or society; 8. Track record of innovation; 9. Exemplary customer focus; 10. Commitment to diversity; and 11. Overall leadership.

Appendix 1 lists the various leaders who received the most Gallup nominations. For each of the individuals cited, we constructed the same analysis as Table 1 to begin to select and prioritize leaders for the book.

The findings from this step of the methodology alone provided fascinating insight into how a broad-based group of peers perceive different leaders and their various strengths.

As Table 1 demonstrates, different leaders are well regarded for different things. Gates, for example, received the highest scores in the key areas of visionary and strategic skills; impact on industry, business, and society; innovation, and entrepreneurship. Welch was the most highly rated for leadership overall, as well as for the areas related to long-term performance, and organizational and people leadership. Gerstner was highest ranked for customer focus and his ability to overcome challenges. And Grove was most highly rated for his entrepreneurial and pioneering spirit.

With the Gallup survey and analysis complete, our next step was then to determine quantitatively how much value the current business leaders added to their organizations.[4] For that, we turned to Lazard Asset Management for assistance.

As described in detail in Appendix 2, Lazard Asset Management evaluated a broad variety of financial measures of corporate performance before settling on the two it felt were most powerful:

1) Total return to shareholders, and
2) Growth in cash flow relative to a company's market value.

To analyze the results of the largest 1,000 U.S. public companies, we cut the data generated by these two measures 10 different ways:

- *Cash Flow Growth to Market Value* as ranked overall and within industry sectors over five- and 10-year periods.
- *Total Return to Shareholders* ranked overall and within industry sectors over one-, five-, and 10-year periods.
- *A Cross-section* of the companies ranked in the top two deciles of Cash Flow Growth and total return to shareholders by industry sector over five- and 10-year periods.

For the purposes of helping select our top leaders, we decided to concentrate on a five-year time horizon for two reasons:

1) It is long enough to be meaningful, and
2) It now approximates the typical tenure of a sitting CEO of a major U.S. corporation. In fact, our research shows that in 1997, 60% of CEOs of America's largest corporations had been in their jobs five years or less. In 1980, that number was only 40%.

We realized early on that it was also important to evaluate results within industry sectors, in order to evaluate the top performers against their competition. This was also essential to ensure that we would not limit our universe to companies from the hottest business sectors over the past five years, industries such as technology or financial services.

---

4. Where we were unable to make this determination, as in the case of private companies and nonprofit organizations, we relied more heavily on the Gallup results, industry references, and the collective judgment of Spencer Stuart.

Since the Cash Flow Growth to Market Value ratios themselves are not really meaningful, we focused more on where companies ranked within the total universe of 1,000 companies and within their industry groups, rather than on the numbers themselves. Obviously, the closer to the top a company appeared in both categories, the higher its ranking.

The following table demonstrates the results for the same four companies we just used and shows how well they (and their leaders) did in growing cash flow relative to their market value at the beginning of the five-year period.

TABLE 2—GROWTH IN CASH FLOW/BEGINNING MARKET VALUE

RANK AMONG 1,000 COMPANIES	COMPANY	INDUSTRY/SECTOR	RANK WITHIN SECTOR (TOTAL # IN SECTOR)
80	Intel	Technology/Components	2 (of 14)
726	IBM	Technology/Hardware	24 (of 30)
164	Microsoft	Technology/Software	4 (of 9)
612	GE	Electrical/Diversified	21 (of 27)

As the table indicates, Intel ranked 80th in growing cash flow, among the largest 1,000 public companies relative to its market value, and was second-ranked among all of the 14 technology/components companies.

Microsoft was also highly ranked, falling in the second decile of the largest 1,000 U.S. public companies. However, General Electric, often cited as the best-managed company in the world, ranked in the middle of the pack among all large U.S. companies. How could this be the case? Is it the company or is it the measure?

The reason is that GE suffered from what might be called a "winner's curse." The company had an extraordinarily high market-weighted enterprise value five years ago, the beginning point in our cash flow evaluation. Its large—and increasing market value—has made it extremely difficult to continue growing cash flow as fast as the market value of the company has grown.

The GE example demonstrates another important lesson in attempting to quantify successful corporate performance and leadership: *No one single measure is sufficient for evaluating performance.*

If we were to use the cash flow growth relative to market value measure alone, a company could achieve a high ranking by having either a large numerator (cash flow growth), or a small denominator (market value). Some companies that were in depressed sectors with low market values five years ago tended to score well against this measure. Airlines, for example, had low market values but managed to grow their cash flows significantly thanks to better revenue management, pricing, operations, and depressed oil prices, and of course the travel industry was aided by a strong economy. As a result, they had extraordinary performance on this measure. Continental Airlines, for example, was 38th among all large U.S. companies in growing cash flow to market value. The General Electric and Continental Airlines examples show why we used *two* quantitative performance measures.

In determining a leader's contribution to the success of the enterprise, the ideal is to be highly ranked both on growing cash flow relative to market value—essentially *what management has control over*—and on total return to shareholders, which reflects *management's ability to demonstrate its strategy and achievements, as well as its growth prospects*, to the investment community.

Let's See How the Stockholders Did

The next step in our analysis was to look at total returns to shareholders.

All four of the companies that we have been using as examples—Microsoft, GE, IBM, and Intel—were among the highest ranked in total return to shareholders, placing well within the top decile of the largest 1,000 public companies in the United States, as the following table clearly shows.

TABLE 3—RETURNS TO SHAREHOLDERS

RANK AMONG 1,000 COMPANIES	COMPANY	INDUSTRY/SECTOR	RANK WITHIN SECTOR (TOTAL # IN SECTOR)	5-YEAR ANNUAL-IZED RETURN
4	Microsoft	Technology/Software	1 (of 9)	69%
21	Intel	Technology/Components	2 (of 14)	51%
32	IBM	Technology/Hardware	9 (of 30)	47%
101	GE	Electrical/Diversified	4 (of 27)	34%

Table 1 of Appendix 2 details all of the annual returns on a one- and five-year basis for each of the companies in *Lessons from the Top*. The performance of this group of companies has indeed been impressive. If you invested in the 46 public companies that are on our final list—we excluded not-for-profit, private, and subsidiary organizations—your returns would have outperformed the S&P 500 by roughly 50% over the past five years, as the following chart demonstrates.

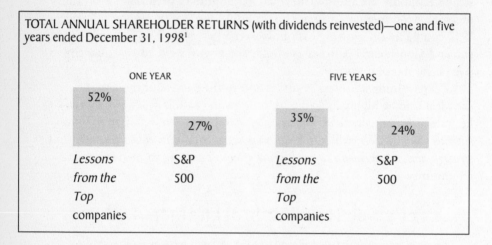

TOTAL ANNUAL SHAREHOLDER RETURNS (with dividends reinvested)—one and five years ended December 31, 1998[1]

ONE YEAR   FIVE YEARS

52%   35%
              27%   24%

Lessons   S&P   Lessons   S&P
from the   500   from the   500
Top   Top
companies   companies

To put this performance into perspective, over a five-year period, $1,000 invested into the S&P 500 would have grown (at a compound annual rate of 24%) to $2,932. The same $1,000 invested into the *Lessons from the Top* companies would have grown to $4,484.

To ensure we captured all the top-performing companies, not just those whose CEOs were nominated in the Gallup survey, Lazard helped us identify companies that were in the top two deciles *in both* growth of cash flow relative to market value, and in total return to shareholders.

That allowed us to capture such top-performing companies as the following:

---

1. In an analysis updating total shareholder returns prior to the publication of the paperback edition, we found that the performance of the *Lessons from the Top* companies moved closer to that of the S&P 500. The one-year returns were 11% for *Lessons from the Top* vs. 12% for the S&P, while the five-year returns were 35% for *Lessons from the Top* vs. 25% for the S&P. For the remainder of this book, we have left the original calculations, since the list of best business leaders was always intended to reflect a point in time.

TABLE 4—TOP PERFORMING COMPANIES

COMPANY	INDUSTRY/SECTOR	5-YEAR ANNUALIZED RETURN	RETURN DECILE	CASH FLOW DECILE
America Online	Leisure/Entertainment	134%	1	1
Charles Schwab	Financial Services	65%	1	2
Cisco Systems	Technology	67%	1	2
Citigroup	Financial Services	33%	2	1
Computer Associates	Technology	29%	2	2
Continental Airlines	Transportation	27%	2	1
Dell Computer	Technology	153%	1	1
Herman Miller	Industrial	30%	2	2
Intel	Technology	51%	1	1
MCI WorldCom	Telecommunications	43%	1	1
Merrill Lynch	Financial Services	28%	2	2
Microsoft	Technology	69%	1	2
Starbucks	Retail	38%	1	2
Tyco International	Electrical/Diversified	43%	1	1

We Now Have the Long List

Based on the Gallup survey and the analysis of corporate performance provided by Lazard Asset Management and our additional research, we compiled a list of *potential* candidates to be profiled. In total, we identified 240 individuals. We took to calling this the "Long List."

Before determining who would be included on the final list and whom we would invite to participate in the book, we had to fill in some relevant information about these 240 people running the companies and organizations that we had identified so far. Specifically, we had to identify the current leadership at each of the high-ranking companies and quantify his or her tenure. After all, our objective was to identify the leaders most responsible for their company making the list.

To do this we went into the Spencer Stuart proprietary database, Quest NT (which stands for *QU*ality *E*xecutive *S*earch *T*racking system—New Technology), to learn more about the leaders, their tenures, career backgrounds, and additional qualitative information.

Once we filled in that data, we completed the Long List information. Here is the way it looked for the four leaders we have been tracking as examples in this section.

TABLE 5

LEADER (TENURE)	COMPANY/ 1998 REVENUES; NET INCOME	INDUSTRY/ SECTOR	WEIGHTED GALLUP POINTS	5-YEAR ANNUAL TOTAL SHARE-HOLDER RETURN	TOTAL RETURN DECILE	TOTAL RETURN RANK WITHIN INDUSTRY SECTOR (TOTAL # IN SECTOR)	CASH FLOW GROWTH/ MARKET VALUE DECILE	CASH FLOW GROWTH/ RANK WITHIN INDUSTRY SECTOR (TOTAL # IN SECTOR)
Jack Welch (CEO since 1981)	GE $99.8 billion; $9.3 billion	Electrical/ Diversified	2,755	34%	1	4 (of 27)	7	21 (of 27)
Bill Gates (CEO since 1975)	Microsoft $16.6 billion; $6.4 billion	Technology/ Software	2,750	69%	1	1 (of 9)	2	4 (of 9)
Lou Gerstner (CEO since 1993)	IBM $81.7 billion; $6.3 billion	Technology/ Hardware	2,314	47%	1	8 (of 30)	8	24 (of 30)
Andy Grove (Chairman since 1997; CEO 1987–97)	Intel $26.3 billion; $6.1 billion	Technology/ Components	2,217	51%	1	2 (of 14)	1	2 (of 14)

Having completed this information, we started to winnow down the Long List by deciding to consider only currently active business leaders rather than the many talented retired CEOs who met our criteria of leadership and success.

We made two exceptions to this rule, at the time of our final selections. The first is Dan Tully, Chairman Emeritus, of Merrill Lynch. Merrill's current CEO is David Komansky, who took over from Tully in 1997 as head of the nation's largest securities firm. Komansky has done an exemplary job, expanding the company globally and providing a steady hand during the tumultuous financial markets in the second half of 1998. He deserves to be on the list. However, the transformation of Merrill Lynch from being a retail-oriented mass market brokerage firm to becoming the world's preeminent, fully integrated investment bank occurred largely during Tully's stewardship between 1992 and 1997. That metamorphosis was nothing short of extraordinary. And Tully, who grew up the son of a steamfitter, is renowned for his leadership principles. That is why we included him on the list (and why we have incorporated Komansky and Tully into one Merrill Lynch chapter).

Secondly, we have included a special brief chapter on Peter F. Drucker, our "51st leader," as part of the concluding section of the book. As Drucker himself pointed out to us, he is not a business leader based on the definitions we are using for the book. However, his influence has been so pervasive—we have several hours of tape from our interviews where the business leaders talked about how Drucker's ideas have influenced their own, and the Gallup survey cited Drucker among the highest-ranked leaders—that not including him seemed to be a serious omission. You will find his chapter beginning on page 357.

The Final Cut

Similar to an executive search assignment, where we have to prioritize potential candidates from a long list of 10 to 20 down to a short list of three or four finalists, we had to make some determinations in order to prioritize our list of 240 potential candidates down to a more manageable number. To do this, we relied on our combined experience of more than 30 years of work assessing people and leadership skills in recruiting top executives to client companies. In addition, our prioritization was based on the analysis of corporate performance just detailed, plus additional research, references, and firsthand experiences that we—or our colleagues—have had with the individuals.

The help from our colleagues proved invaluable. For example, we divided the Long List by industry sector and began reviewing the potential candidates in each sector with our fellow Spencer Stuart partners who serve as practice leaders. As a firm, we have nine global practices: Aviation, Board Services, Communications and Media, Consumer Goods and Services, Financial Services, High Tech, Industrial, Life Sciences, and Energy. Within the firm, most of our colleagues concentrate on recruiting executives and board members for clients whose companies fall into one of these sectors. One or more senior partners works as strategist, account planner, and coordinator for each sector, serving as practice leader.

We asked each of our practice leaders to help assess a list of business leaders against our 10 criteria of leadership and success. Just to take one example, in the technology sector, we asked our High Tech practice leaders to evaluate the following outstanding high-performing executives:

TABLE 6

CEOs (SINCE WHEN)	COMPANY
Jerald G. Fishman (1996)	Analog Devices
James C. Morgan (1987)	Applied Materials
John T. Chambers (1995)	Cisco Systems
Eckhard Pfeiffer (1991–99)	Compaq Computer
Charles Wang (1984)	Computer Associates
Michael Dell (1984)	Dell Computer
Michael Ruettgers (1992)	EMC
Lewis Platt (1992)	Hewlett-Packard
Louis V. Gerstner, Jr. (1994)	IBM
Andrew S. Grove (1987–98)	Intel
Richard A. McGinn (1997)	Lucent
Steven R. Appleton (1996)	Micron Technology
William H. Gates III (1981)	Microsoft
Christopher Galvin (1997)	Motorola
Lawrence Ellison (1977)	Oracle Corp.
Scott McNealy (1981)	Sun Microsystems
Eric Benhamou (1981)	3Com Corp.

Our colleagues came back with insights about why each of the companies had achieved the remarkable success it had; provided assessments of each executive's organizational and people leadership, strategic and visionary skills; and told us what key challenges their organizations faced going forward. This input helped us prioritize the list.

The Results

After countless computer runs, constant checking of the numbers, and vigorous internal debates within Spencer Stuart, we were ready to select our list.

We combined the in-depth analysis of our three distinct sources of information—the Gallup survey; the Lazard Asset Management corporate performance assessment; and our collective judgment based on additional research, references, and not only our personal knowledge but that of our colleagues as well—and assembled the list of business leaders you see on page 32.

A Final Thought

In sharp contrast to most of the "how-to" business books and executive biographies already on the bookshelves, we hope *Lessons from the Top* will encourage and enable an unusually broad range of potential readers—from current as well as future CEOs, managers, entrepreneurs, and board members to investors and business students—to learn from, and pattern themselves after, those profiled as they travel down the path toward achieving their own dreams and ambitions. It is our hope that readers will be able to use what they learn from these leaders to help manage their own careers and lives to reach their fullest potential.

We look forward to hearing your thoughts, reactions, and comments, about who made—and did not make—the list and the subjects we covered with them. You can communicate with us directly by visiting our web site: *www.lessonsfromthetop.com*

Thomas J. Neff		James M. Citrin
New York, New York;	&	Stamford, Connecticut

PART II

Profiles

Overview to Profiles

FROM THE VERY BEGINNING, WE INTENDED *LESSONS FROM THE TOP* to be built around the people who are among the very best business leaders in America. So, rather than identifying themes of leadership and using profiles as examples to support each one, we went straight at it and built a stand-alone chapter for each leader and his or her organization. This way a leader like Mike Armstrong of AT&T has an opportunity to talk at length about what *he* thinks is important for people to know about leading an organization today.

It turns out that Armstrong, who had senior positions at IBM and Hughes Electronics before being recruited to become AT&T's CEO, believes there are five key things every leader must do. If we organized the book by themes, Armstrong would have appeared only in the "vision" or "executing strategy" sections. Both he and you would have been short-changed.

How This Section Is Organized

With all due apologies to Alfred Zeien of Gillette, whose profile begins on page 347, we have organized this section alphabetically by business leader. (That, unfortunately, makes Zeien appear last.)

We considered ordering the chapters along a number of different lines, including by industry group, size, financial performance, geography, alphabetically by company, and even randomly. In the end, however, after many discussions with colleagues and participants in this project, we concluded that presenting chapters alphabetically by leader worked best.

Each profile chapter has four parts:

1) An introduction that not only sets the stage but also puts what the leader has accomplished in context.
2) A résumé box, chronicling the upward progress of the leader's career.
3) The "story" about the leader and his or her company based on our discussions with them.
4) A company-at-a-glance, which summarizes the breadth of product or business line and lists the location of the "home" office, ticker symbol (where applicable), and financial performance of the enterprise.

Each chapter can stand alone. Part III distills the principles of business leadership and common traits that these great leaders share.

Here is the list of the 50 leaders profiled in *Lessons from the Top*.

LEADER	COMPANY
Mike Armstrong	AT&T
Carol Bartz	Autodesk
Hans Becherer	Deere
Gordon Bethune	Continental Airlines
Larry Bossidy	AlliedSignal
Jim Broadhead	FPL Group
Steve Case	America Online
John Chambers	Cisco Systems
Michael Dell	Dell Computer
Elizabeth Dole	American Red Cross
Bob Eaton	DaimlerChrysler
Bernie Ebbers	MCI WorldCom
Michael Eisner	Walt Disney
Don Fisher	The Gap
Don Fites	Caterpillar
Bill Gates	Microsoft
Lou Gerstner	IBM
Ray Gilmartin	Merck
Ace Greenberg	Bear Stearns
Hank Greenberg	AIG
Andy Grove	Intel
Charles Heimbold	Bristol-Myers Squibb
Martha Ingram	Ingram Industries
David Johnson	Campbell Soup
Herb Kelleher	Southwest Airlines
Bill Kerr	Meredith

LEADER	COMPANY
Chuck Knight	Emerson Electric
Dennis Kozlowski	Tyco International
Ralph Larsen	Johnson & Johnson
Ken Lay	Enron
Shelly Lazarus	Ogilvy & Mather
Bill Marriott	Marriott International
Lou Noto	Mobil
Paul O'Neill	Alcoa
John Pepper	Procter & Gamble
Frank Raines	Fannie Mae
Howard Schultz	Starbucks
Charles Schwab	Charles Schwab
Walter Shipley	Chase Manhattan
Fred Smith	FDX
Bill Steere	Pfizer
Bob Tillman	Lowe's Companies
Alex Trotman	Ford Motor Company
Dan Tully and David Komansky	Merrill Lynch
Mike Volkema	Herman Miller
Charles Wang	Computer Associates
Sandy Weill	Citigroup
Jack Welch	General Electric
Al Zeien	Gillette

With this by way of background, let's move ahead with the profiles.

MIKE ARMSTRONG
AT&T

"You've got to have the guts to make a decision."

C. MICHAEL ARMSTRONG DISAPPEARED FOR 90 DAYS IMMEDIATELY AF-
ter being named AT&T's new chairman and CEO in October 1997. He
came to work every day, but no one outside of the company—with the
exception of key clients—saw him. There were no press conferences. No
speeches. No meetings with securities analysts.

"I closed the top management team in a conference room for three months," Armstrong explains. "That's a long time. But during that time we did something extraordinary. We hammered out a complete redefinition of our strategy for AT&T."

Ironically, Armstrong's lack of visibility spurred frenetic press coverage. It seemed that everyone had an opinion about what Armstrong would—or should—do with AT&T. But even the most rabid speculators were surprised. Ultimately, Armstrong and his team decided to turn the company on its head.

Armstrong, who had run Hughes Electronics (which founded satellite television operator DirecTV) and was previously IBM's Group Executive, Communications, understood the telecommunications industry. And having spent nearly three decades at IBM, a tenure which included restructuring the company's

CAREER
OCTOBER 1997–PRESENT Chairman and
   CEO, AT&T Corporation
1993–1997 Chairman and CEO, Hughes
   Electronics
1992–1993 Chairman, President, and CEO,
   IBM World Trade Corp.
1987–1992 President and General Director
   IBM Europe/Middle East
1984–1987 Group Executive
   Communications, IBM
1978–1983 President, Data Processing
   Division, IBM
1961–1976 Various operating and staff
   positions worldwide, IBM

EDUCATION
B.S., Miami University of Ohio, 1961
Advanced Management curriculum, Dartmouth
   Institute, 1976

FAMILY
Married, Anne; children: Linda, Julie, Kristy

Born: Detroit, Michigan, October 18, 1938

operations in Europe, he knew what it would take to turn a business around. So, he was no stranger to what had to be done.

At the end of those 90 days, AT&T started down a path that would do nothing less than make it, once again, one of the world's great companies. Investors have responded—enthusiastically. The company's stock price, which was $34 on October 21, 1997 (the day before Armstrong was named chairman and CEO), stood at $61 less than a year and a half later (May 7, 1999), a market value gain of $92 billion.

WE HAVE TO ADMIT WE WERE SURPRISED. AS PART OF THE INTERVIEW process, we sent every leader a list of questions ahead of time. We wanted to give them an idea of the kinds of topics we hoped to discuss. (See Appendix 3.)

"I don't expect anyone to be perfect. It's not human nature. What I do expect is that you will take risks, correct mistakes, and learn from both. And if you don't—judging by market results—then we'll make a change. It's nothing personal. And I'll do it, even if you're my best friend. We must have this company execute to its full potential."

Some of the leaders just glanced at the questions, preferring that our conversations be spontaneous. Others wrote copious notes in the margins of what we had faxed them and referred to them continuously during our talks. And a handful of others went so far as to pull out slides and talking points from speeches they had given in preparation for our meeting.

Still, we were not quite ready for Mike Armstrong.

"I've looked at your questions as a whole," he began. "It seems what you really want to know is how I go about leading an organization like this one, right?"

When we agreed, Armstrong launched into one of the most concise and articulate discussions of business leadership we had ever encountered.

Mike Armstrong's Principles of Leadership

"In my view, there are five buckets. The first is widely reported and written about, but it's also plainly true: You've got to have a defining idea. Some people call it 'the vision.' Others call it 'the strategy.' I'm not sure it matters how you describe it in its adjectival form. But it must be real, substantive, and something that people can buy into and believe in."

Before Armstrong arrived, the strategy at AT&T was basically built around protecting the company's long distance business, conserving capital, and optimizing cash flow.

"I took a look and I didn't think that the company's strategy was sustainable or durable," Armstrong recalls. "My defining idea was for AT&T to move to facilities-based broadband communications. We wouldn't just be domestic, but global in our reach. We would not just sell narrow-band long distance service, we would operate seamlessly through broadband wireless, Internet, and cable. Instead of being a point-to-point long distance company, we would be an 'any distance company' from wherever a customer was to wherever a customer wanted to go. We'll connect to people and PBXs; to your local area network, extraterritorial network, Internet network, or your personal network. No matter where in the world you are, any service, any distance from AT&T."

In short, the vision could be reduced to this: AT&T will be the only communications provider a customer will ever need.

To Armstrong, the need to position the company this way could not have been clearer.

"Here we are in this marvelous growth industry—telecommunications— the most fabulous growth industry for decades, and AT&T, the largest company in that industry, was not growing. It was defending a business that—on a stand-alone basis—was not even viable, given the technology and deregulation. We had to go on the offensive."

And little more than one year later, the company had invested more than $100 billion to do just that. It invested $12 billion for Teleport Communication, $5 billion for IBM's global network, $5.5 billion in an $11 billion joint venture with British Telecom, and $48 billion for TCI, the United States' second largest cable company. In addition, AT&T agreed to acquire MediaOne Group for $54 billion.

These were huge decisions, Armstrong agrees, but he adds that making decisions of this magnitude is a key ingredient of the CEO's job.

"In the end you have to have the guts to make a decision. You'll never have all the data you need. You'll never be able to sort through all the alternatives and threats and risks that are in front of you. You get the right information and couple it with the right instincts to enable you make a decision. Then you energize your organization to make that decision work in the marketplace.

"I would say that 90% of what we decided coming out of our initial strategy meetings was agreed to. The other 10% were people who weren't used to this new pace of activity. They were used to taking months and months for analysis, homework, and review. To some degree, moving this quickly was a risk, but I felt strongly that this strategy was the only way AT&T could fulfill its potential."

It is clear that Armstrong believes that it is critical to create an overarching strategy that people will believe in.

Moving On

"The second thing you have to do is have the courage to be competitive. There's no strategy, or defining idea, that will overcome a noncompetitive company.

"When I came here SG&A [selling, general, and administrative expenses] was 29.6% of revenue. The industry average was 22%. And so I put a mark on the wall and said, 'We're going to get to 22% in 24 months and have an 18,000 workforce reduction over two years.' "

The company achieved this aggressive workforce objective in just 12 months. Through reorganizations, streamlining, and a 20,000 reduction in head count, the company took out over $1.6 billion in overhead and expense in one year.

These kinds of dramatic moves, Armstrong says, are mandatory.

"Very few competitive businesses have sustainable success if they're not the low-cost producer. This company has no excuse not to be the low-cost producer and use cost as an advantage in its market.

"Of course, this must be an ongoing priority. You don't just become cost competitive and then go on to other things. You have to focus on it every year."

The current SG&A goal? 21% of sales.

"The third fundamental you need to do is understand, respect, and trust your management team. You can't concurrently change a culture and change your entire management team. During my meetings with the board [in 1997, before Armstrong was hired], I made it clear that I wouldn't take the job until I understood who the executives were and whether, in my judgment, we could have the mutual respect and trust to carry forward as a team. It's just like sports. There are a lot of great athletes out there, but usually the team that plays together best gets the Super Bowl ring. It's the same in business.

"This is a $60 billion business. There's no way that this office can execute everything. You've got to have trust and confidence in your team. Of the top 16 executives, eight are in new jobs and four are new to the company. But that means that about half are part of the team that was in place when I arrived."

Part of getting those executives to "buy in" is the way Armstrong does his job.

"You've got to lead by example," he says. "There are CEOs who get to love their office. You've got to get out into the markets. You've got to meet your customers. You've got to understand your competition. You've got to give the same speech too many times. You've got to go to the lunch bag forum with discipline. I write an article every month for the company newspaper. I do videotapes. I do company broadcasts. Communicate, communicate, communicate! You cannot be a remote image. You've got to be touched, felt, heard, and believed.

"And you've got to stand up for what you stand for. When the company comes under attack—whether it's from Washington, the competition, or industry analysts—you've got to be out there taking the brunt of whatever it is and lead by example.

"The fourth thing you must do involves decision making. Big organizations sometimes institutionalize decision making. Businesses are not democratic institutions. Some may choose, because of the momentum of their success, to lead by consensus. But there are very few that can enjoy that luxury. You'd better lead by intelligence, instinct, judgment, and make decisions while there's still risk in them, or you're not going to lead in your markets.

"That was one of the problems here. They had 'one-stop shopping.' Any manager at any level could stop any good idea forever. We had to cut through that and make decisions."

How does Armstrong do that?

"Every single Monday, the company's top executives—eight to 10 people—meet for the whole day. And we pull, drag, and inspect this company to make sure we're responding to the market and the competition. It's not a 'command performance.' You don't have to attend, if the subject matter we are going to discuss that day is irrelevant to your

Company (Ticker): AT&T Corporation (T)

Location: Basking Ridge, New Jersey

Leader: C. Michael Armstrong

AT&T at a glance: With more than 80 million customers and 148,000 employees, AT&T is the largest communications company in the United States. The company has expanded its communications business to include wireless telephony (including cellular, messaging, and air-to-ground services), Internet access (AT&T WorldNet), and local and international telephone services. AT&T acquired the nation's second-largest cable operating company, Tele-Communications, Inc. (TCI), which will enable the company to offer local phone service through cable hookups, boost its Internet access business and add cable TV to its services. Furthering its push into local broadband services and cable television, AT&T acquired MediaOne Group in addition to forming partnerships with Time Warner Cable, Comcast, and British Telecommunications. However, in November 2000, AT&T announced plans to divide the business into four separate companies under the AT&T name.

1999 Financial Results
—Revenues: $62.3 billion
—Net Income: $3.4 billion

area. But it is a command performance if it is. And if you miss the meeting, we just make the decision without you.

"The last thing that I'd say you have to do is to commit to values as you generate both personal and organizational energy. You have to create excitement as well as opportunity. We all spend so much time working, it's got to be fun as well as rewarding for people. They've got to smile more often than they frown. They've got to feel good about themselves as well as where they work. They need to feel that the best day of their week is Monday. If you can create that environment, people just work their bloody tails off for you. And if you've got an organization of people doing that, you're going to win.

"These five things form my view of business leadership."

Not surprisingly, Armstrong believes that if he follows these principles correctly, AT&T will fulfill his vision and thrive.

"Whether you want to be tethered with wires, or whether you want to be wireless, we will be there for you, providing every communications service you need, wherever you are. That's the kind of company we will be. And that's a long way from being a domestic point-to-point, long distance company. The technology is already there to have it take place. And my job is to keep this company on the leading edge of those technologies."

Beyond the leadership and execution required to realize this vision, the company has another major advantage—its brand.

"It's our good fortune that the AT&T brand actually represents *more* than we are. If you go into the RBOCs' [Regional Bell Operating Companies such as Bell Atlantic or SBC Communications] territories and ask, 'Who provides your local service?' 23% of the people say AT&T. We're not even in the local service business yet. If you ask, 'Who provides your cable television?' 14% will say AT&T. We're not in that business yet. AT&T has the most trusted brand, not just in America, but in the world. And to fulfill the potential of that brand is what our strategy has got to execute against. Fortunately, the brand is way ahead of where we are in the market. That's really an advantage and an asset."

Once again, people—be they customers, employees, suppliers, strategic partners, or the investment community—believe in what AT&T stands for today. That, more than anything, may be Armstrong's lasting legacy.

CAROL BARTZ
Autodesk

Leading by example

MAYBE IT IS BECAUSE SHE GREW UP ON a farm.

Maybe it is because she is one of the few senior technology executives with extensive experience in both hardware and software.

Or maybe it is because she is frequently the only woman in the room when CEOs of large companies gather. Whatever the reason, Carol Bartz has unique perspectives on both business issues and leadership styles.

After climbing through the ranks of Sun Microsystems, Bartz was recruited in 1992 to run Autodesk, a leading producer of computer-aided design/computer-aided manufacturing (CAD/CAM) software. Immediately after arriving at the company, she raised manufacturing standards, hired a stronger salespeople force, and began adding new products.

Today, odds are if design software is required for a particular industry, Autodesk makes it.

"Simply, look around you," Bartz says. "Anything designed, built, or manufactured could involve the use of our prod-

CAREER

1992– PRESENT Chairman, CEO, and President, Autodesk, Inc.

1990–1992 Vice President, Worldwide Field Operations, Sun Microsystems

1989–1990 Vice President, Customer Service, Sun Microsystems

1987–1989 President, Sun Federal, part of Sun Microsystems

1984–1987 Vice President, Marketing, Sun Microsystems

1983–1984 Manager, Consumer Marketing, Sun Microsystems

1976–1983 Sales Management Department, Digital Equipment Corp.

1971–1976 Sales Management Department, 3M

EDUCATION

Honorary Doctorates: Worcester Polytechnic Institute and William Woods University

B.S. in Computer Science, University of Wisconsin, 1971

FAMILY

Married, William Marr; one daughter

Born: Alma, Wisconsin, August 29, 1948

> *"I like management. I like the complexity of putting structures together and getting teams going."*

ucts. I don't care if we are talking about the road you drove to work on, the automobile you're riding in, the building you're standing in, the furniture you're sitting on, or the clothes you're wearing, we may have been involved."

Company sales are now approaching $1 billion annually and climbing, as Bartz holds her employees accountable, leads by example, and tries to do everything in her power *not* to be a role model.

THE SUBJECT WAS "WHAT DOES IT TAKE TO RUN A COMPANY EFFEC-tively?" Not surprisingly, Carol Bartz, chairman and CEO of Autodesk, had a well-thought-out opinion.

"First, I think you really have to know the business," she says. "I am not so sure that these hired guns who come in to run one kind of business for a couple of years, and then go off to run another, are effective long-term. I am assuming that by the time somebody's even a candidate for a top-level position, he has experience and brains. Given all that, I look at whether the candidate's management style and the culture of the company he is going to help run are a good match. An autocratic style that might work in one industry or company could really blow up in another.

"This style thing cannot go unnoticed. When you factor everything else out, it may be the most important thing."

Because Bartz believes style is so important, she feels it cannot be faked, or even copied. That is why she is so passionate about mentoring.

She is a*gainst* it.

"I hate the word mentor. I don't think the concept works. We're all snowflakes, and I can't find another snowflake that perfectly matches me. So if I spend too much time copying another snowflake, then I'm not being all *I* can be.

"I've watched people who have been mentored and you just wonder why they are acting the way they are. Often they are trying to copy a style that may work for someone else, but it sure doesn't work for them and they are left with nothing."

Bartz concedes there is a certain irony at work here. She doesn't believe in the concept of mentoring, but by holding the position she does—one of the very few female CEOs running a major corporation—she is a role model for many.

It is not, she stresses, something she sought out.

"The role model mantle is a pretty heavy one. A lot of times I would like to pretend I'm not one, because it is pretty weighty. The sad part is that I don't care what event I may go to, the few women who are there stand out. And by standing out, you feel more pressure. You feel more obliged to be 'on.' To do well.

"And even though I've gotten to this position, I'm still running into yahoos every day who when we attend a meeting want me to run out and get everyone tea. That gets old. I don't try to pay a whole lot of attention to it, but you still get irritated. And then I say, gosh, if people are doing this to me, what the heck are they doing to women further down the organization?"

There are benefits, of course, to being a woman in her position and Bartz tries to take advantage of them.

"Because of the curiosity factor, I can get in to see people who would never otherwise see me," Bartz explains. "And, some people—both male and female—have told me that they came to work at Autodesk because I am the CEO."

Plus, being a woman in a high-visibility position gives Bartz a "bully pulpit." She uses it to advise people about how to get ahead at Autodesk, or any other organization.

"I'm pretty outspoken on career development. I think people really need to build their career like a pyramid, not like a ladder. I think too often they go for the almighty promotion, and as a result stay in a very narrow field. For instance, if they get a job in marketing, they say okay, I can get to be a manager, if I stay here, and then maybe I can be a director, and maybe even a vice president of marketing."

While that approach can make sense, it is limiting, Bartz argues. It certainly will preclude you from a top management position at a company such as Autodesk.

"I think the safest, surest way to the top is to have a strong, broad base of experience. That's why I use the pyramid metaphor," Bartz says. "Pyramids have a stronger base than a free-standing ladder. But to get that strong base, you may have to take lateral promotions, or maybe even take a step backward in your career.

"Too many times, somebody in their twenties or thirties will come into my office and want career counseling. I always begin the same way. I tell them they have 30 or so more years to work here, and every minute of that 30 years is not going to be spent on an onward and upward track. I want you to get that out of your head right now. With that out of the way, let's see what skills and knowledge you might need based on whatever the heck it is you want to do."

The responsibility for gaining the necessary knowledge and skills rests with the employee, Bartz says. While managers can be supportive and helpful, it is up to the employees themselves to make sure they get the kind of grounding they need.

"The other thing I tell them is that you have to have passion, and that passion has to come through. I'll take a smart person with passion over someone with years of experience any day. People with intelligence and passion will get the problem solved, no matter what."

How to Lead

Despite all her protestations, people do spend a lot of time studying how Bartz does her job, in the hopes of learning how they might do theirs better. What they discover is that she is an executive who monitors results closely, and models the behavior she wants her employees to have.

"I frequently say, what you don't inspect, they don't respect," Bartz says. "I do that with my daughter's homework, and I do it at the company. I do it because I value the thinking process. I want my daughter, and the people at Autodesk, to understand the consequences of what they do. If you do this, then that will happen, and getting them to understand the consequences always goes back to what you measure."

There is not one set of measures at Autodesk.

"Every function is different, so it affects what you look at. I don't run around with this huge checklist that says look at revenues today, and operating profits tomorrow. I ask people, based on what their job is and what kind of function they're running, to make a series of commitments. They might be revenue commitments, or it might be soft goals, or it could be a project they're doing. But whatever it is, I expect it to be delivered. I make no secret of that. And I always tell them the bad news better come out real fast. The faster we can figure out that something either has changed beneath us, or needs to change, the quicker we can reassess and get going again."

She is equally clear in communicating what else she thinks is important. All

Company (Ticker): Autodesk, Inc. (ADSK)

Location: San Rafael, California

Leader: Carol Bartz

Autodesk at a glance: One of the world's largest PC software companies, Autodesk is a leading supplier of computer-aided design (CAD) automation software. AutoCAD, the company's flagship product, is used by architects and engineers to perform design, modeling, drafting, mapping, and rendering projects.

In addition to AutoCAD, Autodesk makes software for the multimedia, film, and video industries. Autodesk has created two new Internet portals, buzzsaw.com and redspark.com, which are focusing on the construction, design, and manufacturing industries.

1999 Financial Results

—Revenues: $820 million

—Net Income: $100 million

you have to do is watch how she does her job and leads her life. This is by design.

"You have to show by example what is important. I tell my VPs that if their 10-year-old has a concert, that is only going to happen one time and that the concert takes precedence over an executive meeting. Again, I have to show people what I respect and what I'm interested in. I think that's really important.

"Many times over the years, even before I was CEO, I heard people say, 'Carol wouldn't do that.' I think leadership starts there. Then, you have to have a vision that you are excited about. You have to be so excited about your vision that people can't wait to come and try to achieve it with you. I don't care whether it's a small project or it's running a big company, your people have got to want to stay with you and want to go the extra mile. You have to have people excited about what you are doing, because going to work is not just about getting paid."

What happens when a company's people are excited about what they do? They work harder. They have more fun. And—as the employees at Autodesk are quick to point out—they deliver.

HANS BECHERER

Deere

Creating customers for life

FOR MOST OF THE 1980S, U.S. AGRICULTURE EQUIPMENT SUFFERED a long, slow, painful contraction. At that time, falling asset values and excessive debt in the farm sector together with high inflation and interest rates in a fragile general economy triggered a widespread financial farm crisis. Many farm equipment companies struggled to survive. Deere & Company, the world's largest manufacturer of farm equipment, was no exception.

Deere not only weathered the crisis of the eighties and restructured itself into a global competitor, it came back with a vengeance, so much so that *The Wall Street Journal* recently called the company, "the model American multinational corporation."

Agricultural equipment is still the core product line of John Deere, but the non-ag operations of construction, commercial and consumer equipment, credit operations, and even an HMO now make up nearly 50% of its product mix. (The Heritage National Healthplan HMO was originally established to provide care to Deere personnel.)

The architect of this resurgence? CEO Hans Becherer. A history major, Becherer went to work for Deere after serving in the Air Force in Germany and earning an MBA from Harvard. As the

CAREER
1990–PRESENT Chairman, Deere & Company
1989–present CEO
1987–1989 President and COO
1986–1987 Executive Vice President
1983–1986 Senior Vice President
1977–1983 Vice President
1973–1977 Director of Export Marketing
1969–1973 General Manager, Deere Export, Mannheim, Germany
1966–1969 Executive Assistant, Office of the Chairman, Deere & Company

EDUCATION
M.B.A., Harvard University, 1962
Postgraduate, Munich University, 1958
B.A., Trinity College, 1957

FAMILY
Married, Michele Beigbeder, November 28, 1959; children: Maxime, Vanessa

Born: Detroit, Michigan, April 19, 1935

"I'm proud that I see such a good team around me. I wish I were younger so I could take advantage of it for more years."

son of German immigrants, Becherer says he already had a strong international orientation long before joining the company. That international perspective, in fact, would prove to be a key part of his career. Becherer's early positions primarily involved international marketing, and he believes his company's future will rest on how well it can continue to provide extraordinary customer service, in the growth markets outside North America, especially in Latin America, the former Soviet Union, China, and India.

FOR HANS BECHERER, IT WAS A MATTER OF BEING IN THE RIGHT PLACE at the right time.

"I came in touch with Deere & Company for the first time in France. My wife is French, and we were spending about a month with her family before I was to start at the Harvard Business School. One day, during that stay, her uncle, who was a successful businessman, came by. He said, 'Hans, a number of international executives are coming in for lunch tomorrow. Would you like to join us?' Of course; I did.

"At lunch I sat next to Comart Peterson, vice president of marketing for Deere in Europe, who asked me to keep in touch. I dropped him a note, once I was in business school, asking about a summer job. That resulted in my working for Deere in Moline, Illinois, after my first year in graduate school. That summer I realized that this was a company of immense integrity, with really fine people. It was a company willing to let you run as hard as you wanted. I'm very proud of those observations. As a young man, I saw the lasting values and the mores of this company, and they were exactly what I was looking for. Also, I was interested in international business, and Deere had started its journey internationally.

"So I went with Deere after I graduated and I've never looked back. I've loved every day since. The qualities of Deere I saw in my summer job—integrity, trust, customer focus, superior products, and concern for the employees and its communities—have made my career here fun. That's why my message to young people thinking about their careers is, 'You've got to like where you are, what you're doing, and whom you work for. You've got to have a lot of fun doing what you're doing. When you don't, you've got to pick up and go somewhere else.' I encourage our folks to have fun as we work. If you can't laugh, and enjoy the job, you're not going to do a good job over time."

In Europe, Becherer enjoyed himself immensely as he introduced

Deere's legendary devotion to customer service to geographic and market areas that had never experienced it firsthand.

"Consider the farmer," Becherer begins in explaining what sustains the customer service ethos. "He's out there at harvest time or planting time, the two critical points of the cycle, and he just can't afford to have anything go wrong for very long. Every day he misses planting at the ideal time is going to cost him in yield later on. It's one of the reasons why a farmer owns a $150,000 combine and only uses it for a short period of the year. He doesn't want to depend on somebody else. For the same reason, he *has* to depend on that machine. If something breaks, he needs to have the confidence it's going to be fixed pronto.

"Over the years we have developed the capability to do that well. What's really important is that this capability has been embedded in each of the new businesses we've developed. For example, when we added construction machinery to our product line we stressed being more dependable than our competition."

So, part of Deere's customer service strategy was to provide clients with good products that seldom failed, but would be repaired quickly if anything did go wrong. A second part was giving customers the kinds of products they wanted.

"Just about every addition to our product line was made because we listened to the customer and developed products and business lines that built upon our strengths and capabilities," Becherer said. "We are in the lawn and grounds care business—more than $2 billion in sales today— as a direct result of customers asking why they could put all green (Deere's trademark color) equipment on their farms, but had to mow their lawns with someone else's red mowers. We felt we had to do something about that.

"No matter which field we move into, we're usually the ones with the highest commitment to product support. Our competitors, particularly those in residential products, often come from backgrounds not associated with customers as demanding as the ag customer. They don't have the capability or the heritage of extensive product support and customer service that we've developed to satisfy our customers. This has long been the tradition at Deere. As an example, during the Depression John Deere kept extending credit to farmers, allowing many of them to avoid going bankrupt. There are still thousands of families out there who have a loyalty to us because we helped save the farm when times were tough. We have this tremendous bond of confidence with many customers. And we endeavor to build that trust across our other businesses as well."

You can see this in Deere's decision to create a finance company to help customers pay for their purchases, in providing insurance to protect what they buy, and even in its health care business. That same devotion to listening to and helping customers will contribute to drive the company going forward.

Information-Driven Farming

"What's exciting today is watching technology impact the equipment business develop," Becherer explains. "Information-driven farming is something brand new. Farming has always been an intuitive, 'I-think-I'll-plant-today' kind of environment. Farming is one of the last cottage businesses. You have thousands of individual farmers out there making their own decisions and doing quite well, but we are going to help them improve their productivity even more by providing management tools for information-driven farming.

"What do I mean by information-driven farming? Well, today farmers make decisions based on innumerable inputs involving seeds, fertilizers, weather, row width, and soil conditions. They try different combinations, but there is an inadequate information base upon which to center their decisions or bring clear focus to their judgment. They have to pull it all together from fragmentary information from multiple sources. So today, the farmer is often perplexed about how to gather the information he needs to make a decision. We are working on a solution to this. For example, we have launched what we call Greenstar computer information, which is a precision, satellite-driven farming technique. As the combine goes through a field, it picks up electronically its exact location in the field, and what exactly is going on with growing conditions and yield.

"Farmers are discovering they have been treating the field homogeneously, even though fields vary tremendously from one end to the other. With Greenstar, the farmer will get a prescription for what he should do for each part of the field. It will tell him he should put more fertilizer in this area, and less over there. We're also making planters and other equipment, so he can put that same computer-driven information into his tractor and make those changes automatically, while he is out in the field.

"The net result is going to be greater productivity for the farmer," Becherer says. "He'll increase his output and his bottom-line results. We are in the process of establishing an online service that will enable information-based farming. We want the farmer to have complete access to critical weather information, price, supply and demand information to make the best possible decisions. We expect to be a leader in data warehousing for the farmer."

And, Becherer plans to go even further.

"We're working on a common information backbone system for all of our businesses where you will be able to take data directly from machines and provide information value. You'll know that your tire is leaking; that the bearing is worn on your rear axle; that you're losing oil pressure. We'll be able to track everything and then say, 'Mr. Farmer or Mr. Builder, your machine number so-and-so is showing these signs. We suggest you pull it out and do this and that,' or we'll have the dealer go out and do it for him on the spot.

"So, there's just a tremendous new game being built on information that's going to emerge, and it will be those companies that figure out how to do it well that will thrive. Deere will do this, and we have the advantage of being able to leverage this capability over three equipment divisions. I'm not so sure who else will, but it's going to be a new game. Customers' need for new technology is driving us to provide these solutions. Normally, people don't think that we are in a technology-driven business, but today we are."

When Becherer talks about the future, and how technology can help the farmer, you can hear the passion in his voice. That is not by accident.

"I think CEOs who are successful are all impassioned about what they do and what they believe in. That passion permeates an organization. It's essential to have.

"With passion you need to have a vision, and you've got to know where you're going," Becherer adds. "I don't think there is a successful CEO who doesn't know where he or she is trying to lead the enterprise and who isn't trying to motivate the company to endorse that vision," Becherer says.

"One of the CEO's roles," Becherer says, "is to create new paradigms and present new challenges to the enterprise in order to keep it energized and moving toward the vision."

At Deere, the common vision is what Becherer calls "genuine value" and the strategy that results is "Business Process Excellence."

"At Deere, genuine value sums up our vision. Genuine value captures the essence of what we are trying to do in serving our constituents. We pursue this through financial goals linked to metrics like growth and return on assets. And our goals are established to ensure continuous improvement in quality, through the implementation of Six Sigma, supply management, customer satisfaction, and workforce planning and development.

That will be carried out, Becherer says, through Business Process Excellence.

"BPE is our approach to moving Deere from a functional organization to a more process-driven one. We believe this will provide a powerful differentiator for us in the years to come. We have established the goals for

BPE in continuous improvement, supply management, workforce planning and development, and customer focus. The goals have been linked to performance awards.

"We believe BPE will drive the changes needed for Deere to continue delivering genuine value in the future."

The other thing he believes great leaders have in common is "being very open to change, because the biggest difference between being a CEO today and one a generation or so back is the speed of change. We're all on treadmills; you never 'get there.' You used to get places. You don't get there anymore, because goals change and capabilities change so rapidly. You need a mind-set where you're comfortable with this new kind of an environment. Again, that's a trait most great CEOs have. They're very open and ready to accept change. As a result, they create a learning organization. We have to train, retrain, and then do it over again."

Embracing change is the price of entry for today's CEOs, says Becherer, adding that the situation is going to be even tougher for the next generation of leaders because change will not just be in the external environment.

This leads him to discuss another core belief: "An attitude of inclusion. One can never lose the capacity for indignation on the issue of diversity," Becherer says. "We should be indignant if we aren't able to embrace diversity; it's such an acceptable, proper, and utterly appropriate thing to do. It's the first step to globalism. If we can't accept diversity locally, how can we possibly accept the diversity of working in a global world?

"I think the hardest thing going forward is that there will be a lot less loyalty to companies and more turnover of people. I come from a company with virtually no turnover and immense loyalty. And I wonder how you can convey your values, passions, and beliefs, if you have high turnover. I think the value system

Company (Ticker): Deere & Company (DE)

Location: Moline, Illinois

Leader: Hans Walter Becherer

Deere at a glance: Deere & Co. is the world's largest manufacturer of farm equipment and is a leading producer of industrial and lawn care equipment. The company produces and markets tractors, harvesting machinery, soil-preparation machinery, construction equipment, diesel engines, chain saws, lawn trimmers, leaf blowers, tillers, back hoes, and snow blowers. Market conditions led to the acquisition of Timberjack, which allows Deere to expand into forestry equipment. To further expand itself out of the agricultural market, Deere acquired Sunbelt Outdoor Products and a controlling interest in Shanghai GE Construction Equipment Engineering Co., Ltd. Deere also provides financing, leasing, and insurance to its dealers and customers, and it operates a managed health care program for its employees and others.

1999 Financial Results

—Revenues: $11.5 billion

—Net Income: $239 million

is going to become more important, and the soft skills of executive leadership are going to become even more important, as the workforce churns. It will be more important to communicate your company's value structure. That really is the only thing of permanence within an organization."

In that communication you'll have to be sincere, honest, open, and, Becherer stresses again, passionate.

"I host chairman coffees with randomly selected employees, and I sit there for an hour or so speaking with them in open dialogue. We drink coffee and I tell them what the company is trying to do and what I believe in. Then, I try to make sure they understand their important role in providing solutions to the challenges we face in improving the company.

"When people leave, the response is, 'Yes, you're right. I can help. It's my job.' They are responding to my passion. And that's what it is all about. I believe a company responds to the passion and enthusiasm of its leaders. It's contagious. If you can't stand there and pour your heart into what you're saying we ought to be doing, then how do you expect others to be passionate?"

Care about the customer. Provide genuine value. Sustain lasting values. Be global. Embrace change and be passionate about what you do. It's a formula that has served Deere well.

GORDON BETHUNE
Continental Airlines

It's how you'd run an airline

UNLESS YOU FLEW CONTINENTAL IN THE bad old days—the 1980s and into the early 1990s—it is truly hard to imagine how awful the airline was. Planes were constantly late. Estimated times of arrivals and departures were just that—estimates, that rarely had any basis in reality—and no one who had ever flown on the airline would check their bag if it was humanly impossible to avoid doing so. The reason for that is simple. There was no reason to expect that your luggage would arrive in the same city at the same time you did.

The airline had gone bankrupt twice, and was well on its way to going down for a third—and probably final—time when Gordon M. Bethune was named president and COO on Valentine's Day, 1994, CEO in November 1994, and chairman in September 1996.

A high school dropout—who later earned a G.E.D., high school diploma, college degree, and certificate from the Harvard Business School Advanced Management Program for senior executives— Bethune now concedes in retrospect he had no idea how bad the problems were.

CAREER
1996–PRESENT Chairman, Continental Airlines, Inc.
1994–PRESENT CEO
1994 President and COO
1988–1994 Vice President and General Manager, Boeing Commercial Airplane Group's Renton Division; Vice President and General Manager, Customer Services Division
1984–1988 Piedmont Airlines, Senior Vice President, Operations
1983 Western Airlines, Vice President, Maintenance and Engineering
1979–1982 Braniff Airways, Vice President, Engineering and Maintenance
1968–1978 United States Navy, Aircraft Maintenance Officer

EDUCATION
Advanced Management Program, Harvard Business School, 1992 B.S., Abilene Christian University

FAMILY
Married to Tommie Richardson; three children: Xavier, Michael, and Grady

Born: San Antonio, Texas, August 29, 1941

If he had, he admits, he is not sure he would have ever left Boeing to try to turn around the airline.

"You don't have to beat the horse to run faster. Sometimes he actually accelerates if you stop whipping him. We quit whipping the horse and things improved."

How bad was it?

Continental was nearly out of cash, employees didn't trust management, and the airline ranked dead last in all the categories airline passengers cared about, things such as on-time arrivals and departures, reliable luggage handling, and good food at meal times.

Bethune, who has written his own book (*From Worst to First*) was also featured in a small, much underappreciated book, called *Comeback* (by Martin Puris). We cannot think of a better leader to have been included in any work carrying that title.

HAVING DECIDED THAT CONTINENTAL WAS WORTH SAVING, BEcause of its strong franchise in the marketplace, the question was how to do it, Bethune explains. Over a series of dinners (which he has taken to calling "our last suppers"), Bethune and Greg Brenneman (first a Bain & Company consultant and now president and chief operating officer of Continental) mapped out a turnaround strategy.

In retrospect, their plan seems commonsensical and obvious. But there are two key things to remember. First, the company was in the midst of a crisis. (At one of its darkest moments, the company was less than six weeks away from not having enough cash to meet payroll.) And the second point is this: Straightforward as the plan might have been, no one had ever come up with, nor implemented, such a plan. (The airline had gone through 10 presidents in 10 years.)

"The first step was to figure out exactly what we wanted to do," Bethune says. "We needed to develop a simple clear strategy, one that everyone could understand, and once it was in place, one that we weren't going to deviate from."

Easier said than done.

When you are in the middle of an emergency—and trying to save an airline that is desperately short of cash certainly qualifies as an emergency—there is a natural tendency to grasp at straws, to go after whatever will bring in money to keep you solvent for another week or two.

Bethune understood the temptation and fought it off. The company would focus exclusively on four things which collectively came to be known as the "Go Forward Plan":

- Turning profitable. Part of that was cutting costs. CALite, the company's low-cost division, was eliminated and money-losing flights were taken off the schedule. But that was only half the battle. Continental would also build on its strengths, most notably its hubs in Cleveland, Houston, and Newark.
- Becoming cash-flow positive. Loans were restructured and operations were streamlined. The company went from 13 kinds of planes to six, on the way to four, for example—to simplify maintenance and purchasing, and to increase liquidity.
- Performing. On-time arrivals and departures would improve, incidents of lost luggage would decrease, and the quality of food would get better.
- Creating a new corporate culture. One where everyone won—or lost—together. Says Bethune, "We all were going to win, or nobody would."

With that strategy in place, Bethune went out to sell it to Continental's rank and file.

From the middle ranks down, the employees "got it." Although many passengers who suffered through the Continental of the 1980s and early '90s do not know it, the airline has a rich history of exemplary performance. That excellence dated back to the days when Robert F. Six, a former barnstormer, founded the airline. Longtime employees who remembered Six wanted Bethune to return the airline to profitability, if not glory, and personnel with less experience wanted to keep their jobs.

"There wasn't anything wrong with the people who worked here," Bethune says. "It was a dysfunctional company, but that had to do with the culture more than anything else. Previous management had treated employees badly. As a result, they were like abused children, but they were a good bunch of people."

But while employees were quick to rally around Bethune and Brenneman, senior management was another story. Major changes needed to be made, for both internal and external reasons.

No one likes to admit mistakes and changing the way Continental did things would be an acknowledgment by the old senior management that they had caused the problems in the first place. Because they would be reluctant to admit their mistakes, they were bound to fight new initiatives. Keeping those managers would have caused problems internally.

And keeping them would cause problems outside the company as well. Since it is logical to conclude that the old managers got Continental into trouble in the first place, why would either customers or investors believe they were the right people to get Continental out of its mess.

Wholesale changes were needed.

"The sickest patients need the best doctors, and I hired a team of the best executives to help me put this thing back together," Bethune says. "In the span of a couple of months, we replaced 50 of our 61 officers with about 20 individuals. Because we were replacing so many people, the managers that we hired had to be the absolute best at what they did."

Bethune says there were two benefits that flowed directly from these changes.

"We were cutting bureaucracy and costs, but also putting important stuff, like the right culture, back in. Every company has a culture. And the people who had evolved it here were from a culture that focused on factionalism. Me win. You lose. Most of those people weren't able to play as team members. We had to make changes."

The changes extended throughout the organization from the highest supervisors down to the baggage handlers. Bethune was trying to eliminate all vestiges of the bad old Continental.

And Then Came the Hard Part

But having the right people in place doesn't help you much if you don't have any customers, and Continental had lost them in droves. Frequent flyers had abandoned the airline because of its poor performance in the past.

Advertising that Bethune was creating a "new and improved" Continental would not bring customers back. Consumers—especially Continental's—were too jaded for that approach to be effective.

So the first thing that Bethune and his team did was start calling frequent flyers, and former frequent flyers, to apologize for the way Continental had treated them in the past. However, these new managers used those phone calls to do something else as well. They asked those frequent travelers what they wanted—and were willing to pay for—in an airline.

Both components of the question are important.

If you ask someone what they want from a service provider, you will hear no shortage of ideas. However, if you ask customers what on their "wish list" they are willing to pay for, the list gets shortened quickly.

Looking at what customers said they were willing to pay for, you realize just how bad a job that Continental had done. Customers said they wanted terminals and planes that were safe, on-time flights, reliable baggage handling, and edible food served at normal mealtimes. With the exception of safety, where Continental had always had a good record, the airline was failing miserably.

So Bethune and his team returned Continental to the basics. And an amazing thing happened. With employees working together, instead of fighting with one another, and with a management committed to profit sharing instead of cost cutting, service improved. Dramatically.

Continental went from being ranked worst among the major airlines in customer satisfaction to first. In one year. And its rankings have remained consistently high.

"The only thing that surprised me was the rate of change," Bethune says. "I knew directionally we were correct in having a good product and having people who liked working here. What surprised me was the dramatic change in behavior of our employees and how fast we excelled. I thought it would take a couple of years to turn this place around. But if you take people who are starved for some kind of recognition and appreciation and have them help to develop a plan for what you want to do, the results can be this dramatic."

That, Bethune is quick to add, is consistent with what he had seen at his previous jobs.

"I've worked for some good companies, like Piedmont and Boeing. And I've worked for companies like Braniff who overreached. But everywhere I have seen failures that were 100% attributable to the people element. The single biggest criterion for success as a leader is to recognize and openly appreciate your subordinates. They'll kill for you if you do that. But if you treat them like they're ciphers, they'll let you know in a hundred different ways why you shouldn't have done that.

"Implementation is a bigger issue in being successful than most strategies are. I'm not saying that you don't have to know which is the right hill to take. But knowing which hill to take is only part of the battle. You've got to get your people to want to take the hill. And if

Company (Ticker): Continental Airlines Inc. (Ticker CAL)
Location: Houston, Texas
Leader: Gordon M. Bethune
Continental at a glance: Continental Airlines is the fifth-largest airline in the United States, offering more than 2,200 departures daily to 127 domestic and 79 international destinations. Operating major hubs in Newark, Houston, and Cleveland, Continental (http://www.continental.com) has extensive service throughout the Americas, and to Europe and Asia. Continental recently initiated a strategic global alliance with Northwest Airlines. Continental is in the top half of *Fortune* magazine's "100 Best Companies to Work for in America," and has won first- or second-place *Frequent Flyer* magazine and J. D. Power awards for four consecutive years. Continental has received numerous awards for its BusinessFirst premium cabin (*Condé Nast Traveler, OAG Official Airline Guides, Entrepreneur,* and *Smart Money* magazines), OnePass frequent flyer program (*InsideFlyer*'s Freddie Awards) and overall operations and management (*Air Transport World*'s 1997 Airline of the Year).
1998 Financial Results
—Revenues: $8 billion
—Net Income: $383 million

you know how to do that, you're going to be successful. You can always get someone to help you with the strategy part. There are a whole lot of business school graduates who understand the math, the planning, and the strategic benchmarking. But you better be able to talk straight to people and get them to want to help you."

The results of doing that have been impressive.

LARRY BOSSIDY
AlliedSignal
(Honeywell International Inc.)

"There was a time when I thought brains were everything."

THERE ARE EXAMPLES TOO NUMEROUS TO MENTION OF A WELL-RESPECTED second-in-command at a major corporation who leaves to take over the top position of a struggling firm. Often, those executives fail. As they soon discover, it is one thing to help run a company—even a thriving one—on a day-to-day basis, but it is quite another to be the executive ultimately in charge.

Then there is Lawrence Bossidy of AlliedSignal, the role model for second-in-commands everywhere.

Bossidy came to the New Jersey–based conglomerate in 1991, after serving as Jack Welch's right-hand man at General Electric. Through a host of sweeping initiatives ranging from the introduction of a total quality management program known as Six Sigma to reducing the workforce by 20%, Bossidy turned the company around.

As is almost always the case, righting a listing ship depends on making sure that the 80% of employees who remained were not only focused on the right objective, but also believed in the cause. It is here that Bossidy, the father of nine grown children, excels. Says one investment banker who has worked with him: "Once Larry's done with AlliedSignal, he could go coach football at Notre Dame. He would be just as successful. He has that kind of personality."

The sports analogy is apt. Bossidy was

CAREER
1992–2000 Chairman, AlliedSignal, Inc.
1991– CEO
1957–1991 General Electric, in numerous positions, including running, and as Vice Chairman, overseeing the following divisions: G.E. Capital, G.E. Industrial and Power systems, G.E. Lighting, G.E. Plastics

EDUCATION
B.A. Economics, Colgate University, 1957

FAMILY
Married, Nancy, 1956; children: Lynn, Larry, Paul, Pam, Nancy, Mary Jane, Lucy, Michael, Kathleen

Born: Pittsfield, Massachusetts, March 5, 1935

"Twenty years ago, succession to the CEO position was a ticket to omnipotence. I think that now, to the contrary, it's a real trial. There's more expected and there's more direct accountability."

a star pitcher on his Pittsfield (Massachusetts) High's baseball team. In fact he was so good that the Detroit Tigers offered the southpaw a $40,000 signing bonus. His parents, who never had a chance to obtain a higher education, insisted he go to college instead. Bossidy attended Colgate University on an athletic scholarship.

The AlliedSignal Bossidy took over was essentially a three-legged company with revenues of some $12 billion. The three divisions—aerospace, automotive, and engineered materials—are still there, just more productive than ever before.

Proving that he learned from Welch, Bossidy has followed G.E.'s strategy of forging alliances across the globe. For example, Allied was weak in truck brake systems in Europe; Germany's Knorr-Bremse was not in the United States at all. The two have formed a large—and successful—global joint venture.

LARRY BOSSIDY SAYS HE FOUND "DISAPPOINTED AND DISILLU-sioned employees" when he was brought in to run AlliedSignal in 1991.

"It was not a bad workforce, but it was one that hadn't had much reason to be successful," he explains. "The stock hadn't done anything, and there had been two acquisitions in the prior five or six years [Bendix and Signal] that were not integrated nearly as well as they could have been."

Then there was the issue of "multiple cultures," caused by the numerous divisions that the company had, which people told Bossidy was part of the problem.

"My view, however, was that this wasn't a problem. It was wonderful. You want as many cultures in a company as you can get, because it provides more points of view. We're never going to have our aerospace people be of the same culture as our materials people. They travel in different circles. They have different kinds of education, and I think that's fine."

However, AlliedSignal needed something to unite all those different cultures and people. As a starting point, Bossidy created a vision statement that said: "We want to become a premier company, distinctive, and successful in everything we do.

"We tried to define what premier meant so everybody could buy into it. For example, for our legal department we said premier means preventive law. I don't want the best litigators in the world working here; what I do want is for them to create a good educational curriculum in terms of helping our people comply with the law and comply with the policies of the company, so that we don't get into litigative situations in the first place."

But as clear as the vision statement was, Bossidy knew there "was nothing unique about it."

The company needed something more to serve as a unifying force. The solution: Six Sigma, the quality improvement program.

By implementing it throughout the company, Bossidy not only improved quality—the heart of the program is teaching people how to systemically identify defects and then correct the systems that allowed them to happen in the first place—but also created a common language.

To signify the importance of the idea, Bossidy began at the top.

"We took some of our top people and went to a Six Sigma academy, and then we retained some people from the outside who knew Six Sigma and used them as instructors within the company. Ultimately we developed what we call our own master black belts, and they served as the trainers as we rolled Six Sigma out through the company.

"We started it in manufacturing because we thought we had more to gain there. But in recent years we've expanded it across all the functions, because we learned this methodology works just as well in marketing as it does in manufacturing.

No matter where it was introduced, Six Sigma worked. And it worked on a number of levels. Not only did efficiency improve, but the company also became better at reasoning through challenges.

"It's changed the mind-set and I think that's a positive. When we have a problem in our company now, people apply the methodology that comes from Six Sigma as a way to resolve it. And beyond that, our people feel like they're doing something on the leading edge, which makes them feel better about themselves, and better about the company. So the results are wonderful, and its application has been across the board."

That universality is important in a company as far-flung as Allied-Signal. In total, the company's 77,000 employees operate in 40 countries worldwide producing total revenues of $15 billion.

"In a company as diverse as ours, you need to find ways to bind it together with a common vision, common goals, or common values," Bossidy says. "But then you must make sure that you operate the divisions independently of one another, in the sense that they have different customers to serve and different markets to fill."

The conventional wisdom is that succeeding as a conglomerate is harder to do than operating a company focused on one specific market. (That is why conglomerates have fallen out of favor.) Bossidy has heard the argument before—and rejects it.

"I don't think the management chore is more difficult if you have a multi-product company," Bossidy says. "Arguably, it's easier because you have more strategic alternatives. If you have a one-product company, you don't have a lot of options in the event things go sour on you. There are some disadvantages to being a multi-product company in the sense that you're always trying to explain who you are and what you are, as opposed to being a pure play. But I think there are advantages as well, such as the room to maneuver and the fact that you can protect yourself—to some degree—from economic cycles."

The CEO's Job

But whether you are running a conglomerate, or a start-up focused on a particular product niche, the job of the person in charge is still the same, Bossidy says.

"I think the CEO today has to be far more hands-on than he has had to be in previous eras. He has to be far more communicative in terms of the various constituencies the company serves. And I think he has to be far more nimble.

"Here's an example. Companies used to have five-year strategic plans. Now most people have cut it down to three years, and probably that's too long. With the pace of the world changing as it does, you've got to look at where you are ever more frequently, or the bus goes by.

"So I always ask myself, what can I do to influence this company? I influence the people process. I influence strategy and I influence operations. And I try to put my time into those three things. I don't think the CEO who is in the role of presiding officer works anymore in this country. I think there has to be far more involvement, because of the things I've enumerated."

And as the job has changed, so has Bossidy's belief in what it takes to be a successful CEO.

"There was a time when I thought brains were everything. That view has dimmed recently. I think brains are important, but now I also look for a lot of collateral assets. I look for people who are team-builders, good communicators, courageous people who don't get stuck with an idea. You need people who are more nimble, who have the ability to lead organizations in changing and tumultuous times comfortably, without panicking. That doesn't mean you sacrifice your principles, but it sure means you take a second look at issues and topics. You might have a different view in a year than you do now.

"To secure buy in," Bossidy says, "you've got to tell people where you want the company to go. They need to be able to answer the question: 'What am I doing this for?' If I want to have Six Sigma, I need to explain the purpose of having Six Sigma. Or if I want to grow earnings 10%, employees will need to know why. You not only need to set out what you want to do, I think you've got to set out what it will mean when you get there.

"Beyond that, I think you've got to continually make sure employees understand how important they are. As a CEO, you need people more than they need you. In other words, my job is to keep our people interested in staying, and working, and growing and prospering with this company."

Bossidy takes this philosophy a step further and extends it to the people he moves into senior management positions.

"I want to find leaders who are human beings, and who have an interest in being successful for themselves and want to share that success with others. If I can get people like this, they're easy to lead."

What characteristics is he looking for specifically?

"Positive people, to begin with. I like to see people with smiles on their faces. Business is difficult. It's so much better to greet the world with a smile on your face. You can't show me people with great accomplishments who are negative people. I want to see people who are positive. And even though it's simple, in my mind it's important. I also like to see ambitious people who want to get something done. Then I look to see if they can contain their ego. Do I see a person who can work well with others? Do I see a person who's shown some interest in others? Are these the people who can share their knowledge with other people and do it gracefully and willingly? Or are they very self-centered, very ambitious, but not necessarily to the benefit of anybody else?"

Is there one question Bossidy asks to help him gain insights into the people he is considering for promotion?

"I ask people, 'What are you good at?' It's remarkable the number of people that don't speak to that question

Company (Ticker): Honeywell International Inc. (HON)
Location: Morristown, New Jersey
Leader: Michael R. Bonsignore
AlliedSignal at a glance: Honeywell is one of the world's leading companies engaged in advanced technology and manufacturing. The company serves customers worldwide with aerospace and automotive products, automation controls and systems, chemicals, fibers, plastics, and advanced materials. AlliedSignal acquired the original Honeywell and took its name. Soon after Honeywell purchased Pittway Corporation, a manufacturer of building security and fire alarms. In October 2000, Honeywell agreed to be acquired by General Electric for $45 billion.
1999 Financial Results
—Revenues: $23.7 billion
—Net Income: $1.5 billion

with any degree of insight. You've got to know what you're good at. I've been lucky; I can make things happen. I can get the people to identify with what we want to do, and I can get it done. You've got to know what you're good at, because those are the cards you bring to the party."

In other words, you need a sense of who you are and where you are going in order to be a successful manager.

"I think leadership is about vision. It's a matter of persuading people to your vision. And I think it's choosing the right people to make sure that they can fulfill all the obligations that the organization expects them to have. Being a CEO used to mean you knew everything. But these are humbling jobs. And the more you search, the more you recognize every reason you have to be humble, because there's an awful lot more to do all the time."

JIM BROADHEAD
FPL Group

Execute

In a world of energy deregulation, an engineer/turned lawyer/turned phone company executive probably has the required set of skills to run what was once know as Florida Power and Light.

James Broadhead's background is unusual, but then again, so are his plans for the company based in Juno Beach, Florida. While FPL Group, as it is now known, continues to focus on providing energy to the Sunshine State—with 3.6 million customer accounts, it is Florida's largest utility—its long-term focus is far broader. Broadhead has created a new subsidiary, FPL Energy, to act as an umbrella over the investments he has made in the United States and international markets. That division has purchased or constructed power plants in 12 states, including California, Virginia, Maine, Massachusetts, and New Jersey and has moved overseas as well. FPL owns facilities in Columbia and Northern Ireland.

So all of the skills Broadhead developed before coming to FPL are being called into play as he tries to handle the challenges of running the rapidly growing diversified power company. Besides,

CAREER
1989–PRESENT Chairman, President, and CEO, FPL Group, Inc.
1986–1988 President, GTE Telephone Operations
1984–1986 Senior Vice President, GTE Corp.
1981–1982 President, St. Joe Minerals Corp.
1977–1980 President, St. Joe Zinc. Co. & Executive Vice President, St. Joe Minerals Corp.
1975–1977 Vice President
1973–1974 General Counsel
1970–1977 Secretary
1968–1970 Assistant Secretary
1963–1968 Associate, Debevoise, Plimpton, Lyons & Gates
1958–1959 Mechanical Engineering Sales Department, Ingersoll-Rand Co.

EDUCATION
J.D., Columbia University, 1963
B.M.E., Cornell University, 1958

FAMILY
Married, Sharon Ann Rulon, May 6, 1967; children: Jeffrey Thornton, Kristen Ann, Carolyn Mary, Catherine Lee

Born: New Rochelle, New York, November 28, 1935

"It's virtually impossible to communicate too much. I've never heard a single employee anywhere complain that he or she is being kept too informed."

Broadhead says, the move to FPL allowed him to come full circle. He was trained as an engineer and his first real job was working for Ingersoll-Rand, a supplier to the power business. Broadhead sold pumps, compressors, turbines, and condensers to the power companies like FPL.

THE SITUATION JAMES BROADHEAD INHERITED WHEN HE TOOK OVER AS chief executive at what was then called Florida Power and Light was fairly typical.

"I don't mean to be unkind, but this was an old-fashioned electric utility. We had some skills in quality, which I was very happy to have, but there was very little focus on cost or productivity. In addition, this was a very slow-moving, inflexible, and bureaucratic company.

"Having grown up in a fiercely competitive industry, the natural resource business, and then seeing the changes that were taking place in the telephone business, I figured it was more than likely that at some point we were going to be facing a competitive environment here as well."

Broadhead's response to what he had inherited was also fairly typical of smart executives who find themselves running antiquated businesses.

"We had to prepare for change and we needed to develop a clear strategy. The first thing we did in developing that strategy was to ask a team of employees to try to answer the question: 'What will our business environment look like over the next five to 10 years?' That expected business environment was the basis of our subsequent planning efforts.

"By the time the first year had passed, we had a plan that focused on four things: improving our cost position, enhancing our quality, being more customer-oriented, and becoming faster and more flexible. Those would be our areas of concentration."

And then Broadhead did something that regrettably is not yet typical when a new CEO takes over.

"Once we had the strategy, everything we did from that point on was focused on achieving those four goals.

"I think what separates the winners from the losers is execution," Broadhead says. "Not only do you have to come up with a clear idea of what it's going to take to be a winner, you actually have to do it. There are a lot of good strategic plans in companies around the country, but not a lot of great execution, in my opinion."

The first step in executing the vision was making sure everyone segments."

By defining the mission this way, Broadhead was making several important points: Customers will have a choice, which they did not have in the past when it comes to who will supply them with power; in making that choice, quality and cost will be important factors; and since electricity is a commodity, the company will need to sell more than just electricity to differentiate itself from other suppliers. He did not want FPL to be restricted to just selling gas and electricity. Those are commodities and if all you sell are commodities, all you can do is sell on price.

Where's the Fire?

While the vision was clear, it was not immediately apparent to everyone within the company that FPL needed to execute it, or that change was even necessary.

When you are being faced with competitors who are gobbling up your customers and destroying your margins, it is fairly easy to convince employees you have to change the way you do business. But FPL wasn't facing those demons—yet. In fact, it was very profitable. How do you get people to change dramatically the way they do their jobs, when there is no crisis to motivate them?

"It's a hard challenge," Broadhead says. "Part of the answer goes back to the beginning of the change process. I suppose I could have sat down and said here is the strategy we need to pursue, and then ordered everyone to carry it out. But I didn't do that.

"As you remember, I said we started by putting together a team of employees to examine what the future would look like. We then had another team involved in identifying what our critical success factors would be in that future environment. In addition we formed teams to identify what our strengths and weaknesses were and finally we had another team involved in working on trying to figure out the best organizational structure for what we were trying to do. Overall, there were about 100 people involved in our planning process.

"We also changed our quality program. After talking—in groups of 20 or 25—with about 500 different employees, I put together another team of about 15 employees from across the company, including bargaining unit employees, and asked them to determine how we should change our quality program to prepare for the competitive environment we were going to face.

"So there were many people, besides me, involved from the very beginning, saying we have to change our company.

"At the same time, we started to communicate aggressively about the changes going on in the industry and what those changes could mean for us. We started with a monthly video, and then we changed it to a weekly video. We started with a small monthly newsletter and soon added a bi-weekly tabloid-style newspaper. We also initiated quarterly meetings with the top 150 members of the senior management team. I started sending out key executives to all our offices and the message was always the same. The world is changing. We have to be ready, or otherwise we're going to be in deep trouble. And over and over again we kept focusing on what we needed to do to get better in those four critical areas—improving our costs, improving our quality, being more customer-oriented, and becoming faster and more flexible.

"As I said we did a lot of things. Every time we had a success in one of those areas, we talked about it and kept talking about it with pride. All that communication helped change our outlook and our way of working.

"We also made a lot of changes in the top positions. I would like to tell you that I could come in and make all the changes just by persuasion. But one of the most effective ways of changing an organization, particularly an organization that's been doing things the same way for almost 75 years, is to bring in key people from either the outside, or from lower down within the organization. This provides a diversity of experience and perspective, as well as a greater willingness to do things differently.

"We also modified all the existing training programs to reinforce what we were trying to do. In addition, we put in new and expanded programs to teach necessary skills and behaviors. We even changed our corporate procedures because procedures in an organization can define what's important. As FPL's traditional hierarchy developed over the years, it brought with it a tremendously high number of detailed nonoperating procedures, to ensure that we didn't make any mistakes. We even had a procedures department, and we had procedures for writing procedures!

"We knew that if we retained those procedures people who had been brought up in the old environment of the company would be inclined—really almost compelled—to work in the same ways they had worked in the past. So we put together a cross-functional team of employees to examine all our nonoperating procedures, eliminate the ones that were unnecessary, and streamline the ones we thought we ought to keep. The team eliminated 80% of our corporate procedures and shortened the 20% of them that remained. That effort made a big difference in the way people worked throughout the company.

"In addition, we introduced a compensation program which was much more incentive-based and we eliminated work rules that were barriers to efficiency. The union deserves great credit for being farsighted enough to work with us to try to eliminate things that would stand in the way of productivity."

In short, Broadhead systematically went through every aspect of the way FPL did business and aligned it with the company's new vision.

"As I said, we really tried hard to focus on those four areas of cost, quality, customer service, and speed and flexibility. We undertook many initiatives in every one of those areas, and we are still doing so.

"I would say we probably have made as much improvement in productivity as any electric company that I know. Our unit costs in six or seven years have fallen over 30%, and they're still going down. At the same time, the availability of our plants has gone up significantly. In other words, we are making more effective use of our assets. And almost all quality measures have improved.

"We're constantly benchmarking ourselves against the best in the industry, and the best in the country, if we can," Broadhead states proudly.

"I think one of the reasons we have been successful is that we really did set out to change the corporate culture, to enable ourselves to meet our objectives. I hate the phrase 'corporate culture,' because it has become a buzz word like 'empowerment.' But whatever it's called, our attitude really has changed.

"When we went through the strategic planning process that I discussed, and saw the magnitude of the challenge in front of us, we realized that more than fine tuning was needed. We really needed to change our focus and our core operations."

In other words, the company needed to execute against the vision.

What has been the payoff for all this effort?

Well, throughout the country today, dozens of power companies are desperately trying to convince their customer base to stay, in light of new competition. FPL does not have that problem. The company is a leaner—the number

---

Company (Ticker): FPL Group, Inc. (FPL)

Location: Juno Beach, Florida

Leader: James Lowell Broadhead

FPL at a glance: FPL Group is one of the United States' largest publicly owned electric utilities. The company provides electricity for more than 3.8 million customers on Florida's east and southwestern coasts (about half of the state's population) through its Florida Power & Light subsidiary. Another subsidiary, FPL Energy, develops nonutility energy projects in the United States and abroad. FPL Fibernet, a subsidiary of FPL Group, utilizes their 1,600-mile fiber optic network to provide extra resources to telephone, cable, and Internet providers. In July 2000, FPL Group and Energy Corp. agreed to combine in a $7 billion stock deal that would create the largest electric company in the United States.

1999 Financial Results

—Revenues: $6.4 billion

—Net Income: $697 million

of full-time equivalent employees has dropped by 40% since 1991—more efficient organization, that is providing power at lower costs.

"Our Florida customers are buying their electric power today for 10% less than they paid in 1985," Broadhead says. "That's more than 40% less when you adjust for inflation. There are a lot of people living here on fixed incomes, and we have made their lives a littler easier. I'm proud of that. And we've made it less expensive for entrepreneurs to start up businesses and run them in Florida, because the power prices are lower and the power delivery is more reliable. So I think we have done a very good job of providing a necessary element of civilized society. As the head of the company, I feel real pride in that.

"That's from the customer side. From the shareholder side, I'm proud our company has dramatically improved its productivity and quality, and that the shareholders have gotten returns far beyond our industry index. And I feel good that we are recognized by financial analysts as being a well-managed growth company and that we were voted the most admired electric company in the *Fortune* magazine poll."

When you trace it back, all of these accomplishments stem from Broadhead executing his strategy.

"A strategy is nothing but a piece of paper unless you put it into action," he says. "That's the CEO's job. There are a lot of people who sound good and who have wonderful strategies and seem to be leaders, but somehow it doesn't get done. The company doesn't get better.

"The person in charge not only has to know what needs to be done, he has to get results."

He has to execute.

STEVE CASE
America Online

You've got mail

FOR YEARS, THE TECHNOLOGY COGNOSCENTI WROTE OFF AMERICA ONline as dead. And indeed on several occasions it looked as if the company would prove them right.

First, "experts" argued the company's technology was hopelessly behind the times. Many people use AOL as an entry point to the Internet, and the thinking, in the mid-1990s, was that as people became more comfortable with the new technology, they would go to the Internet directly, bypassing online service providers such as AOL.

Then when the company switched to offering a flat pricing plan—charging one fixed fee a month for unlimited access, as opposed to billing by the hour—it was swamped with potential users. The inability to get online triggered a rash of class-action suits.

Nobody talks about AOL's imminent demise anymore.

The problem of constant busy signals is mostly a thing of the past—thanks to additional capacity—and the company announcement in late 1998 that it was acquiring Netscape has silenced critics who used to refer to AOL as "the Internet with training wheels."

Customers stuck with AOL because of the content and options it offers—the company's "chat rooms" are amazingly popular—and because of the fact that the service is extremely simple to use. In fact, the principles that Case outlined in

CAREER
1985–PRESENT Co-founder, Chairman, and
    CEO, America Online, Inc.
1983–1985 Vice President—Marketing,
    Control Video Corporation
1982–1983 Manager of New Pizza
    Development, Pizza Hut Division of PepsiCo.
1980–1982 Brand Assistant, & Assistant
    Brand Manager, Procter & Gamble

EDUCATION
B.A., 1980, Williams College

FAMILY
Married, Jean; five children

Born: Honolulu, Hawaii, August 21, 1958

"The key to building an enduring new medium is passion, people, perseverance, perspective, and paranoia."

his business plan are still the same. Give customers a product that is:

- Easy to work with,
- Truly useful,
- Fun, and
- Affordable.

Founder and CEO Steve Case not only has earned the last laugh, he has earned something more: the fulfillment of a vision he had 15 years ago. When Case founded AOL in 1985, his goal was to create a mass market for online services—and that is exactly what he has done.

One quick indicator of how successful he has been is the decision in Hollywood to make the service's ubiquitous phrase, "You've got mail," heard every time a user receives an e-mail, the title of the hit Tom Hanks–Meg Ryan movie that opened in 1998.

THE CORPORATE GRAVEYARD IS LITTERED WITH THE REMAINS OF THOU-sands of companies that could not make the transition from entrepreneurial start-up to full-fledged, large, enduring concern. The explanation is frequently the same: The founder does not grow and adapt rapidly enough. As a result, the company he started never evolves beyond the point where one person can manage it.[1]

Steve Case, who has made it a point to study the histories of people who have created new commercial categories—most notably the pioneers of the automobile, television, and computer industries—is well aware of the problem, but he says he found the transition from entrepreneur to manager relatively easy.

"Fundamentally, it came down to an idea I had about five years ago," he explains. "I said to myself, instead of thinking you have to do everything, why don't you assume that there's actually nothing you have to do, and organize things accordingly? It took a little while to put into practice, but the idea turned out to be absolutely right.

"Five or 10 years ago, we only had a few hundred people, and I was involved in every decision. I was writing releases and writing ads. I was just doing the classic entrepreneurial kind of thing. But it gets to a point where there's just too much going on. There are too many moving parts. Things start piling up on your desk and you don't get to them. Peo-

---

1. Intriguingly, overcoming these pitfalls is a sound route to corporate success. Eleven of the 50 leaders in this book, including the heads of Dell, Federal Express, Intel, Microsoft, Schwab, and Starbucks, founded (or co-founded) the companies they are still leading.

ple get frustrated. And you just realize that the only way you're going to create a significant company is to make your role into one where you *guide* things as opposed to *do* things."

The "secret" to making that approach work, Case says, "should not be surprising. The key is hiring great people, people you really have confidence in and can trust. Then you organize things in such a way that one person is in charge of this, and another is in charge of that, until there is nothing that you are absolutely in charge of.

"If you do this, your role as chief executive changes. Instead of measuring your contribution based on how many things you did, and how many decisions you made, you measure your contribution only on how many *key* decisions you made.

"Thinking about my role in this new way really was the key in my transition from entrepreneur to leader," Case adds. "But it does require a different mind-set. When I hear about a problem, I have to ask: 'Is this truly something that requires my personal attention?' And do you know what? It almost always does not. There are a few things that do, but the vast majority do not."

Everyone Must Know What We Stand For

Case is being self-effacing, of course. But his point is valid. The founding entrepreneur needs to let go. But if you are going to have this kind of hands-off approach, your guiding principles must be well known throughout the organization. They are within AOL.

Perhaps Case's two biggest factors are passion and paranoia. He has legitimate reasons for fervently believing in both.

By now it is a well-known tale about what happened when Case went out to visit Microsoft Chairman Bill Gates a number of years ago. As the (true) story goes, Gates told him: "We can buy 20% of AOL, we can buy 100%, or we can bury you."

That kind of comment from the industry leader is bound to get your attention and convince you that not only do you have to stay focused on what you want to accomplish, but that you must also study the competition, no matter its potential source.

"Five years ago, companies that are now major forces in our market like Yahoo and Amazon didn't even exist," Case explains. "Now they're important new brands. Clearly, there's been an acceleration in the creation of markets, and in the number of firms started to serve those markets. Companies can be made—or broken—in so-called Internet time.

"This makes having a sense of paranoia very important. I know that's something you have heard from other people as well. The day this company gets cocky and complacent is the day we're in deep, deep trouble because this is such an intensely competitive market, and one that is changing at such a rapid pace. If we get complacent, then we won't be able to attract the best people. They'll be bored and frustrated and run off. And we'll just become another kind of lumbering giant whose best days are behind it, not in front of it."

But paranoia in and of itself does no good unless the people who are paranoid truly care about the product that they are creating.

"If you look at the reason that AOL has been successful," explains Case, "it comes down to hiring and keeping great people. I'm always pleased when I talk with someone who has just had a meeting with one of our people and he tells me how impressed he was not only with their intellect but also their passion."

The passion is critical.

"If you really believe what you're doing is right, and you believe it's important, and you truly feel that you are a pioneer who is making a difference, you may make some mistakes, but your energy and commitment will help you overcome them.

"That perseverance is important particularly in new industries because there are many times where the so-called smart thing may be to throw up your hands and quit because it's hard, or you've hit a brick wall. But you have to think 'Well, we're just going to keep at it. That is critical.' "

And this perseverance in the face of long odds has been present throughout AOL's history. In the very beginning, even connecting to the Internet was notoriously difficult. And while most people have now forgotten, there were long periods when the conventional wisdom was that AOL would be put out of business by everyone from Prodigy—an Internet service originally created by CBS, IBM, and Sears—to Compuserve to various competing products offered by AT&T, MCI, and others.

Then came the problems associated with the switch to flat pricing, which occurred about the same time that William J. Razzouk, hired from Federal Express to be AOL's chief operating officer, left after only four months.[2] In the light of all these problems, perservance at AOL was more than necessary; it was a matter of survival.

---

2. Case more than recovered from this particular episode by recruiting Bob Pittman—a co-founder of MTV, who went on to run Time Warner's Six Flags theme parks and then later Century 21 Real Estate—to be president and chief operating officer.

But You Need More

Coupled with perseverance, says Case, must be perspective.

"Because I've been doing this for so long, I am able to bring a historical context, and a kind of even-keeled perspective to things, because I've usually seen some version of this movie before. Some of the people who have joined us recently haven't.

"In new industries, it takes a while to get traction," Case adds. "It requires a balancing act. On the one hand, we must believe passionately about the possibilities of what could happen if we had a society where everyone was connected. But at the same time, if we are so focused on the promised land that we forget to perform the steps necessary to get from here to there, we'll never get there. So we have to strike the right balance between vision and passion, on the one hand, and creating a pragmatic approach, on the other."

If you look at AOL's success, you can see that Case has done just that. When asked where his drive comes from, now that he has helped create a new industry, Case has a simple answer.

"I think it would be a real tragedy if 50 years from now, when the history books are written about this medium, people concluded that it had a lot of promise but somehow it didn't live up to its potential. I think it would be disappointing if we were considered to be like television. While I think television has done a lot of good things, people really have a sort of negative impression of it, that it's a kind of this vast wasteland."

Case's vision for online services in general, and AOL in particular, is far greater than that. He wants to create a global medium as central to people's lives as the telephone, one that is even more valuable.

"We are driven by the fact that 50 years from now our people are going to be able to tell their grandchildren: 'I

Company (Ticker): America Online, Inc. (AOL)

Location: Dulles, Virginia

Leader: Stephen M. Case

AOL at a glance: AOL is the world's largest online service with 23 million members. Major products include commerce, e-mail, chat, and Internet access. On a daily basis, AOL's members average 8.9 million hours of usage, send 33 million e-mails, make 1 billion web hits, and send 283 million Instant Messages. In 1999, the company completed the acquisition of Internet software leader Netscape. AOL will become the world's largest entertainment and media group through its agreement to acquire Time Warner. AOL's Interactive Online Services, AOL TV, and partnerships with AT&T, Motorola, Nokia, and Sprint allow AOL to tap into wireless markets and further establish its "AOL Everywhere" initiative.

1999 Financial Results
—Revenues: $4.7 billion
—Net Income: $762 million

was there. I was one of the pioneers who helped build what's now called the Interactive Medium.' "

There are signs Case is on his way to do that.

Growing up, Case, like a lot of children, loved getting mail.

"I never got enough. I don't have that problem anymore. I get something like 5,000 e-mails a day [at Steve Case@aol.com]."

JOHN CHAMBERS
Cisco Systems

"Everybody here knows what we want to accomplish."

MAYBE WE ALL SHOULD ASPIRE TO BE PARANOID. INTEL'S ANDY GROVE borrowed his own personal mantra when he came up with the title for his best-selling book, *Only the Paranoid Survive*. And when asked to describe himself, John Chambers is quick to use the "p" word as well. Maybe there is something in all this paranoia because the performance of Cisco Systems under Chambers's leadership has been no less impressive than Intel's.

When John Chambers joined Cisco in 1991, the company had sales of $1.2 billion. They hit $10 billion eight years later. Chambers's strategic objective is just as impressive. He wants Cisco to be number one or number two in every major computer networking segment, and ultimately provide one-stop networking and Internet shopping for his customers.

To do this, Cisco will obviously have to grow internally. But equally important, it will also have to keep making acquisitions—the company has made as many as a dozen in any given year, since Chambers has been CEO. Managing acquisitions is always tricky, so it is not surprising that Chambers has both a law degree and an MBA, in addition to his technical expertise.

Having bought so may companies, Chambers has a handle on what it takes for them to succeed. He has crystallized his thinking into a five-step formula:

CAREER
JANUARY 1991–PRESENT CEO, Cisco Systems Inc.
1982–1990 Senior Vice President, Wang Laboratories, holding positions in Americas/Asia Pacific operations, and U.S. operations
1976–1982 Various positions, IBM

EDUCATION
M.B.A., Indiana University, 1975
J.D., West Virginia University, 1974
B.S./B.A., Business, West Virginia University, 1971

FAMILY
Married, Elaine; children: Jonathan, Lindsay

Born: Cleveland, Ohio, August 23, 1949

"We have no religion when it comes to technology. If the customers say this is what they're going to do regardless of our engineering views on it, that's what we're going to help them do."

1) There needs to be a common vision between the two companies.
2) Almost immediately you have to produce short-term wins, or people at both companies will lose interest.
3) There has to be long-term strategic potential behind the alliance.
4) There needs to be good chemistry between the people at both companies.
5) Geographic proximity helps a lot to minimize the chances that the acquired talent will leave.

Chambers spends a lot of time on point five. In an industry where talent is key, attracting the best is an art, one that Cisco has mastered. The key? Stock options. After being with the company for just one year, the average employee has over $125,000 in paper profits on unexercised options. That's on top of the company's average starting salary, which is about $70,000. That's not too bad for someone who is in their early 20s.

WHEN YOU ASK JOHN CHAMBERS WHAT HE WANTS TO ACCOMPLISH, HE doesn't hesitate for a second. "We want to create unprecedented opportunities for our customers, our employees, our shareholders, and our partners."

If the answer sounds scripted, it is. Every one of the company's objectives is written down on a small card that every single employee carries around at all times. It is just one small way that Chambers makes sure that Cisco stays focused on its goals.

"By the time I became CEO we had established these goals," he says. "I kind of put the gauntlet down and said we were going to accomplish them. We were going to do what no one else had done and become the clear leader in our industry."

Cisco's success—on Wall Street the company's stock has become a shorthand for the entire high-tech industry—is proof that he has been successful.

The secret? Maintaining the delicate balance between confidence in the company's technological abilities and staying focused on the customers' needs. "From the very beginning I believed that if we could do that—and it requires a healthy paranoia to keep those two things in balance—I was convinced there was almost an unlimited upside. And it has worked out that way. We have become the leader in data networking. And we have had the good fortune to be the fastest-growing, most profitable computer company in history. We were also the first to achieve a market capitalization of $100 billion as quickly as we did."(Cisco reached $100 billion in 12 years of existence; it took Microsoft 20 years.)

To make sure that Cisco remains a leader, Chambers has transformed the company into a living example of where he thinks the overall technology market is going.

"We're the number-one electronic commerce site in the world by a factor of five-fold. We do 20 million orders a day; 64% of our total orders are handled through the Internet. Some 70% of the interfaces we have with customers are over the network without human intervention. And while it took us four years to get here, the customers now prefer to use the network rather than talk to our engineers; that saved us $150 million a year in reduced staffing costs.

"We began to shift the information systems function from an expense item, which it was when I got here, into a competitive advantage. This last year we saved $500 million on an expense base of $2 billion through seven web-based applications. We put that back into R&D and distribution. We *save* more each year than our nearest competitor *spends* on R&D. You don't have to explain to a nontechnology businessperson what that means in terms of competitive advantage."

That commitment to technology has internal benefits as well.

"All communication with employees—from the time they apply to Cisco to the time they get their final benefits—is done through the Internet. Our suppliers are also part of our virtual company, just like all the textbooks are writing about.

"When you explain to people what all this means, and you walk them through it slowly, first using Cisco as an example, and then expanding what we are doing to other industries, people are now beginning to understand why the Internet is starting to change everything. The industrial revolution realigned which countries, and which companies, would be best for individuals. That is what the Internet revolution will do as well. It will level the playing field, and those countries, companies, and individuals who take advantage of it will be those who grow and survive."

And clearly Chambers is positioning Cisco to be at the forefront of that change, and is positioning the company to be one that not only survives, but thrives.

"We Measure Everything"

To make sure that happens, Chambers is relentless in tracking the company's financials.

"We measure everything, in all areas, in real time. For example, by the end of the day I know what my orders have been by geography, by product type, and by margin. And I check every day. We can almost close our books in two days now. No company that I am aware of has ever been able to do that. And we're moving toward being able to do it simultaneously. In other words, we are moving toward the point where we would never really have to close our books. We would know exactly where we are at any given point in time."

Tracking the numbers is one thing, acting on them is another, Chambers concedes. And so he gives an example of how Cisco does just that.

"Customer satisfaction is the most important measure to me, and if you really believe that, then you've got to tie it to your reward system, to your management practices, and we do. Let me tell you how it works.

"We measure customer satisfaction every way imaginable. We measure it, on a scale of one to five, after every customer visit. We track every problem by how well we respond to it and I review how well we are doing with every critical account every night. The measurements are not only done in absolute terms, but relative to our key competitors as well. Once a year we total all these results and we pay managers based on how well they score."

This is all part of Chambers creating the kind of company he wants to build.

"If you were to ask what I'm most proud of, they are the three things that have resulted in our success. First is our almost fanatical approach to customer success. We don't say it, we do it; we walk our talk, we tie it to the reward system, and we tie it to the way we spend our time. It's something I don't have to explain to anyone in our company anymore.

"Second is the quality of the team we've built. As a leader, I am most proud of how broad and deep our team is. We've been able to get the top 10% to

Company (Ticker): Cisco Systems Inc. (CSCO)
Location: San Jose, California
Leader: John T. Chambers
Cisco at a glance: The company is the leading supplier of products that make the Internet work. It has over 75% of the market share for network routers (which tell information and messages where to go) and is also one of the market leaders in local area network (LAN) switches. Its other products include dial-up-access servers and network-management software. Cisco has grown through both aggressive internal development, strategic partnerships with IBM, Microsoft, and Sun Microsystems, and acquisitions to broaden its product line.
1999 Financial Results
—Revenues: $12.1 billion
—Net Income: $2.0 billion

15% of the people in the industry and have been able to motivate them to play together as a team. Because of our company's stock appreciation, almost everybody at the senior level is financially independent, so the only way to keep them is to keep them motivated, to have them want to work together as a team to accomplish something. You can't keep them here just by offering a paycheck. They don't need the money.

"Finally, I am proud that we have a set vision in place; we've determined the key elements by which we're going to measure our success and we are executing against them. You can see that in the fact that we are not the shoemaker's kids. We use our systems to gain a huge competitive advantage. We're saying we know what is going to happen in society. We are all going to become progressively more connected, and information is going to move even faster, thanks to the Internet, and we are the best example of an Internet-based company."

This Strategy Works Everywhere

Keep the customer first. Stay focused. Draw on all the resources around you. That is Chambers's prescription for Cisco success. Not surprisingly, it is also what he tells people when he is asked for career advice.

"The first thing I always say is that within reason, you can accomplish almost anything in life that you want to, as long as you're willing to work hard—and smart—to get it. The second is deal with life the way it is, not the way you wish it was, and if you have hurdles thrown in front of you, learn how to get over them, rather than let them distract you. I had a learning disability [dyslexia]. There was a doubt that I would even be able to graduate from high school. Now my parents never believed that, but some people did. It was a problem for me, and I got it corrected through some hard work with a very wonderful teacher who helped me understand what was going on in my brain, long before learning disabilities were really understood. And I use that as an example with our young people who say 'I can't do it because . . .'

"I tell them that's just an excuse. Third, you really should treat people the way you would like to be treated yourself. The last element? Have fun. Don't take life too seriously."

This approach has undeniably worked for John Chambers—and Cisco.

MICHAEL DELL

Dell Computer

The power of direct

IT COULD HAVE BEEN THE SHORTEST—AND MOST EFFECTIVE—
shareholder meeting ever.

It happened a couple of years ago, as Dell Computer stockholders
gathered for the company's annual meeting. When founder and chairman
Michael Dell took the stage, a slide comparing the performance of Dell's
stock to companies such as Coca-Cola, Compaq, Intel, and Microsoft appeared behind him. It took less than five seconds for the audience to realize that the upward slope labeled "Dell" was at least twice as steep as the
ones for the other companies. Dell had outperformed these better-known
companies by a wide margin.

Just as the "oohs" and "aahs" from the appreciative shareholders
reached their peak, Dell looked out at the audience and said: "And that
concludes our presentation." The applause was deafening.

Dell went on, of course, but he really didn't have to. The chart made
the point.

To revolutionize an industry once is noteworthy. To do it twice—
and do it before your 30th birthday—
is enough to cause anyone pause. But
then, again, Michael Dell is quite impressive, as investors—especially those
who came in early to the computer company he founded—have learned.

By now the history of Dell and his
company are pretty well known. To
please his parents, Dell enrolled as a pre-
med student at the University of Texas in
1983, but by then he was really only interested in tinkering with computers.

CAREER
1984–PRESENT Founder, Chairman, and CEO,
Dell Computer Corporation

EDUCATION
Student, University of Texas. 1983–1984

FAMILY
Married, Susan Lieberman, October 23, 1989;
four children

Born: Houston, Texas, February 23, 1965

> *"We know who we are and what we do."*

During his first semester, he bought remaindered, outmoded IBM PCs from local retailers, upgraded them in his dorm room, and started selling them not only around campus, but in the local business community as well. Revenues were $180,000—*the first month.*

Dell quickly realized that instead of upgrading older machines, he could buy components and assemble the whole PC himself more cheaply. He sold the machines he put together directly to customers at a 15% discount to what established brands were charging, *even though his models had substantially more computing power.*

Inadvertently, he had created his first revolution.

Up until that point, virtually all personal computers were sold like other retail products, through stores (either ones devoted just to personal computers, or consumer electronics outlets). Dell had just proven that this did not need to be the case and his distribution model was in place.

The second revolution came a couple of years later when Dell began selling the computers—which by this point carried his own brand name—made to order. A customer calls up or contacts the company via the Internet and explains exactly what he does—or does not—want in his computer and his customized machine is on its way within 36 hours.

The approach—which allows the company to keep costly inventory to a minimum—has proved so successful that Dell's competitors have started to copy it, although they are nowhere near achieving Dell Computer's success in going direct to consumers.

Personally, Dell has toppled every milestone there is. In 1992 he became—at age 27—the youngest CEO of a Fortune 500 company and he is now universally described as the wealthiest man in Texas.

IF THE DELL COMPUTER CORPORATION WAS LOOKING FOR A THEME SONG, there is one that came out a couple of years ago that seems to work: "The Future's So Bright, I Have to Wear Shades."

Consider these three factors:

1) The company is superbly positioned. While competitors now are trying to figure out how to deal with customers directly, in an attempt to boost margins as computer prices keep falling, Dell is already a master. It only sells computers directly to consumers.
2) The Internet only helps to solidify Dell's position as a direct marketer.
3) The computer company has already overcome many of the diversification/expansion problems that seem to invariably plague

relatively new organizations such as Dell, which, although it seems as if it has been around forever, was founded only in 1984.

Michael Dell takes these points one at a time.

"From the very beginning we figured we could sell to consumers directly without the need for the dealer, and without the need for a dealer's markup," Dell explains. "If you can offer a better price, a better level of service, and the latest technology directly to the customer, why would you have to sell through a dealer?"

Selling direct gives Dell some protection in the hugely competitive computer business. And while competitors—such as Compaq and IBM—have also begun to sell direct, in addition to their traditional channels of distribution, Michael Dell is not overly worried.

"The question is this: Can they really achieve the efficiencies that we have using the system they have? I think just about any analyst that looks at our industry would now agree that to truly get to the efficiency of a model like ours you've basically got to get rid of the dealer, and there are a few problems with that if you are IBM or Compaq.

"For one, the dealers object to this notion fairly strongly.

"For another, it's very hard for a company that has built its whole business around filling a pipeline—that is, selling to dealers—to switch to going direct. It hasn't built a competency in dealing with end users.

"Just to kind of flip this around for a second, let's suppose you took all of Dell's 22,000 employees and put them in a room and said, 'Instead of selling direct, we're going to be indirect.' That's a pretty radical shift. When you grow up in the industry of indirect, direct is the enemy.

"So, what our competitors are trying to do by selling direct as well is a big change. Can you name a company that's gone through a transition from indirect to direct in any industry successfully?" Dell asks rhetorically.

Hidden Advantages

But while Dell's experience in dealing directly with customers is an advantage, it is not the only edge the company has, its chairman argues.

"Dell often gets stereotyped. People say we're just a distribution channel. Well, we are, of course, but we also spend almost $300 million a year on research and development, have 2,000 engineers, and file several hundred patents a year. We lead the industry in product awards, and arguably, product leadership.

"We don't spend a lot of our dollars researching basic materials, or developing computer architectures. Rather, we try to figure out how to apply the tens of billions of dollars that computer companies invest in R&D every year in ways that will solve customer problems.

"So our position in the marketplace is not just about distribution of products, or logistics, or manufacturing, it's a combination of these things.

"I can remember four or five years ago somebody suggested that maybe Dell should kind of divide itself up into a product company and a distribution company, and let each one develop its full potential. I thought about it for a while and said, maybe there's something to that. But later when I thought it through I realized it was all wrong. The reason this company is successful is because we've got these two things working in harmony in a way that nobody has ever been able to achieve before."

The rise of the Internet can only help.

"If you sat back and said, let's design a technology that could radically impact this company in positive ways, it would be hard to create one better than the Internet," Dell says. "It essentially puts us that much closer to our customers. It's the ultimate form of direct for us.

"And because we're already dealing directly with our customers, it's a very natural extension for us. We don't have to change the way we do business in order to do business on the net. Everything is already in place. The result is that the Internet lowers the cost of doing business for our customers and for us, and it speeds transactions, whether we're talking about sales, support, or customers gaining information.

"I'll give you an example. For our large business clients, we have account executives. These are our hired guns who go out and sell the Fords of this world. And for Ford we can have lots of account execs because they buy about 50,000 machines a year.

"Now, a small business may want to buy 100 machines a year, and for that kind of volume, we really can't afford to send out an account exec. So, we've created something we call the virtual account exec. For a small company that's interested in Dell's products, we essentially have a briefing online. We set up this briefing for say 1:30 in the afternoon. His salesperson gets the customer on the phone and stays on the line as we tell him to turn on his computer and point his browser to www.dell.com.virtualae. The customer is dealing with three different types of media at this point. They've got their salesperson on the telephone who is leading them through the briefing. And then they've got a video online, which is essentially video clips of the kinds of people that a large account would see during a live executive briefing. So, for example, they'll see me talking about Dell's business model. And right next to that is a PowerPoint presentation extolling the virtues of what Dell has to offer.

"So, we're using Internet technology in a way that allows us to be much more effective in the selling environment than we ever could before.

We've put the process online. We no longer have the account exec dealing with the mundane, like 'tell me your zip code and I'll mail you this stuff.' Their time becomes more leveraged.

"The result is that we've become more efficient. The customer gets faster access to the information, and we're sort of moving up the value-added food chain. We are using the tools more effectively.

"Another example of that would be our web site called Web Talk. It now has tens of thousands of registered users, and it's sort of an online bulletin board, or a chat room on the Internet, except that it is just for Dell users. Through it a lot of users help other users optimize what they can do with their machines. It's not 'My keyboard broke,' or something like that. It's more like 'I'm deploying this complicated software and it's not quite doing what I'd like, does anybody have any ideas?' Someone posts that and someone else responds: 'Oh, yeah, I did that too, and here's how you get it working just perfectly.'

"These things are not a substitute, and do not take away from the need for us to have face-to-face, or telephone contact, with our customers, but they certainly improve the efficiency of those other activities."

The Internet activities are fully integrated into everything Dell does, a fact that Michael Dell says helps keep his company ahead of the competition.

"Let's suppose you were one of our competitors that sells indirectly through retailers. If you set up a presence on the Internet, it is even worse than going direct. Here's why. Let's say one of your retailers handles Chrysler. It sells them thousands of computers a year. Now, Chrysler has a pretty smart procurement department, and, at some point, they're going to wonder where else they can buy this product? And then they go online and see they can buy it directly from you, the manufacturer, over the net and it's $46 less than they are paying the retailer who handles their product.

Company (Ticker): Dell Computer Corporation (DELL)

Location: Round Rock, Texas

Leader: Michael S. Dell

Dell at a glance: Dell Computer is one of the world's leading personal computer manufacturers and is the world's number-one direct-sales computer vendor. In the near future, it expects to get 50% of sales via the Internet. Led by founder Michael Dell (the longest-tenured CEO of any major U.S. computer company), who owns 16% of the company, Dell sells hardware and markets third-party software and peripherals. Products include notebooks, PCs, and network servers. Dell also markets a variety of peripherals and software for other manufacturers. Approximately 70% of its systems are sold to businesses and government entities. To compensate for the slump in demand of desktop PCs, Dell has expanded into high-end server products and Internet services.

1999 Financial Results

—Revenues: $25.2 billion

—Net Income: $1.6 billion

Do you think that reseller is ever going to sell your product to Chrysler again? Not a chance.

"So, this is the prisoner's dilemma that the indirect companies have. They have to eliminate the dealer that generates 98% of their revenues to get out of the box they're in and start selling directly."

Dell, obviously, doesn't have that problem, although that does not mean the company makes no mistakes. It does. But like all high performers, it learns from them, ultimately becoming more focused as a result.

"If you go back to the late '80s, Dell developed its own version of UNIX, which would seem like a very unlikely thing for our company to do," its chairman says. "At the time it seemed like a pretty good idea, but it turns out it was just a horrible use of resources and a big waste of time.

"We were also the first major PC company to sell PCs through what is now the PC superstore channel. We viewed them as kind of a cross between going direct and traditional retail stores. We fell asleep on this decision. People were telling us that we could get only so big if all we did was sell direct, and we believed them. They were wrong, but we listened to them. That was a huge mistake. Fortunately for us it never became a large portion of our business. When we finally got rid of that, it certainly improved the company's financial results. But the more important change was that it clarified inside the company what our strategy was. We sell direct. And that clarity has proven to be just awesome. It kept us from running off in five different directions. We became incredibly focused."

The result is a very bright future indeed.

ELIZABETH DOLE
American Red Cross

Managing the nation's material, human, and inner resources

IT WAS A MASTERFUL POLITICAL MO-
ment. As she entered the room an announcer bellowed over the loudspeaker,
"Our beloved president of the American Red Cross, Mrs. Elizabeth Dole!"
and more than 500 cheering employees
went wild. So went Dole's departure announcement from the nation's preeminent not-for-profit corporation in early
1999. She turned a potentially mundane
event—the resignation of an organization's CEO—into a veritable pep rally,
where she was repeatedly praised for her
leadership, vision, and impact on the
country. (She also picked a slow news
day to announce she was leaving, guar-
anteeing substantial press coverage.)

Two years after her husband's presidential run, and coming off the best
financial year in the history of the
American Red Cross, (despite it being
one of the worst in terms of natural disasters), Dole effectively cleared the path
for her own campaign for the White
House in 2000 and pushed herself
toward the front ranks of candidates.

At all times, this ultimate Washington
insider strikes just the right note.

CAREER
1991–1999 President and CEO, American Red
Cross
1989–1990 Secretary, U.S. Department of Labor
1987–1988 with Robert Dole's Presidential
Campaign
1983–1987 Secretary, U.S. Department of
Transportation
1980–1983 Assistant to the President for
Public Liaison
1980 Chairman of Voters for Reagan-Bush
1973–1979 Commissioner, Federal Trade
Commission
1971–1973 Deputy Assistant to the President
for Consumer Affairs
1968–1971 Associate Director, Legislative
Affairs, then Executive Director, President's
Commission for Consumer Interests

EDUCATION
J.D., Harvard University, 1965
M.A. in Education and Government, Harvard
University, 1960
Postgraduate, Oxford (England) University,
summer 1959
B.A. with honors, Duke University, 1958

FAMILY
Married, Robert Joseph Dole, December 6, 1975

Born: Salisbury, North Carolina, July 29, 1936

"At the Red Cross, your full-time mission is to make a difference—a positive difference—for people with dire human needs. The reward is in serving those who are in need. Most of the people involved in the Red Cross, and a lot of the people involved in government service, could earn much more if they were in the private sector. But they appreciate the opportunity to be a servant leader, to serve the public."

In part, it is because she is a product of her upbringing. Growing up in North Carolina, intelligent women—and Dole, who graduated from Duke with honors, did postgraduate work at Oxford, and is a Harvard-trained lawyer, is nothing if not intelligent—asserted themselves without fuss.

And, in part, it is because of her innate drive and devotion to make a contribution.

The result is that Dole has asserted herself to the extent where she is perennially cited as one of the most admired leaders in America.

Asked if she is a feminist, Dole replies, "I think if it means that you have some sort of prepackaged answers that are handed down by the political correctness club, no. But, if it means that you want equal opportunity for women, more freedom for women—absolutely."

Obviously, Dole has followed a different path than most chief executive officers. But as her career points out, the parallels between effective leadership of not-for-profit organizations and governmental departments and management in the private sector could not be more clear. And, intriguingly, a major thread throughout her career has been working with the private sector to accomplish many of her goals.

If it were a corporation, it would rank squarely in the middle of the Fortune 500. The American Red Cross, a humanitarian organization that relies heavily on unpaid help, is a $2.1 billion organization with 31,000 paid employees, in addition to the nearly 1.3 million people who work for it on a volunteer basis.

Running the organization deserves tremendous respect, but that was not something always accorded to Elizabeth Dole. Here is how she was greeted on her first day of law school in 1962.

"I had just entered the library, and these were the first words I heard. A male classmate called out, 'Elizabeth, what are you doing here? Don't you realize there are men who'd give their right arm to be here? Men who would *use* their legal education.'

"That man is now a senior partner in one of Washington's most prestigious law firms," Dole recalls with a laugh.

You would be hard-pressed to find anyone today who has either questioned whether Dole has put her education to good use, or how her abilities stack up as a chief executive. Her communications skills and organizational abilities are legendary. In Washington, Dole is known as someone who can work a room better than anyone. And she is also known as a fund-raiser extraordinaire. (While some 70% of the Red Cross's budget comes from earned income—everything from the blood it sells to hospitals to the courses it teaches to the return on its investments—the remaining 30%, nearly $700 million a year, is raised through donations. (The organization is not, as many people believe, a government agency.)

Given her reputation and the organization's reliance on donations, we asked, half-jokingly, what her secret was to being a successful fund-raiser? Her response goes a long way to explaining why the Red Cross is, according to the Jankelovich research firm, the most respected nonprofit organization in America.

"We became good at fund raising once we borrowed one of the critical tools from the business community, and that is market research. We really needed to find out what our customers wanted so that we could be responsive to them.

"In our case, our customers are our blood donors, financial donors, and volunteers, as well as those who receive our blood, our disaster relief, and our training.

"So, understanding what their needs are, and then fashioning our activities to meet and respond to those needs is very important."

Setting the Direction

Charting a course for the organization was critical when Dole took over. Serious questions were being raised concerning how the Red Cross handled its blood program, in light of reported cases of AIDS being transmitted through blood transfusions. Income was declining from the organization's traditional source of funding, the United Way. In addition, the Red Cross was organized inefficiently, with too many and overlapping chapters.

Without question, the problems with the blood program took precedence.

"I cannot begin to tell you what a wrenching change this was," Dole says. "We had to totally change the way we tested, collected, and distributed nearly half of America's blood supply. Our procedures had been in place since World War II and we had to change all of them. In testing, for example, we used to do two tests for each unit of blood. Now we do eight. All in all, we have put seven years and $287 million into the project."

However, these funds were becoming harder to come by. The vast majority of the American Red Cross's charitable donations had originated from the United Way, the umbrella organization that encompasses a number of charities. As the United Way has, in recent years, decided to add many more local and national charities, the percentage it sends on to the American Red Cross has been steadily decreasing.

Given this decrease in funding, the organization had to execute two actions simultaneously to become more efficient and to search for new sources of revenue.

"The way we moved forward was through our visioning and corporate-wide strategic-planning process," Dole says. "We went all over the country holding meetings with people in the field, soliciting their input as to what was required. Out of this came our vision. The organization is structured in such a way that we really need to be responsive to the field and build consensus and ownership. We need to have that ownership because we are an organization that's far-flung with so many volunteers."

What was also clear from both the market research and the meetings with the staffers and volunteers in the field was that the Red Cross also needed to clarify its image. It had to do a better job explaining what it does.

"It is not enough to be seen as that great old organization that's been there for so many years, that's venerable, that does good work," Dole says. "If we are dependent on generating charitable dollars, volunteers, and blood donors by the millions, people need to feel passionately about what we do."

Dole needed the Red Cross to come up with an integrated marketing campaign that would address the needs of all its constituencies. This is something she readily admits was borrowed from private-sector organizations.

"We have much more in common with the corporate sector than we've ever been willing to admit," she says. "We may be a nonprofit, but we must reap the profits of good management practices. Being customer-focused and anticipating change in order to capitalize on it is crucial for any business, for profit or not for profit. I remember Jack Welch saying that if any organization is not changing as fast as the environment in which it operates, the end is in sight. You may have a great name and a long history of service as a venerable, respected organization, but you just won't be here in the next century if you don't make those changes and stay ahead of that curve."

Obviously, you cannot make those changes without people, and if you want employees to feel passionate about the company's mission, the person at the top has to be passionate as well.

"When what you believe comes from the heart, it gives you the energy and the drive, and generates enthusiasm that's contagious," Dole says.

So:

Step 1: Identify the true needs of your market,
Step 2: Be passionate about what you are trying to accomplish, and
Step 3: Effectively communicate your vision throughout the organization.

"You may be the most dedicated person in the world, and have tremendous skills, but if you can't communicate what you are trying to achieve, if you can't reach out to others and explain it so that you inspire your people, your organization is not going to go anywhere."

With the framework in place, Dole set off to accomplish her specific—and limited—set of goals.

Focus, Focus, Focus

"When I became Secretary of Transportation, my predecessor, Drew Lewis, beseeched me to 'Identify no more than five things that you feel are really important, where you can make a difference, and go for it. If you spread yourself across too many initiatives, years later you will have been working night and day and you'll wonder what you have accomplished. You will have dissipated your efforts.'

"I think that's such good advice and it's something that I've tried to do in each of my positions. I try to concentrate on where I really can make a difference and then I put a lot of energy into making sure that those things happen."

This clear focus has paid off in each of the major phases of Dole's career.

Leading the Department of Transportation (where Dole was the first woman in American history to head a division of the Armed Forces—the Coast Guard is part of Transportation), Dole says that her mission was to "oversee the material resources of the United States." This included highway construction, shipbuilding, air traffic control, and much of the country's railroad system. "A main objective was to be the flagship of privatization," Dole explains. Sales of government assets included Conrail (the freight railroad) and the Alaskan Railway.

"During the arduous three-year Conrail process, you really had to become a rail expert, an investment banker, and antitrust lawyer," Dole recalls. "The sale, which was the largest industrial offering then to date, raised $2 billion to help reduce the nation's deficit."

Dole says that the mission at the Department of Labor was the "management of human resources. We were trying to do everything we could to improve the skills of America's workforce."

Again, Dole focused on a handful of major priorities. "What we were looking at was really a potential workforce crisis. One in four high school graduates is functionally illiterate and many do not have the skills to compete in today's competitive global economy. We set up a blue-ribbon commission to develop national competency guidelines that reflect work readiness and then urged schools and educators to utilize these in curriculum development and other programs." The department also worked with America's companies to create extensive programs in work-based training and employee mentoring of at-risk kids.

At the Red Cross, Dole says she spent her time on "the management of inner resources. What the organization has been trying to do is encourage people to give of their time, money, and their blood. Our aim has been to be the nonprofit pacesetter, establishing a new credo of business for businesses of the heart." One way the Red Cross has been pursuing this aim, intriguingly, is via the Internet. "We want to connect every school, office, and home that has access to the Internet to the Red Cross, so that we can offer volunteer opportunities, allow people to make an appointment for blood donations, take courses, or make financial contributions online."

Her other selected area of focus included making sure the organization could move faster.

"We rechartered our chapters for the first time in Red Cross history. Now we do not have nearly as many chapters as we used to—in fact, half as many today—but our service is much more efficient because we have a new field structure that's organized around states. In other words, rather than chapter by chapter, the chapters work across the state, and they collaborate and share resources. So the service delivery is better."

The blood-supply program has been almost completely overhauled, and fundraising efforts have been established

Organization: American Red Cross

Location: Falls Church, Virginia

Leader: Bernadine P. Healy

American Red Cross at a glance: The American Red Cross is a not-for-profit organization committed to helping people, especially after disasters. Though chartered by Congress to provide relief services, the Red Cross is not a government agency. Its staff is made up largely of volunteers—nearly 1.3 million of them. In addition to providing relief to victims of more than 60,000 natural and man-made disasters nationwide each year, the Red Cross teaches lifesaving, CPR, first aid, water safety, and AIDS awareness courses to 12 million people a year, conveys 4,000 emergency messages a day between members of the Armed Forces and their families, and provides almost half of the nation's blood supply.

Revenues: $2.4 billion (1999)

based on meeting customer needs. Dole is leaving the American Red Cross on rock-solid ground. Financially, the organization has just had its best year in its history. And despite the worst year of natural disasters and most expensive, it topped its largest fund-raising campaign ever—$50 million—by $3 million.

Dole can see she made a difference. That is something extremely important to her.

"My mother is 97 and when I get to be her age, the question is going to be, 'What did I stand for? Did I make a positive difference for others?' That is what is going to matter, not all of the other more shallow things."

The only remaining question, as we go to press, is where Dole will apply her considerable energy, drive, intelligence, and leadership next.

BOB EATON
DaimlerChrysler

"You don't want to be a manager. You want to
be a leader."

THE AUTO INDUSTRY HAS ALWAYS BEEN CYCLICAL, BUT SOMEHOW THOSE
economic cycles always seemed to hit Chrysler—the smallest of Detroit's
"Big 3" automakers—hardest.

The government loan guarantees in the early 1980s were just the
biggest example. But the company had been in trouble numerous times
before. That's why when he was asked about his goals, upon coming to
Chrysler in 1992, Robert J. Eaton offered an answer that made insiders
smile. Eaton, who had spent his entire
career at GM, said one of his objectives
was "to be the first chairman of Chrysler
who never has to bring this company
back from the brink of bankruptcy. I
want us to be on the opposite side of
that, the most financially stable auto
company in the world."

Even before the 1998 merger with
Daimler-Benz, the maker of Mercedes-
Benz, Eaton was well on his way. Indeed,
Daimler executives repeatedly cited the
job Eaton did as one of the reasons they
wanted to merge with Chrysler. Eaton,
today, is chairman and co-CEO of the
new DaimlerChrysler.

It is not hard to see why Daimler-
Benz found Chrysler so attractive. In the
automobile business, image may not be
everything, but it sure is important. And
Eaton's mere presence at Chrysler sent a

CAREER
1998–2000 Chairman and Co-CEO,
    DaimlerChrysler Corporation
1993–1998 Chairman and CEO, Chrysler Corp
1992–1993 Vice Chairman and COO, Chrysler
1988–1992 President, General Motors-Europe
1982–1988 Vice President and Group
    Executive, GM
1979–1982 Assistant Chief, Oldsmobile
    Division
1976–1979 Chief Engineer, Cars, GM
1974–1976 Engineer Staff, GM

EDUCATION
B.S. Mechanical Engineering, University of
    Kansas, 1963

FAMILY
Married, Connie; two sons

Born: Buena Vista, Colorado, February 13,
    1940

> *"A leader is someone who can take a group of people to a place they don't think they can go."*

message. First, since he was the former head of GM-Europe, everyone expected him to expand Chrysler's international presence. Southeast Asia and South America looked particularly promising. The fact that Chrysler was in the process of boosting its exports wasn't lost on Mercedes.

Second, Eaton is a "car guy." He owns four, and he'll talk for as long as you want about what makes his two Dodge Vipers, a Plymouth Prowler coupe, and a Jeep Wrangler (complete with gun rack) so much fun to drive.

All those cars draw loving looks from car aficionados, and they also go a long way toward explaining why the average age of the Chrysler customer is far younger than it was when Eaton took over. That, too, was appealing to Mercedes, which is now trying to court a younger audience.

Finally, Eaton is an engineer by training, which explains why, in the words of one U.S. analyst, "more than any other automaker, foreign or domestic, Chrysler has refined the product development process into a potent competitive weapon." For example, the 1993 Intrepid took 39 months to go from concept to market. The 1998 Durango SUV (sport utility vehicle) took 23 months. The industry average is about 30 months. The Germans, also, are noted for their passions for engineering and efficiency.

As Furman Seltz auto analyst Maryann Keller said prior to the merger: "Chrysler is clearly the best of the American trio in empowerment, cost structure, and having the newest products."

When shoppers enter a new market, they go after the best merchandise first. No wonder Daimler went to Chrysler when it went looking for an American partner.

The merger came as a surprise. But it was totally consistent with what Eaton had been saying since he had become CEO. In speeches and interviews he stresses, "I want to be known for having created the best team of any company in the world, a team that is focused on building vehicles that people want to buy, and will enjoy."

That won't change with the Mercedes merger, a fact that he has been able to communicate to Chrysler employees.

"I clearly thought from the beginning that the merger was a great thing for the company, but I felt that it might be a little more difficult to convince our various stakeholders that, in fact, it was a great thing. But it wasn't. From the very first day, our union came out in favor of it, our employees were in favor of it, and so were our dealers. Virtually all the stakeholders had a very, very positive response."

Maybe they understood the days of worrying about Chrysler's solvency are finally over.

BEFITTING AN ENGINEER, BOB EATON DREW UP A PRECISE BLUEPRINT when he began thinking about what it would take to make Chrysler successful.

"We established our key success factors, and what kinds of beliefs and values we wanted to have as a company, and we focused exactly on that for roughly six years," he explains. "We decided the purpose of this company was to produce cars and trucks that people want to buy, will enjoy driving, and will want to buy again. We set an objective of being the premier automobile company in the world by the year 2000.

"Everybody in this company now understands where we're trying to go, and how we want to get there. We don't believe in slogans, or putting things on the walls, because everybody knows them. We've internalized them."

In the broadest sense, the goal was to build a company around the concept of continuous improvement. While that can sound vague, how Chrysler put the idea into practice is anything but.

"I'm a very firm believer that no matter what business you're in, there are five things that you've got to worry about, and only five. I always say, whatever the sixth one is, it never gets up high enough up on the priority list to work on.

"The most important one is product, and that's true in every company, even if you're a service company. There, obviously, your product is service. Then there's cost, quality, customer satisfaction, and people. And we constantly measure how well we're doing in every one of those five categories. For example, with product there are a lot of different measures. We have lots of competitions and awards in our business and we also look at customer preferences. We use a compilation of all of those when it comes to measuring product."

Those five measures drive everything about Chrysler, including the way it is organized, even though it is now part of DaimlerChrysler. You can see this if you take a look at how product development works.

"We're organized into platform teams that contain representatives from all disciplines—marketing, manufacturing, product engineering, design, procurement, and supply—everybody is represented. And very early on, we agree on the major decisions as a company, and we enter into, in effect, a one-page contract with a group of people ranging anywhere from 80 people, who are working on the Prowler (a sports car), to maybe 1,000 people working on something built on a bigger platform, on one of our high-volume vehicles."

But the contract covering production works the same in either case.

"It's called a 12-panel chart," Eaton says. "There are literally 12 little panels on this one piece of paper that covers everything from fuel economy, aerodynamics, cost margins, overall profitability, investment, weight, and pleasability targets. Those include things such as how the ride is going to be, how it is going to handle, and how quiet the car is going to be. We agree on this stuff going in, and as long as the teams stay within the parameters on that chart, they don't have to come back to senior management. They are left alone to execute.

"This really does two things. Number one, it cuts out time—they don't have to return constantly to headquarters for approval and funding—but more important is that it becomes the team's project. They don't have to look over their shoulder to see if we're going to change something, or second-guess them. As long as they stay within those parameters, it's their program. And obviously they strive to stay within those parameters, so they don't have us looking over their shoulder.

"So we've virtually eliminated upper management involvement on a day-to-day basis. We let the team execute."

This relentless focus on what is important now governs everything the company does.

"The biggest mistake made by Chrysler in the last 10 or 12 years also occurred throughout the industry, but probably it affected us the most," Eaton says. "The mistake was diversification. The idea was that this being a cyclical industry, if you had a more diverse business, you would tend to flatten out your earnings if you diversified into other businesses and you wouldn't have quite the earnings swings you get in the cyclical automobile business.

"But in reality, we didn't have the expertise, nor did we really have the scale in many of the other businesses, to be as competitive as we should have been. And so, in our case, we reversed course."

The company, which had sold Gulf Stream Aviation before Eaton got there,

Company (Ticker): DaimlerChrysler Corporation and DaimlerChrysler A.G. (DCX)

Locations: Stuttgart, Germany, and Auburn Hills, Michigan

Leaders: Hilmar Kopper, Chairman—Supervisory Board

Juergen E. Schrempp, Chairman—Management Board

DaimlerChrysler at a glance:

DaimlerChrysler, formed by the 1998 merger of Chrysler and Daimler-Benz, is the world's third-largest car maker in terms of revenue, trailing only General Motors and Ford (it is fifth in terms of units sold). The combination with Daimler—maker of Mercedes—gave Chrysler a major boost in the international arena, while Daimler has benefited from Chrysler's broad product spectrum, marketing savvy, manufacturing efficiency, and U.S. dealer network.

1999 Financial Results

—Revenues: $151.0 billion

—Net Income: $5.7 billion

has gotten out of the defense business as well as car rentals and financial services (other than the financing of cars and trucks).

"We have a core business focus—and we've reduced our vertical integration even in our core business—and I think the collective moves have had a very, very positive effect."

The decision to change the focus of the corporation is characteristic of how Eaton sees the evolving role of CEO.

"I believe the job of the chief executive has changed very dramatically. First of all, there's a huge difference between managing and leading, and I believe that if you went back 20 years most of the people running companies were managing. Now I think people at the top of large corporations aren't—or shouldn't—be devoting very much time to management. Most of their time should be going toward leadership. The world is much more competitive and is changing faster, and there isn't enough time for executives to manage, to control, to track results. You need to focus on vision and beliefs and values and inspiring people and breaking roadblocks for people to be able to accomplish more."

That's what happened at Chrysler, under Eaton's leadership. And now that the company has become DaimlerChrysler, the goal is to do this yet again.

BERNIE EBBERS
MCI WorldCom

"The only real values are the eternal ones."

UNTIL LATE 1997, BERNARD J. EBBERS WAS A WELL-KEPT SECRET OUT-side the telecommunications industry. True, he had, through a series of more than 40 acquisitions, turned WorldCom into a billion-dollar company. And yes, he had made WorldCom the fourth-largest phone company in the United States, behind AT&T, MCI, and Sprint. But being fourth in the telephone industry is much like being fourth in the American auto industry—it does not help you much when most people can only name the top three competitors.

And then Ebbers changed all that in one fell swoop. He acquired—for $43 billion—MCI Communications Corp.

The MCI takeover transformed MCI WorldCom, as the company is now known, into:

- The second-largest U.S. long-distance carrier,
- One of the world's largest Internet companies, and
- A major international force in the telephony market.

This is none too shabby for a company run by a transplanted Canadian who prefers cowboy hats and blue jeans to pinstripes and silk ties.

Ebbers, a basketball player at Mississippi College in Jackson, Mississippi, did not start out as a telecommunications mogul. He taught high school after

CAREER
1985–PRESENT President and CEO, MCI WorldCom, Inc.
1983–1985 Founder and investor, LDDS (precursor to MCI WorldCom, Inc.). Prior to founding LDDS, owned and operated group of Best Western motels and taught high school

EDUCATION
Bachelors, Mississippi College, Jackson, Mississippi, 1962

FAMILY
Married; three children

Born: August 27, 1941

"Since we've been a public company, the average annual increase in our stock has been over 50%. Not only does that make for highly motivated employees, it also makes it very difficult for anyone to acquire us."

graduation, and first went into the hospitality business, eventually assembling a string of motels. Always on the lookout for promising ideas, he and a group of investors launched a small phone company in 1983 to take advantage of the newly deregulated market for long distance services, and soon the acquisition spree was under way.

Following an acquisition—be it Wiltel, MFS Communications, or now MCI—the plan is always the same. Eliminate anything resembling fat, in order to preserve operating earnings and support the company's stock price. Ebbers does not believe in large customer entertainment or advertising expenses and has made it a point to reduce costs in every area, including expensive executive perks, in order to increase profits.

FOR SOMEONE WHO WORKS IN A REMARKABLY COMPLEX BUSINESS— telecommunications—Bernie Ebbers has a remarkably simple approach to what his role should be.

In fact, initially he envisioned no role at all.

"In the earliest days of WorldCom, I was a passive investor and not involved in the company. It was only after the company was in desperate financial straits that I became involved. It was strictly a matter of survival. When I did, my vision was simple. I planned to get our profits up, hoping somebody would buy us. Obviously, that has not happened."

Once involved, Ebbers stayed engaged and imposed strict financial controls to ensure that the company would not run into fiscal troubles again. Perhaps it was because of the company's financial woes, or perhaps it goes back to his beginnings in the motel business, but Ebbers is fanatical about tracking measurements designed to ensure the company remains profitable.

Ebbers knows that the best way to guarantee that a company will hit its financial targets is to make sure employees are rewarded for doing so. That is why he makes sure they are paid like owners. Everyone in the company has stock options.

"You can't go through our building without seeing charts, which are revised every day, showing what those options are worth," Ebbers says. "MCI did not offer everyone stock options. We will.

"To be honest with you, this is the most satisfying part of my job," he adds. "I could show you letter after letter from employees who write 'If it had not been for the options, I never would have been able to send my child to college.' Or, 'I've never had the opportunity to own a home before, and now I can make a substantial down payment, thanks to what my options are worth.' From a company point of view, we are pleased with the return we have produced for our shareholders, and the participation that the board has allowed us to include for the people that work here. The results have been amazing."

The number of options awarded is determined in large part by how well the company executes against its budgets and business plan. Not surprisingly, Ebbers spends a lot of time thinking about the company's performance, and he has reduced those thoughts to one key idea.

"It is not how much revenue growth you can have. The question is how much does it cost you for each dollar of increased revenue that you get? We focus on that because a dollar of revenue is not worth anything unless it's a profitable dollar."

This same philosophy applies equally to acquisitions.

"Anyone who has money can make an acquisition," Ebbers says. "The question is what can you do with [the acquired property] once you get it?"

The answer, at MCI WorldCom, is "quite a lot." Going back to the company's earliest days there has never been a year when sales and earnings have not grown at least 16% a year. The industry average over that time? Just 5%.

New People, New Views

The acquisitions have another benefit: new perspectives.

"If you look at my direct reports, only one has been with me since the beginning. Every other person came through an acquisition. That has been a great opportunity for us because we get many different perspectives about the way things are done."

That, Ebbers says, helps him perform his job better.

"The way I see it, my function is not to be the most knowledgeable in any specific area. My challenge is to make sure that I have blue chip players in each area—and we are fortunate now that we have a lot of Michael Jordans—and then try to get them to play on the same team.

"One of the most difficult things in doing mergers is that you don't know a lot about the people that you are getting with the acquisition. But the opposite is also true. When you grew up from nothing like we did, it's a great concern that the guy who took you to the dance can't take you home. We have to constantly be looking to make sure people are growing. Some people can grow and some don't."

And Ebbers says there is another key aspect to his job.

"The critical thing for me is to recognize that I am not the company. I am a steward of this company. For me, to have an opportunity to participate in something like MCI WorldCom is unheard of. And every day I think about how fortunate I am to have been given this stewardship responsibility.

"I think that's important because as CEOs, we often tend to think we know a whole lot more than we really do. We forget that it's the people that are working with us that really make us what we are. I recognize that I have a stewardship responsibility, and not an authoritative one.

"I would hope not to offend anyone, but I'd like to take this concept one step further. I look at my stewardship of this company as an opportunity that the Lord has given me. And that the fundamental principle in my life is to serve Him and to serve people through the opportunities He has given me."

And where does his own drive come from?

"I am not sure," he replies. "I was born in Canada. My family is all from Canada. My parents, after I finished grade one, moved to California for four years. And then we moved to just outside of Gallup, New Mexico, for five years. And we lived on the Navajo Reservation at a mission post there. My father was the business manager for the mission. We didn't have much. If my dad had a few dollars left in his pocket at the end of the month, we would go out and eat hamburgers as a family.

"I remember the most exciting Christmas for me was the year my sister received a deck of 'Old Maid' cards and I received a deck of 'Animal Rummy' cards.

"I don't know if that fueled a passion. My father and my brothers and I are fairly competitive, driven people. Maybe it's genetics. We've all been very aggressive and worked hard at what we've done.

Company (Ticker): MCI WorldCom, Inc. (WCOM)

Location: Jackson, Mississippi

Leader: Bernard J. Ebbers

MCI WorldCom at a glance: Formed in 1998 from the acquisition of number-two long distance provider MCI Communications by number-four provider WorldCom, the company is the second-largest communications company (behind AT&T). With established operations in over 65 countries encompassing the Americas, Europe, and Asia-Pacific, WorldCom is a premier provider of facilities-based and fully integrated local, long distance, international, and Internet services. The company's global networks and transoceanic cable systems provide end-to-end high-capacity connectivity to more than 40,000 buildings worldwide. WorldCom subsidiary UUNet, through their alliance with AOL's Compuserve, operates one of the largest Internet infrastructure networks available.

1999 Financial Results

—Revenues: $37.1 billion

—Net Income: $4.0 billion

I guess everybody has a desire to be 'successful,' or be able to provide for their family. But I think more than anything, my father and mother taught us that the only real values in life are the eternal values."

Those comments show that Ebbers is really a blend of humility and ambition. Given MCI WorldCom's success, it is clearly something employees respond to. Ebbers has a theory on why that is the case.

"I recognize who I am. And if I do that, and I deal with people on a person-to-person basis, not a title-to-title basis, then people generally participate. If you can work with people, and they participate in making significant decisions in the company, you'll find there is much less resistance than if you do things in a dictatorial manner.

"What has always worked for me is having a very casual relationship with people. Trying to participate in people's lives as people, not as employees. And obviously that's where the reward also comes.

"One of the worst things that can happen is you have people do something because you said to do it instead of having them do something because they agree that it's the right thing to do. That doesn't change as you get bigger. It becomes a little bit more complex, but it doesn't change."

Not surprisingly, when Ebbers is asked to describe, in a word, the personality of the company he has built, he says "egoless."

"We have tried very hard to make sure we do not have an oversupply of ego in the company. For my part, I know I am very fortunate to be here."

MICHAEL EISNER
Walt Disney

"What you are striving for is magic,
not perfection."

MICHAEL EISNER TELLS A STORY THAT ILLUSTRATES THE KIND OF AT-
tention that he and the Walt Disney Company experience as the world's
second-largest (behind Time Warner), but most well-known, media and
entertainment company.

It was 1994, an unusually difficult
year for the company, which included the
tragic death of Eisner's longtime business
partner Disney president Frank Wells, the
public outcry and ultimate withdrawal
of Disney's America, the historical theme
park concept planned for Virginia, and
Eisner's quadruple bypass surgery.

"While I was still groggy from the
procedure, I am told that an editor from
one of the Hollywood trades sent in a
woman reporter with instructions to pretend she was a nurse at Los Angeles'
Cedars-Sinai Hospital and get into my
room and interview me. The next day,
when the reporter returned to her office,
the editor asked, 'Did you get the story?'
'No,' she said, 'I was thrown out by the
doctor from the *L.A. Times.*' "

One of the consequences of Eisner's
and Disney's remarkable success is that
the entire world seems to watch the
company's every move. Because they are
followed so closely by the nation's media

CAREER
1984–PRESENT Chairman and CEO, the Walt
Disney Company
1976–1984 President and COO, Paramount
Pictures (Gulf + Western)
1976 Senior Vice President, Prime Time
Production and Development, ABC
1975–1976 Vice President, Program Planning
and Development, ABC
1971–1975 Vice President, Daytime
Programming, ABC
1968–1971 Manager, Specials and Talent,
Director of Program Development–East
Coast, ABC
1966–1968 National Programming, ABC
1964–1966 Programming Department,
CBS

EDUCATION
B.A., Denison University, 1964

FAMILY
Married, Jane Breckenridge; children: Breck,
Eric, Anders

Born: Mt. Kisco, New York, March 7, 1942

"Nothing matters more than thinking and talking about new ideas."

and a wide variety of interest groups, the company's failures are magnified. And Disney is held to a higher standard because the quality of its services and products has come to be taken for granted.

But what many people tend to forget is that it was not always this way. When Eisner was appointed chief executive officer in 1984, after having just left Paramount Communications as president and chief operating officer, Walt Disney Co. was a small and troubled animation and theme park company. Disneyland and Disney World were languishing and hit movies were a distant memory. Wall Street raiders were looking to take over the company and break it up into pieces.

Over the past 15 years, Eisner has led Disney's vigorous renaissance, growing the company's market value from approximately $3 billion to about $70 billion today. This has been done by reviving animated movies, with such hits as *The Little Mermaid, Aladdin, The Lion King, Toy Story, Mulan,* and *A Bug's Life.* A new film division, Touchstone, has been created to produce movies that are not "G"-rated. The theme parks have been dramatically upgraded and expanded with the addition of new attractions, the opening of the now very successful Disneyland Paris, the recently launched Animal Kingdom, and Disney Cruise Line. All the while thousands of new hotel rooms have been added to the theme parks so that visitors never have to leave. Hundreds of Disney Stores have been added to both sell the company's vast array of consumer products and also cross-promote coming features on the big screen or on cable television's Disney Channel.

The biggest bet was Eisner's 1995 $19 billion acquisition of Cap Cities/ABC, which added both the ABC Television Network and one of the crown jewels of the cable television industry, sports powerhouse ESPN.

Disney has also moved aggressively into book and magazine publishing, the Internet (with Disney Online, ESPN.com, and with Infoseek partner GO.com), sports (with teams such as the Mighty Ducks and Anaheim Angels), and onto the live stage, with hits *Beauty and the Beast* and *The Lion King* on Broadway.

Beyond simply growing these businesses, however, Eisner deserves the most credit for doing something that had never been done in entertainment before—actually driving synergy across the company's various lines of business. While the word synergy is often (rightly) ridiculed as so much business jargon, the way a new Disney animated film is launched, with all of the business units lining up to support and promote it, shows how the concept should be executed.

ONE OF THE QUESTIONS THAT PETER DRUCKER IS FAMOUS FOR ASKING IS: "What business are you [really] in?" We asked Michael Eisner Professor Drucker's question in a slightly different guise: "Whom do you consider competition?"

Eisner's answer goes a long way toward explaining Disney's success.

"I think anybody dealing in the leisure world, or the education world, or the world of dealing with people's available time is a competitor," he begins. "It can be a motion picture company. It can be a music company. It can be a broadcast company. It can be an Internet company. It can be a hardware company that has aspirations to be in software. It can be Microsoft or a phone company. Everybody seems to understand that content is important, and so there are a lot of people that are competing with us. Every industry is in competition for people's time, whether they're shopping at a mall or going to a sporting event. But we, unlike a Pepsi-Cola, which has Coca-Cola as its principal competitor, do not have the luxury of having one individual competitor."

And those competitors can come from anywhere.

"Some of our biggest competitors are *not* based in the United States, such as the Bertelsmanns, Newscorps, and Polygrams. Then there are some key United States competitors such as Time Warner. But any company entertaining or informing people is competition for us."

How do you deal with that competition? Eisner's answer: "You battle it all on fronts.

"We, as a company, decided that there are two places that we can deal with people—in the home and outside the home. Outside the home includes going to sports, concerts, Broadway shows, as well as movies and amusement parks. Inside the home it's television and the influence of the computer and the television set. I think if we're going to be a relevant company, and not a dinosaur, in the future, we need to be a leader in all those places, and in all those technologies, including the Internet. The Internet is a very important place to entertain, to educate, and to communicate. So we are making it a strategic priority of the company. And since the world is getting pretty small, we are looking to be everywhere. A Disney theme park in China may not be a cash cow until our 150th anniversary [which will occur in the late 21st century], but it will probably happen a lot sooner."

You get an idea of how clearly Eisner understands what business he is in, when we followed up with another Drucker-inspired question. Countless leaders have adopted Drucker's "What gets measured, gets done" idea as their own motto. And when a typical manager is asked what he measures, he answers sales per employee, revenue growth, shareholder return, and customer satisfaction.

However, when we asked Eisner, he said, "The first thing I measure is content.

"I want to know, 'How good is the show? How entertaining is the movie? How does the food in the park taste?' I focus maniacal attention on the product because I have learned through my years in the business that a hit in our industry tends to wash away all of our incompetencies.

"So if you can do something that results in a big hit, that's the best way to dig yourself out of any problem you have. Also, what may look like an economic problem today will cease to be an economic problem in our industry if it is based on something where the content is really good.

"Why is that the case? Because you have word of mouth and because quality does win out in the end. So, the number-one thing, maybe the only thing, we judge day in and day out, is the quality of our product. And when we talk about quality we include everything from how we deal with the public in our parks and hotels to how our audience enjoys our films, television programs, books, magazines, and web sites.

"Obviously, there are a series of other factors that are important, everything from financial responsibility to diversity to philanthropy, and the other things that are important to us and make us the kind of company that we want to be. But if you try to pinpoint what it is that will allow us to continue to survive and grow, it is asking whether we have gone the last mile on the Broadway show for *The Lion King*? Have we gone the last mile on the Animal Kingdom? Have we gone the last mile on Disneyland Paris? Making sure we have, that's what it's all about.

"Sometimes we are surprised when something we think is great no one else does. Or there are other times—much more seldom—when something we thought was horrible is actually accepted by the public. But, by and large, if we keep out the peripheral influences—and try not to worry about what the press is going to think, we can make a pretty clear determination about whether we've done a good job."

Interestingly, because of its past successes, Disney is held to a higher standard. Eisner does not see that as a problem.

"On one hand, we are definitely held to a higher standard and we have to be cognizant of that and careful. On the other hand, we can't let it paralyze us. Because if it paralyzes us, we'll do nothing and all of our products will be boring and dull. So, you'd be surprised at how far we go before we say, that's not appropriate. I don't mean gratuitously violent or sexual or anything like that. But there is always a very fine line between what is appropriate and not for our company, because we know that the quality of what we do always will be examined under a magnifying glass.

"By the way, quality—and this is something I learned from [movie producer/director] George Lucas—does not mean perfection. The cost of perfection will drive you out of business. What you are striving for is magic, not perfection."

Going Forward

Given Eisner's and Disney's high profile, and the fact that there is no clear successor, speculation on who will replace Eisner as the company's next CEO has been a topic of discussion for years. Obviously, Eisner is unwilling to offer specific names, but he is happy to talk about the traits that he thinks will be required.

"I hope the Disney board will try forever to have its top people come from the creative side of the company. At the same time, they will need a strong understanding of the financials. Being totally creative and having no financial understanding is a problem. I think the more entrepreneurial

Company (Ticker): The Walt Disney Company (DIS)

Location: Burbank, California

Leader: Michael D. Eisner

Walt Disney at a glance: Disney is the world's third-largest media and entertainment company (following Time Warner and Viacom). The company has interests in television and movie production (including Buena Vista Motion Pictures Group, Buena Vista Television, and Miramax Film), theme parks (including Animal Kingdom, Disneyland, Disneyland Paris, Epcot Center, and the Magic Kingdom at Walt Disney World), publishing companies, a new cruise line, a major Internet business, Disney Internet Group (Disney Online, ABCNews.com, ESPN.com, Infoseek, Starwave, and GO.com), and professional sports franchises. Disney's ABC Inc. division includes the ABC television network, several dozen television stations, and ownership or interests in five cable channels, including ESPN, The Disney Channel, A&E, Lifetime, and the History Channel. Disney also produces recorded music and operates a consumer products division and more than 600 retail stores. Disney has enjoyed continued success with *Who Wants to Be a Millionaire?*, *The Sixth Sense*, *Toy Story 2*, and four new theme parks to be opened by year 2005.

1999 Financial Results
—Revenues: $23.4 billion
—Net Income: $1.3 billion

and more creative you are as a chief executive the better, as long as there's some kind of financial box surrounding you."

This is true of every company, Eisner says, not just those in the entertainment business.

"I think that even in the most mundane industry you could ever find, if the person who's running it is creative I think you'll find that they will come up with products that are interesting."

But regardless of the industry, what will determine success, Eisner argues, will always be the same.

"It really comes down to the striving for excellence in everything you do. If you're making soap operas, make the best possible soap opera. If you're making a toy, make the best possible toy. If you're the coach of your kid's soccer team, be the best possible coach you can be.

"In other words, just strive for excellence at each place you are in your life at that time. If you do, I think you end up doing better."

DON FISHER
The Gap

The Gap Formula for Success is as easy as
1-2-3: luck, common sense, and a small ego.

"FALL INTO THE GAP."

If you are of a certain age, you probably heard those four words sung in a booming bass voice hourly, it seemed, as you listened to a "Top 40" rock station while you were growing up. "Fall into The Gap" was a tag line you just could not escape.

The concept behind the slogan was more clever than the name. (It is a reference to the phrase "generation gap.") Here, for the first time, was going to be a huge store devoted to selling the core item of the counter-culture—blue jeans. Row upon row of blue jeans.

The store was an instant hit.

From there, Don Fisher and his management team added other clothing chains—such as GapKids, Old Navy, and Banana Republic—as the company kept expanding around the world to the point where today it is a $9 billion retailing powerhouse.

Fisher, who started in the real estate business, turned over the CEO title in late 1995 to Millard (Mickey) Drexler, universally recognized as one of the country's best merchants. Today, Fisher focuses on Gap's real estate holdings, long-range strategy, and growing the company's brands both internationally as well as domestically.

CAREER

1995–PRESENT Founder and Chairman, Gap Inc.

1969–1995 Founder, Chairman, and CEO

1957–1969 President, Fisher Property Investment Co.

1950–1957 Partner, M. Fisher & Son

EDUCATION

B.S., University of California, 1950

FAMILY

Married, Doris Feigenbaum; children: Robert, William, John

Born: San Francisco, California, September 3, 1928

STEP 1: LUCK

When asked about the long-term vision he had for his company when he founded it three decades ago, Donald Fisher just laughs.

"What vision?" he asks. "Five things needed to happen for me to even open my first store. If one of those five things didn't occur, there may never have been a Gap.

> *"I am not a gambler at casinos. But I gamble in business all the time. Every store is a gamble. I dislike losing more than I like winning."*

"I grew up in the real estate business, first working with my father and then I went off on my own. When I started my own company, I began by buying old hotel leases. In one of the first ones I acquired (in Sacramento), Levi Strauss had a small office. One day, I bought some clothes from the salesman there, but I bought the wrong size. I went to Macy's and tried to exchange them but the process of exchanging them was awful."

The experience may have been awful, but it triggered a thought. There had to be a better way to sell Levi's. Fisher decided he would become a (self-appointed) franchisee of Levi's.

"So, if I didn't buy that hotel, or if Levi's hadn't had an office, or if I had never bought any clothes from the salesman, or if they had fit, or if Macy's had a good blue jeans department, The Gap might never have happened.

"I'd rather be lucky than smart."

Or have an overarching vision to become one of the nation's best-known brands.

STEP 2: COMMON SENSE—PART I

Why open a store that sold basically nothing but blue jeans? They were the official uniform of the baby boomer generation, so what could be better? To Fisher, this was just common sense.

"I think common sense is a big part of success in business. You can be brilliant in some respects, but if you don't make the right decisions, you'll fail. I had a real estate and construction background, so I knew how to build our stores, and I had a good sense of good locations, as well as a fair amount of business experience."

As appealing as Fisher's retail concept was, there were two problems. Problem number one? Levi's was not granting franchises. That, Fisher decided, did not matter. He would become a de facto franchisee by stocking nothing but Levi's products in his store. "I thought Levi's knew everything about men's pants. That's all they were making at the time."

Fisher scraped together $63,000—most of it money marked for his sons' education—and opened The Gap.

Problem number two. Fisher didn't know anything about being a retailer. "I got a guy to run the store who was a friend of my father. He didn't work out, so about a month after we opened, I fired him. And then I found myself in a position of being the merchant and everything else."

Eventually, Fisher would find Drexler, who had been working at Ann Taylor.

"Until Mickey came along, I never found anyone who understood or could execute what I wanted to do with the business."

COMMON SENSE—PART II

What did Fisher want to do? Grow the business in a way that made sense.

"In 1974, five years after we had opened the first store, we started carrying Levi's for gals, which was their second line, their women's line. We thought Levi's didn't know very much about designing women's clothes. So we decided that we would carry our own line.

"We didn't have enough time to think of a name, so we called our women's brand 'The Gap' jeans and priced them lower than women's Levi's. [In 1980 we dropped 'The.']"

Why go private label? Clearly, skepticism about Levi's ability to market to women wasn't the full reason, was it?

"By this point, we had competition. County Seat (owned by Super Valu) had become a competitor and Levi's had started the concept of Levi's-only stores. In light of this, I decided that I wanted to be different than anybody else in order to have a competitive advantage. Now, I hadn't gone to business school and I'm not too sure I would have articulated it exactly that way in 1974. But I did know that I wanted to be different. I wanted customers to come into our store and find clothes they couldn't find anyplace else so we would be their first choice to shop.

"So every year starting in 1974 we reduced the percentage of Levi's we sold by about 5%, and increased the percentage we sold under our own name by the same amount. It took us almost 20 years, but by 1991 we had sold our last pair of Levi's."

The initial plan was to have The Gap line sell for slightly less than Levi's. "Our strategy was to have 'special value sales,' like they have in the supermarket, where they mark the price of butter down one week and raise it the next. Well, the people running the business would violate the plan because when they marked the merchandise down, it sold so well. So instead of leaving the price down for 10 days, they'd leave it down for 20 or 30 and sometimes they wouldn't mark it back up again. And it was driving me crazy.

"Ultimately, the whole store had these yellow 'special value' tags, and the stores started to look cheap. We were doing great, but I hated the business. I didn't like the concept of selling based on price. Unless you are someone like Wal-Mart, you can't win at that game.

"I wanted to be smarter rather than cheaper. But I never had anybody that understood what I wanted to do until Mickey joined the company. Together we figured out how to do it."

Company (Ticker): Gap Inc. (GPS)
Location: San Francisco, California
Leaders: Donald G. Fisher, Chairman
  Millard "Mickey" S. Drexler, CEO
Gap at a glance: The Gap is an
  industry-leading clothing retailer
  that operates over 2,300 casual
  clothing stores in the United States,
  Canada, France, Germany, Japan,
  and the United Kingdom. Its
  flagship Gap stores offer a wide
  variety of men's and women's casual
  clothing (T-shirts, jeans, khakis).
  The company's other chains include
  GapKids, BabyGap, Banana
  Republic, and Old Navy Clothing
  Co. The Gap is vertically integrated.
  It designs, contracts for the
  manufacture of, and sells its
  products exclusively in its own
  stores. Founder and Chairman Don
  Fisher and his wife Doris own 34%
  of the company.
1999 Financial Results
—Revenues: $11.6 billion
—Net Income: $1.1 billion

COMMON SENSE—PART III

The easiest way to command a premium for your products is to offer a better product. So starting in mid-1984, Fisher and Drexler decided to turn The Gap into a vertically integrated firm that would control everything from design to manufacturing to retail.

"When we started, we would go to branded manufacturers in New York and say, 'We like the pants you are making, would you manufacture 25,000 and put The Gap label on them,' " Fisher recalls. But eventually the company began designing its own lines and contracting directly for the manufacturing. "And at each step of the process we improved the quality. It finally got to the point where clothes with The Gap label were as well made as anything offered by the 'branded' competition."

Since The Gap was controlling the manufacturing process, it didn't have to pay middlemen. It used the money it saved to advertise the brand. Spending now tops more than $300 million a year and brand recognition is the highest it has ever been.

STEP 3: CHECK YOUR EGO AT THE DOOR

Just as Fisher worked hard to integrate every part of the manufacturing process, he has also worked hard to ensure that his company was fully integrated as well from a personnel perspective.

"I think people's egos are a big problem in running a business. I haven't let my own ego get in the way. I'd just as soon have other people get credit for good results rather than me. If I were to take credit for all of it, it would be very discouraging to the person who really did the work. We had a situation where someone created an incredible advertising campaign. But the individual running the department wanted all the credit and never gave any to the other person. The true creator quit because of it. And it wasn't right. The credit should go to where it belongs. I think it's very important that people be recognized for what they do.

"You've got to respect the other person's ideas as well. There's no reason not to fight for your ideas, if you think you're right. But if the other person's idea is better, you should accept it and then be a big supporter of it."

This is something many people—especially newly minted M.B.A.s—fail to understand, Fisher says.

"They think that because they've gone to business school that they're better and smarter than the people who are already in place. But I think that common sense is something you don't get in business school. Common sense is important. Before you start yelling about how things need to be changed, you have to understand the culture. Don't arrive and think you know everything."

DON FITES
Caterpillar

(Earth)Mover

IT WASN'T THAT LONG AGO THAT THE BUSINESS PRESS WAS FILLED WITH stories about how Japanese makers of earth-moving equipment were not only going to take over the American market, but were going to put companies such as Caterpillar out of business in the process.

It did not happen.

In fact, perhaps one of the most surprising performers in the U.S. economy in recent years has been Caterpillar. Credit for that goes to Donald V. Fites, under whose leadership the company increased exports to the point where they account for a third of sales, slashed inventory, and cut manufacturing costs.

Fites implemented a corporate reorganization and cost-cutting program immediately upon taking over as CEO in 1990. His primary objective? To make Caterpillar competitive with Japanese producers. The man, who grew up poor on a farm in Tippecanoe, Indiana, and became an engineer because he liked the idea of working outside, succeeded with a vengeance.

A key reason for that is that Fites, who spent his entire working life at Cat, knows every aspect of the company—and everything about its competition—having worked in numerous capacities around the globe.

CAREER
1990–1999 Chairman and CEO, Caterpillar, Inc.
1989–1990 President and COO
1985–1989 Executive Vice President
1981–1985 Vice President, Products
1979–1981 President, Caterpillar Brazil SEA
1976–1979 Manager, Products Control Department
1956–1975 Various worldwide postings, Caterpillar, Inc.

EDUCATION
M.S., M.I.T., 1971
B.S. in Civil Engineering, Valparaiso University, 1956

FAMILY
Married, Sylvia Dempsey, 1960; children: Linda Marie

Born: Tippecanoe, Indiana, January 20, 1934

"First of all, you have to get the right organization in place. You can have a wonderful culture, and you can pay people very well, but if you have an organization that by its very nature generates a lot of internal—as opposed to external—activity, if you find yourself writing a lot of letters to people in the company, there's something wrong. You ought to be focused outwardly."

That experience came to the fore in the 1980s when a slumping economy, coupled with an aggressive push by Japanese competitors, put Caterpillar's future in doubt. Fites, who had written his master's thesis at M.I.T. in 1971 on whether U.S. manufacturers could compete with Japan, decided it was imperative for Cat to maintain marketshare at all costs.

In response to the Japanese push into the U.S. market, Caterpillar matched prices of its Japanese competitors, even though it meant losing almost $1 billion between 1982 and 1984. Cat recovered as the U.S. economy did and, to make sure the company stayed in shape, Fites launched a five-year, $1.8 billion modernization program, designed to take costs out. Simultaneously, he began a new campaign to decentralize the company and push responsibility down the ranks. Managers suddenly found their compensation tied to return on asset targets. They responded and Cat was on its way back.

"I'VE BEEN HERE 42 YEARS," SAYS DON FITES SHORTLY AFTER greeting a visitor. When his guest points out that long-term commitment to any company today is surprising, it is Fites's turn to be surprised.

"This kind of tenure is not out of the ordinary in a company like Caterpillar," he says. "It's the norm. Almost all of our people come here and spend their entire careers with the company."

Fites thinks he understands why.

"First of all, this is a great company, and you become very connected to the people that you work with, and to the product. People are proud of the products we produce. I think they just really enjoy working for this company."

Leadership has something to do with why people stay with an organization, and since he has been in charge, the company has been routinely cited as one of America's most admired companies and has turned in the best numbers in its 73-year history.

Fites says he has been able to achieve those results because he was prepared to build on the company's strengths, specifically one that had been long overlooked—the people who work at Caterpillar—once he was named CEO in 1990.

"This is a company with a great heritage and a great product line, but that's not enough to be successful, as a lot of U.S. companies and companies around the world have discovered," says Fites, a past chairman of the Business Roundtable, an organization that represents 200 of the nation's largest companies in Washington. "You also, in this day and age, have to be globally competitive. You have to have the right organization. You have to have the right culture, and then you have to compensate people for performance.

"I think we had a great culture but we lost our global competitiveness to the Japanese in the early 1980s and we had to fight our way back to where we are today, the world leader in what we do."

The biggest factor in regaining that competitiveness?

Reorganizing Caterpillar in order to draw on the intellectual capital within the firm.

"We were a company that essentially was run top down, and my philosophy is to push decision making as far down as you can, to really make people feel accountable and responsible for their decisions, and then reward them when they do well. I think we had started down the road of becoming more competitive in our plants before I became CEO."

Fites also pushed that idea a lot further by doing two distinct things: one, actually giving people authority and two, letting them share in the profits that result.

Notice what he did. Instead of ordering changes from above, Fites's vision of Caterpillar's future called for giving employees direct control over how well they—and the company—would perform in coming years.

The Days of "Because I Say So" Are Gone

"Certainly there are some CEOs who run a pretty tight ship, and dictate everything that needs to be done. But to run a company the size of Caterpillar, which has $21 billion in sales, you have to convince people. They have to become part of what you want to do. The idea that you're going to write a memo, or make a speech, and lay down the law doesn't work in this day and age. It's much better if you get everyone on the team."

Paying employees for performance was a key to getting everyone on the team. And to make sure that everyone would truly benefit from their actions, Fites moved on the second part of his vision, pushing authority out to people on the line.

"You have to distribute information, and authority, as far down in the organization as you possibly can to allow people to make the right decisions. That's a cultural thing in a company. When you say you want people to be accountable and responsible, everyone's reaction is 'ho hum.' Employees know that everybody says that. You have to show them you mean it. You really have to let people make decisions at the lowest level possible.

"Now, how do you find out how low level that level is? At some point, people will start making lousy decisions and, of course, that tests your fortitude a little bit, because you can't just jump all over someone the first time they make a poor decision. If they make two or three, then obviously you start moving authority up a level or two. But you have to push authority down to the people on the line. Organizations understand pretty quickly whether you're just talking about responsibility and accountability or whether you're really going to let people make investment decisions, sales decisions, or price decisions, all the key things going into a successful company.

"This kind of change is cultural. You have to get the organization right. And then you have to get the climate right in your organization. And the third important factor—but it's not important if you don't have the first two right—is to compensate people who perform. If they perform better than their peers, they should receive better compensation."

To do that, Fites reorganized the company.

"I wanted to completely restructure the company into profit centers. This company was run essentially by the head office since its inception. And I had labored under that burden during my entire career. I was not a headquarters guy. I had spent 16 years living outside the United States, working on five continents. In the old days, I'd be far from Peoria, Illinois, receiving cables and letters with instructions that didn't make any sense with what I was trying to do, or where I was living. And my driving ambition, and I think my predecessor was coming along the same track, was to dismember this head office organization and put everyone in either a profit center, with their own P&Ls and profit objectives, or in a service center and make them realize that they are people who create costs, and they would have to find somebody to buy their services. If they couldn't convince the profit centers to use them, we'd find an outside vendor to do what they were doing since it was clear we didn't need their services at their cost. Virtually on the first day I became CEO, I announced we were going to do this. Everybody told me it was impossible, and I said we are going to do it anyway."

The company now has 26 separate profit centers and some 200 different compensation plans to make sure that everyone can benefit from their actions.

"Doing this changed the whole operating environment," Fites explains. "We are now results-driven. The key measure we use is return on assets. We use it for a couple of reasons. First, it is easy to explain. You have profit on top and you have assets on the bottom and the only way you improve that ratio is by making the number on top bigger or the number on the bottom smaller. Even engineers understood that." ("I'm an engineer, so I can say that," Fites quickly adds.)

As Caterpillar's results show, all the moves paid off. But instead of coasting on his success as he headed toward retirement, which took effect January 29, 1999, Fites took the opposite tack.

"During the eight years I have been CEO, we've grown from about a $10 billion company to greater than a $20 billion company, and we've also grown to be very profitable. Right now we have on our plate the most ambitious growth program ever in terms of new products, entry into new market areas where we have been minor players—places like the former Soviet Union and China—and new product lines that we have never had. We'll be a $30 billion company well before the end of the next decade. We've told the industry and the Street we're going to grow 6% to 7% a year in real terms. It is absolutely vital during the next three years that we successfully implement all of these investments that we are making. The next three years is not a period for great strategizing, it's a period for great implementation. We've got the organization clearly focused on implementing the growth plans that are already in place."

Setting these kinds of clear objectives is a key part of the CEO's job, Fites says. So is "leading by example."

"Leading by example means that you don't just talk about performance, you demonstrate performance in your own job, and you reward people who perform and you do not reward people who do not perform."

Company (Ticker): Caterpillar, Inc. (CAT)

Location: Peoria, Illinois

Leader: Glen A. Barton

Caterpillar at a glance: The world's number-one maker of earth-moving machinery, Caterpillar operates under the brand names Cat, Solar, Barber-Green, and more. The company makes a variety of construction, mining, and agricultural machinery, as well as engines for trucks, locomotives, and electrical power-generation systems. It also provides insurance for its dealers and customers. It has some 170 plants and more than 270 dealerships around the world. Changes in the agricultural, mining, and oil exploration industries caused Caterpillar to adapt and expand its product line into compact equipment and marine engines and to cut its workforce and production.

1999 Financial Results

—Revenues: $19.7 billion

—Net Income: $946 million

"Another way you do it as a CEO is by who you promote, by who you put into key jobs. Let me tell you, there are an awful lot of people, at an awful lot of companies, who still get promoted based on who likes them and who they know. If you promote people who have demonstrated performance regardless of whether you knew the person, the organization picks up on it pretty fast. They are watching to see if you are really serious about performance. If you are not they'll wonder why you aren't promoting people who are demonstrating superior performance and superior commitment."

Fites's vision was simple. Let people be responsible for their own jobs and their own success, and pay them for succeeding. He implemented his vision, and the people at Caterpillar responded.

BILL GATES
Microsoft

Missionary

BILL GATES HAS BEEN IN THE LIMELIGHT FOR SO LONG THAT PEOPLE often forget:

1) Exactly how significant an enterprise he has created, and
2) He is not yet 45.

It is easy to understand why people gloss over these facts. There is no other businessperson who has achieved his cult-like status. Almost everything written about him focuses on either how smart he is, or how wealthy. (Almost all of his net worth is in the form of Microsoft stock, and as of spring 1999, Gates was worth roughly $80 billion, which at various times has made him the richest man in the world.[1])

CAREER
2000–PRESENT Chairman and Chief Software Architect
1975–2000 Founder, Chairman, and CEO, Microsoft Corp.

EDUCATION
Student, Harvard University, 1973–1975
Graduated from Lakeside High School, Seattle, Washington, 1973

FAMILY
Married, Melinda French, 1994; children: Jennifer

Born: Seattle, Washington, October 28, 1955

---

1. We asked Gates about the fact that people sometimes assume he is to our era what John D. Rockefeller was to his.

"The comparison doesn't make sense," Gates replies. "I'm certainly not as wealthy as Rockefeller was. At the time of his death, Rockefeller's assets accounted for more than 1.5% of U.S. GDP. [Note: According to *Forbes* magazine, Gates's assets equal 0.58% of U.S. GDP.]

"More important, Rockefeller's business was about controlling scarce resources and distribution. His product [oil] didn't change. There is no analogy here to software, where the resources are smart people, innovation is constantly improving products, and there are no barriers to distribution thanks partly to the Internet. The software industry is the most fast-changing, competitive, and vibrant industry in the world, with more companies entering the market every month."

> *"The PC and the Internet will become as fundamental tomorrow as the automobile is today."*

Here is a lead from an early profile that is typical of the kind of press he gets: "Being smarter than most tycoons, richer than several small countries and as powerful as any minor deity, William Henry Gates III . . ."

This kind of adulation has made Gates a full-blown celebrity. Everyone from *Fortune* magazine to Barbara Walters has interviewed him, and he is a frequent target for satire. (In Winblows '98, a software spoof, you get to pretend you are Bill Gates and "rise from Penniless Nerd to Supreme Ruler of the Galaxy.") It is also well known how intense he is, how much homework he does, and how he can be brusque with people who are not prepared. His celebrity is such that he even endorses golf clubs (Callaway's Big Bertha driver).

All this is well and good, but it obscures the essential fact of what Gates has accomplished. He, along with Andy Grove of Intel, led the building of the worldwide personal computing business. The operating system that Microsoft, founded by Gates and his childhood friend Paul Allen, created can be found in more than 80% of the personal computers in this country. (Their market dominance and aggressive business practices led to one of the highest-stakes antitrust trials in U.S. history.)

Gates's leadership style is, like that of almost all of the leaders in this book, permanently intertwined with his personality and intelligence. By approaching his job with such intensity, and doing his homework so thoroughly, Gates has set an extremely high standard that his employees try desperately to emulate. Much more than most leaders we profiled, the people who work at Microsoft often tend to mirror his style and approach.

Part of that approach is a relentless focus on the future: Gates has continually displayed an unabashed optimism about the power of technology to transform everything from the way we live to the way markets perform. This comment, from his book, *The Road Ahead,* about how we will communicate in the future is representative:

> You'll set explicit delivery policies for all incoming communications you receive. You'll decide who can make your phone ring during dinner, who can reach you in your car or when you're on vacation, and which kinds of calls or messages are worth waking you for in the middle of the night.

Intriguingly, despite all the money Microsoft and the rest of the software industry has invested in research, Gates says it is not enough, given how ubiquitous the computer and Internet are bound to become.

BILL GATES CANNOT WAIT FOR THE FUTURE TO GET HERE.

"One of the biggest advances over the next few years will be the extension of the PC model to new intelligent devices of all sizes. You'll see everything from smart pagers and cell phones to "tablet PCs" and electronic books that allow you to read as easily as you do on paper. All of these will be connected to the Internet in ways that are totally seamless and transparent to users. In time, software will allow computers to speak, listen, see, and learn. In the future, we will look back at today's PCs and software as incredibly unnatural and rudimentary."

Gates, who has a good understanding of his place in the business firmament, has read extensively about the development of new industries and, as he points out, "there are some incredible parallels between what the auto industry did and what the PC industry is just at the beginning of doing."

It is a theme that dominates many of his speeches.[2]

"Early cars were bought by enthusiasts, just like PCs. People who bought the earliest PCs kind of got a kick out of doing something with a personal computer, even if it wasn't the most efficient way to do it.

"People used to like to go out in their car and kind of show off. There were some wonderful magazines at the start of this business, *My Automobile* and the *Horseless Age* were just two examples.

"If you go back and look at the *Horseless Age*, it's sort of like the *Byte* magazine of the PC industry, very hard-core. It tried to cover all the models in-depth, and explain what was going on inside them. And although *Horseless Age* didn't have long-term success, it was definitely part of getting things going.

"Early cars had some terrible limitations, and I look back and laugh at the idea now that you had to get out and manually crank the car to get it going.

"I don't know if the boot process in a PC is worse or not, but it's pretty archaic. And we had an era where people, if they wanted to do anything to their PC, had to open up the case, put a card in, understand the different switches that were there, and even understand certain resource conflicts that would take place internally when they issued a command. Even the hard-core people found it daunting to go out and extend their PC and add on the peripherals that could really take full advantage of what their computer could do.

"Early cars didn't have easy going. There were mud roads, and they'd

---

2. Proving that Gates embodies what he preaches, those speeches are available on the Microsoft web site, Microsoft.com.

get bogged down. The original concept of the chauffeur was not somebody who would drive you around. It was much more important that your chauffeur was somebody who could fix the car when it broke, so you could still get somewhere. And, of course, that concept didn't scale very well. They had to make cars a lot more reliable, so that everybody could manage them themselves. We still aren't fully there yet in the case of the PC."

Gates says the parallels between automobiles and personal computers hold, even as both innovations became more established.

"The automobile, as the volume got to be substantial, was the focus of incredible innovation. There were a few centers of activity that were particularly important, like Detroit, but all over the country there were new companies coming in and proposing new things. A lot of those new ideas didn't pan out, but many of them went on to become key elements of the car, things like adding an electrical system, so you could have a radio, and so you could have car lights that would allow you to drive at night, something which wasn't possible initially. They came up with the idea of taking that electrical power and making it so you didn't have to be strong in order to steer, the introduction of power steering, or even to roll the windows up and down.

"We need a lot of these same things in the case of the PC. Certainly the rate of improvement has been amazing, and here our speed is faster. There have been exponential improvements, but there is so much more to be done."

And as a source of new ideas, Gates says the industry could do a lot worse than studying how the automobile business developed.

"One of my favorite books on business is the one Alfred Sloan wrote [*My Years with General Motors*]. He's the person who took General Motors and led it to significant success. Sloan really invented a lot of modern management techniques. He invented the concept of the model year, he thought through what it meant to have used cars in the market.

"One of the interesting things he believed, which I think draws a very strong parallel to the PC industry, was the need for integration. He wrote that the problem with the development of the automobile was to raise its level of efficiency, and this often meant raising the level of its integration. The automobile is a very complex and closely integrated piece of machinery. And we're seeing this in many levels in our industry, such as at the chip level. No longer do you have to go out and buy separate chips for your machine. They are already there. We're certainly seeing it at the software level. If you think about Windows 98 and how many separate pieces of software you'd have to go buy to get the equivalent utility, you'd realize that it's quite a lot.

"Now there were a huge number of related industries that had to grow up, in order for people to get the most out of cars. You needed auto shows and showrooms, drivers' education, service stations all over the place—so you could get gas wherever you wanted—and you even needed places to stop if you were on a long trip. The first motel showed up in 1925.

"For the computer industry, this is an interesting area, because it could be a little bit of a bottleneck. We're having to train lots of people to understand the systems. The number of new jobs and services around high technology is going up even faster than supply. This is an amazing area, and whether it's the new small companies that are providing the services or the large firms, like EDS or Arthur Andersen, they're growing at pretty incredible rates."

The World Will Never Be the Same

"The impact of all this is really hard to exaggerate," Gates explains. "I mean, once something like this happens, your whole mind-set changes, and you can't even really go back and compare, particularly when the change has happened over several generations, because everything is so much different."

Gates quickly ticks off a number of examples that have occurred since the widespread introduction of the automobile.

"For example, we now take the idea of shopping centers for granted. The average size store is now four times greater than it was 30 years ago, and that's because with a car people can go out and carry more. The whole idea of suburbs comes from the freedom that the car provided.

"Now, the equivalent with the PC is that distance doesn't matter at all. You can live in the middle of nowhere, and if you've got the Internet connection, then you're set, whether you want to do your job,[3] or simply to connect up and do a multi-player game. I often play multi-player bridge with some of my friends, who live all over the United States. Some of them have gotten so used to interacting through the Internet that when we meet face to face, they're not used to it at all. They're used to being able to type in little pithy comments, or not have to think about what they're wearing. I think some of them actually prefer to do it over the Internet now. They're a little spoiled by that.

"And although the car reshaped things—changed where people lived and how they shopped—I think the impact of computers and the Internet will be far greater. The idea of going out and finding expertise anywhere in the world, using the Internet to search for somebody who

---

3. It is interesting to note that Gates answered the questions we posed him by e-mail. The authors—based in Manhattan and Stamford, Connecticut, respectively—sent him the list of questions you see listed in Appendix 3, and he answered them online.

has, say, the exact engineering background that can help you out with a problem, is going to be significant. It means that service activities, which were necessarily local because of the need to collaborate and find each other, will move to a global market in the same way that manufacturing has. That's a really very, very substantial change."

When will all this happen? Far sooner than you might think, Gates says.

"It took almost a century between the time the first car appeared and the point where 75% of people in the United States were able to use a car, and thought of it as just part of their normal activities.

"In the case of the PC, the growth—and acceptance—has been far more rapid. There are lots of reasons for that. A PC today is a lot less expensive than when it was introduced, and the country is more affluent, but also the rate of improvement is a very, very big deal here. I think during the next three years, we'll continue to see a rapid rise of penetration. I think we'll get to the point by 2001 where 60% of homes have PCs and 85% of those will be connected up to the Internet. Really this is an unprecedented increase in the number of households that are doing something new.

"So the blast of impact of the PC is going to be amazing. We really are just at the start of this."

And the reason for that, Gates says, are the people making the resources available to software developers on the hardware side of the business.

"It's amazing what the hardware guys are giving us," Gates says. "When you buy a personal computer today, it's hard to buy a machine with less than four gigabytes of storage, simply because the scale economics of making the hard disk are such that a one gigabyte driver, instead of a two, doesn't really save them much in the way of manufacturing costs. And if we take that out for the next five to 10 years, then you're going to have hundreds of gigabytes of local storage. But all this power is pointing out the need for better thinking and better research really in the software realm."

Consumers are demanding it, Gates says.

"People are going to want to keep information of all types. You're going to want to keep your photographs, the music that you're interested in, even video clips, and you are going to want them all to be on one device and you are going to want all those things you've saved to be easy to find. Hardware is not going to be the problem. They're going to give us lots of room to do all the exciting things we want."

The software industry just has to come up with a way of providing it and that will require substantial amounts of research, an area where the industry is lacking, Gates says.

"I'm really a big believer in research and the payback that it can bring. And I'm actually a little surprised about how little the software industry has invested in research. The payoff is very, very clear. The need is very,

very clear. In the information age, the ability to process information, to let people have access to the things they care about, is the most exciting problem of all.

"The info-glut is a big problem. Everything you want will be on the Internet. The question is, will you be able to get to it? And most users will want to get to it either by typing in a question, or through speech—asking for the information in the same way they would ask another human being. The commercial payoff to being able to do that well is very dramatic.

"There really can be no doubt that there's a lot left to be done," he adds. "Information on a PC today is very difficult to find. We've got it stored in many, many different ways. We have different name spaces. Just think about how many search commands you have to know. We have a lot of areas where we need to make further advances. I put 'ease of use' at the top of the list of the places [where the industry needs to do the most research]."

Gates is putting Microsoft's money where his mouth is.

"It was about five or six years ago that we got to the size where we decided we could really try to make these kinds of changes happen. And so we got going in areas like natural language and graphics. And I think it was about three or four years ago we started some of the work in the databases. This has become the fastest-growing part of Microsoft, and that will continue to be the case for many, many years to come. The only thing that is holding us back is how quickly we can bring in great people, but that has always been true of the company, as a whole."

But the benefits of the research Microsoft does extend far beyond the research centers the company has in Redmond, Washington [at corporate headquarters], San Francisco, and in the United Kingdom, he says.

Company (Ticker): Microsoft Corporation (MSFT)

Location: Redmond, Washington

Leaders: William Henry Gates, III, Chairman
Steven A. Ballmer, CEO

Microsoft at a glance: Microsoft is the world's number-one software company. In 2000, it was ordered by U.S. District Court of the District of Columbia to be broken into two companies, one to control the Windows Operating System, and the other to control the MS Office Productivity Suite, Internet Explorer, Expedia, and the Microsoft Network. The court-ordered break-up is currently under appeal. In terms of its products, the MSN web site provides online content, commerce, e-mail, search, and other services to users. With NBC, the company operates cable news channel MSNBC. Microsoft is continuing its expansion into interactive television, e-commerce, television/cable, and home mortgage transaction automation. Founder, Chairman, and Chief Software Architect Bill Gates owns 15% of the company.

1999 Financial Results
—Revenues: $22.9 billion
—Net Income: $9.4 billion

"Really, I think the whole industry gains when companies invest in research. And I would like to see other software companies do more in this area, because most of the good work is shared, and that can really help drive forward the pace at which we're taking advantage of all these computer capabilities."

Why isn't the industry investing more? Part of the reason may be because the payback is far from immediate.

"It's important to have a long time horizon, when it comes to research," Gates says. "You shouldn't expect much in the way of payback for five or 10 years." That can be a difficult sell in an industry where stocks routinely trade at 100 times earnings. In that kind of environment, every nickel you don't plow into research has the ability to boost your stock price by $5.00.

Given the rapid way the software industry is changing, shortchanging research is simply shortsighted thinking, Gates contends.

"You know, when you thought about getting the best insurance policy or buying a car three years ago, you wouldn't have thought about your PC as a tool that could help you get that done. Today, you would, so we are moving along. But I'm going to suggest that we're really sort of at the 1920 stage in this industry, when we compare it to the auto industry. There's a lot more that needs to be done. A lot of things that need to fall into place."

That will require more research. Microsoft is now spending more than $3 billion annually to make sure all these things happen. You get the distinct impression that Gates wouldn't have it any other way.

"I have the most fun job in the world, and love coming to work each day because there are always new challenges, new opportunities, and new things to learn. If you enjoy your job this much, you will never burn out."

LOU GERSTNER
IBM

> "Once you think you can write down what
> made you successful, you won't be."

Louis V. Gerstner, Jr., is an extremely unlikely rock star. In an industry where a buttoned-down shirt and a pair of clean blue jeans pass for formal, Gerstner is almost always photographed wearing a dark blue suit befitting the chairman of IBM—which he is.

Still, at computer shows, customers—as well as programmers who work for the competition—line up for his autograph. And people who run businesses with hundreds of millions of dollars in revenues talk about meeting him in the same tones they would have reserved for spending time with Elvis or the Beatles decades before. The man has even been the subject of a *Jeopardy!* answer.[1]

It is not Gerstner's ability at small talk that inspires this fame and adulation. Before almost every important internal meeting he requests a written briefing as a way to dispense with the background and move quickly to decision making. Similarly, as Gerstner readily admits when he serves on outside boards, "I arrive two minutes before the meeting, and leave immediately once it is over."

But the ability to make small talk doesn't make you the youngest partner in the history of McKinsey, the consulting firm. Similarly, the ability to put people at ease doesn't necessarily translate to turning around American Ex-

CAREER
APRIL 1993–PRESENT Chairman and CEO, IBM Corp.
March 1989–1993 CEO, RJR Nabisco
1978–1989 Executive Vice President, then President, American Express
1965–1978 Consultant/Principal/Director, McKinsey & Company

EDUCATION
M.B.A., Harvard Business School, 1965
B.A., Dartmouth College, 1963

FAMILY
Married, Elizabeth Robbins Link, 1968; children: Louis III, Elizabeth

Born: Mineola, Long Island, March 1, 1942

---

1. "In 1993, Louis V. Gerstner became the first outsider to head this computer giant."

> *"We are constantly challenging what we do—building a culture of restless self-renewal."*

press and managing the leveraged buyout of RJR Nabisco, all of which Gerstner had accomplished by the time he was 50.

In fact, it seems everything he had done in his past was in preparation for his current job.

Gerstner's tenure at "Big Blue" can be divided into two major halves:

1) Turning around IBM, and
2) Making it—once again—one of the world's preeminent corporations.

Many people have forgotten, but IBM was well on its way to being broken up into individual parts and then spun off—à la AT&T (minus the government mandate)—before the board hired Gerstner in 1993.

The first goal—righting the ship—has clearly been accomplished and the company is well on its way to achieving the second one. Products are getting to market faster, and equally important, they are once again being praised for being on the cutting edge. The company's service business is climbing and talk about breaking up the firm is now a distant memory.

As a business magazine cover story put it not so long ago: "IBM is back."

PERHAPS THE BIGGEST DECISION LOU GERSTNER EVER MADE WAS TO DECIDE to do nothing at all.

Hired by the IBM board, after what may very well have been the most publicized executive search in history, Gerstner was under tremendous pressure to move, and move quickly, when he took over the job on April 1, 1993.

Investment bankers (from Morgan Stanley) had been hired to help break up IBM and spin the pieces off to the public. Various divisions (such as the microelectronic and disk drive businesses) had been identified to be jettisoned and the investment community—and everyone else it seemed—waited eagerly for Gerstner to make his mark.

But Gerstner never pulled the trigger on the breakup.

He did the things you would expect: He announced downsizing and ambitious new goals, but the man who readily describes himself as "intense, competitive, focused, blunt and tough" ultimately never dismantled Big Blue.

The reason was simple, say those who were privy to Gerstner's thinking at the time.

"Lou kept thinking back to his days at American Express when he was

an IBM customer," says a colleague. "He didn't buy from IBM just because of one product or one service. He bought because of the depth of
their product line, their research, and the company's legendary customer
service."

In short, he bought solutions. He did business with IBM because of all
the pieces that made up the company, not just one. After studying the
company he had been hired to run, Gerstner concluded that IBM was,
indeed, greater than the sum of the parts, and that, in fact, the last thing
the information technology industry needed was more niche products.
He believed that IBM's customers valued integration. After validating
that instinct in a series of meetings with key customers and industry leaders during the first two months on the job, Gerstner announced he would
keep IBM in one piece.

Having made that surprising decision, Gerstner then made another
one. He was not going to create a new, overarching vision for IBM. It
wasn't that the company did not need one—which was the interpretation
that many people put on Gerstner's comment ("The last thing IBM needs
right now is a vision") made at an early press conference. Rather, Gerstner's analysis of IBM's situation convinced him that the priority was not
"vision"—some dreamy, utopian view of the future shaped by information technology. IBM's customers and shareholders did want to know
where computing was going, but there were a lot of bases to touch first.
IBM had to stabilize, return to profitability, and grow. It had to reconnect
with the marketplace and its customers. It had to build better products
and deliver them faster—all prerequisite steps to a return to leadership,
and a legitimate platform from which to offer a vision.

After all that was finally done in the fall of 1995, Gerstner unveiled his
vision. It was called network computing (later e-business) and it was the
first clear articulation of a computing model dominated by powerful
global networks like the Internet. (This was before Netscape's IPO and
before Microsoft reoriented its strategy to the Internet.)

Here is how Gerstner put it during a recent television interview. "We
have focused this company maniacally on the customer," he told CNBC.
"Everything we've done in this company has been driven by the identifi-
cation of who our customers are and what they want. That's what got us
in front of this whole network computing/e-business world. That's why
we're leading this field. It's because that's what our customers said they
wanted."

And Gerstner added that an interesting thing happened as IBM began
to rebuild the company from the customer's point of view. "We eliminated a lot of the internal focus that was in the company," something that
everyone—including longtime IBM employees—agree got the company
in trouble.

From Now On, We Will Only Look Outside

Gerstner has taken pains to ensure that the company will remain outer-directed.

IBM executives point to small but telling examples of how Gerstner re-oriented the corporate culture. He has changed the way the company conducts meetings, banning the use of overhead projectors and what IBMers call "foils," the transparencies that are used with the projectors.

The point is not that Gerstner is biased against overheads. What he did not particularly care for was the institutional motif of company meetings: darkened room, lengthy presentations with all attention directed to the charts rather than the speaker, and an obviously extravagant expense of staff time to create the pitch in the first place.

By getting rid of the overhead projectors—and truth to tell, they are still used from time to time—Gerstner forced the organization to clarify its thinking, prior to calling a meeting, and ensured that those people attending the conference would be prepared to make a decision and not merely share information or bog down in internal debate.

All these changes are fine, in theory. But they will remain just that—a theory—unless the people in the organization believe in the thinking behind them.

Most of the people Gerstner inherited did. Some were disheartened by the changes he was making, and others took the buyout packages that were offered in the days immediately after he took over. But the majority of IBM's employees bought into what Gerstner had in mind, and did so with more vigor than most people expected.

Gerstner, however, was not surprised by the response.

"We've energized an incredibly talented group of people who were here waiting for the leadership that would bring the company back again," is the way he puts it. "And they've been great. I haven't done this. It's been 280,000 people who have done it. We took a change in focus, a change in preoccupation, and a great talented group of people, merged it together, and changed the company."

The numbers speak for themselves. Since Gerstner became CEO, total shareholder returns have grown at an annual rate of 47%, resulting in a $146 billion increase in market valuation from the time of the 1993 restructuring to the end of 1998. Equally important, IBM is once again a major force in every area in which it competes, most notably coining the term e-business and becoming a leader in the way individuals, industries, and institutions derive value from the Internet.

Lessons Learned

When asked if he was surprised that IBM had run into trouble, Gerstner says no.

"I think what happened to us relates to many large enterprises today. I call it the 'success syndrome.' You have a program that's working, it's trusted and proven, and then you stay with it too long. It's one thing to see that the world is changing. It's another to rewrite a code of conduct that has been in place for decades."

That was something that IBM did not do.

"We measured IBM against internal measures. We had built an internal structure that dictated behavior that had worked in past. This was powerfully successful for a while—but when the industry and customer needs shifted, our bureaucracy kept old behavior patterns in place despite the fact that they no longer had any connection to the marketplace. So, in the spring of 1993, we had a crisis on our hands. Fortunately, when we had to react, we had thousands of people who were not only capable of changing, they were ready and eager to do so."

Not surprisingly, Gerstner says that in going forward IBM will guard against any thoughts of complacency. As he explains, once you believe the job is finished, you are bound to run into trouble.

"Once you think you're at the point that it's time to write it down, build the manual, and document the formula, you're no longer exploring, questioning the status quo," Gerstner says. "My belief is that all large, successful companies run the risk of trying to codify their success. And when you try to codify your success, you become internally focused. You become preoccupied with what's happening inside. When that happens, you are in trouble. This company going forward will be driven from the customer back and not from the inside looking out."

Company (Ticker): IBM Corp. (IBM)

Location: Armonk, New York

Leader: Louis V. Gerstner, Jr.

IBM at a glance: IBM is the world's leading provider of information technology solutions. It is the largest computer hardware manufacturer and the second-largest software provider following Microsoft. The company produces a broad range of computers, including PCs, mainframes, and network servers. IBM also makes software and peripherals, and generates 35% of its revenues from a rapidly expanding services arm. Nearly 60% of the company's sales are to customers outside the United States. IBM is a leader in the Internet business under the umbrella marketing campaign e-business.

1999 Financial Results

—Revenues: $87.5 billion

—Net Income: $7.7 billion

RAY GILMARTIN
Merck

"Working for a higher purpose"

IN SHOW BUSINESS AND IN SPORTS THERE IS A SAYING THAT GOES: "You never want to be the person who replaces a legend. You want to be the person who follows the person who replaces the legend."

The thinking is sound. If you follow a superstar, you are destined to be compared to him forever. That's why most performers—be they athletes, entertainers, or even businesspeople—are reluctant to follow in a superstar's wake.

Raymond Gilmartin is not most people.

He didn't have the usual qualms after he was picked—following a confidential CEO search—to succeed P. Roy Vagelos, the man who had helped steer Merck & Co. to greatness.

In many ways, Gilmartin, an engineer by training, was a surprising choice. Gilmartin had run hospital and medical device supplier Becton Dickinson & Co. for the previous five years, prior to his appointment at Merck in 1994. He was a company outsider with no direct pharmaceutical experience.

But in the changing world of health care, Gilmartin came with an impressive track record. While he was at BD he was credited with restructuring the

CAREER
1994–PRESENT Chairman, President, and CEO, Merck & Company, Inc.
1992–1994 Chairman, President, and CEO, Becton Dickinson & Company
1989–1992 President and CEO
1987–1989 President
1986–1987 Executive Vice President
1984–1986 Senior Vice President
1982–1983 Group President
1979–1987 Division President
1976–1979 Vice President Corporate Planning
1968–1976 Senior Consultant, Arthur D. Little Inc.
1963–1966 Development Engineer, Eastman Kodak Co.

EDUCATION
M.B.A., Harvard University, 1968
B.S. in Electrical Engineering, Union College, 1963

FAMILY
Married, Gladys Higham; three children

Born: Washington, D.C., March 6, 1941

> *"We're not going to consume our talent or people in the sole pursuit of achieving financial results. We have a higher purpose that we're committed to."*

company—a move that included eliminating several layers of management—which allowed BD to respond quickly to the demand for lower medical pricing. Since more than 80% of BD's United States sales came from managed care organizations and large buying groups, Gilmartin was familiar with what customers—especially corporate customers—expect of drug companies today.

GILMARTIN UNDERSTOOD THE SCRUTINY HE WOULD FACE WHEN HE TOOK over as CEO of Merck, but to his credit instead of thinking about how he would top the record that Vagelos had left behind, he decided to concentrate on the task at hand. "The challenge was not so much the legacy, but what the future was going to look like. We needed to develop breakthrough drugs, because we hadn't had any for a while. We had to make the Medco acquisition work and we had to deal with cost-containment issues. [At the time, President Clinton was talking about a major overhaul of the medical delivery system, as part of an overall effort to drive down medical costs.]

"So the biggest challenge I faced was uncertainty that surrounded the company and the industry, not how I was going to succeed someone who had been so successful."

What has happened since? The stock has increased fourfold. New drugs are on their way, and Medco has been successfully integrated.

How did he do it?

"When I arrived here, June 16, 1994, I started by interviewing around 30 or 40 executives at a couple levels of the company. Basically, I asked them two questions:

1) What are the major issues that we face? And
2) If you were me, where would you spend your time?

"That allowed me to gather a lot of information about the company.

"Because I was from the outside, and because people were genuinely committed to our success, the people I spoke with were very candid and straightforward. What they told me helped set some priorities in my own mind. But in addition to that, it gave me a good feel for the management of the company. It gave me the information I needed to move to the next step, which I also felt a great urgency about: putting a management team in place. Creating a great team was one of the key ways to resolve the uncertainty around Merck. People wanted to know who was going to run the company.

"I had a couple of criteria in mind, as I thought about who I wanted to be on the team. One of them obviously was ability, and a track record of accomplishment. But also very important was the fact that I wanted to be sure to name people to key positions who would be seen by others within Merck as being absolutely the right person for the job. They needed to be people who demonstrated the core values of the company, people who would inspire our employees."

The point Gilmartin would be making with his picks would be as profound as it was simple: Even given the change in leadership, one of the things that would never change at Merck was what the drug company stood for.

In fact, in preparation for picking the new management team, Gilmartin went back and studied the core values articulated by founder George W. Merck, the company's president from 1925 to 1950.

"One of the things he said was that 'medicine is for people, and not for profits. If you remember that, profits will follow.' And that's true of my own personal philosophy as well. And the more we have remembered that we are producing medicines to improve people's lives, the more profits we have made. Our share price is a reward for doing that well.

"*Fortune* ranked Merck as one of the top 10 best companies to work for and in their summary they said that employees like the fact that we are working toward a higher purpose. They spoke to the reporter about our low-cost AIDS drug, which was consciously priced lower than the other protease inhibitors on the market. We could have gotten more money for it, because of the characteristics of the drug. It's something that we discussed, but we talked about the George W. Merck philosophy and considered the need of getting the drug to the people who needed it, as well as what kind of financial return we wanted to generate, and we came down on the side of the lower price. And I think that not only had a positive impact both outside the company but inside as well. This is a very reinforcing concept. So not only do we talk about this stuff about having a higher purpose, but we base our actions on it."

To make sure the company continued to do so, Gilmartin looked at potential candidates to see if they shared these values, and how they went about achieving the results that got them on the short list in the first place.

What were the things Gilmartin was looking for in an executive?

He spent a lot of time on the question.

"We literally sat down as a management committee and thought through in several sessions the attributes that are particularly important for leadership at Merck. This is not something that we took off the shelf, or asked some human resource function to do. Our fingerprints—for better or worse—are all over this stuff. And we've characterized the traits as falling into four basic categories:

1) Know and develop yourself;
2) Know and develop the business;
3) Know, develop, and support your people; and
4) Communicate.

"Under know and develop yourself, one of the key attributes is conducting yourself according to the highest standards of ethics and integrity. And that means in the area you are responsible for, you'll set up an organization where this is well understood. And it's also well understood that you will act if you have any indication of any deviation from those principles.

"As to the second point, it is obvious that we expect good businesspeople to have good judgment, competence, and so on. And we expect our leadership to develop their organization and their people, to set up the right enabling conditions for people to grow professionally and personally. That's the third point.

"It is the last leadership principle that is often the hardest. We try to communicate heavily throughout the organization so that everyone knows what we are trying to accomplish, and so that everybody has the information they need to contribute. That takes a lot of energy and a big investment of time."

It was only after Gilmartin was clear what he wanted the world inside of Merck to look like that he started addressing the strategic direction—the outer direction—of the company.

"I had the management team in place just after Labor Day, and we then went off-site in early October and started the process, which continued over a couple of months, of setting the strategic direction of the company. We basically made three key decisions, which were somewhat counter to the conventional wisdom at the time.

"We decided that the key to our success was going to be investing in breakthrough research, the same thing that had made the company successful in the past. It seems pretty obvious now that this was the right decision as far as the whole industry is concerned. But at the time, because of the changes that were taking place in the health care delivery system, and in the emergence of managed care, there was conventional wisdom that breakthrough research would not be bought by managed care companies. We didn't believe that, and so we decided breakthrough research was the way to go. That was a major shift for the company, because it led to a decision to get out of the generic drug business right away.

"The other thing that decision did was make us get out of all businesses that didn't fit our research base, the ethical pharmaceutical focus we wanted. So we divested our specialty chemical businesses, and everything else that didn't fit.

"The second key decision that the company made was to invest in internal development and not to try to grow through mergers and acquisitions. And that decision, made in 1994, was based on the fact that we had the potential, because of our research pipeline, to achieve our growth objectives through internal development. And that's completely against a lot of the conventional wisdom.

"But the history across all industries, including our own, is that those companies that are able to grow through internal development create greater shareholder value than those companies that have had to grow because of mergers and acquisitions.

"We don't buy the argument that pharmaceutical companies are getting together because scale is more important than it ever was. First of all, managed care buyers don't pay any attention to breadth of line. They look for the best value of each therapeutic category. Breadth of line, or size of company, is meaningless to them, and that has been borne out. Also, once you get beyond a certain size in research, you've got the critical mass to discover new drugs and you've got the resources to bring them to the market. So getting ever bigger in research doesn't mean you're more productive.

"The third key decision was what to do with Medco. How were we going to make it reach its full potential? We decided that Medco was not a distributor, as the press often describes it, but that it was actually a managed pharmaceutical care organization. And the way we were going to make it pay off was that both companies had to grow faster together than either company could grow on its own.

"So the question became not only what could Medco do for Merck in terms of helping the pharmaceutical business grow faster, but also, what does Merck contribute to Medco in order to help it grow faster? And with that came the idea that in the near-term Medco can help Merck grow faster through its formulary management programs that help companies control their drug costs.

"So those three decisions basically framed our strategy," Gilmartin explains. "And then it became a question of setting a financial goal, retaining our top-tier growth status. That meant contributing to work on creating an organization that could respond quickly and easily to opportunities, which means breaking down the barriers across the major divisions of marketing, research, and manufacturing. And in the process of doing that, delegating more responsibility and authority."

The key result of doing all three things would be to invent better drugs. "We now have excellent drugs, which is a direct result of the research strategy that we followed. We decide to go after drugs that have large patient populations, where there's new knowledge about the pathway of the disease, and novel chemistry is usually required to attack it. So this means we have high sales potential drugs that are novel.

"In addition to that, the design criteria are oral, and once a day, so they're convenient. And the other part is highly specific to the target we're after: They are highly potent, and highly specific. That means they're well tolerated. There are few side effects. These are common characteristics that run through our drug discovery process. They are a mantra that's understood at all levels of Merck research laboratories. They are also important in dealing with the cost-containment pressures."

"The Largest Hurdle to Doing All This? Us."

"The biggest obstacle to creating this kind of company was the sheer complexity of what we're about. We'll be in 24 therapeutic categories by the end of 2002. In addition, we've been expanding worldwide. So you've got the complexity of geography combined with many therapeutic categories. And it's fair to say that in each one of those categories we have a dedicated competitor who is going to be pretty tough. So how do we maintain the focus in each therapeutic category and do that on a global basis? That really keys into our organizational philosophy, which says it is important to be able to work easily across divisional boundaries and focus around therapeutic franchises, and delegate more responsibility and authority.

"And in order to accomplish that, particularly as you get larger, you've got to have a management style that allows the organization to assume more responsibility, make more decisions through delegation of authority, so that the people who are making decisions are close to the action.

"Therefore, my job is really to set the overall strategic direction of the company, to ensure that we are organized

Company (Ticker): Merck & Company, Inc. (MRK)

Location: Whitehouse Station, New Jersey

Leader: Raymond V. Gilmartin

Merck at a glance: Merck is the world's largest pharmaceutical company. The company develops products for both humans and animals; almost 40% of sales come from treating ailments associated with American eating habits, such as high cholesterol, as well as treatments for AIDS, hypertension, and heart failure. Merck's major products include Zocor and Mevacor, two prominent cholesterol drugs.

1999 Financial Results
—Revenues: $32.7 billion
—Net Income: $5.8 billion

to carry out that strategy, and that we have the right management processes in place. I need to create an environment where everyone in the organization can achieve their full potential, so that our company does."

This seems far different from managing a business and Gilmartin agrees. "The demands on the CEO in terms of delivering are probably tougher today than they have been before. But I think the CEO's job has become more interesting."

Gilmartin is happy to explain.

"I think one of the things that has happened in the business press recently is a decision to single out the CEO as the most important person in the organization for why things do or don't happen. And I think that's a distortion, because if I were to put somebody on the front cover of *Business Week* or *Fortune* it would be Ed Scolnick, the person who heads up our research organization, not me. Or I would put a team of people on the cover.

"I see my task as one of mobilizing an entire organization. I don't possess all the knowledge in terms of research and could never hope to do that. I don't need to know firsthand what's going on in Thailand right now, but I do have to be good at selecting people and having the instinct for people as to who can do the job and getting the right people in the right slots. I think the CEO has to be a pretty good strategic thinker. I think there are a variety of leadership styles that work, but I think it has to be a leadership style that inspires confidence and trust on the part of the organization, so that people are willing to make significant commitments such as getting a project up and running in 15, instead of 24 months.

"A leadership skill that inspires confidence and trust can be expressed in a variety of ways. It doesn't have to be charismatic. It can be pretty low key. But it has to be there."

ACE GREENBERG
Bear Stearns

"We hire PSDs: people who are poor, smart,
and have a deep desire to be rich."

THERE WEREN'T A WHOLE LOT OF SURPRISES WHEN WE ASKED OUR
50 leaders to tell us about their personal lives. A lot of them played golf.
Most of them were active in both civic and business activities, and more
than a couple were happy to brag about how well their children were
doing.

We thought we would discover the same sorts of things about Alan C.
(Ace) Greenberg when we saw at the beginning of his bio that he was a
member of Sunningdale Country Club, and the Deep Dale Club.

And then we looked a little further.

Among his accomplishments Greenberg listed winning the national
bridge championship in 1977, and among his memberships he included
"the Society of Amateur Magicians."

Greenberg fell in love with magic at the age of nine after watching
Harry Blackstone, Sr., perform. When we asked the chairman of the securities firm what was his favorite trick, he
replied: "I don't do tricks. I do miracles."

While he is deadly serious about
magic, he is less so about himself.

When it came time to pose for the
author photo for his own book, Greenberg put on a sports coat and slacks—
not pinstripes—and refused to pose in
his award-strewn office. The photogra-
pher shot him out in the hall playing
with a yo-yo.

And what was that book? *Memos from
the Chairman*. This is one case where
you can judge a book by its cover. *Memos*

CAREER
1993–PRESENT Chairman of Executive
   Committee, Senior Managing Director, Bear
   Stearns Companies, Inc.
1958–PRESENT Partner, Bear Stearns
1949–1958 with Bear Stearns

EDUCATION
Student, University of Missouri, 1949

FAMILY
Married, Kathryn Olson, June 27, 1987;
   children: Lynn, Theodore

Born: Wichita, Kansas, September 3, 1927

"What advice would I give my grandchildren? That's the easiest question in the world. Do something you enjoy—music, business, public service, whatever. If they don't enjoy going to work, I don't care if their IQ is 30 points higher, the guy with the inferior IQ—who loves what he is doing—will beat them to death."

is a collection of notes that Greenberg—using the voice of Haimchinkel Malintz Anaynikal, H.M.A. as he is known within the firm, "the famed business consultant" whom Greenberg invented out of whole cloth—has sent to his staff over the last 20 years.

We quote one in its entirety.

TO: Senior Managing
Directors
Managing Directors and
Associate Directors

FROM: Alan C. Greenberg

DATE: August 14, 1991

Two important milestones were reached last week. McDonald's sold its 70th billion hamburger and Bears Stearns bought its 10,000th fax machine.

I do have some sad news to report. The fax machine salesperson who was servicing Bear Stearns has retired. He is burnt out—he is 33 years old. He has purchased Donald Trump's yacht, and the overworked soul just wants to cruise and take it easy for a while.

(A relative of H.M.A.) read this and thinks there is a moral hidden somewhere between the lines. Can you find it?

When we cut expenses we have a direct, equal and positive impact on our bottom line. If we forget this fact, we will be stupid and a member of the "Loser's Club." This is one club we are not joining.

While H.M.A. is fictitious, the advice he offered is sound: Be courteous to customers. Watch expenses, especially when times are good. Ignore what everyone else is doing. Do what you think is right instead. And in a conversation, Greenberg even expanded on one of his memos, giving us a bit of financial advice in the process: "There are only two good tax shelters. Municipal bonds, and the Greenberg. What's the Greenberg? You pay your taxes, then you don't have to worry anymore."

The intriguing thing about the memos—besides the fact that they are often quite funny—is the tone varies inversely with how well Bear Stearns is doing. When times are good, Greenberg relentlessly harps on the need to control expenses, promptly return customer phone calls, and present the best possible image of the firm. When times are tough, he tries—and often succeeds—in being inspirational.

> "Ace Greenberg does almost everything better than I do—bridge, magic tricks, dog training, arbitrage—all of the important things of life."
> —*Warren Buffett*

To that list, Buffett might also add leading and inspiring people.

In an industry that has, as Greenberg puts it, more than its fair share of prima donnas, Bear Stearns has never been hit with an ethical scandal. Greenberg says this is his proudest accomplishment. The man who has spent his entire working life at the firm is blunt when asked why Bear Stearns has been able to avoid the woes that have plagued much of his competition.

"Mark Twain said, 'Fish stink from the head,' right? It's people up top who set an example of how a business should be run. And if they're sloppy, or throw money around and have big expense accounts, I think it permeates the whole firm. So I think employees are inspired by the people up top and their conduct—how they act is extremely important."

And Greenberg, who turned the CEO title over to James Cayne in 1993, believes who these top managers hire is just as important as the example they set.

"I have always looked for smart, poor people who have a personal desire to become rich. That is still my standard. Some other people here go visit the various business schools, and I don't hold it against somebody if he has a master's degree from some prestigious school, but I certainly don't think it should be the end-all as far as hiring people."

Instead, Greenberg says, "If you really want to understand what someone is like, you should talk to people who do business with him, his customers, and the people who work for him. How someone comes over in an interview in my office, that's nonsense."

Once hired, Bear Stearns employees are expected to work hard, and above all, be ethical. How do you make sure that those ethical standards are upheld? By making sure ethics are everybody's responsibility and reward people—immediately and with cash—when they identify lapses.

"That's the best way to find out what's going wrong. You don't want to rely on an internal audit committee where it takes years to find some-thing. The quickest way is for somebody who sits next to somebody to tell us he's doing something wrong.

"In some firms that's a no-no, they don't want to be known as a com-pany where people tell and become whistle blowers. That isn't the case here. We're very much in favor of whistle blowers. We encourage it, we pay them 5% of whatever error they uncover, and we pay them on the spot in cash—I have written checks as large as $50,000 and $60,000.

"When I first started doing this we were criticized by large firms who said turning employees into informers is a terrible thing. Well, the Naval Academy, West Point, and the Air Force have a policy—and some colleges do too—that if you don't turn people in you get in trouble. If it's good enough for them, why isn't it good enough for us? If somebody is trying to put us out of business, what's wrong with having somebody tell us he's trying to break us? I have no sympathy for employees who are trying to break us."

The result of this approach has made the employees—and shareholders—of Bear Stearns quite wealthy. Greenberg is happy for the shareholders (he's a large one, as he never fails to remind people in his memos) and equally happy for employees, who are compensated based on how well the company does.

Company (Ticker): Bear Stearns Companies, Inc. (BSC)

Location: New York, NY

Business Leaders: Alan C. Greenberg, Chairman
James Cayne, CEO

Bear Stearns at a glance: One of the United States' leading securities trading, investment banking, and brokerage firms, Bear Stearns serves a worldwide clientele of corporations, financial institutions, governments, and individuals. The firm also provides asset management, clearing and custody, fiduciary, securities lending, mergers and acquisitions, and trust services.

1999 Financial Results
—Revenues: $7.8 billion
—Net Income: $673 million

"Our package is different than any-body else's in the world. The executive committee's compensation is based on how the firm does. If the firm doesn't make any money, they get $200,000, period. No phantom options, no gim-micks, no nothing. If the firm does well, we participate.

"In many cases, when a firm does lousy, they give their top guys an extra bonus. When the stock is down they cancel their options and give him new ones, which is ridiculous, but they do it. We don't. I know of no other group of senior executives who are will-ing to let their compensation rise and fall solely based on the profits of the company. They want a sure, secure thing. We don't work that way."

When you make millions of dollars a year—as many of Bear Stearns' employees do—it is natural to pat yourself on the back, and try to figure out ways to make even more. That's also true for Bear Stearns' employees, but their money comes with one string attached, a string that is unique.

"All the senior managing directors, there are about 300 of them, are required to give away 4% of their total gross income to charity every year," Greenberg explains. "Most of them give much more. We don't care what they give it to, but we audit them to make sure they do.

"Why do we insist upon this? I just think we're the luckiest people in the world to be in this country. Since most of us are not Native Americans, we had to get here somehow, and we're very lucky. And I think we owe something to those less fortunate. It's just that simple."

Let's see. Work hard. Take care of your customers. Behave ethically. Give something back. All this sounds like nothing more than a common-sense formula for business success. Greenberg doesn't disagree, although he did add one comment to our analysis.

"Somebody once said, the most uncommon sense in the world is common sense. So I guess we have to believe that."

HANK GREENBERG
AIG

"You look for white blackbirds."

IT SOUNDS LIKE AN OLD JOKE.

Q: How do you run the world's most profitable insurance company?
A: Very carefully.

But there is a lot of truth in that wheeze when it comes to describing the success of the American International Group, Inc. (AIG). Chairman Maurice R. (Hank) Greenberg has grown the business almost entirely internally, opening new markets one by one and installing AIG-trained managers to run things. There have not been many pricey acquisitions.

Once the company has established a beachhead, he markets aggressively, but guards against taking on excess risk. A quick look at the company's combined ratio—a key measure of underwriting profitability in property/casualty insurance—tells the story. The combined ratio, which is expressed as a percentage, compares policy losses and expenses (the numerator) to premiums (the denominator).

A combined ratio of less than 100 indicates an underwriting profit and the smaller the fraction, the more profitable the business. AIG's combined ratio on its foreign business is an industry leading 90—meaning it is making 10 cents on every dollar in premiums it takes in.

CAREER
1989–PRESENT Chairman of the Board and
  CEO, American International Group, Inc.
1967–1989 President and CEO
1962–1967 Senior Staff Positions
1952–1960 Continental Casualty Co.

EDUCATION
Honorary Doctorates from Brown University,
  Bryant College, New England Law School,
  New York Law School, and Pace University
LL.B., New York Law School, 1950
Prelaw certificate, University of Miami,
  Florida, 1948

FAMILY
Married, Corinne Phyllis Zuckerman; children:
  Jeffrey, Evan, Scott, Cathleen

Born: New York City, May 4, 1925

"Usually if everybody is going in one direction it's wrong."

Most companies are happy to break even, relying on their investment income to make an overall profit.

AIG's tightfistedness is a direct reflection of its chairman, who earned a Bronze Star in Korea.

IF EVER A COMPANY AND A CHIEF EXECUTIVE WERE A PERFECT MATCH IT IS AIG and Hank Greenberg. They both are innovative, fearless, and extremely individualistic.

Normally when a company and its leader share the same personality it is because the CEO is the founder and has created the firm in his image. That is not the case here. This is a situation where the company and leader found each other. The result? One of the most profitable—and most respected firms—in the insurance and financial-related services industry.

AIG began life in Shanghai in 1919. "C. V. Starr, an American out of Fort Bragg, California, started the company because he was looking for something to do after World War I," Greenberg explains. "He found his way to Japan, and then Shanghai, which was kind of the pearl of the Orient. After exploring the landscape and making some inquiries, Starr opened a small insurance company, since it went hand in hand with what was already in place.

"This decision had a profound effect because it meant that AIG started as an international company rather than a domestic one.

"Starr came back to the United States and talked a company called the Globe and Rutgers into giving him a general agency [a franchise] for overseas business. And you've got to remember at that time, it took a couple of months to get from Asia to the United States. So it took a great deal of courage, and a lot of salesmanship, to sell an American company on giving you a general agency to write risks in Asia. They didn't know what they were writing for maybe a year or a year and a half. It could have broken the company."

But in addition to being a great salesman, Starr had another remarkable characteristic. He was fiercely independent. He was more than willing to work halfway around the world, with almost no support from the home office. "Eventually he turned his general agency into the AIU, American International Underwriters, which, in essence, was a general agency that represented Globe and Rutgers and a number of other American companies doing business overseas," Greenberg explains.

So those were AIG's roots. "The company, by definition, attracted more independent-thinking people who operated in a global environment at that time. You didn't have reliable communication. And that was true in the 1950s, '60s, and to some degree in the '70s. Air travel became easier, but communications were still uncertain. As a result we had to build our company around independent, self-reliant individuals and that's the way it remains today."

Greenberg himself serves as a case in point.

He grew up on a New York farm "and I've been on my own since I was a kid. My father died when I was very young. When I was about 13, I'd get up at four o'clock in the morning and tramp through the woods for hours until dawn trying to trap muskrats and mink."

Greenberg enlisted in the Army during World War II. After earning a law degree, he went looking about for something to do and eventually found AIG.

"Back then, we had one company in the United States, that was American Home, but it never made any money, and that was embarrassing. How do you represent other companies when you can't run your own?"

Greenberg was put in charge of American Home and turned it around. How? By hiring iconoclasts. "It was a very lackluster industry, nothing creative about it at all. Anybody who was creative was bound to win. We gradually built a core of people who were prepared to break with the past."

Profit Is Good

Greenberg made over American Home from top to bottom, starting with the most fundamental decision of all. The company, he decreed, should be able to turn a profit on the insurance it sold.

"Historically, very few insurance companies made an underwriting profit. They didn't hold their management accountable for underwriting. The thinking was you would break even on the insurance you sold, and your profit would come from the way you invested the premiums. We never did that. I didn't do it then, and I don't do it now. Every profit center manager here is measured only on the underwriting results. The investment side is totally separate, they get no credit for that. They get credit for bringing in a premium that's profitable, collecting their premiums, and managing their areas in the most efficient way possible. We build leaders, we don't build a bunch of clerks."

Regardless of what the rest of the industry thinks, it just doesn't make sense to run a company any other way, Greenberg says.

"Our core business is underwriting, that's the basic business. If you fail in your basic business, how in the world are you going to succeed long term in anything? The basic business is not investment, the basic business is underwriting risk. So you want to have the best people who understand risk, and develop the best products to make a profit on that business."

Those are the people he sets out to hire.

"It doesn't matter if we are talking about hiring a manager in Japan, Eastern Europe, or Latin America, we want somebody who's different than the run of the mill. There isn't one trait, or one single thing that we look for, other than what I call 'white blackbirds.' We want people who have the conviction and the ability to continue to do things that bring about change and create profits. That's what it's all about."

Clearly not everyone fits. And equally clearly not everyone is cut out for the AIG working environment. AIG, Greenberg agrees, can be a demanding place to work. He sees nothing wrong with that.

"There's a price you have to pay to succeed. You can't have too many deviations that attract you to other things. You can't go wander in the woods for 30 days thinking about nature. That may be wonderful, I'm not saying it's not a great thing to do, but not if you want to get ahead around here. There are other things that are priorities. Is it a demanding environment? Yes. Does it take a total commitment? Absolutely. And is there a self-cleansing apparatus at work? I think so. We attract a certain kind of person who wants to work in a certain kind of environment. They want a fully charged environment that challenges them totally. They want the company to do well. They want to be around people who think and feel and work that way."

And that includes the CEO, Greenberg says. "I don't believe a CEO should be living in some kind of an ivory tower thinking great thoughts. I believe in a hands-on management approach. You've got to be out there doing it. In the insurance business, everybody starts on the same level. You get a charter and you get capital. That's where the similarities end and the differences begin. What you do with what you're given makes the difference."

And the payoff, if you make a lot out of those limited resources? Success and money, of course, but Greenberg stresses something else.

Company (Ticker): American International Group, Inc. (AIG)
Location: New York, New York
Leader: Maurice R. Greenberg
AIG at a glance: AIG is a leading international insurance and financial services organization, and among the largest underwriters of commercial and industrial insurance in the United States. Member companies write property, casualty, marine, life, and financial services insurance and are engaged in financial services businesses in approximately 130 countries and jurisdictions around the world. The company recently acquired Sun America, Inc., one of the largest United States issuers of tax-deferred fixed and variable annuities and guaranteed investment contracts.

1999 Financial Results
—Revenues: $37.5 billion
—Net Income: $5.0 billion

"Building an international business is exciting. You're breaking new ground, you're opening new areas, and you're dealing with different problems every day, different cultures. If there's an underwriting problem, it's a challenge, because the political systems are different in every way. It's not just doing more of the same.

"Doing business in Minnesota versus Kansas is not that different. This is more challenging, it's more exciting. It's got to be fun. If you don't like it, you can't do it."

ANDY GROVE
Intel

The boss must be in charge of training.

IN THE WORDS OF FORMER *FORBES* EDITOR JAMES W. MICHAELS, INTEL'S Andrew S. Grove will go down in history as the man who made paranoia respectable. Indeed, thanks to Grove's success, the affliction is no longer a psychosis, argues Michaels, "it's a survival trait."

Now it is one thing for Michaels, widely recognized as the father of today's business reporting, to hail Grove's *Only the Paranoid Survive* as the best business book since the publication of Alfred Sloan's *My Years with General Motors*. Michaels is, after all, a journalist, and Intel is truly one of the great corporate success stories of the second half of the 20th century. But when *Time* magazine recognizes someone as Man of the Year, as it did with Grove in 1997, you know you are dealing with someone who has had a lasting impact on all of America.

And Grove has. Intel's semiconductors have changed every single aspect of American life.

President and CEO of Intel for 10 years, before assuming the duties of chairman in May 1997, Grove has run just about every major division of the company over the last 30 years. He was present at the beginning, when Intel began life with $2,790 in revenues in 1968. Today, the company is a fixture in the American economy, and Grove is credited with a large share of that success.

This is not too bad for someone who emigrated to the United States from Hungary at the age of 20 with little

CAREER
1998–PRESENT Chairman, Intel Corporation
1997–1998 Chairman and CEO
1987–1997 President and CEO
1979–1987 President and COO
1968–1978 Participated in the founding of Intel and held various senior positions
1963–1968 Fairchild Camera and Instrument Co.

EDUCATION
Ph.D., University of California-Berkeley, 1963
B.S., CCNY, 1960

FAMILY
Married; two children

Born: Budapest, Hungary, 1936

When it comes to training and performance reviews, "I think we have our priorities reversed. Shouldn't we spend more time trying to improve the performance of our stars? After all, these people account for a disproportionately large share of the work in any organization. Put another way, concentrating on the stars is a highly leveraged activity; if they get better, the impact on group output is very large indeed."

money and even less understanding of English.

Perhaps his personal story explains the origins of his "only the paranoid" survive motto. Born Andras Grof, he left his native Hungary following the 1956 uprising and came to America on a decommissioned troopship bound for New York.

Grove, who quickly Americanized his name, moved in with an uncle and entered The City College of New York, like tens of thousands of immigrants before him. He received a degree in chemical engineering from CCNY before heading west to earn a doctorate from the University of California-Berkeley.

As a co-founder, Grove was one of Intel's first employees, and from the very beginning the fear of being overtaken—either by a competitor, or by what he calls a "strategic inflection point," a change so fundamental that it alters the very nature of your business—has been a governing force in every decision he has made.

You will see a brief example of that vigilance here, in our decision to focus on Grove's belief about the need for managers to spend a substantial amount of time on an area that rarely captures their attention—the training of their employees.

There is a lot to be said for being vigilant. Intel controls 85% of the microprocessor segment of the United States semiconductor market.

IN HIS FIRST BOOK, *HIGH OUTPUT MANAGEMENT*, ANDREW S. GROVE tells a story about going out to dinner that makes plain why employee training is so important.

The woman who took reservations over the phone seemed flustered and then volunteered that she was new and didn't know all the ropes. No matter, we were booked. When we showed up for dinner, we quickly learned that the restaurant had lost its liquor license and that its patrons were expected to bring their own wine if they wanted any.

As the maitre d' rubbed his hands, he asked, "Weren't you told this on the phone when you made your reservations?" As we went through our dinner without wine, I listened to him go through the same routine with every party he seated. I don't know for sure, but it's probably fair to assume that nobody instructed the woman taking calls to tell potential guests what the situation was. Instead, the maitre d' had to go through an inept apology time and time again, and nobody had wine—all because one employee was not properly trained.

Situations like these occur all too frequently in business life. Insufficiently trained employees, despite their best intentions, are inefficient, since they do not know the best way to do things. At the very least, that leads to higher costs. And often, as was the case when the Groves went out to dinner, it leads to unhappy customers—or worse, as Grove pointed out in the coda to his story.

In an instance at Intel, for example, one of our sophisticated pieces of production machinery in a silicon fabrication plant—a machine called an ion implanter—drifted slightly out of tune. The machine operator, like the woman at the restaurant, was relatively new. While she was trained in the basic skills needed to operate the machine, she hadn't been taught to recognize the signs of an out-of-tune condition. So, she continued to operate the machine, subjecting nearly a day's worth of almost completely processed silicon wafers to the wrong machine conditions. By the time the situation was discovered, more than $1 million [of material] had passed through the machine and had to be scrapped. Because it takes over two weeks to make up such a loss with fresh material, deliveries to our customers slipped, compounding the problem.

Given the problems of insufficient training—everything from petty inconveniences to major disasters—it is hard to find a senior manager who does not believe that training is important. But when asked who should do it, already overworked executives typically nominate someone else, either because "they don't have the time," or because they believe training is best left to a specialist.

Grove says that is exactly *the wrong* way to go. He argues that training is precisely what managers should be doing.

That statement, he says, is not as strange as it first seems.

Grove begins his explanation by returning to basics, and focusing on what it is a manager is supposed to do. He says a manager is responsible for "the output of his organization—no more, no less." Therefore, it follows that a manager's own productivity depends on getting more out of his team.

If you start with that premise, a manager basically has three ways to increase the output of the people who work for him:

- Leaving everything else the same, he can work them harder.
- He can inspire them to do more.
- He can increase their individual capabilities so that they can work smarter and increase their productivity.

The last point, of course, is where training fits in.

If motivating employees—one of the ways to increase productivity—is seen as the manager's job, why isn't training! Grove wonders. It is, as he says, "one of the highest-leverage activities a manager can perform."

Being the engineer he is, Grove quantifies the statement by using an example of a manager who is going to deliver a series of three lectures to 10 members of his department. In the example, Grove assumes that the manager is going to prepare three hours for each one-hour talk, for a total investment of 12 hours.

If those talks just result in a 1% increase in productivity for each of the 10 members of the manager's team, the overall results are tremendous.

For example, let us assume—realistically—that each of those 10 people works 2,000 hours a year. So, their combined work time (the 10 employees times 2,000 each) is 20,000 hours. A 1% gain means that their total productivity will increase by 200 hours of work, as a result of the 12 hours of time the manager invested. *That is a 1,667% return.*

When you look at training this way, it is hard to argue against it being a manager's job.

This Assumes the Manager Knows What He Is Doing

Implicit in Grove's argument, he concedes, is that the manager is concentrating his training on the right things. While you certainly want to correct something, when it goes wrong, the kind of training Grove is talking about is "systematic and scheduled, not a rescue effort summoned to solve the problem of the moment. In other words, training should be a process, not an event."

And the boss should do it to show it is important.

Intel practices what Groves preaches. In 1997, for example, Intel spent more than $500 million on employee training. Intel University offers 3,000 courses for all employees, whether they are engineers, technicians, administrators, or managers. There is an extensive, and mandatory, new-hire orientation program to help employees assimilate into the Intel way of doing business. All functional groups develop training plans for employees to teach job-specific skills, and all managers are *required* to teach at least four courses per year.

Does Grove lead classes?

Yes, as this passage from *High Output Management* indicates:

> My own training repertoire includes a course on preparing and delivering performance reviews, on conducting productive meetings, and a three-hour-long introduction to Intel, in which I describe our history, objectives, organization, and management practices. Over the years I have given [that talk] to a sizable proportion of our professional employees. I have also been recruited to pinch-hit in other management courses. (To my regret, I have become far too obsolete to teach technical material.)

Interestingly, Grove and Intel make a distinction between two types of training. The first is teaching new employees—at all levels—the skills they need to do their jobs.

Company (Ticker): Intel Corporation (INTC)

Location: Santa Clara, California

Leaders: Andrew S. Grove, Chairman
Craig R. Barrett, CEO

Intel at a glance: With the dominant share of the world's microprocessor market, the company's trademarked motto—"Intel inside"—is apt. The company also designs and markets computer flash memory chips; microcontrollers; and networking, communications, and graphics products. Intel is also the largest e-commerce company, producing over $1 billion monthly in online sales. Intel continues to expand and upgrade its products and facilities to maintain its leadership position over rival chip makers such as Cyrix and Advanced Micro Devices. This dominance prompted the Federal Trade Commission to file an antitrust complaint against the company. About 55% of its revenues come from outside the United States.

1999 Financial Results
—Revenues: $29.3 billion
—Net Income: $7.3 billion

The second involves teaching new ideas, principles, or skills.

The distinction is important, Grove says, because the goals of each task are different.

The Payoff

Having bought into the idea of training, what do you do?

Grove's first piece of advice is the most basic: Make a list of everything you believe your subordinates, and/or members of your department should be trained in.

But while the idea is basic, the list should not be. It should include everything from what seems simple—telling the person taking reservations to remind customers to bring their own wine—to the more abstract, such as the values of your company and your department.

Do not make this list alone, Grove counsels. Ask the people working for you what they feel they need. They are likely to surprise you by telling you they would like training in areas that you never thought of.

Finally, he argues, take advantage of something else managers tend not to pay sufficient attention to—performance appraisals—in order to gain more insights into what your people need. As Grove wrote: "Giving [performance reviews] is the most important form of task-relevant feedback we, as supervisors, can provide."

Why?

Because, Grove says, it is the single best way to identify areas where an employee can improve his or her performance. And while you can give your worst performers a detailed roadmap to follow as they head off toward improvement, he argues that more time should be spent on the company's top performers. Since they are the people who do most of the work in the company, a 2% increase in their performance will have much more of an impact on the company than a 2% increase by a marginal employee.

Grove claims it will be fairly easy to see which areas of your company need improving by drawing from all these sources. Once you have the list, Grove's advice is simple and direct:

1) Prioritize the areas that need improvement,
2) Start with the items that are going to have the greatest impact on productivity, and
3) Get to work.

CHARLES HEIMBOLD
Bristol-Myers Squibb

Rallying—and leading—the troops

CHARLES A. HEIMBOLD, JR., HAD SPENT HIS ENTIRE WORKING LIFE preparing to run Bristol-Myers Squibb.

One of his first jobs at the health and personal care company—after working as an attorney for the major New York law firm Middle-bank, Tweed, Hadley, & McCloy—was secretary of the executive committee of the company that sells pharmaceuticals, beauty care products (Clairol), consumer medicines (Excedrin), and medical devices. There he had the chance to listen "to the deliberations of these very senior, very experienced businesspeople and then see what worked and what didn't." He also got to compare their decisions to what he would have done.

The experience was invaluable, Heimbold says, because "you could see the difference between people who really have terrific ideas and values, and the people who might not be at the same level."

The other advantage to sitting in on those meetings was that it exposed Heimbold to the annual budget and planning meetings, which allowed him to learn firsthand the inner workings of the company. By the time he was named CEO, Heimbold not only knew how each part

CAREER

1995–PRESENT Chairman and CEO, Bristol-Myers Squibb Company
1994–1995 President and CEO
1992–1994 President
1989–1992 Executive Vice President
1984–1988 President, Health Care Group
1981–1984 Senior Vice President, Planning and Development, Bristol-Myers
1963–1981 Various legal and operating positions
1960–1963 Attorney, Milbank, Tweed, Hadley, & McCloy

EDUCATION

LL.M., New York University, 1965
LL.B., University of Pennsylvania, 1960
B.A., Villanova University, 1954

FAMILY

Married, Monika Astrid Barkvall, 1962; children: Joanna, Eric, Leif, Peter

Born: Newark, New Jersey, May 27, 1933

of the company operated, but he also had a good idea of where he wanted to lead it.

WHAT CHARLES HEIMBOLD WANTED TO ACCOMPLISH UPON BEING named CEO was clear.

"We were trying to grow the company and move it toward becoming more of a scientific-based pharmaceutical company with very strong consumer franchises," he says. "That meant we had to move away from some of the lower margin, slower-growth businesses that we had.

"A great business leader has to be attuned with the times."

"We had made some good progress toward that goal, with the Squibb merger being the latest and most important move, a move that was accomplished before I became CEO. Dick Gelb [Heimbold's predecessor] had done that and it really was a superb accomplishment."

Heimbold wanted to continue down that path, but he faced three major hurdles from the outset upon becoming CEO in 1994.

"First, we had health care reform. That knocked $100 billion off the market value of companies in this industry. And it looked like it was also going to kill R&D because it would put price controls on breakthrough drugs. How in the world would the company know how much it could afford to invest in the development of a new product, if the whimsy of a government bureaucrat was going to determine the price that could be set?

"The second issue we faced was a major patent expiration. Our largest single product, Capoten [a blood pressure medication], which accounted for between 14% and 15% of our worldwide sales, was going off patent. It was our most profitable product. The year before it went off patent, United States sales were about $650 million. And in the year after the patent expired, it was down to about $125 million. So we had to devise some kind of aggressive plan to compensate for that.

"And the third obstacle we were facing right off the bat was the breast implant situation. We owned about 25% of the sales in that industry. And for a part of our company that only had sales of about $20 million, we ultimately incurred charges of nearly $3 *billion*.

"All of these things were threatening to impede our growth when I became CEO. I decided that I needed to take people's attention away from these very negative influences, and set some clear and ambitious goals that I knew, or had a strong belief, we could attain.

"At my very first management meeting, within two weeks of the time that I took over, I brought everyone together and said, 'We're going to aim to have a doubling of our sales and our earnings per share by the end of the year 2000.' That implied a growth rate that was quite a bit greater than we had had the prior couple of years.

"This goal was greeted by general disbelief—both outside and inside the company. But I said that we were going to attain this so-called 'double-double' goal by focusing on increasing revenues to establish ourselves as one of the preeminent growth companies in our markets and we would finance the growth through a major, ongoing productivity program.

"There was widespread skepticism. But I stuck with the double-double goal and pushed. Today, we are known for our strength and balance; as a result, we have 36 products or product lines each with at least $100 million in annual global sales. And we have another 20 with sales of $50 million or more, and another nine with sales of at least $500 million a year. So, we have great breadth. It's kind of like an aircraft carrier with lots of watertight compartments. You know that while you can take a blow here or there, you can still press on; you can attack the enemy or competitors and satisfy your customers and win the campaign."

Given the ambitious goal, Heimbold undertook a number of different strategies to achieve his growth objectives.

"We acquired a few small and medium-sized companies, including a small pharmaceutical business in Argentina and one in Peru, and a fairly substantial one in France. We took a terrific group of new managers and moved them up the ranks inside the company, and we went outside to get others. We took existing products and moved them into new markets. We licensed new products and introduced them into the Bristol-Myers Squibb distribution systems. It's not rocket science. It's basic good business practice. These are the kinds of moves that give quality and endurance to a company."

It also got employees of the company focused on the potential and positive aspects of the future, instead of having them dwell on the problems of the past. Heimbold encouraged that optimism by constantly speaking with employees, and by offering training and support—so that the company could exploit the new opportunities to the fullest—and most important, by nurturing their belief that the future would be far better than the past. He constantly told everyone that the goal of doubling sales and earnings was achievable. "When you repeat these expectations frequently enough, you can get people to understand and buy in," he says. "People start to say, 'Yeah, maybe we can do that.' That's the feeling I wanted to create. I wanted our people to believe."

And to make sure that they keep the faith, Heimbold does two things. He makes sure Bristol-Myers Squibb shares its success with employees—

everyone in the company now has stock options—and he leads by example, modeling the behavior he wants to see within the company.

"People see that I go out on customer calls with the sales force. They see that when there are devastating ice storms in Quebec I am on the phone right away to find out what happened to our people, and making sure we're getting emergency supplies up there. They can see that I am as committed to my co-workers and to our success as they are."

What Gets Measured Gets Done

Hope in the future is one thing; making sure that the future turns out the way you project is something else. That is why Heimbold constantly probes and relentlessly keeps an eye on how well the company is progressing toward its goals.

"I ask a lot of questions. If you ask somebody to do something, you need to follow up fairly quickly to see whether it is done. You must let people know that you expect results in a given period of time.

"If you are inspecting and measuring, people are going to pay attention. They are going to remember that you do look at the performance you told them you'd be measuring."

But, as always, the inspecting—just like the new focus Heimbold instilled in the company—is directed with the competition in mind. For example, Heimbold's long-term goal is for Bristol-Myers Squibb to have the fastest earnings per share growth of any major company in the industry.

"I'm sure you have heard the line that one of the CEO's biggest jobs is to keep the lions from eating one another. What you try to do is focus people's natural competitive energies on the outside world, instead of the inside. The way you do that is twofold: First, you make sure you have the right number and caliber of people in place. If you have too many people it is almost like too many lions going after one bone.

Company (Ticker): Bristol-Myers Squibb Company (BMY)
Location: New York, New York
Leader: Charles A. Heimbold, Jr.
Bristol-Myers Squibb at a glance:
Bristol-Myers Squibb is a world-leading health and personal care products company. Seventy percent of its sales come from pharmaceuticals, where the company has significant leadership positions in cardiovascular treatments, anticancer drugs, and infectious diseases. Among its major consumer brands are Clairol hair care products, Excedrin analgesics, and Enfamil infant formulas. The company is also a world leader in orthopedics and ostomy products. Bristol-Myers Squibb is currently contemplating mergers and acquisitions in an effort to stay competitive due to impending patent expirations and consolidation of the industry.
1999 Financial Results
—Revenues: $20.2 billion
—Net Income: $4.1 billion

"And the second way you do it is through accountability. It's not empowerment that is magic, it is accountability. Give people the responsibility and the resources to get something done. Let them understand that they will be held accountable for it, that you are expecting those results, and that they are going to share in the success. Then watch what happens."

Clairol's Herbal Essences hair care line is a case in point. An extremely popular shampoo in the 1970s, its sales fell off sharply in the 1980s and into the early 1990s. However, a new reformulated product—backed by a revitalized packaging and marketing plan developed by a new management team—was launched in 1995 with a campaign designed to appeal to "Generation Xers" and "30-somethings." Sales are now more than $500 million annually and Heimbold feels Herbal Essences can easily become a $1 billion brand.

The revitalization efforts extend to the company's core pharmaceutical business as well.

Under Heimbold, Bristol-Myers Squibb has increased pharmaceutical research and development spending—it was up 16% alone in 1998—and has stepped up it licensing efforts as well. Glucophage serves as a case in point. Bristol-Myers Squibb introduced the licensed diabetes drug into the U.S. market in June 1995, with what Heimbold says were modest expectations. However, in just six months—thanks to intense efforts by the company's sales force—revenues were $90 million. Building off that success, with a strong physician education program and increased marketing efforts, the company grew sales nearly 10-fold over the next three years. They totaled $861 million in 1998 and Heimbold expects Glucophage's revenues will top $1 billion in the year 2000.

By setting tough goals, prioritizing opportunities, rallying, and then leading his team, Heimbold has led Bristol-Myers Squibb to new levels of growth and performance.

MARTHA INGRAM
Ingram Industries

Keeping everything in balance

THE "GRANDE DAME" OF NASHVILLE IS THE WAY *FORBES* USED TO describe Martha Ingram, focusing on the fact she was the arbiter of both the performing arts and social taste in the city. That description made some sense. Ingram helped found the Nashville Ballet, the Tennessee Performing Arts Center, the Tennessee Repertory Theatre, and enhanced the Nashville Symphony Orchestra.

But then the magazine went digging a little deeper and found this charming self-effacing woman ("I am pretty undistinguished compared to all the other people on your list," she said when we first asked to interview her) was one of world's richest people. (*Forbes* estimates her fortune at better than $3 billion, and calls her the wealthiest businesswoman in the United States. Maybe that is why *Fortune* described her as the quintessential steel magnolia.)

Following the death of her husband, Bronson, in 1995, Ingram took over the company's sprawling distribution empire that she divided into three parts to accommodate her sons. David, 37, runs the video wholesaler Ingram Entertainment; John, 38, runs the nation's largest book distributor (600,000 titles in stock); and Orrin, 39, handles the family's inland waterway barging operations. Impressive as those three divisions are, the company's largest business interest is Ingram Micro, which handles 20% of all computer products sold in the

CAREER
1995–PRESENT Chairman, Ingram Industries Inc.
1995–1999 CEO, Ingram Industries Inc.
1979–1995 Director of Public Affairs, Ingram Industries
1971–1979 Coordinator, Tennessee Performing Arts Center Project

EDUCATION
A.B., Vassar College, 1957

FAMILY
Married, Bronson Ingram, October 1958 (deceased 1995); children: three sons, David, John, Orrin; one daughter, Robin

Born: Charleston, South Carolina, 1935

"All you can do is the best you can. Stay on the balls of your feet as you might in a tennis game. Be ready to change directions if you need to, but don't do it in haste (as one might have to in tennis), and above all, worry about your customers. Customers can go away in a drop of a hat."

United States. The company was spun off to the public in 1996, but the Ingram family still owns or controls about 65% through Ingram family trusts.

Martha Ingram is a key part of all four businesses, but then again she always was, as Frances Fergusson, president of Vassar College (Ingram's alma mater) is quick to point out. "Martha is an extraordinary woman, and one of the unheralded facts is that Ingram Industries has taken off because of her leadership. We're awfully proud to be able to claim her, and shamelessly take some of the credit for what she has become."

While her husband was alive, Ingram had an office next door and was in charge of, among other things, the company's corporate donations. (Ingram companies traditionally give 2% of their pretax income to charity.) While people tended to focus on that, they overlooked the fact that she served as the go-between for management and the company's workers. She installed a toll-free line (which is still in use) that rings only in her office for employees who want to discuss problems that cannot go through normal channels. Some of the calls she received have led to investigations, which in turn led to disciplinary action and dismissals.

Her ombudsman role also had an unexpected result. All this contact with employees gave her a better understanding of the company, which, of course, made her better prepared to take over the company following her husband's death.

Although it was not until recently that Ingram's management ability became widely known, her skills have long been recognized within Tennessee. While working with her husband, Ingram was offered the chance to run part of the state's college system.

"Are you going to pay me?" asked Ingram, who drew no salary from the family business.

"Of course," came the reply from a state official who offered a salary in the six figures.

Ingram turned down the offer, but she did mention it to her husband.

"Do you want me to match it?" he asked.

"Yes, I think I do," she said.

Bronson Ingram paid up. Willingly.

As the company's results show, it was a sound decision.

CONSULTANTS HAVE MADE A LIVING OFF APPLYING THE MILITARY STRA-
tegies of everyone from Lao Tzu to Ulysses S. Grant to the marketplace.
Business writers have constructed management books about the wisdom
of Winnie-the-Pooh, and academics have even turned television shows—
such as *Star Trek* and *The Andy Griffith Show*—into sources of executive
education.

Far be it from us to question any of those works. But we would like to
suggest a more likely source of wisdom that can be found closer to home.
We even have a title. How about, *Everything I Know About Running a
Company I Learned from Mom.* If you were ever to write such a book, your
first research visit would ideally be with Martha Ingram. If you incorporated her lessons, your book—or the business you run—would do very
well indeed.

"I never ever had any intention of joining the business, but I did in
1979," she explains about her background with Ingram Industries. "I had
just finished an eight-year project of developing—and then coordinating—
the Tennessee Performing Arts Center. We went from dream to reality.
We got a $36 million bond issue through the state legislature, raised a
$5.5 million private endowment, and we had just hired a professional
manager when my husband said, 'What are you going to do now?'

" 'I want to go to the beach.'

"And he said, 'That won't last long. Why don't you come work for me?
You've proven that you've got a lot of energy and a strong aptitude for
business. Why don't you come to work here, just in case something were
to happen to me. Come in one or two days a week and try it.'

"I had real serious reservations about it because we had four children.
And I wondered if it would be a good idea being together 24 hours a day
and eliminating the boundary between work and family. But I figured I'd
try it one day a week. Once I started, however, I never stopped going, because I kept finding areas where I could be helpful."

Ingram was instrumental in expanding the company's book business.
Computer books were the company's first big push. "That led us into
software because it seemed that it was also something that might be com-
patible with bookstore goods for our retail customers.

"At the same time," Ingram adds, "we got into the video distribution
business to enhance the product line for book retailers, our original customers. And then, there were freestanding computer and video stores. So
we added hardware to the software. And all the businesses just kept on
growing."

And Ingram kept working alongside her husband, who learned he had cancer in December 1994. Upon his death six months later, Ingram took over the company.

"It was not my choice, but someone had to step in. Bronson had told me before he even became ill that if anything were ever to happen to him I should make myself chairman and surround myself with the smartest people I could find. So, I've tried to do that. And fortunately, I'd been in the office for about 16 years at the time of his death, so, I felt comfortable with the business. But the big thing was that there were decisions that had to be made."

Short-term, those decisions involved running the business until her children were ready to take over. Longer-term, it meant determining how the family's holdings would be administered.

In both cases, a balancing act was required. That was something Ingram had lots of experience with.

"I'm really quite serious in saying that I think one of my main jobs has been to try to keep the family in balance," she says. "That's always been my role, even before I was with the company. I think that's the mother's role, to try to keep a family in balance. That certainly was my role. We had four children in five years. There was a lot of stabilizing going on all the time. I know I sound like a pacifist, but I can also fight like the dickens if I have to. But I think that's a last resort. The real role is to try to keep it all steady.

"I have often said that my greatest training for the job I have now was being a mother," she adds. "In both jobs, you have to keep everybody feeling good about themselves and doing their best and you try to get them to maximize the talents they have. This is also the role of the person in charge of a business.

"My other challenge is to try to bring my sons along as fast as I can because I have no long-term interest in remaining chairman, and certainly not CEO. They are taking more and more of the CEO role. They're in operations. That's their job. I want to know what's going on. I'm not going to second-guess them, but I want to know. We have regular reporting routines.

"You can imagine how it would be to be running a company and have your mother in charge. But, they've been very sweet about it. Right after my husband's death, I said to my children, 'Look, you guys can just have the business. I'll just step aside.'

"And they said, 'Not so fast, Mother. You think the banks want to loan a bunch of 30-year-olds the kind of money that we borrow?'

"And I hadn't really thought of it that way. They said, 'Look, whether you want to or not, you've got to stick around until we've got a few gray hairs—at least until we reach somewhere around forty.' "

A Sense of Fun

With her children agreeing Ingram would be running things for a number of years, she began putting her own stamp on the company.

"I would say that the thing that I've probably added, at least in my mind, is a sense of fun. I want people to love to come to work. I want them to have a good time. Bronson wanted them to have wonderful working conditions, and fine salaries. I think they enjoyed themselves, but I think we're all talking a little bit louder in the halls now and laughing a lot too.

"Sometimes when I walk in my sons', and son-in-law's, offices—they are all on the same floor as mine—I hear their cackling and laughter. You never used to hear that. Before, when you worked for Ingram, you were serious. I don't fault Bronson's style, but I can't work that way. I have a different style and that maybe is a result of having had a family. I want my children to be happy and have a good time and I think this attitude has permeated throughout the company. I think a sense of fun can be good. People become more productive. They have a sense that it's okay to be jolly."

Is that because women are more nurturing?

Ingram is not sure. While the fact that she is one of the very few women running multi-billion-dollar organizations is frequently commented upon, she says it is not something she has given a lot of thought.

"I'm asked about that every now and again, particularly in the school setting. I'm on the board of two girls' schools, in addition to two colleges—both now co-ed—Vanderbilt and Vassar. And I myself really haven't had a lot of the stress points that I know a lot of women have. I've never had any sense of feeling that I was somehow given a bum deal. I've always felt very privileged.

Company: Ingram Industries Inc. (Privately held)
Location: Nashville, Tennessee
Business Leader: Martha R. Ingram
Ingram Industries at a glance:
Ingram Industries Inc., one of the largest companies in the United States owned and led by a woman, is a leader in distribution, barge operations, and insurance. Ingram Book Group is the nation's leading wholesale book distributor, annually shipping more than 115 million books, audiotapes, and CD-ROMs. Ingram Book handles approximately two thirds of the books that go to United States retailers via wholesalers. Ingram Marine Group operates 2,600 barges on a for-hire basis; Ingram's Permanent General insurance company covers high-risk automobile drivers. The company is privately held by the Ingram family, which also owns about 65% of computer products wholesaler Ingram Micro, Inc. ($22 billion in revenues).
1999 Financial Results
—Revenues: $2.0 billion

"I grew up as the oldest in my family. And my father never said to me, 'Oh, too bad, you're a girl.' He just said, 'Look, we've got a successful radio and television business and I've got a lot of money borrowed. Pay attention in case something happens to me. Your mother doesn't have any interest in running our business. You'd be in charge.' Even when I was going to Vassar, he made me sit down and look at a balance sheet and P&L. At the time, I thought it was the most boring thing in the world. And sometimes I still feel that it's boring—until I stop to understand what it really represents.

"But in terms of being at a disadvantage as a woman, I've never felt any problem. I guess that's because my father never made me feel it was a problem. I was to be his successor when I got out of Vassar. But then I married Bronson and moved away. My dad really was glad for me, but it meant that he had to hire somebody to come in."

Does she see herself as a role model?

"It's sort of a curious question in a sense because a lot of young women will make appointments to come to see me, and they want to know, 'When did you know you wanted to be chairman and CEO?' I always tell them I never wanted to be chairman. I just wanted to be a wife and a mother. That was my generation. I wanted to be an active volunteer and a community leader. That's what my mother had been. It's what my mother-in-law was. I really had no business ambitions.

"What I do remember thinking was that I wanted to make a difference. However, it never occurred to me that it would be in the business world. I didn't know what it would be in. But I had this Protestant challenge that says, 'To those to whom much is given much is expected.' At the end of your days, this world should somehow be better because you passed through it.

"So certainly I had ambitions. But it was never to be a business leader. I saw working in business as more of a duty, something I would have to do, if something happened to someone else. But what has ended up happening of course is that I enjoy the business world much more than I thought I would. And while I never sought this position, and would not have leaped to have taken the CEO role in another company, I really do enjoy it.

"I wanted to make a difference. I'm not sure that I've done that yet, but I'm still working on it."

DAVID JOHNSON
Campbell Soup

Winning

DAVID JOHNSON, 66, CAN'T SIT STILL. THE CHAIRMAN OF THE $6.7-billion-in-sales Campbell Soup Co. is bounding about his office. First, he makes sure his visitors have something to drink. Then he pushes back from the small conference table in his office to get a piece of paper that will show exactly how much market share Campbell Soup has won from its peers over the last 10 years. Then there is a quick call to make sure that lunch is on its way. . . .

Even when he is listening to questions, Johnson is rocking back and forth, and rummaging about for notes that will convey precisely what he wants to say.

It is exactly this energy—and focus—that has been responsible for Johnson's success—and Campbell Soup's success. After becoming CEO in 1990, Johnson moved tirelessly toward one single objective: gaining on, and ultimately beating, every other consumer products company. (Scoreboards comparing Campbell Soup quarterly net-profit increases versus other food companies are spread throughout the company's headquarters in Camden, New Jersey, just outside of Philadelphia.)

To make sure Campbell Soup would be able to beat the competition, Johnson slashed costs. He closed more than 20 fac-

CAREER

2000–PRESENT President and CEO, Campbell Soup Company

1997–2000 Chairman, Campbell Soup Company

1993–1997 Chairman, President, and CEO

1990–1993 President and CEO, Campbell Soup Company

1987–1989 Chairman and CEO, Gerber Products Co.

1982–1987 President and CEO, Entenmann's division, General Foods

1980–1982 President, Specialty Foods Group, Warner-Lambert Co.

1973–1980 President, Warner-Lambert/Parke-Davis Asia

1959–1973 Numerous executive positions for Colgate-Palmolive Co. in Australia and Africa

EDUCATION

M.B.A., University of Chicago, 1958

B.Ec., University of Sydney, 1954

FAMILY

Married, Sylvia, March 1966; children: three sons

Born: August 7, 1932

> *"If you want to be a world-class performer, and I don't want to have anybody with me who doesn't dream of that, then you're not going to set goals that are easy to achieve. You won't do that, because you wouldn't be able to live with yourself. You would not be worth knowing."*

tories, eliminated layers of management within the corporate structure, fired hundreds of managers, and sold $500 million worth of poorly performing businesses and products—many of them soups. Johnson used the savings to buy other companies—such as Pace Foods of San Antonio, the nation's leading maker of salsa—that had better prospects and higher margins. Johnson's mantra: "20-20-20." 20% annual earnings growth; 20% return on equity, and 20% return on invested cash.

That relentless focus on numbers is one reason for Campbell's turnaround under Johnson. The other is unabashed boosterism, coupled with setting aggressive goals for all his managers.

Hit your target, and Johnson will literally hire a brass band to serenade you. Miss more than once, and expect to find another job.

Johnson, who relinquished the CEO title in 1997 and now serves as a very active chairman, doesn't see this approach as harsh. For one thing, employees share in the company's success; a large part of a manager's compensation comes in the form of bonuses and stock options. For another, as Johnson says, "The competition is always plotting to kill you. You have to work harder."

This self-reliance, which Johnson imparts to his troops, is something he learned growing up on a ranch in Australia. This "owner mentality" is something that he believes all companies need.

DAVID JOHNSON HAS AN M.B.A. (FROM THE UNIVERSITY OF CHICAGO).

He has run divisions throughout the world (for Colgate-Palmolive, Warner-Lambert, and General Foods).

And he has worked his way up the ranks, starting as a salesman and ending up a CEO (twice).

So what does he think is the best preparation for running a multi-billion, multi-national corporation?

Spending your entire childhood on a ranch in Australia.

"If you grow up in the country on a ranch—I call it a ranch, you call it a farm—you get introduced to what I call an owner mentality from the very beginning of life. We learned early on that what we earned and how well we did depended upon our talents, and our capabilities—with a little help from God."

And Johnson learned something else. Doing your best was not good enough. At the very least you had to do better than your competition, if you wanted to survive.

"If you live in the country, your prices are published when you go to the sale yards. The prices for your fat lambs or your veal, and those of everybody else, are right there out in the open, so you know how good your prices are versus somebody else. We were constantly being measured on a comparative basis."

That requires you to be vigilant, a lesson that was reinforced in the 1960s at one of his first management jobs, head of the detergent business for Colgate-Palmolive in Australia.

"We were succeeding incredulously. We were succeeding so well that we were out of stock, couldn't produce anymore, and were importing all we could from other countries. So, we'd have a board meeting and sit around, with our feet up on the table, being self-congratulatory. We joked around about how we really could take a month off because the thing was humming, zinging, roaring, and life was wonderful. But you know what happened? The competition—stung by this unbelievable defeat we had imposed on them—worked nauseatingly well through the night. And in six, maybe eight months, they began to unfold a series of new product movements that caught us by surprise. We weren't prepared for it. We had been relaxed, overconfident, and complacent. That was one of the great lessons of my life. Because never again would I underestimate the competition. I imagine the things that the competition must be plotting right now, and I never, or I try to never, let the team anywhere relax.

"Everything we do is done with the competition in mind. You have to constantly compare yourself to them, and worry about them. I'm telling you the competition will sap your lifeblood, would be delighted to stop you from making money, and would be delighted to kill you if they could."

The need to be self-reliant, and outperform the competition, has governed everything Johnson has done. And he looks for people who see the business universe the way he does.

"When nighttime comes, the competition plots while we sleep. Therefore, we're going to have people working around the clock, and it's not just going to be the fact that they are working that matters, it is the quality of the work and their inventiveness that's important, otherwise you quickly can be outmaneuvered."

To ensure that doesn't happen, Johnson insists that all managers set aggressive goals. Merely trying to grow their units 2% faster than inflation isn't going to cut it. Johnson draws a circus analogy to show what he is after.

"It's like the staff is trapeze artists and I tell them we are going to do triple summersaults. This is what we are really all about: the high trapeze of business. And to add risk, I tell them you get no pay if you don't perform. [Johnson is exaggerating—but not by much. As little as 20% of an executive's compensation comes in the form of fixed salary. The rest is tied to his or her performance, and that of the company.]

"I tell them, this is the way it is. If you have faint heart, leave now; don't come forward, because it's going to get tougher and tougher and tougher. But if we are good it will be unbelievable.

"My message to them is that you've got to be prepared to take risks, train together, and live and die together by the results that we deliver. And if you set tough goals that stretch you on an escalating basis and you succeed, the feeling is unbelievable, because we're talking about accomplishment.

"I ask everybody: Didn't you get turned on when you got an 'A' in school? Didn't you get turned on when you were selected for the first team or you got a letter? Didn't you get excited if your marching band won? Okay. It's the same for us. We've got to get to the finals.

"The question for me is how do we convert business into a form of fun and sharing and stretching and fulfillment that is as touchable as graduating summa cum laude. That's when you get the buy in. That's when people say, 'I am going to do incredible things.' "

To obtain that buy in, Johnson calls on his initial training—as a teacher. He doesn't think that should be surprising. "What is my job if it's not teaching and coaching on a constant basis? That is what I was trained to do. I've gotten my Ph.D. from the business battlefield and I'm a professor in terms of coaching and mentoring and communicating and growing people and teaching them."

As all teachers know, motivation is the key to getting people to perform, and Johnson has a huge motivation tool at his disposal—money. And a lot of it. Given the fact that a huge part of everyone's compensation—both in terms of bonuses and stock options—is based on the company's performance, and given Campbell's terrific performance over the past decade Johnson has made a lot of people wealthy.

"I'm proud of the fact that I've made a lot of people rich. I am not talking only about shareholders, although they have done fine, too. I'm talking about hundreds of people who work at the company. We have made their lives more meaningful. They are so much better off. They can educate their children. The money means if they really want to take early retirement, they can retire. And I don't begrudge anybody if they have had their fill. They've taken the risks. They've stretched. They've lost hair. If the time has come, isn't it wonderful that we have made them a few bucks so if they want to do something different, to go on with another life, they can."

To Johnson, the fact that employees have shared in the company's success is only fair. It is the logical culmination of their doing the highest-quality work they can, and besting the competition in the process.

"In a way, what I've preached about here is having a group of professionals who will put themselves at risk. People who at first go on the high trapeze and perform triple summersaults, or whatever, and do it safely while the crowd watches in amazement.

"And if your people are truly good, you say, 'Take away the nets.' The silence is pervasive as the crowd watches in horror and wonders if you can perform. And when you do that triple summersault, the exultation and feeling that you share with your team—and everybody associated with it—calls for a celebration, one that's mixed with the pride of knowing that you've done it.

"I believe our work is part of our life and has meaning. I believe what we are doing together is truly meaningful and not just the mechanical habit, going through the motions of work."

It's inevitable when someone reaches 66, and steps down as CEO, to ask about their future plans. Will they retire? What will they do from here on out? Not surprisingly, Johnson stays right in character as he answers.

"You know, I'm the luckiest person in the world. It's a dream. I can't believe that this has happened to me, that I've been given this opportunity. Now, there were times when people have looked at the darkness under my eyes—I'm very pale and at the end of days of working on some challenging problem, I will be drained and gray—and they'll say, 'You look terrible.' And I'll reply, 'But I feel terrific.' That's the essence of it. I feel terrific. I'm wired, turned on, juices flowing, stretched by the challenge. Excitement surrounds me. Work is fun.

"More than that, today I am con-

Company (Ticker): Campbell Soup Company (CPB)

Location: Camden, New Jersey

Leader: David W. Johnson

Campbell Soup at a glance: Led by its soup stalwarts—tomato, chicken noodle, and cream of mushroom—Campbell accounts for about 85% of all condensed soup sold in the United States and 10% of the total prepared soup market outside the United States, where it is expanding. Campbell's other key businesses are sauces (Pace Mexican sauces, Prego spaghetti sauce), baked goods (Pepperidge Farm and Arnotts), food service products (restaurant soups, Stockpot Refrigerated Soups), Godiva chocolates, and other food products (SpaghettiOs and V8 Vegetable and V8 Splash juices).

1999 Financial Results

—Revenues: $6.4 billion

—Net Income: $724 million

nected to Campbell as chairman of a board that is famous for its governance. And I have free time to explore life's greatest opportunities to grow—like going with my wife to a Wagner opera festival in Bavaria, or white-water rafting with my sons, or exploring the North Pole."

HERB KELLEHER
Southwest Airlines

"Culture is your number-one priority."

IT IS A TOSS-UP AS TO WHAT HERB KELLEHER IS BEST KNOWN FOR—HIS management skills, or his I-am-having-more-fun-than-anyone-on-the-planet style.

On the one hand, you have a man who was twice named CEO of the year by *Financial World* magazine (1982 and 1990) and has shown the world how to build a major airline, when people such as Don Burr of People's Express, and countless others, came up short.

But on the other hand, you have an executive who has dressed up at company functions as everyone from the Easter Bunny to Elvis.

What people who may be aware of Kelleher may not realize, however, is how well he knows his job. At one time or another he has supervised or held just about every position at South-west, so he understands the company better than anyone. And the stories that stress his good ol' boy image—this is a good ol' boy who was born outside of Philadelphia and was educated in the East—also tend to ignore the discipline it took to build the airline market by market. Kelleher typically opens a hub in a city close to where his competitors have a near stranglehold. That puts off competing head-to-head for as long as possible. Direct competition has doomed just about every other start-up airline you can think of.

That geographic positioning is one reason for Southwest's success. Here's an-

CAREER

1967–PRESENT Founder, Chairman, and CEO, Southwest Airlines Company
1961–1978 Senior partner, Oppenheimer, Rosenberg, Kelleher & Wheatley, Inc.
1959–1961 Partner, Matthews, Nowlin, Macfarlane & Barrett
1956–1959 Clerk, New Jersey Supreme Court

EDUCATION

LL.B. cum laude, New York University, 1956
B.A. cum laude, Wesleyan University, 1953

FAMILY

Married, Joan Negley September 9, 1955; children: Julie, Michael, Ruth, David

Born: Camden, New Jersey, March 12, 1931

> *"What employees are looking for is sincerity, and you don't demonstrate sincerity through making something programmatic. It has to come from the heart rather than the head."*

other. In a business where everyone has the same planes, same gates, and basically the same fares, Kelleher knows that the only thing that differentiates one airline from another is the people who work there. That's why employees have a huge say over who is hired. The assumption Kelleher makes is the background checks will determine whether someone has the technical skills to do the job.

The employees' input is designed to see if the applicant will fit into the Southwest culture, which is nonbureaucratic, fun-loving, and built on the assumption that everyone will do the right thing for both the customer and their colleagues.

It is clear that Kelleher fits in. Like every other Southwest employee, he is willing to share the burden. Here is a simple example. People like to fly on Thanksgiving to see their families. That means someone at Southwest has to work while the rest of the country is home eating turkey. Kelleher has been on the job Thanksgiving Day taking tickets or handling bags.

"It's interesting," Kelleher says. "People have come to visit Southwest Airlines saying they want to establish a culture similar to ours. When we tell them all we've done is just treat people right, it's too simplistic for them. They want something far more complex. They want a program. We always felt that making it 'a program' murders it."

HERB KELLEHER ANSWERS A QUESTION WITH A QUESTION.

When asked where the idea of creating a fun work environment—the hallmark of Southwest Airlines—came from, he answered:

"Do you think people work better, and they're more productive, if they enjoy what they're doing, or if they don't?

"I've always felt that you shouldn't have to change your personality when you come to work. So we decided we are going to hire good people, and let them be themselves, let them be individualistic. We were going to create an environment where we pay a great deal of attention to them, their personal lives as well as their business lives. We wanted to show them that we don't regard them just as work automatons. We wanted to create an environment where people can really enjoy what they're doing.

"People used to make a lot out of it, and question how we could run the company this way, but now I'm starting to read books advocating it."

But, Kelleher is quick to stress, you cannot just provide lip service to the concept, in the hope of scoring higher profits.

"People know whether you're treating them this way for some kind of purely economic reason or whether you're doing it because you like people and value them. And that's why we say that this approach has to be spontaneous."

Kelleher provides an example. "Our people captured a bunch of gates at Midway airport in Chicago a while ago. When Midway Airlines stopped using them, our folks just went in and seized them, so that we would have more room for our customers. And when they got back from doing that, we had a gigantic banner in the lobby saying 'Hail Chicago Banditos.' That's what I mean by doing things spontaneously."

Those kinds of decisions may be spontaneous, but the decision to applaud initiative and individuality is anything but.

"There's been a real change in American society in the attitude people have toward work, and what they are looking for out of their working lives," says Kelleher, who began his working life more than 40 years ago. "So you have to change in order to accommodate that.

"Some years ago, I told one of our officers, who was kind of from the old school, the more militaristic school you might say, that I was not going to argue with him whether what's going on in society is right or wrong. My focus is on being successful at Southwest Airlines, and making our people's jobs secure and prosperous, and to do that we have got to adapt to society. You know, we're not going to be very successful leading a war against it, so we have to change. It doesn't mean that people are any better or any worse than they used to be. It just means they have different drives and a different focus than they used to. And you have to learn to accommodate yourself to those desires.

"I don't really believe in, or pay much attention to, the folks who say that there's no work ethic in America today, because we get marvelous applicants all the time," Kelleher adds. "But they are driven, they are motivated, they are inspired by different things than people used to be. And so you have to be aware of that."

This is particularly important at Southwest, which is in basically a commodity business. In a commodity business, the only thing that differentiates you from the competition is the service you provide.

"I know it sounds simple, but I keep saying follow the golden rule of service. Serve others as you yourself would like to be served. I'll ask our people, 'Do you like to go into a restaurant or department store and encounter salespeople who are indifferent to you, who don't care about your needs and wants, who treat you as if you're an object?' Well, everybody has to answer that one way. 'No, we don't like that.' Then I say, well then, don't be a hypocrite. Provide better service. Provide the service you yourself would like to receive."

But preaching, no matter how sincere, only takes you so far. Southwest needs people who truly want customers to have a pleasant flight, so it spends an inordinate amount of time interviewing potential employees to make sure they have the right attitude. That is true not only for the people who deal with customers directly, but also for those who work behind the scenes.

"We've always operated on the theory that everybody has a customer," Kelleher explains. "That means from a customer service standpoint it is just as important to get the right people in the finance department as anywhere else, because the way that they provide customer service to other people within the company eventually manifests and reflects itself in the service that you provide to the public. So that internal customer service is where you start. Your employees are your most important customers."

"We Look for Attitude"

"This is a huge area of focus for us. We're religious about hiring. Just to give you an example, years ago a then vice president of the People Department told me that she was a little bit dismayed because they had interviewed 34 people for a ramp agent position in one of the smaller cities that we serve, and they hadn't found anybody. Of course she was concerned about the delay, but also about the cost associated with the delay. And I told her, if you have to interview 134 people to get the right ramp agent, do it.

"We look for attitude. You know, we really focus on attitude. It's wonderful to have somebody with a good education, don't misunderstand me. And it's wonderful to have someone who has experience, and maybe even some expertise, but if they have a lousy attitude, we don't want them. We'll take somebody with lesser education, lesser experience, and lesser expertise, because the one thing that you cannot change is attitude. We hire for attitude and teach skills if we have to.

"The interviewing process may seem rather idiosyncratic to you, but there is a system to it. Here's an example. We had a group of pilot applicants, and we told them that we don't interview people in suits. They had to wear Southwest Airline shorts instead. And so there they are, they had their suit jackets and ties on, and Southwest Airlines shorts. Well, the people that were happy to do that, we hired, and the people that weren't, we didn't."

No matter how technically proficient, the pilots had to fit into the Southwest culture.

In addition to this offbeat approach, Southwest employees spend an inordinate amount of time "just talking" with applicants. "We might talk to you about baseball, if you're interested in baseball. We might talk to you about your family, or an article that was in the newspaper. You can learn so much about what a person's values are this way. We're looking for people who are altruistic and idealistic. And just by talking to them about how they conduct their lives, and the things they're interested in, you can find out whether they are."

This focus hasn't changed a lick as the company has grown. "For years, I have had people say to me 'Yeah, what you're doing when it comes to hiring is great, but wait until you have 500 employees.' And then it was 'Wait until 5,000.' They were saying that you couldn't maintain your culture, and your espirit de corps, as you get big. Well, of course, if you think that way, you're doomed. You can't do it. But if the culture is your number-one priority, you can."

Maintaining this approach to the business, Kelleher says, is what the chief executive of Southwest should be doing. "We're not at all loath to talk to people in terms that involve love, or idealism, broader philosophical concepts. I think leadership by example is very important. But, you know, we believe that it's important for everybody to realize that they're involved in an enterprise of some magnitude, which has some meaning and significance beyond what you do every day in a mechanical way."

It's all part of being a leader. "I'd describe leadership as servanthood," Kelleher says. "The best leaders, I think, have to be good followers as well. You have to be quite willing to accept other people's ideas, even when they're in conflict with your own. You have to be willing to subjugate your ego to the needs of your business. You have to be willing to take risks for your people. If you won't fight for your people, then you can count on your people not fighting for you. The thing that I am most proud of in my business career is that in this very tumultuous, very cyclical industry, Southwest Airlines has never had any furloughs. That we've provided total job security for our people.

"You have to genuinely believe all this because you're going to be with your people for a long, long time, and obviously they're going to find out

Company (Ticker): Southwest Airlines Company (LUV)
Location: Dallas, Texas
Leader: Herbert D. Kelleher
Southwest at a glance: Southwest has refined the low-cost, no-frills, no-reserved-seats approach to air travel, providing over 2,500 flights daily to about 55 cities in 29 states. To curb maintenance and pilot training costs, the airline uses only fuel-efficient Boeing 737s. It has a fleet of 320 aircraft. The airline boasts about its participative corporate culture and a strike-free, unbroken string of 27 years of profits. The airline has recently begun flying coast-to-coast, building off its regional heritage.
1999 Financial Results
—Revenues: $4.7 billion
—Net Income: $474 million

whether you're a wind bag or a hypocrite or a mountebank, if you're going to spend tremendous amounts of time with them."

And the last thing you want to do is lose the commitment of the people you are leading.

"I wrote everyone a note a while ago where I talked about competition. And we have lots of it, of course, from other carriers, but I also talked about how high-speed rail and even telecommunications were potential competitors. But I said the principal concern that I have about the future is 'us.'

"As Pogo said, the enemy is us. The world will change, and you have to be adaptable or you don't survive. But you know, the main thing that we have to avoid is complacency, cockiness, arrogance, and the assumption that success is final. As Winston Churchill said, 'Success is never final,' you have to keep earning it over and over again.

"In other words, it's a cultural thing," Kelleher adds. "If you believe that your culture is the most important thing at your company, then of course, that's the thing you worry about most. That's the thing you focus on the most, and that's the thing you address the most.

"In our business, the customer service business, the intangibles are far more important than the tangibles. It's not just providing a good value—providing a good product at a reasonable price—you need to offer an infusion of spirituality. In other words, if you're in the customer service business, you don't want people just to fly from A to B and say, 'Woo, we made it.' You want them to get off the plane with the feeling that they were welcome, that they enjoyed great hospitality, that they were, perhaps, entertained. You want it to be a warm event in their lives, so that they will come back. And that's the hardest thing for a competitor to emulate. That's why I say the intangibles are more important than the tangibles. Obviously you can buy the airplanes, the Boeing Company will sell them to you, and you can lease ticket counter space, and you can buy computers, but the intangible things—the esprit de corps if you want to call it that—is the hardest thing for people to imitate."

BILL KERR
Meredith

"We have to keep earning the trust of our customers."

THERE ARE VERY FEW THINGS STRONGER THAN BRAND LOYALTY. IF YOU ask someone why they have bought the same kind of ketchup, or the same brand of dishwasher, or have used the same accounting firm for years on end, you are bound to hear something like "It's a good value"; "I know what I'm getting"; "They know what they're doing"; "They're dependable, I trust them."

If you sell anything—be it to a consumer or another business—you can't ask for more than that.

But as strong as brand loyalty is, it can be severed; and once that happens, it is extremely difficult to get those customers back. That is something that thousands of American companies learned the hard way during the 1980s as once-loyal customers deserted them in droves, turned off by poor quality and high prices.

William T. Kerr, who once thought he was going to teach medieval English history, spends a great deal of time thinking about brand loyalty. The Meredith Corporation—which publishes more than 50 home-and-family-oriented magazines, including *Better Homes and Gardens* and *Ladies' Home Journal*, and owns a dozen television stations—has had a long and profitable relationship with its

CAREER

1998–PRESENT Chairman and CEO, Meredith
  Corporation
1997–1998 President and CEO
1994–1997 President and COO
1991–1994 Executive Vice President, and
  President, Meredith Magazine Group
1985–1991 President, The New York Times
  Company Magazine Group
1979–1991 Vice President
1973–1979 Consultant, McKinsey & Company
1969–1973 Vice President, Dillon Read

EDUCATION

M.B.A., Harvard University, 1969
M.A., Harvard University, 1967
B.A., M.A., Oxford University, England, 1965
B.A., University of Washington, 1963

FAMILY

Married, Mary Lang;
  children: Susannah Gaskill Kerr Adler

Born: Seattle, Washington, April 17, 1941

customers. When Kerr joined Meredith in late 1991, after running The New York Times Company's magazine division, he joined a company facing a tricky task: the need to revitalize and increase profitability without alienating the people who had been Meredith customers all their lives.

IT WAS A MATTER OF FINE-TUNING, RAISING THE BAR, AND, MOST OF ALL, keeping the faith, Kerr responds when asked why Meredith has become so successful.

"The first thing we did was focus on what really mattered. In the 1980s, we were in a bunch of industries tangentially related to our core publishing and broadcasting businesses. We were in the fulfillment business. We were in the printing business. We had a residential real estate operating group. We were in and out of the cable business. We looked at all that and said what we really excel in is publishing and broadcasting. We decided to focus on the core businesses. In a process initiated by my predecessor and accelerated in recent years, we exited everything else.

> "*I think we've been able to make this a company where people are eager to work, are excited to work, and want to work. At the same time we've established Meredith as one of America's absolutely top-performing media companies.*"

"Secondly, we were able to establish and fulfill a strong set of financial expectations for the company. Historically, we were light in thinking about financial expectations. To change that, we did a variety of things. We started by taking the necessary steps for aligning the interests of our managers more directly with the shareholders. This meant a shift to clear performance-based compensation and a heavy reliance on equity ownership. As a result, we've been able to raise the level of financial focus and performance. Over the last several years, we compounded our earnings per share at 33% per year and tripled our profit margins to 15%. At the same time we've visibly strengthened the quality of our products and launched a host of new ones.

"But while we began to focus more on the financials, we were also able to keep the small, hometown, family feel of the company, which was quite important.

"In today's world, people have to agree to perform for us. They have to choose to be our employees. And, therefore, we've got to create an environment where they want to work for us. I don't know what you hear about Meredith, but in the publishing industry today, we are a company where the best people want to work. That helps us perform."

The caring atmosphere that Kerr works hard to maintain internally also carries over to the way Meredith treats its customers.

"I am always talking to our people about the issues of care and commitment," Kerr explains. "I think you really have to care about what you do. And you've got to show that you care. That means caring about your customers, be they external or internal. It also means caring about the quality of our products.

"Nobody has to read our magazines. Nobody has to watch our television programs. And nobody has to give us advertising. As much as I love our properties, and as much as I think our magazines are better than anyone else's, there are 4,000 other magazines out there in which to advertise. Some companies don't even have to advertise. They can use promotion. They can use discounts. They can use a whole variety of approaches. So we have to create an environment where advertisers choose us. And that's true with customers and employees. You have to care."

The subject of caring prompts Kerr to talk about one of his favorite topics: trust.

"I think the whole question of trust is critical," Kerr says. "One of the reasons we do well is that our customers trust us. And I think one of the reasons we have great brand franchises is that trust is implicit in those brands.

"In a way, while we certainly own our magazines, we hold them in trust for our readers. It's interesting to look at reader responses after we do something they don't like. They don't ask, 'Why did you do this to *your* magazine?' They ask, 'Why did you do this to *my* magazine?' The reader views it as her magazine, or his magazine. So I think we've got to show that we care about it at least as much as they do."

And you have to be vigilant about that care, Kerr says.

"We hold ourselves up to some fairly lofty values on how we serve the homes and families of this country. That standard is important to us. I'll give you an example. Recently, our CBS-affiliated television stations were pushed very hard to take the Howard Stern television program. Some of our managers thought we could make good money from this programming, even though it would be inconsistent with our corporate philosophy.

"I didn't think we, as a company, needed this kind of programming to make money. I think there are lots of other ways to make money. When we declined to run Stern's show on any of our stations, we made it clear we would not sacrifice our values to meet short-term financial objectives. That sent an important message throughout our organization."

This trust and consistency is important because it allows Meredith to build off its core franchises. Once Meredith earns a customer's trust, that customer is more willing to buy line extensions that carry a Meredith brand's name.

"In the publishing arena, our approach is to take a 'parent' magazine that embraces a general field, and then introduce an 'offspring' magazine into a subsegment of that field," Kerr says. "Sometimes, we split the subsegments into even smaller segments and introduce still more magazines, often using the same parent umbrella name. Along the way, we have moved into related ancillary publishing businesses."

Kerr uses his company's *Better Homes and Gardens* magazine as an example.

"We expanded into books. We have probably 300 books in print, which are mostly *Better Homes and Gardens* books. We also have about 100 special interest publications. These are newsstand-only magazines that also carry the *Better Homes and Gardens* name and focus on sharply defined home-related issues.

"We've created conventional magazines out of *Better Homes and Gardens*. We introduced *Traditional Home*, a magazine focusing on traditional decorating styles, under the auspices of *Better Homes and Gardens*. We launched *Country Home*, which is also what it says it is—a magazine focusing on country decorating styles. *Country Home*, which is a decade old, has now spawned *Country Gardens*, its own spin-off magazine. This gets us down into another segment.

"We can make a very significant profit with an 8-million circulation magazine. And we can make a really nice profit with a 200,000-circulation magazine if it is done right.

"As much as we have taken slices out of the market, we think there are a lot more opportunities to slice. Consider two of our newest offerings. *Family Money* is targeted to mainstream Americans with a fairly heavy female readership focus. This is a big opportunity because women control the majority of the portfolios, but they're fundamentally undermarketed to by financial institutions. A similar situation existed with auto advertising 15 years ago in Detroit. Back then, the automotive industry did not believe in selling to women. Now, automotive is one of our 10 largest advertising categories among our women's magazines.

"The other slice last year was *MORE*, which is targeted at women over forty. *MORE* isn't a name that describes what it is, but we didn't want to have a magazine called *Older Woman's Magazine*. But the concept is right. The health issues these women face are different. Their lifestyle concerns are different. And they represent one of the most dynamic demographic segments of our society. *MORE* looks like a tremendous launch at this point.

"So we have a pretty good handle on who are customers are."

What else accounts for Meredith's success?

"There have been a couple of other things that have been operating in our favor," Kerr says. "Certainly, we have had a wonderful marketplace to be operating in for most of the decade, and we've taken advantage of it pretty well. This has been especially true on the publishing side due to the home and family publishing franchise we have. There has been a great deal of focus on remodeling homes; acquiring second homes; families; and second families, as the case may be. We are exceptionally well-positioned to deal with that market."

Where Does Meredith Go from Here?

"The question is, how are we going to keep all this going? We're unlikely to be able to make many magazine acquisitions. There's been so much consolidation in the industry. We will be required to grow internally. For us, that will mean focusing heavily on creating new magazines. We've been creating about a new magazine a year and we have to keep that creative process going. Money is not the issue. Good ideas are the real issue, and good editors who can execute those ideas.

"We will continue to look for broadcasting acquisitions that have the potential for significant revenue increases. Our purchase in 1998 of WGNX-TV (CBS) in Atlanta is one example. It's an underperforming station in a large, fast-growing market. It's up to us to mine that potential. But there are fewer and fewer of these opportunities left.

"That makes improving the performance of our existing stations crucial to continued operating profit growth. We are engaged in an initiative to build clear brand identities for our stations in their markets.

"After seven years of strong advertising growth in this country, we will, undoubtedly, have an advertising slowdown some time in the next few years.

Company (Ticker): Meredith Corporation (MDP)

Location: Des Moines, Iowa

Business Leader: William T. Kerr

Meredith at a glance: Meredith is a leading media and marketing company. Its publications, targeted principally at the home and family market, include 20 national consumer magazines, such as flagship *Better Homes and Gardens* and *Ladies' Home Journal*. In addition, the company publishes more than 300 book titles. Meredith's Broadcasting Group consists of six Fox-affiliated TV stations, five CBS stations, and one that carries NBC programming. Meredith has been creating online versions of several of its print publications and other initiatives to develop its online business.

1999 Financial Results

—Revenues: $1.0 billion

—Net Income: $89 million

I don't believe the business cycle has been repealed. And the key is to manage through that slowdown. That is one of the things I spend a lot of time thinking about. What we've tried to do, in broadcasting and publishing, is make our advertising business less dependent on simply selling time and selling space. We've gotten into custom publishing and integrated marketing arrangements, where we use our database and create specific products for companies and advertisers. They are wonderful businesses and it strengthens us for advertising downturns.

"The other thing we are trying to do is maintain our number-one position within the categories in which we compete. Typically, in a downturn, advertisers cut back on where they spend. Instead of going with the top five magazines in the women's service field, they may only go with two or three. We want to make certain we're in a leadership position. Our real challenge is to maintain the growth. We need to take the cash we generate and invest it intelligently. We need to continue the flow of ideas and continue to attract quality people. Those are the challenges I think about.

"In other words," Kerr concludes, "we need to keep improving on what we currently do well. That will help us not only maintain but grow the trust that our customers have placed in us."

CHUCK KNIGHT
Emerson Electric

"Keep it simple."

CHARLES F. KNIGHT TELLS A WONDERFUL STORY ABOUT WHY HE THINKS he ended up being named CEO of Emerson Electric, a position he has held now for 26 years.

It seems the board of the St. Louis–based company was not sure who should replace the outgoing CEO, so it decided to interview four or five prospective candidates to hear where they thought the then $900 million company should be heading.

"I think I went last, or next to last," Knight recalls. "And all the fellows who interviewed before me talked about the major overhauls they would undertake, once they were in charge. That, I learned later, made the board nervous.

"I had been consulting with the company for eight years, and served on two internal boards, so I had a pretty good handle on Emerson. And when the board members asked what I would do if they named me CEO, I said, 'I am not sure I would make any major changes. Things are going pretty well. We should build on our successes, instead of tearing things down.' "

Knight got the job.

This approach has served Emerson, and Knight, well during the 26 years he has held the top job. Knight has methodically built on the company's success and has done it without a misstep. Emerson, a $13.7 billion company in 1998,

CAREER
1974–PRESENT Chairman, Emerson Electric Co.
1973–PRESENT CEO
1962–1972 CEO, Lester B. Knight and Associates
1959–1961 Management Trainee, Goetzewerke A.G. (Germany)

EDUCATION
M.B.A., Cornell University, 1959
B.S., Cornell University, 1958

FAMILY
Married, Joanne Parrish; children: Lester, Anne, Steven, Jennifer

Born: Lake Forest, Illinois, January 20, 1936

> *"The guy with the most resources doesn't win. The guy who utilizes his resources best wins."*

routinely places in the top 10 in polls of most admired companies. And the company's 41 consecutive years of increased earnings and earnings per share and 42 consecutive years of increased dividends are unparalleled among U.S. industrial manufacturers.

Knight's secret? A methodical approach to everything the company does. Emerson calls it "the management process." It includes planning, continues through implementation, and extends to holding people accountable.

It also works.

"OUR MANAGEMENT PROCESS CONSISTS OF A NUMBER OF THINGS, AND you are going to think the first one is silly, but it's terribly important," Knight says. "You have to keep things simple.

"At Emerson, this means setting tough targets, developing plans and programs to achieve them, constantly following up to ensure that we reach our goals, and paying for results. This may sound easy, but we find that keeping it simple requires enormous discipline, because people often want to complicate things. We constantly focus on the importance of simple plans, simple communications, and a simple organization.

"So keeping it simple is step one in our management process, which really shouldn't be surprising. It goes right to management's job: to identify and implement successfully the investment opportunities required to achieve the growth and levels of profitability that it has targeted to create value. That's it. Nothing more. There are probably 150 other things we could talk about in terms of our employees and other constituencies. But, fundamentally, we feel we must have the capability to identify and implement investment opportunities that create value for our stockholders. And if we do that, we will create a winning environment.

"What flows out of this approach is a rigorous planning process, which is the second point in the management process. Planning is where we identify investments.

"I don't think any company is more focused on planning than we are," Knight says when asked why his company has been successful.

Can you plan too much? Absolutely, Knight says. But it is just like (department store magnate) John Wanamaker said about advertising. "I know 50% of my advertising doesn't work, I just don't know which half. If I did, I'd eliminate the half that doesn't."

Knight, too, would cut down on planning if he could only figure out what part of the process is ineffective.

"Now, there is no question that we plan too much. Anybody who takes a five-year plan and puts it in the wastebasket after one year and does it over has to be a little nuts. But I have never seen a plan that lasted longer than a couple of years.

"And I've never seen a plan that didn't get better in that process. So, it's a wonderful management training technique."

Knight, as chairman and CEO, is an integral part of the planning process at each division's planning conference.

"I'm there. The person running the business and his or her direct reports are there. And the people the business leader reports to are there. And since we are all present, decisions get made. And if something doesn't work, there's no audit of who's at fault because I'm as much at fault as anyone.

"Let me emphasize that point or you might not think it's important," he says. "We are a 'blameless company.' When we make decisions, there won't be any second-guessing if something doesn't work. When we make a mistake, we discuss it, but we don't point fingers."

What's Next?

Okay, once there is a plan, then what happens?

"From there, it's a question of implementation. This is where many companies fail. Often, management knows what needs to be done, but for some reason does not do it.

"We're good at implementation. When we set our sights and focus on some objective, we usually succeed as a result of the commitment of our people. They know we at corporate will do our part. And they respond."

This relationship, Knight says, is built on mutual trust.

"One of the few things we won't stand for is trying to hide a problem or failure, instead of acknowledging that something went wrong and fixing it. Remember our planning process? We all agreed on the decision. Nobody will be blamed if something isn't working. Instead, we step back and rethink the situation and start over.

"The fourth point of the management process is the creation of an action-oriented organization. We don't care about structure or form—we worry about getting things done. It is absolutely better to do something, recognizing that it may not be exactly right, than to do nothing.

"For example, we don't have an organizational chart for our corporate organization. Now, if you want an organizational chart of Ridge Tool [one of the company's divisions], we'll give you that. But we never wanted to build a corporate structure and all of the complexities and bureaucracy that come with it. We organize around issues and opportunities—not around an organization chart."

Knight cites three tests of how bureaucratic a company is. First is the size of the corporate staff; the minimum possible number is best.

"Our corporate staff has been the same size for the last 10 years, and that's for a reason. If we hire a staff member at corporate, then we need to create a comparable position at all 70 divisions. And then those people create work for others. The only result of bureaucracy is to slow everything down, or to stop progress. We can't have that.

"Second is whether communications are through strict channels as opposed to dealing with real issues. We communicate around plans and programs.

Company (Ticker): Emerson Electric Co. (EMR)

Location: St. Louis, Missouri

Leader: David N. Farr

Emerson at a glance: Emerson Electric is a global manufacturer of a wide range of electrical and electronic products, systems and solutions for commercial, industrial, and consumer markets. Major products include process control equipment and systems, motors, drives, alternators, sensors, compressors, and heating, ventilation, and air-conditioning equipment. Major brand names include Emerson motors and fans, Fisher controls, Rosemount instruments, and In-Sink-Erator waste disposers. Approximately 40% of sales come from outside the United States. Emerson completed 16 acquisitions in 1999 focusing on electronics, software applications, and communications.

1999 Financial Results

—Revenues: $14.3 billion

—Net Income: $1.3 billion

"And third is the level at which a company plans and controls profits. This may be the most important decision a company makes. We plan and control profits at the lowest possible level—our division presidents are responsible for identifying business investment opportunities and planning and controlling profits by product line."

The management process also includes, as a fifth point, the Emerson Best Cost Producer strategy, which the company adopted in the early 1980s to ensure consistently high levels of profitability in the face of challenges from low-cost offshore competitors. In brief, the Best Cost Producer strategy concentrates on issues such as reduction of material costs, knowledge of the competition, a focused manufacturing strategy that deals with process as well as product design, a commitment to capital expenditures, and intensive internal communications.

The sixth and final point of the management process requires the creation of an environment where people can and do make a difference. This requires leadership on the part of managers, Knight says.

"Leaders need to have a sense of urgency, and the ability to manage priorities," he says. "There must be a commitment to success and to high standards without compromise. A winning environment also requires attention to detail. In my experience, almost all bad decisions result from not understanding the details.

"And a key part of leadership, of course, is dealing with employees. You have to be tough but fair in dealing with people. I've been challenged many times for using the word 'tough.' People sometimes think you are talking about being unjust, but that's not it at all.

"James W. Michaels, the longtime editor of *Forbes*, understood this and, in fact, wrote about it in the magazine's coverage of Emerson in 1978. He cited the Webster's dictionary definition of 'tough' as 'having the quality of being strong or firm. . . .'

"Toughness—strong, firm—is what it takes to make a company run efficiently, to make capital productive, jobs steady and remunerative, and to produce quality products at a low cost for the benefit of society,' Michaels wrote in *Forbes*. 'Being tough does not imply being heartless or irresponsible. . . . But it does mean being supremely rational. . . .' "

Holding people accountable, Knight says, "helps them grow. People want to know if they haven't done a good job and how they can do better. It helps them to be measured against appropriate norms or standards. Our responsibility is to encourage and drive them to achieve, and help them where they fall short, so they can ultimately succeed. That kind of toughness is very important to our organization's morale and ultimately to our performance."

Finally, Knight says, a good environment is one in which people have fun. "I've enjoyed every division planning conference over the past 26 years. These sessions take about 60% of my time. Some would view them as tiring, but I get reenergized. There is no better experience than working with people who care about the business, and who want to make a difference. There's no question about it, people like to be part of a winning team."

DENNIS KOZLOWSKI
Tyco International

"There is a lot one person can do."

"MR. DEAL-A-MONTH," THAT'S HOW *BUSINESS WEEK* DESCRIBED L. DEN-nis Kozlowski's aggressive growth strategy in a profile of the man who heads the largest company you may never have heard of.

While the nickname is hyperbolic, it does make the point. Kozlowski has, indeed, expanded the company rapidly through acquisitions. Tyco International Ltd. is now a diversified company that has become the world's largest manufacturer and installer of fire protection systems; the largest provider of electronic security services in North America (it owns ADT) and the United Kingdom, and has strong leadership positions in disposable medical products (U.S. Surgical), packaging materials, flow control products, electrical and electronic components, and underwater telecommunications systems. The company operates in more than 75 countries and had revenues of $13.4 billion in 1998.

A key reason for this success, Kozlowski believes, is the company's "pay-for-performance" compensation system, which promotes individual goal setting that can also motivate an entire team to perform better. "Our management-incentive program works because it is driven by one overriding credo: The financial interest of our managers, who have unusual autonomy, and of our shareholders is identical." The more managers earn for shareholders, the more they earn for themselves.

"Incentive compensation must, however, be directly linked to each business

CAREER
1993–PRESENT Chairman, Tyco
  International Ltd.
1992–PRESENT CEO
1990–1992 President and COO
1985–1989 President and CEO, Grinnell Corp.
1980–1985 CEO, Ludlow Corp. (subsidiary of
  Tyco International)
1976–1980 Vice President, Finance, Grinnell
  Fire Protection Systems

EDUCATION
B.S., Seton Hall University, 1968

Born: Irvington, New Jersey, November 16, 1946

unit's performance rather than overall corporate results," Kozlowski says, "so that an individual can receive immediate feedback for his actions."

THE POWER OF THE INDIVIDUAL IS AN IDEA THAT COMES UP FREQUENTLY in conversations with Dennis Kozlowski.

You hear it when he talks about the traits that will be required for the next generation of leaders.

> *"I'm not looking over our employees' shoulders and neither is anyone else. We find the best people in the world, and pretty much leave them alone."*

"I think versatility will be important. But I also think somebody who has grown up in a few different cultures, who might have lived in Asia or Europe, or Latin America—someone who has a view of the planet that's not parochial—is going to be important."

You also see it in the way he manages.

"I really believe in finding the best people in the world to run our businesses. We are very decentralized and leave them alone. Of course we make sure there can be no big surprises. We are a public company after all. But we really believe in putting our trust in the people we're hiring and helping them through the difficult times, and rewarding them in good times."

And those rewards are based—not surprisingly—on individual performance.

"We tell everyone who joins us, or who comes to us through an acquisition, that this is a capitalistic system, and if they are actively involved in creating value in the company, they will share significantly in that value. There is no cap placed upon the value that they themselves can realize. There's no upward limit on our incentive programs.

"And we also tell them that with the exception of me, and a couple of people who work directly with me, there's no one whose compensation is tied to Tyco's overall performance. If you're working in the medical business for us, or in the fire and smoke control area, you are only tied to the performance of what you can control yourself.

"Now, most employees are also shareholders of the company. We've found various ways to get them shares, but that would be less than 10% of their compensation. Ninety percent of it specifically comes from what they themselves have responsibility, authority, and control over."

Kozlowski has thought for some time that this is the best way to manage and motivate people.

"In college, I read Ayn Rand's *The Fountainhead* and *Atlas Shrugged* and then I read them again in my late twenties. Those books had an influence on me. They really focus on the contribution that the individual can make. Individuals do make a difference."

Because they can, and do, Kozlowski doesn't see any need for a huge centralized management staff to watch over his thousands of employees.

"We only have about 50 people at headquarters, and about 40 of them handle taxes and all the compliance things you have to do when you are a public corporation. There's about 10 of us who are involved in overseeing the operation from a corporate standpoint, doing strategy and making acquisitions."

And Kozlowski is ruthless about the discipline he brings to doing those acquisitions.

"We believe an acquisition must be immediately acretive [add to earnings]. Therefore, costs have to be taken out; synergies have to be realized quickly. It must be long-term and sustainable to us, and it must be more valuable than buying back our own stock. We use that as sort of a sanity test, to make certain we're doing the right thing.

"When we identify a company and we negotiate a deal, we begin the integration process almost immediately. If you wait beyond the initial point, you lose some of your discipline, and lose earnings that could be realized through the integration."

"Our Biggest Challenge"

Not surprisingly, Kozlowski thinks "maintaining our very disciplined acquisition strategy, only doing acretive deals, and staying focused," are the biggest challenges Tyco faces.

"Maintaining our low-cost producer position, which we have in most of the products we manufacture and the services we provide, is also important. And we want to maintain our significant market share within the businesses."

That is especially important in light of a decision that Kozlowski made in the early 1990s, a decision that was to allow Tyco to put together its long string of successes.

"When I became CEO [in 1992], I made a commitment to really change the nature of the company. Back then we were about 85% in what I would call cyclical businesses, today it's the complete reverse. About 15% of our revenues come from cyclical business and 85% of our revenues are recurring. Recurring revenues come from people who pay their ADT security charge each month or from the companies who pay us to maintain their underseas fiberoptic cables. So we have a very large service component. We can earn more money servicing a product than from making the product. In general, that's just more profitable for us than trying to get an extra 2% or 3% of market share.

"Back in 1992, I really wanted to get out of the cyclical businesses and get more into service and long-term sustaining businesses. The start was we bought the Kendall Companies, which made disposable medical products, and had revenues of about $1 billion a year. We were doing $100 million of disposable medical products in Tyco at the time we acquired Kendall. The acquisition gave us the platform to buy other disposable medical businesses. Today they account for more than $5 billion of our revenues and we have some of our best margins in the business.

"I remember clearly why I wanted to change our business. In 1991 and '92, we were feeling the after-effects of the construction recession that had hit the English-speaking world, and yet, our small medical business was continuing to grow nicely. And I thought, being a new CEO, this would be an ideal time just to shift the emphasis.

"I was sitting in my office and a light-bulb went off. I was thinking about our disposable medical business, and that same day, Kendall happened to announce its earnings. Kendall wasn't on our radar screens at that time, but I researched it and called up the leveraged-buyout firm, Clayton, Dubiler and Rice, who owned it, introduced myself and said, 'You probably don't know Tyco, or you have no idea why I'm interested in this. However, I really would like to sit down and talk to you about Kendall.' And they invited me to New York, we negotiated a deal, and the rest is history."

And Kozlowski was well on his way to restructuring the company, a decision that is ultimately responsible for Tyco's long string of successes.

One individual can make a difference.

Company (Ticker): Tyco International Ltd. (TYC)

Location: Hamilton, Bermuda

Leader: L. Dennis Kozlowski

Tyco at a glance: Tyco is a market-leading, diversified industrial and health care products company. Among other things, it is the world leader in security and fire protection systems. Its Electrical and Electronic Components group makes undersea fiberoptic cable and complex printed circuit boards, and includes its 1999 AMP acquisition. Its Health Care and Specialty Products group makes wound care, adult incontinent, adhesive, and plastic film products. Tyco's United States Surgical subsidiary makes sutures, surgical staplers, and laparoscopy devices. Its Flow Control Products group makes pipe, pipe fittings, valves, steel tubing, and other equipment for commercial and industrial applications.

1999 Financial Results
—Revenues: $22.4 billion
—Net Income: $985 million

RALPH LARSEN
Johnson & Johnson

"Edicts don't work."

"WE DON'T VIEW OURSELVES AS ONE $20 BILLION HEALTH CARE COM-
pany. We see ourselves as 170 small ones."

This counterintuitive thumbnail description of Johnson & Johnson, given by its chairman and CEO, goes a long way toward explaining the company's remarkable growth. While Johnson & Johnson is known for its consumer brands—Band-Aids, baby powder, shampoos, and Tylenol—it has grown into a true health care giant. In fact, consumer products now represent less than a third of total revenue. The company has become one of the largest manufacturers of medical devices—everything from artificial hips and knees to products for neural surgery—and is also one of the world's largest pharmaceutical companies.

To make sure its growth continues, every unit is allowed to be as autonomous as possible. But then this approach is consistent with how the company was created. As far back as the 1930s, longtime chairman Robert Wood Johnson promoted the idea of decentralization and pushing authority to the lowest levels. At those lower levels the question is, "How can we leverage what we have." As Ralph S. Larsen puts it: "We don't look at ourselves as being in the product business. We are in the knowledge business."

To make sure that the boss is up to

CAREER

1989–PRESENT Chairman and CEO, Johnson
   & Johnson
1986–1989 Vice Chairman
1985–1986 Company Group Chairman
1983–1985 President, Chicopee Division
1981–1983 President, Becton Dickenson
   Consumer Products
1977–1981 Vice President, McNeil Consumer
   Products Division of Johnson & Johnson
1962–1977 Staff and management positions,
   Johnson & Johnson

EDUCATION
B.B.A., Hofstra University, 1962

FAMILY
Married, Dorothy M. Zeitfuss; children: Karen,
   Kristen, Garret

Born: Brooklyn, New York, November 19, 1938

date on everything in the company's arsenal, Larsen books a hotel room in New York for days on end each year and reads the business plans of every single unit, writing down suggestions, questions, and flagging potential problems.

TO THE NEWLY NAMED CHAIRMAN AND CEO OF JOHNSON & JOHNSON the problem was obvious.

"We were entering a period [starting in 1989, when Larsen was named to the top jobs] where it was clear that the price increases we had been getting in our business were not sustainable. And it was also clear that you could not continue to see this tremendous rise in health care costs, both on an absolute basis and as a percent of GDP, continue forever. In the United States health care was up to 12% or 13% of GDP. In the United Kingdom it was 6% or 7%

"By the time any decision reaches this office, there are no longer 'right' and 'wrong' answers. There are just shades of gray."

and climbing, and we had been able to continually increase prices to cover the inflation rate. There appeared to be no limit to what you could do.

"This kind of environment can hide a lot of sins and make you sloppy. I was concerned that we were not anywhere near as competitive as we needed to be. And I was also convinced that we needed to take huge chunks of costs out of this business in order to live in the coming economic world, a world in which it would be extremely difficult—if not impossible—to get price increases."

The new world Larsen was envisioning would represent a totally new environment for Johnson & Johnson, a company that had never faced a serious austerity program before. And one that was used to good news not bad.

"Everybody at the company had read these wonderful stories about us, how we were one of the 10 most admired companies. The company got very good press, much of which was deserved, some of which was not. But it led, I felt, to an unhealthy sense of well-being in the company. It's very tough to get people to change when they think everything is wonderful.

"We finally came up with a process to fix that. We decided to periodically perform a case study on the company. We called the first one *Setting the Competitive Standard*. In it we talked about all the stupid things we had done, the mistakes we had made, how our costs were out of line. For example, our SG&A [selling and general administrative expenses] was

40%, where our competitors were often in the low 30s. The list went on and on. This experience dramatized the fact that all was not as good as it appeared. It was an important process, because people left feeling very sober.

"But at the same time it was a tremendous learning experience. It began to sensitize senior management to the fact that we were not as good as we thought we were, and we needed to change this company."

Not surprisingly, though, some of Johnson & Johnson's employees and some of its senior executives held management responsible for creating the bad news.

"Some of the blame was fair, we had let things go on too long," Larsen says. "But we also turned it around and asked employees and managers 'What are *you* going to do about it?' "

It was important for everyone to be involved in deciding the company's future direction, Larsen explains.

"Edicts don't work well inside Johnson & Johnson. You can pass edicts until you're blue in the face. You can get people to do optically what you want them to do, but if their hearts aren't in it . . .

"We've got this tremendous history of decentralization. People are very independent around here. You have to convince them of the rightness of your cause, otherwise not much of substance happens."

To make sure that did not happen, Larsen convened a second case study called *Creating Your Future*. "Essentially, we took the employee feedback from the first conference, repackaged it, and said, 'Okay, this is what you told us was wrong. Now you design the Johnson & Johnson of the year 2005. You tell us how to solve these problems.'

"Ironically, we were greatly helped during this period because this was when the Clinton Health Care Reforms were being debated," Larsen continues. "And that gave us the crisis we needed to get people's attention. In a way, that was the most wonderful thing that had ever happened to Johnson & Johnson because it focused our attention on this issue of spiraling health care costs. It got us engaged, on a worldwide basis, in trying to design rational health care systems. Instead of being defensive, we began thinking about how we could be a productive part of the solution.

"This unleashed an enormous amount of energy within the corporation and led to a major restructuring. I didn't do that. Our people did it. Not simply by working harder or longer but by challenging virtually everything we did."

Larsen provides a couple of examples.

"We had more than 20 domestic companies, all of which had their own payroll departments issuing their own checks. I think we had more than 100 people in that function. And as our people began looking at costs, they asked: 'Why are we doing this?' With information technology we knew we could do it all in one place. We could print checks with different company names, do it all in one center, and save a lot of money.

"And we had thousands of people filling out time sheets every day. Thousands of pieces of paper had to be processed. Somebody said, 'Why do we need time sheets? Most people come to work every day and most employees come to work on time. And if they're going to take vacation or work overtime, we could have an 800 number. They could just call in and register the exception.' Then somebody else said, 'How can you be sure? People will cheat.'

"We said, people aren't going to cheat, because if you cheat you get fired. So, how many people are going to cheat? The net result is that we reduced the number of people there by 60%. Very few people are filling out payroll notices, or time sheets, anymore. We largely eliminated the function."

Once pointed in the right direction, and emboldened with some quick victories, employees discovered potential efficiencies everywhere.

"We found that every division was buying their own chemicals. I bet we had 20 divisions or more buying from firms like Dow or FMC. So we set up commodity buying groups where we had a small team buying chemicals, and we negotiated contract prices for the entire corporation. Really simple stuff."

All this duplication stemmed from Johnson & Johnson's decentralized approach. That independence let divisions set up their own payroll and purchasing departments.

That same independence let them solve the problem once Larsen and his team flagged the issue for them.

Is It in Keeping with the Credo?

Intriguingly, the approach employees took to making Johnson & Johnson more competitive was consistent with the company's famous Credo, a code of ethics that provides a blueprint of how the company should be run.

Larsen was not surprised that was the case.

"The Credo underpins everything we do. And in this complicated world, if there's any guiding principle that allows Johnson & Johnson to run on a decentralized basis, it is the Credo. We can operate 170 or 180 different divisions because we have the glue of the Credo to hold them together.

"If you don't think the Credo is important, or you don't believe in its values, you are not going to last at Johnson & Johnson. The organization will reject you, because sooner or later you will do something that will bring harm to the company. The organization will expel you, just like the body expels foreign organisms.

"For us, the Credo is the North Star. We'll often sit around and try to come up with a course of action and somebody will say, 'How do you square that with the Credo?'"

And so it was with the streamlining of Johnson & Johnson. "The Credo says that the company's first responsibility is to our customers and so we said to ourselves that we wanted to be the best and the most competitive broadly based health care company in the world. There was a lot of pressure for us to get into genetic products, to have an 'okay' product line and different quality levels. We sorted through all that and said, 'No, we want to produce products of the highest quality. We want to be the best, most competitive health care company in the world.'

"Each of these words had meaning. For example, when we said, 'most competitive,' people said, 'What do you mean? Does that mean ruthless? Does that mean that we're going to cut the quality?' And we said, 'No, when we say most competitive, we are talking about competing in the Olympic sense. That we want to be the best trained and capable of the best execution.'

"We wanted to be not only the best, we wanted to be the most competitive. We also wanted to be broadly based. And many people were arguing, and the investment analyst community was suggesting, that we should be solely a pharmaceutical company. That's where the high margins are. We should keep that, and get rid of those other businesses. And we said, 'No, we want to be broadly based. We're not smart enough to pick where health care is going.'"

With the direction set, Johnson & Johnson employees set off with a vengeance in making the company more efficient. Over the last five years the company has reduced annual operating costs by $2 billion.

Surprisingly, Johnson & Johnson employees did not get a bonus that was tied directly to all those cost-cutting measures.

Company (Ticker): Johnson & Johnson (JNJ)
Location: New Brunswick, New Jersey
Leader: Ralph S. Larsen
Johnson & Johnson at a glance:
Johnson & Johnson is one of the world's largest and most diversified health care companies. The company operates in three segments: consumer products (with brands such as Tylenol and Motrin analgesics, Reach toothbrushes, Band-Aid bandages), professional products (AcuVue contact lenses, surgical instruments, joint replacements, diagnostics), and pharmaceuticals (including Risperdal, an antipsychotic, and Sporanox, a treatment for fungal infections, and Ortho-Novum oral contraceptives).
1999 Financial Results
—Revenues: $27.4 billion
—Net Income: $4.1 billion

"We do not have a formula-driven compensation program, which probably makes us different than most companies," Larsen concedes. "We've looked at every plan under the sun about how to tie specific objectives to bonuses, but I have a natural aversion to that, given our lines of businesses. We're in the health care business; the products that we make are life-saving products. They are not products that you can cut corners on, in order to reduce costs and gain a bigger market share. So, we pay people based on their long-term contribution to the business. It's highly subjective. We recognize that there's a lot of judgment that goes into it.

"We are not formula-driven. And we often put our very best people into our most troubled businesses. For example, we were doing nothing in endo-surgery. U.S. Surgical had really pioneered that business; we were hopelessly outclassed and getting nowhere fast. I think we had a 10% market share.

"We turned to one of our talented executives, someone who had a good track record, and asked if he would take on the challenge. He said he would, and he put together a terrific team.

"We asked him, 'How long will it take us to become a major player in this business? We want market leadership.'

"He said, 'I think we can do it in five years.'

"And then we talked about compensation. We thought about tying the team's bonus to making some tightly figured number each year. The flip side, of course, is that they would be penalized if they didn't 'make that number.' I just don't think that's how you bring out the best in people. Obviously targets have their place, but we have people around here who are highly motivated, who will break their backs to do a great job, and who generally set tougher goals for themselves than we would ever set for them. And to me it's demeaning and wrong to set tightly crafted financial objectives, to squeeze people like lemons. Besides, it turns into a game, where people then want to keep the goal lower rather than higher.

"We pay well, and we pay our good people very well. To me compensation is the least expensive thing we have for good people. And it is the most expensive thing we have for mediocre people.

"Oh, about our endo-surgery team. They delivered in four years. The first couple were pretty bleak—and they would have been penalized if we had a rigid bonus system. But they got the job done."

And over the past 10 years, so has Larsen.

KEN LAY

Enron

The $30 billion corner store

Pop quiz: Name America's most innovative company.

The executives running Fortune 500 companies are asked to do just that each year, and the number-one answer three years running surprised a lot of people (but not their peers). The majority voted for Enron.

Enron? The Enron that is one of the world's largest integrated natural gas and electric companies? That Enron?

Yes.

By nominating Enron, the heads of the Fortune 500 companies were publicly recognizing the job that Kenneth L. Lay has done in taking his company into new countries, new businesses, and in executing new business strategies.

If there is one thing that those moves have in common it is that they each involve a new way of thinking about the energy business. For example, Lay has constantly pushed for deregulation, an idea frequently opposed by other executives who run utility companies. They fear that their firms will not be able to compete in a free marketplace. Lay is

CAREER
1986–PRESENT Chairman and CEO, Enron Corporation
1984–1985 Chairman and CEO, Houston Natural Gas
1981–1984 President and COO, Transco Energy
1979–1981 President, Continental Resources
1971–1979 Executive Vice President
1976–1979 President, Florida Gas Transmission Co.
1974–1976 Senior Vice President
1972–1974 Deputy Undersecretary for Energy, U.S. Department of the Interior
1971–1972 Technical Assistant to Commissioner, Federal Energy and Regulatory Commission (FERC)
1968–1971 U.S. Naval Officer and Assistant Professor of Economics, George Washington University
1965–1968 Economist, Exxon Corp.

EDUCATION
Ph.D., University of Houston, 1970
M.A., University of Missouri, 1965
B.A., University of Missouri, 1964

FAMILY
Married, Linda Ann Phillips; children: Robyn, Mark, Todd, Elizabeth, Robert

Born: Tyrone, Missouri, April 15, 1942

"Driving tractors during the summer while I was growing up gave me a lot of time to think about what I wanted to do with my life, and I decided pretty early on that I didn't want to be a farmer."

convinced his company will do better without regulatory shackles.

To prove the point he has added a financing component to the business to help other energy companies build and maintain facilities. The division—Enron Capital & Trade Resources—provides risk-management, long-term contract financing, and other financial services to gas and electric companies in the United States and around the world.

In addition, Lay has broken up the company's profit centers into smaller units in an attempt to give more managers—both on the regulated side of the company, as well as the nonregulated—a chance at being entrepreneurial. Their compensation packages are tied directly to how well their units do.

All these changes are designed to make Enron feel—and operate—like a corner store, instead of a $30 billion energy company.

EARLY EXPERIENCES—ONE POSITIVE, ONE NEGATIVE—HAD A HUGE EFFECT on the way Ken Lay manages today.

What he remembers most fondly about one of his earliest jobs, a period spent as an executive of Florida Gas, was how cozy the company was. All told, there were approximately 1,000 people at the oil and gas company and they all worked in small groups. The overall feeling, Lay says, was that you were working down at the local store on Main Street, rather than inside a big, faceless firm where no one knew your name or what you did.

Lay liked that small-company feeling. What he did not like was the boss's choice of priorities. Lay gives an example.

"Let's say we were trying to fill a position and we got it down to two candidates. The boss would pick the more inexpensive one, if he thought that guy could do the job, even though the other candidate might be two or three times as good. I always promised myself, if I ever became a CEO, I'd try to get a game breaker in every key position. I'm not saying you can always do that, but that's what I've tried to do at Enron.

"When you have a key position come open, you want to get the very best person you can get to fill it. If you do, odds are all kinds of good things will start happening underneath them. And if you don't, invariably you pay a big price for it."

And when Lay sets out to hire that top performer, odds are that person is going to end up running a unit that is as small, and as entrepreneurial, as possible.

"Enron is organized into a number of different companies and businesses," he explains. "And within those businesses we do everything we can to keep the organization flat, and make sure that management has as much contact with employees as possible. In addition, we delegate authority as far down the ranks as possible.

"I think, as a management team, all of us have put a lot of effort into trying to create a working environment where our employees feel—just like I did when I was at Florida Gas—that they are part of a small company, or operating division, instead of a very large bureaucratic company. You can just sense that in the energy level when you come into the building. You can see it at the kickoff rally for our United Way campaign, or in the people who show up to support the company basketball team, or in the number of people who show up for any of the community activities we are involved in.

"To make sure that feeling stays in place," Lay says, "we put a lot of emphasis on our value system and on the importance of the individual. We work hard to create an environment that is conducive to individuals communicating, both within their peer groups and up and down the organization. What we are trying to do is create an environment that will, as I like to put it, really allow our employees to realize their God-given potential. We make sure that Enron provides them with training, encouragement, and incentives that will permit that.

"I'm sure a lot of that comes from my basic value system, but it also comes from my early experiences. I had a boss one time, I'm not going to tell you where it was, who was convinced that there were only six or eight people in the entire company that were indispensable, and everybody else was interchangeable. We've all known organizations where the boss thinks that way.

"I think quite the opposite is true. I think *everybody* in the organization can make a contribution. And the more you can create an environment where everybody believes that, the more impact you're going to have on the overall performance of the company.

"The person at the lowest level of the company, all the way up to the highest level, can make a difference. And we do our very best to try to give them an environment where they can do that."

Putting the Words into Action

To give employees—and the company—more opportunities, Lay has aggressively moved Enron into nonregulated businesses. Melding regulated and nonregulated businesses is never easy. People on the regulated side can find it hard to adjust to businesses where decisions are made faster, and people placed in a regulated environment for the first time can find it frustrating.

Still, Lay says, the attempt to integrate the two different parts of the business "has been good on both sides. An awful lot of people haven't made the transition. We might as well start with that fact. There are a lot of people that could not, at least on the commercial side, make the transition from a regulated business to more of a market-driven, risk-taking environment. But the real positive has been that increasingly we've got the traders and the transaction people looking at all of our assets and trying to figure out how we can maximize their value. And now the operating people are increasingly looking at what the traders are doing and trying to find ways to mitigate risk in our regulated businesses.

"Over time those two have come closer and closer together. We're not totally there yet, but we are getting there."

One of the ways to achieve that integration is by shifting people from one side of the business to the other, Lay says.

"We've moved people around a lot, including internationally. The person heading up our European operation right now, not too many years ago, was in the Florida Gas Transmission Company, which is a regulated pipeline. He now heads up all of Enron Europe, which is one of our major profit centers, and is only now just beginning to be deregulated and become competitive.

"I think one of the secrets to our success has been creating big pockets of

Company (Ticker): Enron Corporation (ENE)

Location: Houston, Texas

Leader: Kenneth L. Lay

Enron at a glance: Enron, the largest buyer and seller of natural gas and electricity in the United States, also builds and manages energy facilities worldwide. The company produces and distributes energy products and commodities, and provides risk management, construction, engineering consulting services, and financial services to customers around the world. Although most of its revenues come from domestic gas operations and power services, Enron focuses aggressively on emerging markets with power plant and pipeline projects in Bolivia, Brazil, China, and India. It also operates a natural gas pipeline in Argentina, markets gas in Europe, and has oil and gas exploration and production units. The company has also entered the water business through a major acquisition in the United Kingdom. Enron is selling off Portland General Electric to raise capital to invest in faster-growing enterprises. Enron Broadband Services is also building a national fiber-optic, Internet protocol-based network, as well as operating a market for the trading of communications bandwidth.

1999 Financial Results

—Revenues: $40.1 billion

—Net Income: $893 million

entrepreneurship throughout the company. That is, in large part, the result of the kinds of people we recruit. We start off recruiting very smart, very results-oriented, very creative, high-performance people. And then we create an incentive system that rewards performance, one that lets them share in the company's success."

This, Lay says, is simply the right way to run a business, any business, regulated or not.

"If you don't have the right environment, where you don't have consistency, where you don't have values, then people get pretty turned off and don't put out the work product."

The responsibility for ensuring that the right environment is created falls squarely on the shoulders of the person in charge, Lay says.

"Your job as chief executive is to provide leadership, and part of that is having a, hopefully, compelling vision, one that will really energize everybody."

This responsibility, says Lay, continues right down the line.

"I will always look for leadership over management skills in my senior people. You've got to have some of both, but I want people who really know where they want to lead an organization and make their vision sufficiently compelling to get everybody else excited about it.

"After that, you want your top managers to have strong 'strategic thinking skills and stamina,'" Lay says. But creating the right environment is far and away the most important trait.

"What we are trying to do is create an environment where we stimulate people to act like entrepreneurs, even inside a $30 billion company," he says. "It's just a matter of taking a very large organization and chopping it up into different chunks and making sure, within those individual pieces, each team has everything they need to act like—and perform like—a small company."

In other words, you can take one of the largest companies there is and have it act like the corner store.

SHELLY LAZARUS
Ogilvy & Mather

360-degree branding

THE EXACT NUMBERS VARY, BUT IT IS NOT HARD TO BELIEVE THAT THE average American is exposed to hundreds of commercial messages every day. There are, of course, the spots on radio and television. But that's just the beginning. There are the billboards we pass on the way to work, the ads in the newspapers and magazines we read, the corporate logos imprinted on the clothing our friends and colleagues wear: even the office equipment we use. Everywhere we turn there is another bit of advertising.

It is not surprising then that all those commercial messages start to blur, and when asked, we are hard-pressed to recall a fraction of the ones we have seen even in the past 24 hours.

This is not good news, if you are in the advertising business where clients pay you to make a *lasting* impression.

While some firms are determined to "break through the clutter" by screaming louder at us, others use humor, or offbeat approaches, to get our attention.

Shelly Lazarus has a different idea. She starts with the premise that a client does, indeed, emit a constant stream of messages about its products. She is not just referring to its advertisements, but everything from the company's packaging and brochures to its sales materials and order forms. If you are going to send out all these messages, she says, they all should work together whether at home or globally. That way when a potential

CAREER

1997–PRESENT Chairman and CEO, Ogilvy & Mather Worldwide

1995–1996 President and COO

1994–1995 President, Ogilvy & Mather North America

1991–1994 President, Ogilvy & Mather New York

1989–1991 President, Ogilvy & Mather Direct U.S.

EDUCATION

M.B.A., Columbia University, 1970

B.A., Smith College, 1968

FAMILY

Married, George Lazarus; three children

Born: Brooklyn, New York, September 1, 1947

customer receives one impression, it reinforces all the other ones that came before.

With an international roster of clients that includes such leading companies as American Express, Ford, IBM, and Unilever, it is clear that Lazarus's approach has made an impression with clients.

IT IS EASY TO IMAGINE THE ENGINEERS AT THE FORD MOTOR CO. starting the meeting with a hint of skepticism. What was *an advertising person*—a woman at that—going to explain to them about the process of running an automotive company better?

"The real trick to marketing is finding a core idea which the world can use. You find the universal, and then you make it the core of what you do."

To her credit, Shelly Lazarus knew her audience.

"One of the first things I said to them was, I'm relatively new to the car category, but here's something I don't understand. If a Ford is different from a Jaguar, is different from a Mazda, is different from a Buick and a Volkswagen, why do all the showrooms look the same?"

There was silence as the group came to the same conclusion simultaneously. All dealerships do, in fact, look the same.

Lazarus then drove the point home.

"You have an audience that's so interested in what you are selling that they have actually driven to your place of business to give you an hour of their precious time to check out what your product is all about. And what do they see once they get there? These faceless showrooms.

"Now, contrast that with Nike Town, which is a store but is really a living brand filled with interactive experiences. Why can't you do a Nike Town for Ford?"

You can, of course. And calling for that kind of all-encompassing brand experience is at the center of Ogilvy's mission in planning and executing Ford's advertising strategy.

"On-brand" showrooms are only one example of what Lazarus calls "360-degree branding," which is not just about advertising. It is about making a significant impression every time a company comes in contact—directly or indirectly—with a customer.

"The process we have gone through with Ford is simple. We go through every point of contact, study it, and ask, 'Is this "Ford"?' And in most instances it's not, just because no one ever asked the question before. Here's one example. We're doing some really interesting work for them right now on their web site. The site was composed of all these disparate images."

That was not surprising. It is hard to find a corporate web site that has the same look and feel as the rest of the company's marketing materials. That, Lazarus argues, is a waste of resources.

"It goes back to 360-degree branding," she says. "If you believe every point of contact should reflect the brand, it seems to me we have to be able to do that on the Internet as well.

"Early on we had some people here at Ogilvy who were very interested in interactive. This was 10 years ago when no one was even talking about it. And in the last 12 months interactive has just taken off. It has become a very significant part of our business.

"Because it was a new technology, a lot of our clients initially went to shops that consisted of four guys with earrings. They went there because they thought these guys knew how to create web sites with all these spinning images. But the clients are now realizing that that's not really what it's all about. They now know the web site must be informed by all the insight they have into their customers and the insights they have into their brand. So a lot of them are coming back to us, as the brand keeper for them. I expect this part of our business to grow enormously, although I don't think it's going to stop the growth of the other disciplines we have. I think all of our marketing tools are going to play a role, it's just that the communications portfolio that we construct for any one client going forward is going to be so much more interesting, richer, or more varied."

Here's What the Brand Represents

But whether it is web sites, showrooms, brochures, the price sticker on the car, or television commercials, the objective is always the same: to make sure the client is clearly communicating what their brand is and what it stands for.

Lazarus adds another example to illustrate what she means.

"One of our most senior creatives on the IBM account has been working with the client to bring the brand mind-set to places that fall between the classic 'marketing communication cracks.' One of his projects for six months was to be the on-site brand consultant to the team developing IBM's new exhibit at Disney World's Epcot Center.

"Now he doesn't know anything about theme park design or interactive installations. But he does know the brand—and by this I do not mean that he just approves the blue color scheme or typeface.

"He worked intensively with the architects and the designers. His job was to question each decision, the layout, the ergonomics, the language, the signage, the total experience. His job was to make sure that everything said 'IBM brand,' said 'friendly,' said 'accessible,' that it offered a smile. In short it all had to make a visitor feel good about IBM."

Lazarus returns to Ford to further elaborate on the power of brands.

"I love talking about brands to people who don't ever think about them. Because as soon as you talk to them about it, they're right with you because they're consumers at heart. They understand how these things work if you actually take a moment to explain it to them."

And because they understand, the working relationship between Ogilvy and Ford has grown even closer.

"Some of our guys have been invited to join the product development groups. This has happened because management beyond marketing is saying, 'Okay, I get it.' The engineer says, 'Why doesn't someone who understands the brand stay with me when I'm first thinking about designing products? If they did, I'd design products that actually represent the Ford brand.' As opposed to designing a product—and this is the way it has traditionally happened—and then asking what mark we should put on it? Jaguar? Mazda? Mercury? Lincoln? Ford?

"It's very interesting for us, because our world is becoming much larger."

And intriguingly, 360-degree branding gives Ogilvy's clients a way to break through all the commercial message clutter that is out there. When you live in a world where company names or mottos can be found on fresh fruit, where banner ads jump out of every web site, and where you would be pressed to spend an hour of your day without seeing a commercial impression of some kind, making your message stand out becomes even more important.

This is something that Lazarus keeps uppermost in her mind.

"About a year ago, we asked our managers at Ogilvy to track and show us what percent of a client's total budget they're working with. I'm no longer interested just in how fast the advertising budget is growing, because I think that's a short-term objective. I'm more interested in what they're doing that integrates everything where the brand touches the consumer. Asking this question has changed our focus and attention."

Will These People Fit?

Ogilvy, like most advertising agencies—indeed, like most companies in general—has a particular way of doing things. How does Lazarus maximize the chance that people who join her firm will fit into the culture?

"It's so much in the fingertips," she says. "I don't know that there are any particular questions we ask, but I do know that you can sense the fit right away. I have spoken to any number of people who I would deem brilliant and provocative. These are people I'd like to have dinner with who I wouldn't necessarily bring into Ogilvy because of my sense that they wouldn't thrive within our culture."

What is that culture like?

"Like many great companies, ours is a very value-driven culture. And when I hear people talk disparagingly, even if they're humorous about people they work with or about their clients, I know that person won't do well here. We have such inherent respect for each other and for our clients. It might work elsewhere—in fact, there are agencies that pride themselves on that attitude—but it just doesn't work here.

"This is a nonpolitical culture, a place that hates politicians, hates politics. You don't play people against each other. You just don't do that here. It's an organization that holds its people accountable. We have a very hard time keeping people here who are not contributing. Not because of senior management holding people's feet to the fire, but because the people around them actually resent it and they resent it vocally.

"Sometimes you might want to keep somebody because you see that a year from now they'll really be in a position to make a contribution, but it's hard in this culture to do that, because everyone holds each other accountable."

If it sounds as if Lazarus spends a lot of time paying attention to the corporate culture, it is because she does. She has decided the culture creates an environment that allows employees to do their best work. She says you can trace the origins of this nurturing culture back to the founding of the agency.

"We've just had our 50th anniversary, so I have been thinking about David Ogilvy a lot. His genius was taking a very strong point of view about how to run an organization and from that point of view developing a set of principles—such as the amazing amount of intellectual rigor that is required—that have actually lived on in our people."

Ogilvy wasn't Lazarus's mentor. By the time she joined the firm, the advertising legend was only working about three months a year, about three weeks at a time. But it is clear that he did have a lasting influence on her.

"I did get to know David because he's very democratic in the sense that he had no idea what titles or positions anyone ever had in the agency. I think he made it a point *not* to know. And he would just find people who interested him. I got to meet him because one of the times he came back, I was nine months' pregnant. And he had never seen anybody nine months' pregnant working in his agency. So every afternoon at six o'clock I would look up from my desk and there was David standing in the doorway. He would just stand there and stare and when I looked up he'd ask, 'Is everything all right?' He'd come in and we would just talk. And I got to know him extremely well because of that.

"I always talk about this place as a meritocracy, and that's because of the way David ran it. Not only did he not care that I was a woman and pregnant, he actually liked it, because it was like a challenge to what everyone else believed. Remember, this was a lot of years ago. My son is now 24. There were still companies that made you leave when you were pregnant. At General Foods, at that time, as soon as you wore maternity clothes you had to leave the building. To David, this was another way of challenging the status quo."

In David's Image

As a woman, CEO Lazarus knows that she is a role model, although it is not something she is particularly comfortable with.

"I'm not presumptuous enough to think that what I choose to do, what I wear, and how I lead my life are things that should be modeled by other people. It's the way I live. Still, I accept it and I'm aware of it. I'm a very private person. The fact that people are watching is probably what surprises me more than anything. But just this morning, at an industry conference I was attending, some woman came up to me and she was practically in tears and she said to me, 'I just wanted to introduce myself. I heard you speak at an event four years ago, when I was pregnant. And I heard what you said about balance and I have led my life for the last four years based on the things I heard you say. It has made a huge difference to me, but more importantly, to my daughter.'

"I was actually a little bit surprised because if I give a speech I just don't think about the fact that there may be people sitting in the audience who are going to take what I have to say as a way to live their lives. But I have come to accept it.

"I know that work-family balance is important and it cheers me when I hear that because I choose to always go to the school play, and field day, and all that, that it gives other women in the company, or clients, the confidence to be able to say, I'm going too."

Since Lazarus is a role model, young women ask her all the time for career advice.

Company: Ogilvy & Mather Worldwide

Location: New York, New York

Leader: Rochelle Lazarus

Ogilvy & Mather at a glance: Ogilvy & Mather is a worldwide marketing communications company founded by David Ogilvy in 1948, and now wholly owned by U.K.-based WPP Group. Its client roster includes such well-known brands as American Express, Ford, Hershey, IBM, Kodak, Mattel, Sears, and Unilever. The agency employs over 10,000 people based in 377 offices in 97 countries worldwide.

Gross Billings:

$11.1 billion

1999 Financial Results (WPP Group plc):

—Revenues: $3.5 billion

—Net Income: $279 million

"There's one thing I say all the time: You have to love what you're doing in your professional life. If you ever want to find balance, you have to love your work, because you're going to love your children, that's almost a given.

"When things get out of balance, and where women become miserable, is when they actually don't like what they're doing professionally. They then resent every minute that they're away from the things they love and, therefore, the job gets worse and worse, because more resentment fills their lives.

"From this, I have made two observations. The people—men or women—who are most successful, are people who love what they do and are passionate about it.

"So the first bit of advice I give is to find something you love. Don't stay in something where you find it a little dreary and not particularly interesting.

"And the second thing I say is that loving your professional life is the way to find balance. Because even when you have those difficult moments and you have to choose between something you want to do in your personal life, at least it's an approach/approach problem, which is much more satisfying and fulfilling than to have an approach/avoidance conflict with the whole thing."

It is clear that Lazarus has found the right balance for both herself, and her clients.

BILL MARRIOTT

Marriott International

Taking care of the customers, and the people
who take care of the customers

AROUND MARRIOTT INTERNATIONAL, EMPLOYEES TELL A STORY ABOUT their CEO that goes a long way toward explaining the company's success.

It seems J. Willard Marriott, Jr., was right in the middle of negotiations that would determine whether or not he would be able to build what could become the flagship of the hotel chain. He was juggling several calls simultaneously. On line one, he had his potential New York City landlord. On line two, his management consultants. And then, his father called on line three.

"I figured I should take the call from Dad first," Marriott recalls. "Dad was calling from a Marriott down in Virginia and he wanted to tell me that the carpeting out by the pool needed replacing. I listened for a while and then I said, 'Dad, I promise I'll take care of it, but it may take a couple of days. I'm negotiating what could be the biggest deal in our company's history."

" 'Son,' he told me. 'If you don't take care of the little things, you won't have a company.' "

The carpeting got fixed right away.

And, by the way, the Marriott Marquis—which was built when no one was sure that Manhattan's Times Square revival would work—is one of the most successful properties within the chain.

Attention to detail, and a willingness to change, have been the hallmarks of Marriott International under Bill Marriott. He has greatly expanded what

CAREER
1985–PRESENT Chairman, Marriott International, Inc.
1972–PRESENT CEO
1964 President
1956 Joined Marriott; oversaw construction of its first hotel
1954–1956 United States Navy

EDUCATION
B.S., University of Utah, 1954

FAMILY
Married, Donna Garff; four children

Born: Washington, D.C., March 25, 1932

> *"We've got three stakeholders: employees, guests, and stockholders, and the stakeholders are all related. If we take care of our employees, they'll take of our guests, our guests will come back, as a result the stockholders will benefit."*

the company has become. Not only does it operate 11 different brands—including the Ritz-Carlton and Renaissance Hotel Group—it is also the leading developer and operator of senior living communities. In addition, Marriott's Pathways program hires welfare recipients and trains them to become Marriott employees. The program, the oldest and largest in the country, has been hailed—and copied—throughout the United States.

But while the company is certainly different from the A&W root beer stand his father started almost 75 years ago, one of its trademarks remains the same. Bill Marriott says that his father's first priority was to make sure his employees were happy. Marriott Senior's thinking was if the employees wanted to come to work, they'd take care of the guests. Happy employees? Happy customers.

The idea was true then. It is true now.

IT IS ALWAYS INTERESTING TO ASK LEADERS, FREQUENTLY THE SOURCE OF adulation, who they themselves admire. Bill Marriott rattles off the names of four people, while barely pausing for breath.

He begins, of course, with his father. Bill Marriott, Sr., who got what has become Marriott International going with a small roadside stand that he opened in the 1920s.

The second figure he names is more surprising.

"Besides my father, I've always talked about Germany's General Rommel and how he crossed Europe at the beginning of World War II. He took France in 45 days. It was an incredible feat. Nothing got in his way. If the French blew up a bridge, he went upstream and found another way to get across. He was in the first tank, leading the charge.

"I also had a lot of respect for Conrad Hilton, although I don't think he was an especially good manager. He put together the first real chain of hotels. But unfortunately, he had no succession plan. The people who came after him basically thought hotels were a risky business and didn't have a big enough return on capital in it, and went into something else. But I admired him. He said that the most important thing was location, location, location. And he was right, he had some very good locations.

"And then there was Ray Kroc, the man who created McDonald's. He was a real genius. He worried about quality, the cleanliness of the bathrooms, and that the hamburger was cooked just right. He would insist that the french fries be cooked in just the right kind of oil. That was the kind of stuff I was brought up with. I think he created a tremendous company."

You can see influences of all four men in the company Marriott has created.

Like Hilton, Marriott remains committed to expanding his leadership position in the hotel business where the company controls some of the best locations. Marriott takes after Rommel in making quick decisions and overcoming obstacles. And like Kroc, Marriott's CEO is relentlessly focused on his product. But in analyzing the performance of the company, it is clear that Bill Marriott's father had the biggest influence.

While the company got caught up in the diversification trend of the late 1970s and into the 1980s, Marriott is now, once again, primarily focused on the hospitality business. (It spun off its real estate division into a separate public company—Host Marriott—in 1995.) And you can hear Marriott Senior's thinking reflected as his son speaks about the company's future.

"Today our vision is to be a global lodging company that provides great service, has a multiplicity of brands, and continues to espouse the culture that my father and mother established back in 1927. We want to take care of the customer, and take care of the people that take care of the customer.

"My father believed very strongly that if people were happy in their work they would take good care of the customer, and the customer would come back again and again. He believed that, and he made it happen. He had tremendous loyalty to our employees, and I think we still do.

"This is something we really stress and work on. Although we're a financially oriented company, and we're worrying about shareholder return, not having too much debt, and growing the business, it all comes back down to this. We don't manufacture anything. We're a service business. And our people are interacting every day with millions and millions of customers who are away from home and the people they love. They're tired. Their feet hurt. They've had a lousy plane ride, or they didn't get the car rental they wanted, or they got lost on the way to the hotel. And maybe they lost the deal they came to do. Whatever it is, by the time they get to our front desk they're whipped and we've got to take care of them. And to do that—to make sure it happens—we have to take care of our employees; otherwise how can we expect them to take care of our customers?

"If you've got a grouchy room clerk, or you get up for breakfast and go downstairs when you've got a big day, and the waitress doesn't say hello, you won't enjoy your stay. All these kinds of things make a big difference."

It is one thing for the man who has his name on the door to talk about the need for providing excellent customer service, it is another to have it implemented through the nearly 2,000 hotels Marriott manages.

"It has to come all the way down through the ranks to all our people. The majority of our general managers in our hotels have come up through the ranks, believing in this culture, understanding the culture, working with the culture. And every time I make a speech, I mean every time, I talk about these things and what we believe in. We want to help people—not only our customers but also the people who take care of our customers, our employees. We want our people to feel that this is a company where there's opportunity. That they can grow, develop and contribute, be trained, and learn and do better in life by working for Marriott, because Marriott cares about them as people, as individuals."

Not surprisingly, a large part of everyone's compensation package is based on the customer satisfaction scores they receive.

"We track customer satisfaction very carefully. And every hotel has goals; if you go back behind the front office, you can see speed of check-in, speed of checkout, and scores of how friendly the front desk is. If you go to the housekeeping department, they'll have a graph up there showing their scores on the cleanliness of the room, and the cleanliness of the bathroom. In the food and beverage department, you'll see charts showing whether we are providing a good breakfast experience. A good lunch experience. You'll see how people rated the service and the hostess. These are very, very accurate measurements. I'm amazed at how accurate they are."

They are monitored closely by everyone, including the CEO. But the company has internal measurements as well.

"In addition to customer satisfaction scores, we have an associate opinion survey that goes out about twice a year, where we survey everybody in our hotels about their working conditions and their boss."

While Marriott clearly wants his hotel managers to run profitable facilities, "about 30% to 40% of how they are rewarded is based on the other items, such as employee satisfaction and guest satisfaction."

So the compensation system reinforces the values that Marriott is trying to get across.

Bill Marriott reinforces those values—without words—every time he visits one of his hotels.

Walking the Walk. Literally.

"I walk the properties. I visit the kitchen, the laundry, the housekeeping, the front office, the back office, the rooms, the parking lot, the receiving dock. What am I looking for? I want to know, is it clean? Is it sharp? What are our people like? Are they happy? Are they enjoying their work? What's the general manager like? How well does he know his people? My favorite general manager is the guy that can stand 50 yards away from an employee and say, 'Good morning, Sam. How's Joan, is she feeling better? And how's little Jimmy, is he still on the baseball team?' This is the kind of stuff that I think makes our hotels and our managers very different from a lot of the others.

"The hotel business, in a lot of cases, particularly outside the United States, is a business of princes. The general managers of the big European hotels, or Japanese hotels, they're kings. They really are. They sit in their office and have room service for breakfast, and it comes in on a silver tray.

"When we bought the Essex House in New York, I went into the dining room and the maitre d' said to me, 'What table do you want?'

"I said, 'What do you mean, which table do I want?'

"Well, we have the park-side table, which the manager uses to entertain. Or we have a regular table over on the side, which he uses when he has no one with him.'

"I said, 'Who uses these tables the rest of the time?'

"Oh no, nobody uses these tables. They're always reserved for the general manager.' "

This is exactly the attitude Marriott works hard to prevent.

How?

"You do it by trying to energize the company to make it a dynamic, proactive, entrepreneurial-type company. I do it every way I can. I jump around a lot. I don't just talk to the people who report to me. I'm talking to hotel general managers, and I'm talking to clerks. I'm talking to brand managers. The majority of my meetings are with people

---

Company (Ticker): Marriott International, Inc. (MAR)
Location: Bethesda, Maryland
Leader: J. Willard Marriott, Jr.
Marriott at a glance: With more than 1,900 owned or franchised hotel properties worldwide, with plans to add 200 more in the year 2000, Marriott International is the largest lodging company in the world. Marriott's hotel brands include Courtyard, Marriott, Ramada International, Renaissance, Residence Inn, Ritz-Carlton, and more. Other operations include Marriott Vacation Club International (time-share resorts), Marriott Senior Living Services (senior living communities), and Marriott Distribution Services (a food services company).
1999 Financial Results
—Revenues: $8.7 billion
—Net Income: $400 million

who don't report directly to me. And the guys around here accept it. I think it's very important for the CEO to have contacts down the line.

"Recently, I spent a whole week in Europe with our vice president for Europe. He's three layers down from me, but we talked about how we could do better over there and what we have to do to improve. We visited 26 hotels. It was a full week. We were in 10 countries, and we had a great time together. I learned a lot. And I think we got a lot done in a short amount of time."

That, Marriott says, is by design.

"Energy is probably the most important thing in a CEO," Marriott adds. "He has to have the energy to get up every morning and hit the deck running and run hard all day long. It's the energy that makes companies perform. It's like an athlete. If you get an athlete who's kind of listless, he might as well not be on the field. But if you've got a hard-charging linebacker, or quarterback, or fullback, or whatever, you've got a successful guy.

"And, of course, honesty is just paramount. People have to trust a CEO. They've got to know he walks the talk, or she walks the talk. They've got to know the CEO believes in something besides profits. We try and foster a very strong belief in the importance of the individual and the importance of our people. We think profits are important, but they're not as important as the individual.

"So, energy, integrity, honesty, and caring for employees as much as you care for profits is what it takes to succeed today. These are the things I am trying to get across."

LOU NOTO
Exxon Mobil Corporation

"You've got to do what you do well."

ON DECEMBER 1, 1998, AT ONE OF THE MOST HEAVILY ATTENDED PRESS conferences in American business history, Mobil and Exxon announced their agreement to merge, creating (upon completion of the transaction) the world's largest corporation.

Just weeks before, the authors were sitting with Lucio A. Noto, chairman and CEO of Mobil Corporation, in the company's Fairfax, Virginia, headquarters, discussing his company's transformation over the previous five years.

Little did we suspect that many of the things that Noto, a gregarious man and terrific storyteller, shared with us about Mobil's successful asset redeployment, marketing and exploration strengths, and global reach were apparently some of the assets that Exxon most coveted.

The notion is that the combined company, to be known as Exxon Mobil, will boast over $200 billion in revenue, $12 billion in net income (*before* nearly $3 billion in estimated pretax synergies) and nearly 120,000 employees in more than 140 countries around the world, and will have the scale and clout to be a leading global competitor in a volatile world economy that is bulging with cheap oil.

While the sheer size of the future company initially gave many industry

CAREER
1999–PRESENT Vice Chairman, Exxon Mobil Corporation
1994–1999 Chairman and CEO, Mobil Corporation
1993–1994 President
1989–1993 Chief Financial Officer
1988 Vice President, Finance
1986–1988 Vice President, Planning and Economics
1985–1986 Chairman, Mobil Saudi Arabia
1981–1985 President
1962–1981 Various worldwide postings— including Japan and Italy—for Mobil

EDUCATION
M.B.A., Cornell University, 1962
B.S., Physics, University of Notre Dame, 1959

FAMILY
Married, Joan; five children

Born: Brooklyn, New York, April 24, 1938

> "Alliances have always been a part of the oil business."

analysts pause, a closer review reveals that the companies fit together well in almost every facet of the business.

As regulatory restrictions limit what information the companies can disclose before merger proxy statements are mailed to shareholders, we can only guess at how Lee R. Raymond, chairman and CEO of Exxon, and his team actually evaluated Mobil.

We suspect that they based their ultimate judgment, in large part, on how Noto developed the company after his appointment as CEO in 1994.

SOMETIMES THE STAFF OF A COMPANY THAT HAS JUST NAMED A NEW CEO must feel like they are living in Lewis Carroll's Wonderland. New leaders often go (figuratively) running through the halls yelling "Off with their heads. Off with their heads," and scores of managers suddenly find themselves leaving the company "to pursue other interests."

Because this has become so relatively commonplace, it does not get much attention anymore. A new CEO is entitled to name his own senior team, the reasoning goes, so no one spends a lot of time wondering if it was a good idea to fire all those executives.

Lou Noto knew how the game was played when the board named him chairman and CEO of Mobil. But there were no wholesale firings, no radical restructuring. "Why would I want to do that?" Noto asks in typically direct fashion. "The company was in good shape."

So instead of tearing the company down—which might have been the predictable thing to do—he decided to build on the strengths of the oil giant instead. Noto knows that his decision to keep existing senior managers in place struck some people as odd. But as you listen to him speak, you realize the decision not to change much at first was done for a number of well-thought-out reasons.

"I knew much less about Mobil, as a company, than did many of the people I found on my management team," Noto explained. "I knew some of the pieces, like international operations and finance, but I had spent more time outside the home office than in it. I would have to have been a complete jerk if I didn't take the attitude, 'Look, fellows, I just happen to be here. I was chosen for this, but if we don't operate as a team, I don't see how we are going to get anything done.' There's often an implication there that you have to throw out everything you find when you are named the new CEO, but I didn't."

There was no reason to.

"I found a strong company. Allen Murray, the CEO between 1986 and 1994, had spent a good amount of his time really doing a fabulous thing for Mobil—cleaning up our act. When Murray took over, we owned Montgomery Ward, Container Corporation, and a number of ancillary businesses that we had gotten into during the days of President Carter. At that time, everyone thought the industry was going to be regulated down the drain. So, the company sought to engage in businesses that were counter-cyclical to the oil industry."

When it was clear that the company was not going to be overly regulated, the company's ancillary businesses were sold off and Noto found himself in charge of a relatively well-focused company that revolved around oil, gas, and chemicals.

But focused as it was, there were still some pieces that did not fit.

"We still had a big real estate business and we still had a plastics business. At the end of the day, the management group figured that we really would be better off focusing a little bit more. But we had the luxury of doing so because Murray had done the hard stuff. Selling plastics and real estate were a breeze compared to getting value for Ward and Container Corporation."

Once Mobil had been streamlined into its core strengths, Noto set out to make the company more nimble. The first thing he did was strip away a startling amount of bureaucracy.

"We had three relatively clean operating divisions, but there was a lot of duplication. When I first got the CEO job, the management team went off to Williamsburg for two days of honest face-to-face talk about what we had to do. One of the things that came out very clearly was that we had to take a new look at our staff delivery model. We had great support people in corporate functions, but they were also generating a lot of staff work. The corporate controller would ask the division controller, 'Why is it that your costs are 13 cents instead of 12 cents?' And then there would be a big study."

Noto concluded that the company had to reorganize. He says there were three factors that governed that decision.

"Number one, we said that we could not afford to have each of these three businesses—oil, gas, and chemicals—be burdened with a superstructure out of line with their earnings expectations. Number two, we decided that instead of having a controller here, and a controller there, a PR guy here and a PR guy there, we could share services. And number three, we weren't consistent. We might have best practices in one division that were not being applied in the division next door.

"The structure was adding cost and complexity and slowing down the way things were done. When we looked at it carefully, we concluded that everyone was doing a pretty good job inside his or her own cell. But nobody was looking at the process across the whole organization. We weren't optimizing things as well as we could.

"We figured out how to realign everything, but to tell you the truth, it was a nightmare. This has been a cradle-to-grave industry. I've been with Mobil 37 years and it's pretty typical to have a career that lasts a lifetime with the company. The reorganization broke with that. When you break that bond it's tough on people."

In all, 4,700 employees, about 7% of the workforce, were let go.

"All of a sudden, the old social contract we had with employees had collapsed," Noto said.

"The questions then became: 'How do you put the feeling of commitment and meaning back together? What are you going to promise your employees?'

"Number one, you can offer them a stimulating and challenging business assignment. That's good, because if you don't have fun at what you're doing, you're probably wasting your time. Number two, you can offer them a chance for self-development. And that was tough, because we didn't have a history of professional development. Managers didn't typically say to employees, 'Jim, you are doing a great job, but I don't think you have a chance of moving two levels up unless you develop these particular new skills.' The process wasn't done, but we are starting to do that now."

This new social contract raised a significant question. Where did Noto want to lead this new, leaner organization which still had 62,000 employees?

The answer: He wanted to turn Mobil into an organization that was as efficient externally as it was internally and one that would make "educated risks."

"I try to tell folks, 'If you bet $100 with a real chance of winning $500, and you lose, I want your supervisor to encourage you to try to find another opportunity like that. Because that's the kind of risk we want to be taking. But if you risked $100 and made $105 or $101, I'm going to fire you. I don't care if you made the goal. It was just a stupid risk.' "

"We had a culture that was solely success-oriented. But the downside of this was that the company took fewer risks. You were not willing to set stretch goals because you had to set a goal you could meet, because if you couldn't meet it, it was the end of the world. I'm not saying that we want to encourage failure. We want to encourage the right kind of risk. To do that, we have to break this ironclad rule that says if you don't succeed, we're going to put you in front of a firing squad.

"If you don't change that rule, you get less than optimal performance."

Noto set out to see that Mobil achieved ultimate performance, and that resulted in some major changes in the way the company does business. No place is that more evident than in the retail gasoline business.

Listening to the Customer

"When you go back to the first days when I was named CEO, one of the things we had to get away from was looking at our navel all the time. We had to look at competition, and more importantly, we had to look at our customers. That was one of the significant breaks with the past. We started to listen to the customer. And the customer, frankly, could give a hoot about the little guys running around in the automobile engine, the basis of Mobil's commercials. He or she wanted convenience, wanted speed, and they wanted to do a lot of things at the service station site that, frankly, we never thought they wanted. They said, 'Give me electronics.' And that started a revolution in our marketing. First, it was pay at the pump. Today, pay at the pump looks relatively simple. Everyone has it. But it was Mobil that started it.

"The next step was 'Speedpass.' This product reflects the fact that technology is developing at an incredible rate. Here's how it works. You tell us who you are, how you want to charge your gasoline purchases, and (in some places) what grade you want, and we'll give you either a little tag that you can put on your key chain or on your car visor. You don't need a credit card. You just pump your gas and off you go. We track who you are and what you bought electronically. Speedpass, which was introduced in 10 key markets in May 1997, went national later that year. In the first year alone, some 1.3 million people activated their Speedpass transponders.

"Why are we doing this? Not because people like gizmos, but because they tell us they want convenience and they want speed.

"Now, the other side of this coin's a little different, and it shows you how fickle the customer is. Customers want speed at the pump and they find Speedpass convenient. But they also want to do as much shopping in one stop as they can. So as long as they are stopping for gas, they want to pick a few things up. What did we do? We put retail markets in our gas stations. Of course, we had the Mobil name on the products we sold. We are Mobil and we're proud of our name. But we learned some important lessons getting into this business, such as customers don't like to have Mobil on food. They tell us, 'Mobil's okay for the oil. But don't give me Mobil on my food.'

"So, miraculously, we actually listened to the customer. We went out and hired some people who knew something about merchandising, as opposed to oil, to build the store that would be part of the gas station. The first thing they told us is: 'You need a new franchise. You need to throw out what you have and go with new colors.' You can imagine how that played with people like me who have Mobil printed on their foreheads. They brought me over to an experimental site, and I almost had a heart attack. The gas station was this cool clean, crisp white Mobil station with the blue and red accents. I loved the way it looked, clean as crystal. Next door, the company's "On the Run" convenience store was a circus. It was yellow and green and purple with lots of lights, lots of action, and a lot of merchandise. But that's what the customer told us she wants.

"The customer wants to go in there in the morning and be able to buy brand-name coffee and breakfast food. She wants to go in there at lunch and buy brand-name sandwiches and fast food. And she wants to go in for dinner, buy take-out for the night, and see a brand that she recognizes. No one's interested in Mobil chicken.

"So we had to revolutionize the way we did business with our customers. We put in Lotto and every other thing customers told us they wanted. We are building parking spaces on service station sites in front of the markets. If anybody worked in this business 20 years ago, they would be turning over in their grave. But we are starting to deliver real results."

Was the repositioning part of a grand vision?

"I hate that word 'vision' because I think it implies sort of a formalistic, 'Now we're going to start the Vision Quest' thing. But, fundamentally, when you are responsible for a company, you have to figure out what you do well. You also have to determine what you don't do that well and get rid of it. You have to learn to listen to the customer and react quickly. And internally, you need to emphasize the positives because nobody is perfect. I guess if I had to sum it all up, you need to build on your strengths."

As Mobil and Exxon plan to come together, this lesson seems to be the watchword.

Company (Ticket): Exxon Mobil Corporation (XOM)
Location: Irving, Texas
Leaders: Lee R. Raymond, Chairman, President, and CEO
Lucio A. Noto, Vice Chairman
Mobil at a glance: The purchase of Mobil by Exxon led to the formation of Exxon Mobil Corporation (both companies originated from Standard Oil), making it the world's largest oil company. Exxon Mobil's core businesses are oil and gas exploration, production, supply, transportation, and marketing. Exxon Mobil has gas holdings in Europe and North America. Exxon Mobil also produces and sells petrochemicals, coal, and other minerals. Over 6 million barrels of oil are refined every day to be sold at over 45,000 service stations in 118 countries.
1999 Financial Results
—Revenues: $160.8 billion
—Net Income: $7.9 billion

PAUL O'NEILL
Alcoa

"The test is how you connect with people."

IT IS FUN TO LOOK AT ALL THOSE FILMS about the future that were made 20 or 30 years ago. One constant—among the robots that were going to do all the housework and all the depictions of commuters driving to work in their hovercrafts—is that everything is going to be made out of aluminum, a truly "space-age" metal.

Well, aluminum is found in more places than ever before today, but sales are growing slower than GDP as a whole.

When it came time to pick a new CEO in 1987, Alcoa's board took that disappointing fact into account. It went searching for someone who could pay relentless attention to not only commodity costs, but cost-cutting, in addition to all the other traits demanded of today's business leaders. They found Paul O'Neill—on their own board of directors.

As someone who had been president of International Paper, O'Neill knew all about commodity prices. And as President Gerald Ford's deputy director of the Office of Management and Budget, he

CAREER
1999–PRESENT Chairman
1987–1999 Chairman and CEO,
   Alcoa, Inc.
1985–1987 President, International Paper Co.
1981–1985 Senior Vice President
1977–1981 Vice President
1974–1977 Deputy Director, U.S. Office of
   Management and Budget
1973–1974 Associate Director of OMB
1971–1972 Assistant Director of OMB
1969–1970 Chief, Human Resources, OMB
1967–1969 Examiner, Bureau of the Budget

EDUCATION
Hon. Ph.D., California University of
   Pennsylvania, 1998
Clarkson University, 1993
M.B.A., Indiana University, 1966
postgraduate George Washington University,
   1962–1965
Haynes Foundation Fellow, Claremont Graduate
   School, 1960–1961
B.A., Fresno State College, 1960

FAMILY
Married, Nancy Jo Wolfe; children: Patricia,
   Margaret, Julie, Paul

Born: St. Louis, Missouri, December 4, 1935

> *"The bigger you are, the more important it is that you don't become bureaucratic and layered with levels of decision-making processes. That is the real danger as you grow."*

could crunch numbers with the best of them.

In his 12-year tenure at Alcoa, O'Neill has worked with other industry executives to reduce a glut of product, and he has been relentless in both trying to raise prices and minimize costs. The results have been exceptional. While investors are not going to award an aluminum company a market multiple equal to a pharmaceutical company, Alcoa's stock consistently trades at a higher price/earnings ratio than the aluminum group as a whole, and O'Neill has almost tripled the company's market capitalization.

Building on that solid performance, O'Neill has taken pains to make sure that Alcoa is an industry leader when it comes to environmental performance and safety. Intriguingly, he sees both issues as a good way to test how successful management is.

"THE SINGLE MOST IMPORTANT CHALLENGE IS TO MAINTAIN MOMENtum," O'Neill says when asked about the challenges facing Alcoa. "We have done okay. Over the last 12 years, our biggest competitor has gone from a $4.5 billion market capitalization to one that is $5 billion or $5.5 billion today. We've gone from $4.5 billion to $12 billion or $13 billion, depending on what day of the week you look at the market. Over that time we have emerged, hands down, as the world leader of our business, not just in terms of sales, and profitability but also in terms of reach around the globe."

Given this success, some executives might feel smug. O'Neill, in contrast, is concerned.

"I think we need to be careful that we don't become self-satisfied. We can't become complacent. We need to keep pressing ourselves to improve to reach levels that other people can't imagine."

Taking nothing for granted is something that comes naturally to O'Neill.

"I grew up in a military family, which meant a whole lot of different schools in a lot of different places—Illinois, Missouri, California, New Mexico, Hawaii, and Alaska for grade school through high school. Not everyone likes that, and I didn't like everything about it, but there were some aspects that I think were important in developing the way I think. You develop flexibility and adaptability from being pulled out by the roots all the time and taken someplace else and being exposed to different kinds of people and kinds of ideas."

And that repotting, if you will, has been a constant in his professional life as well. O'Neill spent 15 years working for the federal government—most notably in the Office of Management and Budget—before moving to the private sector.

While O'Neill's background and experiences have provided him an openness to new ideas and experiences, he has found that this is a perspective not often shared in the business world.

"I think more and more that it's necessary to organize around customer needs and not become fascinated with yourself. Ironically, I find the hardest place in the world to implement change is the United States. It's partly our independence, I suppose, and the need to know why. I think that's a distinguishing characteristic, but it can be frustrating, and it's not that way everywhere.

"In Brazil, for example, they don't need to be able to answer 'the why question' at five levels before they observe that somebody else is doing a better job with something than they are. They immediately adopt it. They don't even give it a second thought."

It isn't surprising, given his own background, that O'Neill looks for "energy and enthusiasm" in the people he is thinking about hiring. And he looks for something else as well.

"In the best people I see a commitment to a continual learning. I don't mean, education, necessarily, in a formal way, but they are people who are constantly in search of new information and new ways they can integrate it into a framework that they carry around in their head."

In other words, they never become complacent.

Core Beliefs

Flexibility, adaptability, and a willingness to learn are important, of course, but you need to have core beliefs. One of O'Neill's is the need for Alcoa to be the safest manufacturing company possible.

But while he is driven to reduce accidents, for all of the usual reasons, he really sees the safety issue as a shorthand way of providing leadership.

O'Neill concedes that this is not intuitively obvious, so he provides some context.

"Safety is the most important performance measure that I use to drive the business. In fact, it's even narrower than that. It's lost workdays. I believe that this number is a leading indicator of whether you're leading or managing. I think if it's improving, then you have some basis for believing you're leading. If it's not improving, then you're what I call managing, and I use that word with a sneer.

"Now why do I focus on this? Because the difference between ordinary companies and great companies is whether people are connected to each other, and whether they believe in something more important than making money or getting paid. And I think the place where you have the best prospect of getting connected is in an area that everybody cares about, and I haven't found anybody who wants to volunteer to be an accident.

"If you can connect with people and show them that their organization cares about them first as human beings, and everything else is second to that, then you have a chance of being a great organization. If your objective is to build an institution that lasts forever, then I think that the first brick in the wall is the brick of connecting with people and connecting with them on the grounds that you care about them, and the organization cares about them as human beings first. You need to find a way to demonstrate that the belief is real, and not just some syrupy sentiment that everybody puts in their annual report."

So safety is the highest internal priority at Alcoa.

"And, you know, it's not just a syrupy sentiment. On my desktop computer is a real time safety data system that tells me every minute of every day, how we are doing. How many lost workday cases we've had, where they occurred, under what circumstances, and what remedial action was taken.

"This is something I've been working at since the day I came here. At that time, everybody said, 'Oh yeah, we care a lot about safety but, you know, we're in a dangerous industry and we can't be any better than we are.' And I said, 'Well, we're operating with incident rates that are one third of the U.S. average, and we shouldn't have any at all, and so from now on, the objective is zero.'

"There weren't a lot of people who believed I was serious. For about the first 18 months, people were wandering around the halls, saying, 'You know, I think O'Neill is some kind of a wild hair, and when he figures out how tough this industry is, when he goes through his first pricing cycle, he'll shut up about this and we can go on to other business. But, you know, today we no longer have one third the industry average of injuries, it is maybe one twentieth, and improving every month."

This Is Part of a Broader Issue

Related to the concern about safety is O'Neill's desire for Alcoa to be seen as an impeccably solid corporate citizen. Yes, being environmentally responsible is a worthy goal, but again, he sees it as a leadership issue as well.

Environmental stewardship is really important and, I guess, in a broader sense, this and the safety issue meld together into having a sense of integrity. I know everyone says that, but we mean it.

"Let me give you an example. Maybe three years ago now, an order of sisters in Texas sent me some correspondence indicating they believed we had had an incident in one of our Mexican plants where people had been overcome by fumes, and had to be hospitalized. While no one was hurt, they said it was a serious situation and they said they didn't think I knew about it.

"I simply didn't believe it. But it turned out they were right, and it also turned out that the division president responsible for this business knew about it and had an outside report done, by an independent environmental consultant, God bless him. The report indicated that it was probably a temperature inversion, combined with carbon monoxide from forklifts inside the plant, that had, in fact, overcome people. The business unit president didn't share the report with company headquarters environmen-

tal and safety people, as he was required to do by policy. This is a guy who'd been with the company 28 years, who had grown businesses from $100 million to $1.5 billion, but when it was clear he had not shared what had happened, he was fired.

"Firing people is not fun, but we don't do business this way. A company must live by its values.

"We don't pay people bribes, even where it's legal to do so. And we hold every branch of this company to the same standards. When we made acquisitions in Hungary we found that many of the buildings had asbestos in them. We removed the asbestos, even though it's not required by Hungarian law. We don't treat people by what the local law is, but by what logic says is the right thing, and logic says people shouldn't be exposed to asbestos."

You have to do these things, O'Neill says, to show you are consistent in what you believe.

"If people can find even trivial examples of deviations, those deviations will

Company (Ticker): Alcoa, Inc.
Location: Pittsburgh, Pennsylvania
Leader: Alain J. P. Belda
Alcoa at a glance: Alcoa, the world's leading producer of aluminum, participates in all major segments of the industry: mining, refining, smelting, fabricating, and recycling. The company provides customers in automotive, aerospace, construction, and other markets with a variety of fabricated and finished products. Nonaluminum businesses include alumina chemicals, plastic bottle closures, packaging machinery, vinyl siding, and electrical distribution systems for cars and trucks. Alcoa acquired Reynolds Metals to retain its position and is buying Cordant Technologies to upgrade its aerospace offerings.
1999 Financial Results
—Revenues: $16.3 billion
—Net Income: $1.0 billion

become the norm, so you can't have them. I think the values you have must be transparent, and they have to be practiced all the time. If you do that, it gives you the potential of being a great company. It won't make you a great company, but it gives you the potential. Without it, I think you may be able to be good, but only for so long."

JOHN PEPPER
Procter & Gamble

"What do you want to achieve?"

To people under 45, the phrase "company man" doesn't have much meaning. There is no reason it should. They entered the workforce at a time when it seemed people began changing jobs about as often as they traded in their cars.

But if you want to see what the résumé of a true company man looks like just take a look at how John Pepper has spent his working life.

In his 36-year career with Procter & Gamble, the only company he has ever worked for, Pepper averaged a promotion every three years. Along the way up the corporate pyramid he ran everything from P&G's soap and detergent units to all of the company's international divisions—and he succeeded at every level. For example, the company's international business doubled both sales and earnings during the five years he was in charge, as Pepper established inroads into new markets such as Central Europe, Russia, China, India, and Latin America. P&G's revenues in Asia have increased 10-fold in the past decade. Sales in China alone, which the company entered in

CAREER
1999 Chairman, The Procter & Gamble Company
1995–1998 Chairman and CEO
1990–1995 President, International Business
1986–1990 President, U.S. Business
1984–1986 Executive Vice President
1981–1984 Group Vice President, European Operations
1980–1984 Group Vice President Packaged Soap and Bar Soap and Household Cleaning Products
1977–1980 Vice President, General Manager Packaged Soap and Detergent
1974–1977 General Manager, P&G, Italia
1963–1974 From Staff Assistant to Advertising Manager, P&G
1961–1963 U.S. Navy

EDUCATION
Hon. Ph.D., Mt. St. Joseph College
Hon. Ph.D., St. Petersburg (Russia)
Hon. Ph.D., Xavier University
B.A., Yale University, 1960

FAMILY
Married, Frances Graham Garber; children: John, David, Douglas, Susan

Born: Pottsville, Pennsylvania, August 2, 1938

> *"You have to be careful not to lose balance. You are always the victim of your own best attributes."*

1988, now exceed $1 billion annually. In fact, P&G now generates over half its revenues outside the United States and Canada.

Following his appointment as chairman and CEO in 1995, Pepper continued P&G's aggressive overseas expansion. But he did something else as well. Together with Durk Jager, Pepper's successor as CEO, Pepper moved ahead with the most important change in P&G's history. Called "Organization 2005," P&G is streamlining its structure and changing its culture to promote speed, risk-taking, and entrepreneurialism.

THE QUINTESSENTIAL P&G COMPANY MAN ARRIVED AT THE FIRM ALMOST by accident.

"Life is a series of coincidences," Pepper begins. "In college, I became the head of the *Yale Daily News* on the business side. That proved terribly important, as luck would have it, because one of the groups I targeted for ads was P&G.

"After graduation, I spent three years in the Navy. I planned to be a lawyer. I was accepted at Harvard Law School with a scholarship. Almost at the last minute, I said, 'You know, I'm just not ready to go back to the stacks in the library right now.' I decided to take another year and try a business thing.

"Then I thought, what business should it be? And I thought back to my time in school and said, 'Procter & Gamble.' They seemed like really sharp people. And I liked the brand management thing they talked about. You could run your own business. So I called Harvard, and they said they would hold my place for a year. I called them six months later and said, 'Don't hold my place next year. I don't know if I'll be here forever, but I'm going to be here for a while because this looks pretty good.' "

What convinced Pepper to stay? The opportunities? Yes. The fact that he could, indeed, run his own show? That, too, played a part. But it really was something more fundamental.

"It was the values of the company," Pepper says, and then he tells a quick story to explain what he is talking about.

"One of my first jobs was as a brand assistant on Cascade [dishwashing detergent] and I quickly spotted what I thought was a fine business opportunity—coming out with a second, larger-size box for Cascade. It was a novel idea then.

"I took this proposal up to Jack Hanley, who was company vice president. He sat me down and asked about my idea and after we had gone over a lot of things he said, 'I have only one more question.'

"I said, 'What's that?' thinking he might ask about profit margins.

" 'Are you certain that this product is going to be good for the consumer?'

"I said, 'Of course. It's the same product that's in the other, smaller size.'

"But then he asked me, 'Have you thought about the condition of the product if somebody buys it and only uses the dishwasher once a month and the product sits in their kitchen for six months?' "

"And I thought, 'Holy cow, I have no idea what that would do to the product.' He told me to find out. We weren't about to offer the product until we really could be sure this was right for the consumer.

"This scene was repeated many times within P&G. Hanley, and the hundreds of people like him, cared about doing what was right for the customer. I liked that."

And so Pepper stayed and worked his way quickly up the ranks. As he progressed, he realized that one of P&G's core strengths—the desire to cover every conceivable base before acting—could also be one of the company's greatest weaknesses.

"Our principles and values are exactly what we want to live. But in the most established parts of our business, we need a culture that is more stretched, faster, and more willing to take risks. A big part of the recent reorganization was designed to free this culture to be what we really want it to be. We need to be more conscious of our behaviors, which some people have described—I think accurately in some cases—as our 'narrow perfectionism.' "

Pepper has always tried to operate in a way that was consistent with the culture he was trying to create. That is one of the many reasons P&G executives placed him on "the fast track." Still, he says, he never thought about the possibility of being named CEO until he had been at P&G for nearly 20 years.

"I guess I first thought about it in 1981, about the time I went to run Europe. It didn't occur to me before that. I know there are people who come in dedicated to becoming CEO of the company but it was not what I did, although I can respect that. I will say I think it's a great mistake to expend energy on that idea for any length of time.

"My view has always been to try to do the job that I'm in as best I'm able to and do it with an idea of anticipating the job ahead of it. It's not that I wanted to take that other job. It was because I wanted to have a framework for the work I was currently doing—I want to know how it fit in—and I wanted to make sure I was learning and growing."

Pepper figured, and rightly so, that his superiors would take care of him.

"If you're in a company where managers are really concerned about the individual, and know that the company's future depends on finding people who are doing well and moving them ahead, you shouldn't have to worry about managing your career. And in this company, by and large, people don't have to."

His ultimate promotion to CEO is proof of that.

Once in charge, Pepper focused relentlessly on improving the company's performance.

"Our most important measures of success are total shareholder return, and market shares," he says. "Market shares are the best litmus test I have found to see if we are indeed doing better than the competition in giving consumers products of superior quality and value.

"There are other measures. A very critical measure for us is the percentage of our product sales that have clear-cut superiority to the competition as the consumer sees it. We're looking for that number to be up in the nineties. We measure that through blind consumer testing. And we watch the results like a hawk. If that number falls, we are really unhappy campers."

A Higher Purpose

Success in business has a lot to do with picking the right strategy, but even when you pick right, you still have to execute. How do you manage—and drive—superior execution?

"Obviously, it starts with having chosen the right people," Pepper responds. "I can't overemphasize that. We can give two of our market development teams the same product, initiatives, and resources and, yet, the results can differ by 50%. The biggest single factor in that difference—and we know this is true, because we've tracked it—is the leader of that unit.

"The successful leaders are people who feel enormous ownership of what they're doing. They feel they're trusted and respected enough to really go for it. They feel the person they are reporting to is supportive, and that they are going to do it together, but they own the mission.

"Then they exercise personal leadership. They bring their people together as a team and focus on the result. They communicate that achieving the goal is not only doable, but the process of getting there is going to be great."

Intriguingly, Pepper is describing exactly what he does.

He has spent a lot of time trying to convince P&G employees that they are involved in something more important than just creating products. Why? It is the only true way, he says, of getting people to give their best.

"It comes down to purpose. Why do we exist as a company? There are multiple reasons, but this one is key: We exist to provide service. I believe that deeply. Service to me is an anchor. We have to serve our consumers through our products. The only way to do that is by giving people better products. We have no business offering parity products."

Related to that is something that Pepper stresses frequently, the thought that "ethical business is good business.

"There are several aspects to this. One is that your ethics will help you keep good people. There are any number of people in this company who came here—and stay here, because of our ethical standards. When we move into places like Eastern Europe and ask new employees why they sought us out it's wonderful to hear them say, 'Because of what you stand for.'

"I know, this is going to make us sound like we think we're perfect and nothing goes wrong. And that's not the case. But we really do believe in these things. I remember a former P&G chairman saying if it ever came to a point where we didn't think we could uphold good ethics and stay in a country, we'd leave that country. This way of thinking creates an ethos, a purpose about the company that is terribly important."

This approach to business, Pepper says, helps P&G attract and retain good people—people who share the company's values—and "ensures you are doing the right thing by the consumer."

It also lets the company move faster.

"It takes things off the table. It's wonderful to have things that you don't have to talk about. When we are discussing a product and there's something wrong with it, you know it's not up for discussion anymore until it's fixed. And in a discussion about meeting profit

Company (Ticker): The Procter & Gamble Company (PG)
Location: Cincinnati, Ohio
Leaders: John Pepper, Chairman Alan G. Lafley, President and CEO
P&G at a glance: P&G is the United States' leading manufacturer and marketer of household products—brands include Tide, Folgers, Pampers, Tampax, Iams, Eukenuba, Pantene, and Cover Girl—and is one of the world's largest advertisers. P&G main product categories are: fabric and home care (detergents, bleaches), baby care (diapers, wipes, feminine protection pads, tampons), beauty care (skin care, shampoos), food and beverage (coffee, juices, snacks), health care (toothpaste, over-the-counter medicines), pet care (dog and cat foods), and prescription drugs. P&G also produces *As the World Turns* and two other daytime dramas (which explains why they are called "soap operas"). Roughly half of P&G's sales come from outside the United States. P&G has restructured its organization by product lines rather than by regions in order to cut costs and promote growth.
1999 Financial Results
—Revenues: $38.1 billion
—Net Income: $3.7 billion

forecasts solely by laying off people, our ethos eliminates debate. We don't do that."

Appealing to this kind of higher purpose is a vital part of the CEO's role, Pepper says.

"Clearly the leader must be able to define the vision for the company, where it needs to be in terms of purpose and financial goals. You, along with your top team, have to be able to articulate a very robust strategy. You have to establish an environment with a balance between a sense of pride and a sense of dissatisfaction with the status quo. You want to be proud of what you have accomplished, yet have a real thirst for continued dramatic improvement. You have to be able to create a cultural environment—certainly within our company anyway—that allows you to be able to attract terrific young men and women and provide them, through the experiences and opportunities they have, the chance to spend a whole career here. There are not many companies for whom that's as important as it is for us."

And what does Pepper look for in these hires?

"You start with the obvious, their record of accomplishment. But then you look for their intensity of conviction, purpose, and what kind of curiosity they have. You try to get some sense of their values, where they are coming from and what they really believe." To do that, Pepper says he always asks: 'What do you want to achieve?' "

FRANK RAINES
Fannie Mae

Reluctant role model

THE HALLS OF POWER IN OUR NATION'S capital are littered with the remains of businessmen and women who had come to Washington determined "to make government run more like a business."

The reason they failed, says Franklin Delano Raines, CEO of Fannie Mae, which used to be known as the Federal National Mortgage Association, is that these executives never understood that there is little relationship between what goes on in the public and private sectors.

"In government, you spend an enormous amount of time on policy-making, and much less time thinking and implementing," explains Raines, a former municipal official, lawyer, and investment banker. "In a well-run company, you spend more time on thinking and putting those thoughts into action. The process of making up your mind takes far less time.

"In a company, if someone has an idea, you set it forward, you debate it either for five minutes or five weeks, and you do or you don't put it into action. In government, the President presents a budget in February that he starts work-

CAREER
1999–PRESENT Chairman and CEO, Fannie Mae
1998 Chairman and CEO–designate
1996–1998 Director, U.S. Office of Management and Budget
1991–1996 Vice Chairman, Fannie Mae
1985–1990 General Partner, Lazard Frères & Co.
1983–1984 Senior Vice President
1979–1982 Vice President
1978–1979 Associate Director, U.S. Office of Management and Budget
1977–1978 Assistant Director, White House Domestic Policy Staff
1976–1977 Associate, Preston, Thorgrimson, Ellis, Holman & Fletcher
1972–1973 Associate Director, Seattle Model Cities Program

EDUCATION
J.D., Harvard University, 1976
Postgraduate, Oxford University (England), 1971–1973
B.A., Harvard University, 1971

FAMILY
Married, Wendy Farrow, 1982; three children

Born: Seattle, Washington, January 14, 1949

> *"A big part of the job of being a leader is being a teacher."*

ing on the September before. Congress, which gets that budget when the President presents it, finishes making their decisions on it in October, and then leaves town. So, by the time Congress has decided what it wants to do about the first budget, the President is working on the next one, even though they haven't implemented the last one."

The frustration of the budget process is something that Raines understands firsthand. Before being named head of Fannie Mae, Raines was President Clinton's Director of the Office of Management and Budget.

"When I was in government, I gave some speeches on the need for us to direct more of our attention to implementation, as opposed to debating whether or not we should do something."

Raines now gets a lot of chances at implementation. Fannie Mae's basic mission is to help low-, moderate-, and middle-income people become homeowners. The company, one of the world's largest financial institutions ranked by assets, owns about $400 billion worth of mortgages and guarantees about $800 billion more.

While the organization started life as an agency of the federal government, it has been privately owned since 1968. However, it is federally regulated, and the President of the United States appoints five of its 18 board members.

It is clear that understanding how government works, in addition to his success in business, made Raines a very attractive candidate when Fannie Mae went looking for a new CEO in 1998 to succeed the well-respected and highly regarded James A. Johnson, who had led the company since 1991.

As anyone who has ever had to deal with the federal government knows, the public sector is different. Raines agrees, but intriguingly, he thinks his private sector peers can learn a few things from leaders who are in public service.

"If you are in government, you have to be flexible," he says. "There are a number of business leaders who are successful because they are *inflexible*, i.e., they have a vision and the ability to impose that on their organization. However, there is a growing consensus that this is not the most effective way to lead.

"If you are in the public sector, no one has the ability to impose his will on the whole government, so you have to be collegial. And you have to be able to deal with diverse groups of people who have diverse interests. Plus, you have to deal with an enormous amount of uncertainty.

"In this kind of environment, you have to learn how to exert influence. In the early 1960s, Richard Neustadt wrote a book called *Presidential Power: The Politics of Leadership*, and in it he argued that presidential power was the power to persuade. And that is what power is within the government—it's the opportunity to persuade other people to do things the way you would like. So in this sense, we may find that this new generation of business leaders will be much more comfortable in government than the older generation, who were much more command- and control-oriented."

Raines spends his time persuading Fannie Mae employees to carry out his vision, a vision that has three parts.

"First, our goal is to increase home ownership. This is our eternal mission, and it helps to focus everyone. Second, we have to maintain our financial strength. And depending on where the stock market is right now, we have roughly a $72 billion market capitalization. Our stock is held by pension funds, mutual funds, 401(K)s and IRAs and the other things that people invest in. And then third, we've got to motivate our employees and get them to focus on getting goals one and two to happen. In some ways we're unique, and in others we're not that different than other regulated financial institutions. We're just a little more focused and we're a lot bigger than most."

Focus and Communicate

"A leader has to have a real vision, or a sense of what it will look like to be successful," Raines says when asked what it takes to be an effective executive today. "Organizations need to have someone at the top who can keep everybody on track, and who will determine whether a particular item being discussed is part of its focus or not. People lose track of what the goal is after a while. They start to get caught up in doing the day-to-day things and forget what you were ultimately trying to do as an enterprise.

"So being a leader isn't about sitting back and thinking grand thoughts. It's more of a discipline. Does this fit, or doesn't it fit? Are you doing things that advance your organization toward its goal, or are you doing things that are moving it toward something else? This intellectual discipline is an important part of leadership.

"And it's an even more important part now as people—and resources—become more and more scarce. In this kind of environment, you can't afford to waste a lot of time, effort, and money on extraneous things. You've got to be focused on your most important items. If a competitor is focusing on what is important, and your interests are spread all over the place, they are going to beat you.

"The kind of focus I am talking about is the kind small companies have because everybody is always in the room, everybody knows what they are supposed to do, and the owner is sitting right there to make sure it gets done.

"In big public companies, where everybody isn't in the same place, people can have different ideas about what they are supposed to do. So the leader's intellectual discipline of being the arbiter of 'on-message/off-message'—deciding whether the organization's mission and strategy are on or are off target—is very important."

This kind of focus is important everywhere, says Raines.

"I think you need to have a pretty good idea of where you're going in all aspects of your life. For example, if you want to spend some time with the kids, you need to organize your life in a way that gives you the opportunity to do that."

Once You Know Where You're Going, You Need to Tell People

Having clarified the mission internally, leaders—whether they are in or out of government—need to communicate their objectives to the rest of the world. This is an area where Raines excels, but as he says, it is also an area where he has had a lot of practice.

"One thing I learned in government is that members of Congress are very busy. They don't have a chance to know half of what you'd like them to know about your particular circumstance. So we make it a point to make sure that members, when they go home to their districts, can see examples of what it is we do. And then they say, 'Okay, now I know. Now I understand what Fannie Mae is about and how that works.'

"So our success comes in part because we're good communicators, but a lot of it is simply a result of this wonderful mandate that we have. If your mission is home ownership, it's pretty hard for people not to be in favor of that. So we just try to make sure that everyone understands, on an issue by issue basis that affects us, whether any proposal affecting us is a good thing for home ownership or not.

But it is not all altruism. Like other companies, Fannie Mae has to balance achieving its vision and making money. Interestingly, Raines says it is not that hard.

"We have focused on trying to maximize our service to the housing finance system," he says. "We made the decision that if we do that well, it will yield about average returns, and that's proved to be true.

"I think companies that focus on maximizing returns very often are short-term oriented and over the long run their returns are below average. By focusing our attention on the answer to the questions: What is our product? What is our service? What is good for our customers? And how do we have a big impact? we get everyone focused on the creative end and on the value-added. Our returns, in a sense, come from that."

So staying on message clearly helps. So too does Fannie Mae's commitment to hiring the best people in the marketplace, regardless of race, color, creed, or gender.

"Diversity is a major business goal of this company," Raines says. "We manage it in the same way we manage our other objectives. We track our progress, and we try to benchmark ourselves against others, and we put a lot of investment into making it work.

"As a result, we probably have one of the most diverse workforces in the country, with a very high percentage of women and minorities in executive positions. And it's been very helpful to the company, because when everybody in the country potentially benefits from your product, it's very important not to have just some narrow group of people sitting in a room trying to figure out, how do we make that work? And also, by being committed to diversity, we expand the pool of talented people that we can draw upon.

"We're in Washington, D.C., not in New York, and we don't pay what New York investment banks and others are paying. But we want the best people. And so, if other firms are going to discriminate against women, or minorities, or not be actively seeking them, we will actively seek them. This way we can get more than our share and, therefore, improve the overall quality of our workforce. Diversity is a core value here and it's proven to be very helpful."

And it doesn't hurt that Raines, who is black, could be the poster child for the benefits of diversity. In fact, the company probably draws more than its fair share of attention because he is black. That, in turn, brings with it pressures of its own.

"I never thought of myself as a role model until I had several young people come up to me over a period of time and say, 'I read this article about you and because of that I decided to go

Company (Ticker): Fannie Mae (FNM)
Location: Washington, D.C.
Leader: Franklin D. Raines
Fannie Mae at a glance: Fannie Mae is the largest nonbank financial institution in the world, with more than a *trillion* dollars in assets. A publicly traded corporation, Fannie Mae was created by the U.S. government, but was privatized in 1968. It is charged with supporting home ownership among Americans. It does so by providing liquidity to the mortgage market by buying mortgages from lenders and holding them in its portfolio or packaging them for resale as bondlike securities. This frees lenders to manage interest rate fluctuations and allows them to offer mortgages to people who would not otherwise be considered.
1999 Financial Results
—Revenues: $36.9 billion
—Net Income: $3.9 billion

into law school.' Or, 'I heard you give a speech at my high school and you said this and that led me to stay in school till I graduated.'

"When they told me these things my first reaction was to say, 'Really? I gave a speech, but I didn't think you guys were going to do something as a result.' But what they told me really impressed upon me the power people in high-level positions have to influence the decision making of young people. When that became clear to me, I embraced this notion of being a role model. I decided to be an example to young people regarding a set of decisions they might choose to make."

Raines makes sure his organization also reflects that idea.

"There's a high school here that Fannie Mae has been involved with for the past 10 years. It's called the H. D. Woodson Senior High School, and it's over in the poorest area of the city. We have created something called the Future's 500 Club, which rewards students for getting all A's and B's on their report card. We set aside $500 a semester, each time they do, that can be used as part of their college fund, and then we make it a point to hire them in the summer, and after they have finished college. We have an induction ceremony each semester and I've spoken at that several times.

"For a lot of these kids, the message they take away after hearing me talk is 'Well, he doesn't look like any great shakes. If he can do it, I can do it.' A lot of these kids have never seen anybody in a significant business position, so they never thought about what they might be able to achieve. And for these kids, our involvement makes them think about being in business. Most of them have never thought about that. For others, it's a chance for them to increase their life goals, to shoot higher.

"So, depending on the audience, you can try to either directly or indirectly have an influence on their decision making. In that sense, I embrace the role-model notion. It's not something I look for. I'm not going out there every day saying, I want to be a role model for somebody, but it's something that's going to happen anyway, and so I might as well try to do it right." And with Raines doing the right things, Fannie Mae has continued its tremendous success.

HOWARD SCHULTZ
Starbucks

Sharing success

POUR YOUR HEART INTO IT IS MORE THAN A CLEVER TITLE FOR THE BEST-selling book Howard Schultz wrote a couple of years ago chronicling the rise of Starbucks. It is also a phrase that explains his operating philosophy.

Schultz grew up in Brooklyn, where he watched his father hold down a series of unsatisfying jobs, such as working for a diaper delivery company and driving a cab. When Schultz was seven, his father broke his leg at work. Since his job did not provide either health insurance or workers' compensation, the family's subsequent financial struggles left an irreversible impression on Schultz.

"I watched my dad's self-esteem fracture and I watched his self-respect deteriorate," Schultz recalls. "I believe his reaction had a lot to do with how he was treated in the workplace as a blue-collar laborer."

Schultz remembered how his father felt, as he built Starbucks.

He took a circuitous route to creating the company that is named after the coffee-guzzling first mate in *Moby Dick*. After graduating from Northern Michigan University, Schultz spent three years in sales with Xerox, before moving on to a housewares company that sold coffee grinders to companies such as Starbucks, which had four stores back then, and sold coffee by the pound, not the cup. Schultz eventually joined Starbucks, serving as its director of retail operations.

CAREER
1987–PRESENT Chairman, Starbucks Corporation
1987–2000 Chairman and CEO, Starbucks Corporation
1986–1987 President, Il Giornale Coffee Company,
1982–1985 Director, Retail Operations/Marketing, Starbucks
1978–1981 Vice President/General Manager, Hammarplast USA
1976–1978 Xerox Corp.

EDUCATION
B.S., Business, Northern Michigan University, 1975

FAMILY
Married, Sheri; children: Jordan, Addison

Born: New York City, July 19, 1953

> *"I think it's very difficult to lead today when people are not really truly participating in the decision. You won't be able to attract and retain great people if they don't feel like they are part of the authorship of the strategy and the authorship of really critical issues. If you don't give people an opportunity to really be engaged, they won't stay."*

After viewing Italy's wildly popular coffee bars—the relatively small country has more than 150,000 of them—Schultz tried to persuade his bosses to open a series of coffee bars in Seattle. When he could not, he left in 1986 to open his own stores, Il Giornale, which were successful enough for him to buy out the Starbucks Coffee Company a year later, with the help of local investors. Schultz continued to open stores using the Starbucks name.

In growing Starbucks nationally, Schultz paid what some people might call an inordinate amount of attention to the people side of the business. That was the smartest thing he could do, he argued in his book. "If people relate to the company that they work for, they will form an emotional tie to it, and buy into its dreams, they will pour their hearts into making it better."

To make sure that happens, Schultz gives everyone—including part-timers—benefits and stock options through a company plan called Bean Stock.

YOU DO NOT HAVE TO SPEND MORE THAN FIVE MINUTES EITHER READING Howard Schultz's book, or visiting with him, to realize that values drive Starbucks. He says it is not hard to understand why.

"I grew up literally on the other side of the tracks," he says. "And if you saw where I came from, you would never place a bet on me becoming as successful as I have. As I grew older I swore to myself that if I were ever in a position of responsibility, I would want to do something that would guarantee people would not be left behind, that they would be respected. I always wanted to build the kind of company that my father never got a chance to work for. I never lose sight of that. Because of that decision there are more than 30,000 people who work at Starbucks today who are partners.

"We open one new store a day. We hire 500 new people a month. And the driving force of the company has always been trying to achieve this very fragile balance between recognizing the company's responsibility for long-term value and profitability for the shareholders, and the most important constituency and responsibility for me, which is making sure that the people who do the work get rewarded. What we have done is link taking care of our people with creating value for the shareholders.

"But we know that if we lose sight of taking care of and rewarding our employees, we won't be the company we're capable of becoming, whether we achieve long-term value for the shareholders or not. I believe that if I, and the organization, can create value for the people who work here and tie that to shareholder value, then the company will be much stronger."

In other words, putting his employees first, Schultz believes, is the best way of achieving the greatest shareholder returns.

While the interests of Starbucks shareholders and Starbucks employees ultimately end up in alignment, they take different paths in getting to the same spot, Schultz says.

"What we've talked about inside Starbucks is building an enduring company. That is very different than creating long-term value for the shareholder. Endurance cannot be achieved without lowering attrition, and creating passion in the environment that people work in. And, perhaps, the most important thing in creating endurance is strengthening the trust between management and the people who do the work.

"I think my job is to do everything I possibly can every day to give our people better tools, and make them feel better about management decisions. I want to do everything I possibly can to improve the feeling of equity within Starbucks."

This philosophy would seem to work best inside a small firm. Can it work inside the international company Schultz is creating?

"That's the greatest challenge facing Starbucks today, and I would characterize it in the form of two questions. One, can a company get big and stay small? And, second, how do you maintain the intimacy? We started fiscal 1988 with 100 employees and 11 retail stores; today we have more than 2,000 stores and more than 30,000 employees. In an enterprise of this size, how can you possibly maintain that kind of intimacy?

"It can't be the same level of intimacy, because the methodology of how you do things changes. But the level of trust and confidence in management's decisions must remain the same, and I think you've got to create a platform to do that. It's much more difficult and much more challenging now that we have become this big. But through the use of technology, and traveling, I am trying.

"I try and reach as many people as I possibly can every single hour of my workday. And the only way I can do that is by human contact. That's important to me, because in the world we are living in, human interaction and human contact are being lost. One of three great aspects of what Starbucks does every day is touch people. People come into our stores not only for the coffee but for the experience, for the interaction, for the social context of it, and we try and play that up with our people.

"We're providing something of value and something that people are very hungry for in their day. If you think about Starbucks and what we've become, you'll see that in many ways we've become "the third place" in America. It's this comfortable place between home and work, and it's the one part of the day where you really can get a respite—you can gather, you can meet over coffee, you can have a private moment.

"In the focus groups we've done people talk about how social Starbucks is. And then we say, 'How many people did you talk to while you were in the restaurant?'

" 'I didn't talk to anybody.'

"So we have learned that it's the experience—the music, the theater, the romance of coffee and the break that we provide."

The True Source of Competitive Advantage

All this sounds great, but anyone can open a coffee shop with exotic blends. And indeed, as the proliferation of coffee shop chains shows, Starbucks is not immune to competition. Why, then, isn't Schultz overly worried?

"The essence of what we do, and the competitive advantage we have, can be traced to a decision we made in the late 1980s, which changed the course of our company. We decided to provide equity, in the form of stock options and comprehensive health care, to part-time workers. As a result, we've developed a culture and value system that's very unusual. It's not an accident that the attrition rate at Starbucks is four to five times lower than the national average for retailers and restaurants in America."

Schultz is happy to explain how that competitive advantage—the decision to treat employees, including part-timers—as partners came about.

"Again, this goes back to my dad. I grew up in a family that had no health care, and I saw firsthand what that did. So I know the fragility and the insecurity of a family not having health insurance and what can happen to them. And I felt very strongly that if people can come to work feeling totally secure and confident that they have health insurance, that they're a part of the action and they have a piece of ownership, however small or large it is, it would give us a huge competitive advantage.

"So in 1989 we created a benefit package called Bean Stock. At the end of the fiscal year, everyone is awarded up to 14% of his or her base pay in stock options, with the strike price being set at the end of the first day of trading in the fiscal year. Those options vest evenly over five years. In addition to that we created comprehensive medical, dental, vision, and a 401(K)."

Instead of being an expense, these benefits actually reduce Starbucks cost of doing business, Schultz says.

"We concluded very quickly that the costs of those benefits were dramatically lower than the cost of hiring and training new people. And most importantly, the performance in terms of the passion and the commitment was so much greater. Prior to having those benefits our attrition was almost 150% to 175% a year and it's been below 60% every year we've had those benefits. The national average is 250%. Because of this benefits package I think Starbucks has become an employer of choice. We've attracted and retained great people."

Schultz concedes that offering these benefits did not make him wildly popular with his shareholders—at first.

"When we made the decision to give equity to part-timers—we were the first company in America to do it by the way—we had to stand up to the shareholders and say this was going to be dilutive. But we told them if we do it right it will be accretive, because it will lower attrition and increase performance. It was a difficult thing for them to decide to agree with me on."

But it was—in all senses of the word—the right thing to do—Schultz says.

"Success is best when it's shared. I have found that if we want to inspire our customers, we have to inspire our people. They can't be left behind. One of the outgrowths of the last 10 to 15 years in business is that there has been a fracturing of trust between senior management and rank-and-file employees. And I would also say that fracturing of trust exists between high levels of management and the inner circle. And you have to change that, but it can't be in words, it has to be in everyday actions in the environment in which people work and live. I think once you break that trust, the ability to inspire people is over.

"I take these kinds of issues very, very seriously, because we are such a values-

Company (Ticker): Starbucks Corporation (SBLJX)
Location: Seattle, Washington
Leaders: Howard Schultz, Chairman Orin Smith, President and CEO
Starbucks at a glance: Starbucks is the United States' number-one specialty coffee retailer. It operates more than 2,800 coffee shops in a variety of locations in the United States and 15 other countries. Starbucks sells coffee drinks and coffee beans, fresh pastries, and other food items and beverages as well as mugs, coffeemakers, coffee grinders, and storage containers. Starbucks has expanded into coffee ice cream (in a partnership with Dreyer's) and makes Frappuccino, a bottled coffee drink (in conjunction with PepsiCo), joined Kraft Foods in order to sell its coffee products in supermarkets, and entered into an alliance with Kozmo.com to deliver Starbucks coffee to your door.
1999 Financial Results
—Revenues: $1.6 billion
—Net Income: $101 million

and culture-based business. And the ability to get people to think passionately and do things as if it were their own business can only be achieved when they are truly part of the business.

"In today's world you've got to be close to the customer and close to your people. We feel we have to be closer to our people, more than we've ever been before."

At the end of the day, everybody wins.

CHARLES SCHWAB
Charles Schwab

"I am the customer."

WHAT CHARLES SCHWAB REALIZED ON "MAY DAY" 1975 WAS THAT THE secret to being in the securities business in the years ahead would have nothing to do with better research, more charming brokers, or even having the inside track with Fortune 500 companies and their ability to steer underwriting deals your way. The secret would be having better computers.

May 1, 1975, was the day that fixed commissions—that is, the law requiring all brokerage firms to charge the same fees when they bought or sold stocks for their customers—were repealed. That meant that every firm was free to charge as much—or as little—as it wanted. The better your computer system, Schwab realized, the more you could afford to offer lower commissions.

So Schwab set out to buy the best computers, and he continues to do so, spending up to a quarter of a billion dollars a year upgrading his information technology systems. Today those systems allow Schwab to do more than just handle trades over the phone. The San Francisco–based company has taken the lead in offering both online brokerage and a supermarket of mutual fund choices to its customers.

Schwab sold his firm to Bank America in 1980, but bought it back seven years later. Since then he has been taking advantage of not only technology, but also demographic trends. With individuals

CAREER
1971–PRESENT Founder, Chairman and CEO, The Charles Schwab Corporation (Co-CEO since 1997)
1962–1970 Principal, Mitchell, Morse & Schwab
1961–1962 Vice President, Foster Investment Services

EDUCATION
M.B.A., Stanford University, 1961
B.A., Stanford University, 1959

FAMILY
Married, Helen O'Neill; five children

Born: Sacramento, California, July 29, 1937

"The question I always ask myself is, what would a customer, someone like me, want us to do."

taking more control of their financial life—as companies continue to do away with defined benefit programs such as pensions, and shift to defined contribution retirement plans such as 401(K)s—customers are looking for more than low prices. They also want advice and Schwab has been adding it to the company's offerings.

EVERY COMPANY TALKS ABOUT WANTING TO GET CLOSE TO THE CUStomer. At The Charles Schwab Corporation, Chuck Schwab is the customer.

"When I look at potential products or services, I see them through the eyes of the customer, because that's who I am, a customer. I am like a chef. I like to taste the food. If it tastes bad, I don't serve it. I'm constantly monitoring what we do, and I'm always looking for better ways we can provide financial services, ways that would make me happy if I were a client.

"Take the idea of offering our customers mutual funds from other financial services firms. In 1984, I wrote my first book and in it I talked about mutual funds. I thought then, and I think now, that for the average investor, mutual funds are the perfect solution. But buying a mutual fund was a very cumbersome process back then. Still, I had been studying mutual funds since 1960, and I knew they were right for most people. They were perfect for all the IRAs that were created starting in 1982.

"So I kept wondering how we could offer our customers no-load mutual funds. Back then, the fees the brokerage firms were charging for mutual funds were excessive. If you asked me for investment advice at that time, I would have said: 'Buy no-load funds.' So, I had to figure out a way to offer no-load funds to our customers. I couldn't say, 'Well, maybe you should buy a *low*-load fund through us.' I had to figure out a way of providing what was best for the customer.

"So we went to a number of funds, such as Fidelity and T. Rowe Price, and said, 'We would like to offer your funds.' They just laughed at us. They couldn't understand why they should pay *us* for bringing them customers, when customers could come *to them* directly.

"As we got a bit more market power, which wasn't really until around 1990, we decided that we had enough clients to go back to the funds and say, 'Look, we now have access to a lot of customers. They like the idea of getting one statement from us. Let us offer your funds, and handle the paperwork, and you give us a percentage—it is 30 basis points [0.30%]—

of the money our customers put in your funds. You'll win because you'll get a huge amount of new money. Our customers will win because they get a much better deal. And, by the way, we'll win, too.' "

This time Schwab got lots of takers. Today, the company handles more than $200 billion in customer funds through its OneSource accounts. It was simply another example of creating a product that his customers wanted.

Schwab is quick to point out that his company has been the beneficiary of perfect timing. "In the last 25 years, we have been in the dead center of the changes in the financial services industry—things such as deregulation. At the same time there have been technological improvements that have allowed us to do things in new ways, starting with the decision to charge less for executing trades."

In the Beginning

That decision, back in 1975, made Schwab a classic entrepreneurial company. "There were four or five of us working out of a small office at the very beginning," he says. Often when companies grow as rapidly as Schwab has, they run into trouble because the founder/entrepreneur finds himself unable to keep up with the company's dizzying growth. Chuck Schwab was able to avoid the problem.

"I recognized early on what I was good at and what I wasn't good at. And that, sometimes, is an awful realization, because you'd like to think you're great at everything. I was pretty fortunate to see in about 1976 that I needed some people to help me in all the operational things. I knew what we wanted to do and where we wanted to go and I brought in people who were particularly good at operations, and others who were good at systems, to help us get there. I consider myself pretty good at the marketing side—not sales—but marketing. And I was really good at understanding what the customer wanted. So I stayed focused on that, and brought in people to do everything else. The combination seemed to work, so I kept doing it. Over the last 20 or 25 years, I've tried to surround myself with really talented, smart people who take concepts and turn them into actual things."

This clear delegation of authority is important. There are countless company founders who don't make the necessary transition from entrepreneur to manager, as their company grows. Invariably, this failure limits what their firm becomes.

From the beginning Schwab accepted his limitations.

"The day-to-day implementation of business strategies takes a tremendous amount of focus, and sometimes I'm not as focused on that sort of thing as I should be. I am always focused on our mission and where we are going. But the grinding away, the day-to-day stuff, sometimes is difficult for me. So I like to delegate that to the other talented people on our deep bench.

"There is just no way, shape, or form that this could be a one-person company, and it never has been," Schwab adds. "Our rapid growth demands teamwork and cooperative thinking. For many years, Larry Stupski was a terrific partner. Then in 1997 we recognized my existing partnership with David S. Pottruck [who was then COO] and named him co-CEO. While I am very engaged in the business, and intend to be until they carry me out, Dave and I have a very complementary and well-tested partnership."

This partnership has helped Schwab build the kind of company he wants.

"If there is a central tenant here it is that we have a sense of fair play, a sense of ethics, a sense of fairness. The word fair is really important to me, with respect to employees, and with respect to customers. I think people feel good about that. And this extends to how we project ourselves to the marketplace. We really work hard at never putting our employees in a conflict of interest position with our customers."

In fact Schwab has frequently said that he created his discount brokerage business to "offer customers a way to move your financial affairs from some guy who has a very clear interest in converting your capital into his personal income."

Consider, for example, how most brokers are paid. They receive a commission on each trade, which can lead them to encourage their clients to make as many trades as possible. Schwab employees don't get paid on commissions. They do get bonuses, however, based on how much money their clients have invested with Schwab. That strategy, of course, encourages better customer service.

With the company's goals and his clients' goals in perfect alignment, Schwab can concentrate on providing the kinds of services that his customers want. Securities trading via the Internet is an example.

"While it is convenient to pick up the phone and say, 'Buy 100 shares of XYZ,' often it would be even more convenient to make the trade yourself through your computer," Schwab points out. "We've adopted—lock, stock, and barrel—Internet capabilities and have integrated them into our entire offerings. Not only can Internet trading be more convenient for our customers, it is also a cheaper service for us to provide, and so we can charge less. In our traditional transactions, where the customer buys or sells over the phone, the average commission ends up being $68 to $70. Through the Internet, it is about $30. Five years from now I think 70% of our customers will be doing all their business with us through the web."

Passion

As Schwab talks about the future, indeed as he talks about any part of his business, you can sense his total commitment, involvement, and passion. When that is pointed out, Schwab says that observation should not be surprising.

"If you look at the CEOs who have been successful, they all have incredible passion about their business. If you don't have that, I don't see how you can possibly be a leader. I mean, a lack of passion just shows through. Think about the people in this very book: Welch, Gates, Fisher. They all are in different businesses and they all have different skills, but they each have an unbelievable passion for what they are doing. Fisher loves retail properties. Gates lives and dies according to the technological advances his company makes. Welch loves the company he has put together.

"In the financial services business, I think the lack of passion among our competitors is one of the great advantages we have. There aren't too many of our competitors who have passion for this business. Most of the banks are run by old credit card guys who don't have a real sense of the needs of the millions and millions of people who are their customers."

A lack of passion and a lack of understanding about whom he is trying to reach are two things that Schwab will never have to worry about. Charles Schwab, chairman, is passionately committed to providing the best possible products and service to Chuck Schwab, customer.

Company (Ticker): The Charles Schwab Corporation (SCH)
Location: San Francisco, California
Leaders: Charles Schwab, Chairman and Co–CEO
David S. Pottruck, President and Co-CEO
Schwab at a glance: The Charles Schwab Corporation, through its principal operating subsidiary Charles Schwab & Co., Inc., provides a variety of financial services to individual investors, independent investment managers, retirement plans, trading and financial services available by telephone as well as online, and institutions through the Internet, over 360 branch offices, touch tone and speech recognition telephone. Its online business, Schwab.com, is the largest online broker in the United States with $418 billion of customer assets handled online, up from $48 billion in 1996. Other services, such as Schwab's OneSource (mutual fund distributor), offer approximately 1,900 no-load mutual funds. Through a partnership with E-Loan, mortgages are available through its online financial services. Schwab introduced Velocity, a desktop system with streaming quotes designed for the active investor. In 2000, Schwab purchased U.S. Trust, which targets its more affluent clients.
1999 Financial Results
—Revenues: $4.7 billion
—Net Income: $588 million

And because he is, that passion has created a successful organization which has paid him enough money to help him fund a personal passion: helping people with learning disabilities.

It is something Schwab knows about firsthand.

"I'm the chairman of a nonprofit organization called All Kinds of Minds. It's a program that we are trying to have put into school systems to help kids—especially kids who have learning problems—understand how they think and let the teachers know about how different kids perform differently and process information in different ways.

"I didn't know anything at all about this until my youngest son was tested when he was in third grade, and we discovered he had a problem."

As Schwab began studying learning disorders, he realized that both he and his sister had suffered with the problem since birth.

Ironically, that realization brought both his academic career—and his determination in both school and business—into focus.

"I flunked English. I couldn't write worth a darn. My reading speed was incredibly slow," he recalls. "So you look back and say, 'Well, maybe this is why I was so focused; I learned subject matters and stuck with them. I wasn't bopping around with 18 different ideas. I sort of narrowed on some areas and got to know them pretty well [to compensate for the fact] I was learning-disabled. So when I got to understand economics pretty well, I stuck with it. But, if you gave me a book on a new subject matter, there would be a whole new language there and I would be very slow at processing it.

"In some ways, I am glad I didn't know how severe my problem was. I might not have accomplished as much. There is a lot of research that shows things like dyslexia have a huge social outcome. You go into prisons and find 40%, 50%, 60% of the people there have learning problems. It's not a small deal."

Not surprisingly, Schwab is attacking the problem in the same way he built his business.

WALTER SHIPLEY
Chase Manhattan

"If people feel valued, you have a much
stronger company."

IT IS HARD TO CHARACTERIZE SOMEONE WHO IS 6'8" AS HAVING A LOW
profile, but for Walter Shipley—all 80 inches of him—the description
certainly fits.

While Hugh McColl of NationsBank and John Reed now of Citigroup
usually come to mind when people first think of bankers, Shipley is all
but unknown outside of corporate America, even though he runs the nation's largest bank. In fact, he is the man who created it.

Shipley orchestrated two huge bank mergers—Manufacturers Hanover
with Chemical in 1991, and then Chemical with Chase in 1996—and even
that was not enough to make him a household name.

Shipley's style and management philosophy help to explain his relative ano-
nymity. While almost every CEO talks
about the importance of people—and always makes it a point to refer to his
employees as their company's biggest resource—Shipley actually acts as if the
people who work at Chase make the
difference.

You can see that in the way that
he handled each of the megamergers.
Even though Chemical was the acquirer
in each case (it took Chase's better-
known name after the second merger)
Shipley worked extremely hard to deal
with the acquired employees as equals.

It simply was the right thing to do, he
says. If you treat people well, he argues,

CAREER
1999–2000 Chairman, Chase Manhattan
    Corporation
1996–1999 Chairman and CEO
1994–1996 Chairman and CEO,
    Chemical Bank
1983–1993 Chairman and CEO,
    Chemical Bank

EDUCATION
B.S., New York University, 1961
Student, Williams College, 1954–1956

FAMILY
Married, Judith Ann Lyman; children: Barbara,
    Allison, Pamela, Dorothy, John

Born: Newark, New Jersey, November 2, 1935

> *"Ideally, you want to rise above the parochial self-interest of the unit or group that you're a part of and demonstrate the ability to make judgments that are in the best interest of the corporation."*

employees are far more likely to accept the pain that comes with mergers and those who remain will "put heart and soul into making a more powerful institution."

Similarly, while most CEOs talk about the need to delegate, Shipley actually does it. In fact some of his lieutenants, such as Chase's investment banking chief Jimmy Lee, have become better known—and better paid—than the boss.

Shipley comes to the industry naturally. His father and brother were in the business and Shipley began working in banks long before he ever received his college degree.

WALTER SHIPLEY REMEMBERS WHAT IT WAS LIKE WHEN CHEMICAL BANK took over New York Trust Co. in 1959. He had just finished working his way through New York Trust's training program, while earning his B.A. at night from NYU, and all of a sudden his image of rising quickly through the ranks was dashed by the acquisition.

"For the longest time after we were acquired, I felt I had a sign stuck to my back which said, 'Kick me, I'm from New York Trust.' Being acquired was demotivating. If you are part of the firm being taken over, you can feel that there is a check mark against you."

Shipley vowed, should he ever be in charge, that no one else would ever experience this feeling.

"When we bought Texas Commerce Bank, I always referred to it as a merger, even though we were three times their size and even though we bought them. My philosophy is to be inclusive, if you can. I know it's different. Most people would say, 'We bought you, now do it our way.' But if you are in a service-oriented business, you have to motivate your people. It's not about building a better widget, or an airplane engine, it's about motivating people. If people feel valued, and feel that they are being treated fairly, we will have a much more powerful company.

"In a merger, the idea is to take the best of both organizations. Honor and respect their histories and traditions, but don't dwell on the past. You want to get *all* your people to rally around the goals and opportunities of the new company instead of wasting time arguing over 'We are better than you, or we have a better approach.'"

This can be difficult, Shipley concedes, because in merging two organizations you inevitably find there are redundancies and people have to be let go.

"When that has to happen, we look at the downsizing to see whether there is bias in favor of one company or the other," he says in explaining how his company handles mergers. "We don't force a balance, but we try to make sure that negative biases aren't happening."

There is a business reason for taking an even-handed approach, Shipley argues.

"Human nature is human nature. One of the greatest challenges in mergers is getting to a point where people trust each other. Trust is absolutely key, and it doesn't happen overnight. If you spent 15 years working alongside somebody, and then all of a sudden somebody you never knew before is sitting at that desk, you don't have the same knowledge of the person, you don't have the same appreciation of his or her competencies, or integrity. You don't have the same level of trust."

Shipley feels it is the CEO's job to make sure that trust is in place.

How do you do it?

Sell, Don't Tell

"Ben Love, who was chairman of Texas Commerce when we merged with them, had a great saying: 'Sell, don't tell.' Tell is command and control. Sell is building consensus. Most people like to do something when they think it's their idea, rather than when they've been told to do something," Shipley says. "I'm a great believer in the softer side of leadership, in creating an environment that allows people to constructively challenge each other and to constructively receive a challenge. Creating an environment that allows this to happen can be very powerful."

In fact, Shipley believes, it is the only way you can lead a large organization.

"We have 68,000 employees. With a company of this size and nature, I'm not 'running' the business. My job is to provide strategy, motivation, and leadership. My job is to create the environment that enables people to leverage each other beyond their own individual capabilities. As good as our people are, we can make them better if we create an environment that allows their talents to be leveraged. The idea is to work beyond your individual ability to get something done.

"I think that in a way I've been lucky. My tenure as CEO has been a time of rapid change. It has given me the opportunity to reposition the company. I get credit for providing the leadership that got us there. But our people did it. And I think the company today is more amenable and accepting of change, because of the mergers we have gone through. In our case there is no Chemical, there is no Manny-Hanny, there is only Chase."

Company (Ticker): Chase Manhattan
  Corporation (CMB)
Location: New York, New York
Leaders: William B. Harrison, Jr.,
  CEO
Chase at a glance: Chase Manhattan
  is the second-largest bank in the
  United States (until the 1998
  merger of NationsBank and
  BankAmerica it was the largest).
  Chase, itself, is the product of the
  1996 merger of Chemical Bank and
  Chase Manhattan. The bank offers
  commercial, consumer, and
  investment banking services to
  clients in more than 50 countries.
  In the United States Chase is the
  largest financier of auto loans, is the
  fourth-largest issuer of credit cards,
  and is a dominant player in the
  syndicated loan business. Chase
  Manhattan has expanded into
  investment banking with its
  subsidiary Chase H&Q and the
  acquisition of The Beacon Group,
  LLC. Also, Chase has entered the
  Internet industry aggressively,
  offering online trading, banking,
  and money management through its
  chase.com service. Chase also has
  become a leader in money
  management, mergers and
  acquisitions consulting, and
  investment research.
1999 Financial Results
—Revenues: $33.7 billion
—Net Income: $5.4 billion

And employees have a responsibility to make sure it stays that way, Shipley says.

"I start with the presumption that you wouldn't be here unless you had some brain power and competency. You've made the cut to get here. The thing that will separate you from everyone else is a combination of innovativeness, creativity, and self-motivation. Some people need to be told all the time what to do, and if that describes you, that's okay. We'll give you lots of direction. But the people who are going to stand out are those who take the initiative and are self-motivated to anticipate what the next need is, or anticipate how they can be supportive. They will be recognized for reaching down and helping, mentoring, and developing people.

"One of the great differentiators today, and even more so going forward, will be people who recognize the value in, and promote, diversity within their group."

Diversity, Shipley believes, can be another source of competitive advantage.

"The business case for having a diverse workforce is compelling. Let me give you an example. The opposite of diversity is Dolly the cloned sheep. If I was surrounded by clones of myself, or if we all grew up with the same backgrounds, the same family, same cultures, same education, religion, etc., think how narrow this company would be.

"There is a tendency for people to think that there's a cost to diversity and that they have to compromise to create a diverse workforce. I don't believe that's true. It requires a lot of hard work. It requires attracting the best people into the organization. But the payoff from new ideas and perspectives can be amazing.

"If you can create an environment where diversity is valued, not only do you get the benefit of different thinking and different problem-solving capabilities, but you liberate the energies of people who were like me when Chemical took over the New York Trust Company. I felt like I'd come from the wrong side of the tracks, and I was self-conscious about that.

"We don't want that to happen again."

FRED SMITH
Federal Express Corporation

"Not to be an entrepreneur is to begin the
process of decline and decay."

IN NOVEMBER 1998, FREDERICK W. SMITH CONFRONTED ONE OF THE
turning points of his career. His company, FDX Corp., parent of express
delivery carrier Federal Express, was in the midst of intractable labor negotiations with the company's pilots. Christmas—his company, and the
country's—critical holiday shopping/shipping period was fast approaching and the pilots were threatening to strike if their wages and work rule
demands were not met.

As Smith and his top management team plotted their strategy, the
memory of arch-rival UPS's debilitating strike in the summer of 1997, and
its impact on Federal Express (volume increased 11%, with part of that gain
being directly attributable to the UPS strike) was fresh in mind. Should they
grant the pilots their demands and get on with what looked like a record
year? Or should they stick to their convic-
tion that the terms offered to the pilots
were already among the most attractive in
the entire transportation industry including the passenger airlines?

What gave Smith the courage not to
cave in tells volumes about the company. Thousands of FedEx employees
in the company's hometown, Memphis,
Tennessee, staged a spontaneous—and
unsponsored—rally in support of the
company. FedEx's drivers, package sort-
ers, and corporate employees congregated
to make it known that the company and
Fred Smith have been a model of fairness
over the company's 26-year history and

CAREER
1998–PRESENT Chairman, President, and
  CEO, Federal Express Corporation
1973–1998 Founder and President, Federal
  Express Corporation
1969–1971 Owner, Arkansas Aviation
1966–1970 Served in the U.S. Marine Corps

EDUCATION
B.A., Yale University, 1966

FAMILY
Married, Diane Davis

Born: Marks, Mississippi, August 11, 1944

> *"I think business is fun and I really enjoy what I'm doing. It's a good job, they pay me well, and I work with people who I like. I also have a lot of planes to ride around in. Most importantly, I think what we do is hugely important to people."*

that the pilots did not enjoy the support of the rest of the company. What drove this attitude? FedEx's customer-focused culture, which can be traced to Smith's long-standing "People-Service-Profit" philosophy.

Shortly thereafter, the pilots backed away from their threat to strike and the Christmas season was the best Federal Express ever had.

It is truly hard to believe that FedEx, which now enjoys nearly universal recognition (in the United States and increasingly internationally) and is recognized as a verb in many dictionaries, was created less than three decades ago. The story of how Smith outlined what the business could look like when he was an undergraduate at Yale is now a business legend. What is less known, is how pervasive the company has become and how wide-ranging its services.

The company is now called FDX Corp., which is a holding company for its various lines of business. These include Federal Express, of course, which now employs more than 140,000 workers worldwide and delivers more than 3 million packages and documents a day in 210 countries via its fleet of more than 625 aircraft and 40,000 vehicles: RPS, the second-largest ground package delivery service in North America: Viking Freight, the leading less-than-truckload (LTL) freight carrier in the western United States; Roberts Express, the world's leading carrier for time-sensitive and special handling shipments (like critical medical shipments), and FDX Global Logistics, all of which were acquired as part of the January 1998 $2 billion acquisition of Caliber System.

FedEx has also long been a leader in the utilization of information technology. From the company's earliest days, Smith has maintained that "the information about a package is as important as the package itself." Not only has this enabled the company to tell every customer where his package is at any point during shipment, but this very ability has eliminated the need for many companies to maintain warehouses full of inventory at all. In the process, Smith and Federal Express have created an industry which in turn has helped spawn such leading companies as Dell Computer, which ships products directly from the manufacturer to the customer.

WE WERE SURPRISED THAT MORE THAN 20% OF THE LEADERS IN THIS book—including Federal Express's Fred Smith—were founder/entrepreneurs. Smith, however, was not. For his entire working life, he has been hearing that entrepreneurs rarely make the transition to running a large enterprise successfully. But Smith has known from the beginning that this is not true.

"I always point out to folks that a lot of the commentary that entrepreneurs can't be good managers is related to some spectacular examples of entrepreneurs trying to make a transition and not being successful. It makes good reading, but there are probably more examples of people who do make the transition than those who don't.

"There are great generals who have been very effective wartime leaders and have gone on to be very good in the corporate or political world. Eisenhower is the most dramatic example probably, but certainly that was true of General Omar Bradley as well. Then there are other examples like Patton that you could cite, who were exactly the opposite, more like the wild entrepreneur who was only good for the start-up phase but was a disaster in the building or expansion phase. It is difficult to generalize accurately."

Smith has observed a few things about the entrepreneurs who make the transition successfully.

"Number one, there's a process of continuing self-education. They find out what's necessary to run bigger enterprises through lots of different educational and resource channels. Second, they surround themselves with people on the board, or within management who have a lot of experience. For example, Michael Dell, who's a good customer of ours, brought in some professional managers and helped him make the transition. So I think there's a pretty clear path how you get there. The difficulty comes in the personal discipline that's required to do it."

In fact, while many people focus on how difficult it is to move from being entrepreneurial to managerial, Smith thinks the problem is quite the opposite.

"Quite frankly, the bigger question is how you retain an appropriate level of entrepreneurialism inside the company," he says. "Because to not be an entrepreneur, even at the Jack Welch level, is to begin the process of decline and decay. You always have to be an entrepreneur; otherwise you will fall behind. The question is how you manage to be entrepreneurial in a progressively larger enterprise, and still provide the appropriate administrative oversight and direction."

Smith learned firsthand how difficult that could be. "In our early days we brought in some 'seasoned management' and most of them did not work out, because they weren't entrepreneurial enough."

The converse was also true. "One of the most difficult things for an entrepreneur to do is recognize that some of the people who were important in the early stages will not have the skills to function effectively when you become a larger organization."

"Systems, Not Smiles"

Those skills are especially important at FedEx, which is as much an information company, as it is a transportation one. While the transportation component—getting packages from here to there—is better known, Smith says that you must understand the information component, to truly know FedEx.

"The first recorded example, I think, of what might be referred to as a fast cycle, or a just-in-time approach to business was actually done in the late 1940s by a professor at MIT. He showed that the vast majority of functions inside any business—the bureaucratic and administrative functions—were waste. He argued that if you could shorten those things, the old proverb was indeed true, that time is money.

"There's been a natural progression forward. Companies such as Wal-Mart, Dell, and FedEx are places where the velocity of business has been steadily increasing and people have gone to great lengths to take mass out. And the reason information is so important to us is because what we are really doing is providing fast cycle transportation and distribution, in lieu of inventory investment for our customers.

"The only reason a warehouse exists is that it's a place to put something so that you know you've got it. It has no economic value in its own right. Now, if it's a store, like a Sam's Warehouse, that's something else, a point of sale. But most distribution centers are nothing but cost. They have nothing whatsoever to do with the value-added proposition the customer wants. The next time you go shopping for a car, I defy you to find a salesman who says, 'We've got a fabulous-looking warehouse in Ohio full of parts.' You don't care about that. All you want is your car to run. If it breaks, you want it fixed promptly and the part to be there. All the stuff that's in Ohio is nothing but waste and investment. We understood that if you could let everybody know exactly where their product was, people could begin to do away with this huge investment in warehouses."

That is what FedEx does with its parcel tracking systems. At any given moment, it can tell you exactly where your package is.

"That's why information has always been important to us. It allows our customers to keep near custodial control of things in transit. They don't need to have inventory stuck someplace. Our trucks and planes are really 550 mile-per-hour warehouses."

There is a second advantage to running the company with a heavy dependence on information. It allows Smith, and his managers, to apply manufacturing quality techniques to their service company.

"It is impossible to manage a business toward progressively higher levels of quality unless you actively measure the activities of the enterprise. That's been proven over and over again. And so, in addition to providing instantaneous accessibility to the customer, we also wanted the information to create a complete record of each transaction we handle, so we could use that mathematically to improve the quality of our business day after day. That's why we won the Malcolm Baldrige Award. Most service businesses are qualitatively measured, not quantitatively measured. You go to a restaurant, it's good food or it is not. You go on an airline, it's a good flight or it's not. We want to improve quality just like Motorola and Toyota, based on actual measurements, not anecdotes."

How does he measure performance? "There are three measures we use to make sure we are going in the right direction," Smith says. "The Service Quality Index is the first one. The SQI is made up of 12 mathematically measured factors on every shipment. Second is the CSI, that's the Customer Satisfaction Index, which is comprised of about 36 ratings customers give us on a repetitive basis. And the last one is our PQI, Process Quality Indicators, where individual operating units monitor the subcomponents that go into the service system. For instance, the Los Angeles terminal will have Process Quality Indicators on the 242 trucks coming into that terminal. And every day they'll want to have those 242 trucks be on time or early. They're constantly working on those PQIs, because if the trucks are late, the containers don't get loaded. If the containers don't get loaded, then the last plane out doesn't get loaded, which causes our packages to be delayed.

"Those are our three gauges, and if they're all going in the right direction then market share should go up. And our results track pretty darn well to these measures."

"We Were e-commerce Before e-commerce Was Cool"

As Smith correctly notes, the company's extensive use of computers, doing business computer (the customer's) to computer (FedEx's), streamlining the supply chain, and fulfilling transactions for Internet companies, makes Federal Express a major factor in the exploding field of e-commerce. It took most people a while to figure that out, but once they had, investors awarded FDX the so-called "Internet premium." For example, when *Barron's* made the point explicitly in December of 1998 that FDX was a major factor in e-commerce, the company's stock jumped 8% the next trading day.

Smith seems a bit bemused that it has taken investors so long to catch on. "All this talk about electronic commerce, it's a little bit like that country and western song, we were country before country was cool. We were in EC a long time before EC was cool. We have the largest online interactive network in the world, and have always had."

Company (Ticker): FedEx Corporation (FDX)

Location: Memphis, Tennessee

Leader: Frederick W. Smith

Description: FedEx Corporation was formed expressly to unite overnight package delivery leader Federal Express (FedEx) and trucking company Caliber System. FedEx consists of five main subsidiaries. FedEx delivers more than three million express packages to more than 210 countries each working day. Subsidiary FedEx Ground is the second-largest ground carrier of small packages (those under 150 pounds) in the United States. Viking Freight is a less-than-truckload carrier in the western United States. FedEx Custom Critical, the largest surface-expedited carrier in North America, provides delivery of time-critical shipments. FDX Global Logistics designs, develops, and applies integrated logistics and technology solutions for customers worldwide. FedEx Trade Networks provides custom brokerage and trade consulting services.

1999 Financial Results

—Revenues: $16.7 billion

—Net income: $631 million

What It Takes to Be a Business Leader Today

What kind of CEO does Smith think it takes to lead a major company both now and in the future?

"I think the CEO of any organization must be above all a strategist. He or she must have, to quote Peter Drucker, some theory of the business. Every business changes and every business is required to change more often than most people would like to think is the case. So you have to have someone who has a vision, whatever it might be, and a strategic, analytical capability.

"The second thing that they've got to do is surround themselves with excellent people, and be willing to delegate a lot of authority. Very large organizations are never the product of one person's executive ability. They're always the product of a team of executives.

"The third thing that you have to do is be highly energetic, because this job does take a big strain. And the fourth characteristic is that you have to be a good communicator, particularly with key external publics, as well as the internal ones. Most of the dangers for big companies today really don't reside internally, they reside externally, among competitors and particularly in Washington.

"And there is another attribute that is required, that has never really been the case before: a basic understanding of what information and telecommunications technology is capable of doing. Maybe 10 years ago you didn't need to know that. Today not knowing it, or at least not keeping abreast of it, is a huge mistake. You don't have to be a technologist, but you have to know that technology is going to allow certain businesses and processes to change fundamentally and see what that does to your business. I don't think you would have had to have been as concerned about the communications and externalities 10 years ago. You always needed to be a strategist and I think you always needed to get good people and give them a lot of authority."

It is rare for someone to create an entirely new industry, but that is exactly what Smith did back when he was an undergraduate at Yale and wrote a paper explaining how it would be possible to start a business that would deliver goods and packages anywhere in the country (and now the world) overnight.

Smith got a "C" on the paper.

He has earned significantly better marks in the real world.

Entrepreneurs aspiring to become corporate leaders can—and do—look to Smith as a role model. He created a breakthrough idea, designed a revolutionary organization to execute it, uses information and technology better than the competition, and consistently measures quality and performance—quantitatively.

And if that is not enough, he lets employees ride in the jump seats of company planes for free.

BILL STEERE
Pfizer

"Fads come. Fads go. We concentrate on what
we do best."

RESEARCH. RESEARCH AND MORE RESEARCH. THAT IS THE WORD—OR
three—that Steere uses to explain Pfizer's success. A few years ago, when
nearly every other major pharmaceutical company was frantically merging or buying generics companies or distribution networks, Steere refused
to play, saying he would rather spend his money on research.

And Steere's singular focus has paid off big time. The company is now
the world's third-largest pharmaceutical company, and Steere's goal is to
make it number one. Under his leadership, Pfizer is committed to developing new drugs to treat a variety of illnesses associated with aging. The
research he talks about is team-based and
multi-disciplinary and often deals with
improving quality of life and lifestyle issues as much as illnesses.

If you take a look at the aging process,
it is easy to see why that is the case. The
good news is medical research has figured out ways to extend our life. The bad
news is that living longer forces us to
deal with problems of its own. More
and more people are being confronted
with the problems of Alzheimer's, cancer,
diabetes, heart disease, as well as hair
loss and impotence, and so Pfizer is devoting its attention to the genes that
govern these problems. It was this commitment to molecular biology—a commitment that is now equal to the one
Pfizer has made to chemistry and other

CAREER
1992–2001 Chairman and CEO,
   Pfizer Inc.
1991–1992 President and CEO
1986–1991 President, Pfizer Pharmaceuticals
1984–1986 Executive Vice President
1982–1984 Vice President, Director of
   Operations, Pfizer Labs
1962–1981 Various staff positions, Pfizer
1960–1962 Sales representative

EDUCATION
B.S., Stanford University, 1959

FAMILY
Married, Lynda Gay Powers; children: William,
   Mark, Christopher

Born: Ann Arbor, Michigan, June 17, 1936

> *"I think the worst thing you can do, when you think about hiring the person who is going to replace you, is to go looking for a clone."*

disciplines—which led to the discovery of Viagra, an impotence treatment.

The company now has about 6,000 researchers around the world at three "campuses." Not all of that research is directed at humans. Pfizer's animal-health business is the largest in the world.

But in either case, the company is now completely focused on discovering, developing, and bringing to market innovative research-based products.

THERE ARE A LOT OF ADVANTAGES TO SPENDING YOUR ENTIRE CAREER working for a single company. For one thing, you get to understand the business pretty well. For another, you watch fads come and go. Those two facts have governed the way Bill Steere has led Pfizer.

As a long-term employee—Steere began working as a Pfizer sales rep after graduating from Stanford—he knew that pharmaceuticals were at the very heart of the company. And as someone who had been around for a while, he knew that management trends tend to come and go, and, unfortunately, have the tendency of leaving inappropriate things in their wake.

"My predecessor, Ed Pratt, did a really good job with the company, but he was in charge of Pfizer during the 1970s, and early 1980s, when CEOs were into diversification," Steere explains. "So we had diversified into a bunch of businesses that, if you reached, you could say were related. When I became CEO, we had businesses from cosmetics to chemicals to talc mines in Montana.

"But that was the operating fad at the time. Everybody was trying to create big conglomerates. The rationale was that if one of your businesses failed, or had trouble, then the others would fill in the slack. The result was financial, rather than strategic, acquisitions and all these other businesses took an enormous amount of time.

"It was clear to me that our pharmaceutical business was our key business, and if anything happened to that, nothing would save us."

And so immediately upon becoming CEO in 1992, Steere began streamlining the company, selling off the 40% of the company that was not directly related to making drugs for either animals or humans.

"That's our core competency," he says simply. "There is a lot of pressure to move beyond that. I remember when I became chairman the first thing people said was, 'You've got to buy a generic company [a firm that makes nonproprietary drugs, some of which may be sold over the counter]. You've got to get into generics.' But generics are not our business. We're a research-based pharmaceutical company. We spend well over $2 billion a year on research and the antithesis of that is a company that makes generics. I mean, they're scavengers. They live off patent expirations, and intellectual property is the life blood of our company.

"Making our products is not very expensive. It's one of the lowest costs in our P&L. Researching the products, finding the products, bringing them to market, and then marketing them is where the real costs are. That's where our real value-added is."

That is something other drug companies recognize. The Japanese pharmaceutical company Eisai enlisted Pfzier's aid in co-promoting Aricept, its Alzheimer's treatment, and Warner-Lambert sought Pfizer's help in co-promoting its product Lipitor, which reduces cholesterol and triglycerides.

"We are absolutely the best when you look at our discovery efforts, our development efforts, and the marketing of drugs. Generics don't fit what we do. Research does."

The company is now spending better than $2 billion a year on research. And the research it does is tightly focused.

"I think we probably manage research better than other companies," Steere says. "We have 6,000 researchers on three continents. And with 6,000 people, you've got management issues. You have the first-line supervisors, and then there are the managers, assistant directors, directors, senior directors, vice presidents, senior vice presidents, and, ultimately, they report in to a board member. And that board member reports to me. So, the research has to be managed. If we've got some really interesting research that's going up a blind alley, then the researchers have to be pulled back from it and put on another track.

"On the other hand, a lot of research is serendipitous. Take our drug Viagra. That was a drug for angina. It had a unique side effect—causing erections in our normal volunteers. That was serendipitous. We knew very well the effect the drug had on the heart. We knew where the receptor sites were and how the drug worked on the heart. We just didn't know that there were more of these receptors in the penis than there were in the heart. So the science is terrific. But now we know about these receptor sites and where they are and how they react. So then, that generated a whole new line of research.

"So, as the Viagra example shows, you can't cut projects off so soon that they can't find other stuff. However, once it becomes clear in the view of the management groups that the research is going down a blind alley, they've got to do something else."

The reason for that is simple, Steere says.

"Our job, and this is well understood by our researchers, is to discover, develop, and bring to market new pharmaceuticals. We aren't doing pure research."

The research Pfizer is doing is designed to satisfy its customers—people, animals, and, intriguingly the Federal Drug Administration (FDA), the federal agency that regulates U.S. pharmaceutical companies.

"One of our core values is customer focus," Steere explains. "And I view the FDA as a customer. Even though they're our regulators, they're our customers. So, the question is, how do you deal with this customer? You have to find ways of satisfying them. We are getting a lot better at it."

It Doesn't Get Any Easier

You might think that reducing Pfizer to a single line of business, one with a directed focus, would make managing the business simpler. Steere says that is not the case and that his successor is going to find managing the company more difficult than he did, even if the next CEO does not change the firm's focus.

"I think everything's getting more complicated," Steere says. "Even in a single line of business like ours, the regulatory complexities, the research complexities, the marketing complexities, and the fierceness of the competition make it a very difficult business. It is complex and getting more so. You have to be able to deal with ambiguity. And if you can't deal with ambiguity, then it's going to be tough to be a CEO in this business. There's just nothing that's really straightforward. It may be true of all the businesses, but it certainly is in ours."

Does he have any advice for aspiring business leaders?

"I believe that you've got to manage to people's strengths. Everybody's got weaknesses. And if you focus on his or her weaknesses, you're just going to make everybody unhappy. Focus on

Company (Ticker): Pfizer Inc. (PFE)
Location: New York, New York
Leader: Henry McKinnell
Pfizer at a glance: Pfizer is one of the world's premier research-based pharmaceutical companies. Its pharmaceutical product line includes Norvasc (its leading product) for cardiovascular disease, antidepressant Zoloft, antibiotic Zithromax, Lipitor, a cholesterol-lowering drug, and Viagra, designed to combat impotence. The company is also one of the world's top producers of veterinary medicine for farm and domestic animals. Pfizer also makes consumer health products, such as Unisom sleep aide, Plax dental rinse, BenGay muscle rub, and Visine eyedrops. Pfizer acquired Warner-Lambert in the year 2000 for $90 billion.
1999 Financial Results
—Revenues: $27.6 billion
—Net Income: $4.9 billion

their strengths. If you gradually understand that their weaknesses are more profound than their strengths, then you have to reassign them. But if you have good people and focus on what they do well, and kind of work around their weaknesses, they'll be happy and do better and so will the company."

Especially if that company is focused on doing what it does best.

BOB TILLMAN
Lowe's Companies

Bet the company, with everyone's help

TO ROBERT L. TILLMAN, THE COMPETITION IS ALL OVER (EXCEPT FOR the shouting) in the home improvement do-it-yourself market. The career veteran of Lowe's, who started with the company as a store manager and has held just about every operating position, sees the industry quickly shaking out into just two companies—Lowe's and Home Depot. Industry analysts say the country can support about 2,000 "big boxes"—those huge retail home improvement centers that spread across the landscape, and Home Depot and Lowe's combined will top that number in a couple of years. Lowe's, alone, will have 700 to 800 stores—located in all 50 states—in the foreseeable future.

To make sure that Lowe's is one of the last two standing, Tillman is committed to not only opening more superstores, but also to providing better service. But those two moves, he believes, are just the cost of entry. To truly succeed, Tillman argues, Lowe's will have to capture four key market segments:

- Female consumers, because he believes they will be making more and more of the home improvement purchasing decisions in coming years.
- The aging baby boomers, who want the convenience of one-stop shopping everywhere, including the do-it-yourself market.
- Generation Xers, a group that he thinks has been underserved, and who are

CAREER
1998–PRESENT Chairman, President, and CEO, Lowe's Companies, Inc.
1996–1998 President and CEO
1994–1996 COO and Executive Vice President, Merchandising
1989–1994 Senior Vice President, Merchandising
1962–1989 Various operating positions,

EDUCATION
B.A., University of North Carolina, 1962

FAMILY
Married, Sandy; children: one daughter

Born: Mount Olive, North Carolina, September 4, 1943

"As its leader, I never expected to make it all the way through our change process. I never thought I would survive. But as long as I did what was in the best interests of the company, I knew that I could defend any recommendation, or decision, with pride."

obviously both getting older, and buying homes in increasing numbers.
• People who shop online.

But no matter which segments he targets, he is going to make sure to ask customers what they want—and then give it to them. Says Tillman: "If you give the consumers credit for being intelligent and smart, they'll reward you with their business."

YEARS AGO, CHARLES GRODIN, THE ACTOR AND TALK SHOW HOST, wrote his autobiography. He took his title from an incident that happened when he was filming in England.

The producers had rented a castle that was still being lived in by minor royalty who could use the money. One day during production the woman of the house came across the crew shooting a scene downstairs.

It was clear that the woman resented the scores of technicians, actors, and support people being there. But there was no doubt that she would never forget her manners. The dowager walked up to Grodin, introduced herself, and gave Grodin his title when she said, "It would be ever so nice if you weren't here."

It was clear that Bob Tillman felt much the same way about our visit, gracious and engaging though he was.

"Let me say, first of all, I would not have done this [interview] if our public relations folks had not pressured me," he said, almost immediately after we met. "And the reason for that, quite frankly, is philosophically I don't agree with singling out leadership when it comes to talking about our success. Leadership is important inside our company and externally as it relates to the financial community and our customer base and the customer franchise. But one person neither builds nor manages a business. You have to have a team that does that. And the more you embellish or highlight one person, the more you detract from the whole team itself."

And the last thing that Tillman wants to do is detract from his team because it is in the midst of carrying out—extremely successfully—his bet-the-company decision.

There was a time, not that long ago, that Lowe's, based in North Carolina, was the number-one do-it-yourself home repair chain in the country.

But as Tillman puts it with characteristic directness, "We allowed our-selves to slip into the number-two position [behind Home Depot]. They are a great company, but we are trying awfully hard to overtake them."

Step one in the plan was for the board to appoint Tillman, who had been chief operating officer and executive vice president of merchandis-ing, to the CEO position.

Step two was for Lowe's to solidify its position in the market, and in essence guarantee that ultimately there will only be two big national play-ers. Tillman has done that through Lowe's 1999 acquisition of Eagle, a West Coast home and garden retailer, a purchase that will bring Lowe's annual revenues up to about $15 billion.

And then comes step three, which is still underway. Tillman is com-pletely restructuring the company—changing everything from what the stores look like to what they sell. The move is necessary, he says, if the company is to survive.

Some background will help.

The Good Old Days

In 1989, Lowe's had 295 stores, all of them were less than 20,000 square feet, and it was facing Home Depot, which was starting to build complete one-stop, do-it-yourself centers that were five times as large. Tillman could see the writing on the wall.

"We were, at the time, the largest do-it-yourself retailer in the world. And we were doing a little less than $2 billion a year by principally offer-ing a way of doing business that our customers didn't particularly like," Tillman says. "We were basically a lumberyard with a retail store on the front.

"In 1989 I was given the job of running the merchandising and mar-keting area of the business. I had been in store operations forever. One of the first things I did was hire a research firm to do a lot of work for us. We had always done research internally, but nobody believes internal infor-mation. You have to have somebody authoritative from the outside to confirm what you should already know.

"Consumers told the researchers that 'We like you, Lowe's, but we hate your stores. We like you, Lowe's, but we hate your merchandise. We like you, Lowe's, but you're not my complete home improvement store.'

"They liked us because we'd been at it a long time. We had credibility. They felt that we were honorable and that our stores were good commu-nity citizens, but they felt we weren't listening to them. They told us, 'You're okay for lumber building materials, but you're not worth a dime for plumbing or electrical or hardware or home decor—all the other things that I need for my home.'"

That wasn't a problem, if everything in the market stayed the same. As long as chains stayed in their own area of the country—Scotties in Florida markets; Lowe's in the lower Mid-Atlantic and Southeast, and Pay Less in the Midwest—and everyone offered the same sort of merchandise—not listening to the consumer wasn't fatal.

But the market was not staying the same. Home Depot, with its huge stores and national plans, was in the process of changing everything, much in the same way Staples changed the way office supplies are sold, and the retailers who sell nothing but athletic shoes have altered forever the way people buy sneakers.

It was clear from the research that Lowe's would have to change dramatically in order to survive. Either it would give consumers what they wanted, or someone else would.

Understanding that you have to change is one thing, changing is something else. But as Tillman explains, the company did have some advantages going for it.

"One, we had employee owners, because of our ESOP [Employee Stock Ownership Plan]. [In total, the company's 65,000 employees own about 15% of the company.] Employee/owners are willing to change far quicker than traditional employees because they have a vested interest. Second, most of the senior managers back then were not really merchants or store operators, so they had no real ownership of what we carried or even what the stores looked like. They were not standing in the way saying, 'No, you can't change the store. You can't change the merchandise offering.'

"And three, once we knew what we wanted to do, we had the capital to do it. Lowe's was a well-managed company with very, very low debt ratios."

At the direction of the CEO at the time, Tillman, without the rest of senior management initially knowing about it, went off with four other executives and wrote a new vision for Lowe's, one that called for larger stores, much more merchandise, and a commitment to everyday low prices, the retailing strategy that eliminates most "sales."

"To the credit of the then CEO, he agreed to accept the new vision for the company. This was in early 1990. And this new vision became our guide for growth. And we used that vision like a hammer to move the company forward. Because everybody in the company was not in favor of what we had in mind."

How do you gain acceptance, when you are talking about tearing down what has worked for generations?

"One thing that helped tremendously is that the chief executive officer gave me access to the board of directors of the company. I was allowed to bring the board up to speed on the new vision, where we wanted to go, and what the plans for growth were. There were 120 different growth plans because we had to change every single thing, in order to realize the vision. The board, which included retailers such as John Schumaker, who had been a vice chairman of Wal-Mart before he retired, was very supportive. And the CEO ran interference for me. I think the reason everyone became supportive was that after we laid everything out, and showed how the market was changing, the team understood that even though we were a great company, we really had to start all over again. We didn't have the luxury of standing still anymore. Everything had to change and we didn't have a lot of time to change it. Our biggest store at the time had 10,000 SKUs [stock keeping units; an SKU is assigned to each individual item that a store sells]. We had to get to 40,000 SKUs in every store—in a hurry."

And the prices on those items had to change as well. As Tillman put it: "We were a high-low price retailer," meaning that everyday prices on items were fairly high, but when the company had a sale it had the lowest prices in the area.

"We had to switch to everyday low prices. But in the history of retailing, very few companies have done that successfully. It took Wal-Mart eight years. Sears tried it for a few months and quit. We had to do it successfully in 18 months."

The company had to change, because the customer demanded it.

"Growing up in retail, I have known from the very beginning that the customer is far smarter than the retailer is. When retailers fail, it's because of their own personal arrogance that they believe they know what the customer really wants. That's why they fail.

"Our customers told us they didn't want to wait for sales. So, we bet the bank on things like everyday low prices. We didn't go pick selective items within a category and say we'll mark them down and feature them. We reduced the entire category, and guess what happened? Within a week, sales on those items went up 30% and 40%.

"And we had to replace all those small stores. We've spent billions doing it. We were probably overcognizant of recognizing that the change we've experienced in the last 10 years will be amplified and accelerated in the next five. In the 1950s, if you came up with a concept, it might be good for 20 years. In the 1960s and 1970s, it might be good for 15 years. Now, it may only last five years, so we had to design a vehicle—complete with systems and capabilities—to give us maximum flexibility. If the customer doesn't like the merchandise in the category—bam! We'll just put a new one in. If the customer doesn't want to shop one way, we have to be able to modify our stores quickly to let them shop another.

"So building large stores was not just about having category dominance. It was also about building stores with maximum flexibility. It is our vision that in our stores, over the period of the next five years, every-thing in that store will change completely. You have to have a lot of peo-ple thinking strategically, who understand how we will have to modify our business in advance of customer trends.

"It's a real challenge for us. The moment you fix any particular prob-lem, you have to start finding even a better way to be able to handle that business process or get that new assortment to market quicker. The diffi-cult thing about the business environment today is that you never really reach fulfillment. There's no such thing as 'I've finally got it done.' Be-cause the minute you reach that pinnacle of thinking you've got it exactly the way you want it, it's got to start changing. It has to change."

For the immediate future, what do the new Lowe's stores look like? They are the biggest in the industry, some 115,000 square feet, more than two acres of selling space. To put this vast size in perspective, the typical Wal-Mart or Kmart is about 40,000 square feet. "Superstore" is the term usually applied to anything larger than that, and a "big" superstore is 80,000 square feet. The typical Lowe's store then is half again as large as a big superstore. Home Depot stores, on average, are in the 80,000- to 100,000-square-foot range.

Not only are the stores larger than Home Depot's, they are decidedly different. For one thing, they are deliberately designed to appeal to women.

"All our research told us that women make the decisions in terms of major projects. I mean, how often does a man come home and say, 'I think we need a new kitchen.' Or, 'I want to put some new draperies up.' Or, 'We need to put a new floor down in the bedroom.' It just doesn't happen. Women drive those decisions.

"And we learned something else. We learned that the most discriminat-ing shoppers are female. We knew that if we could win over the loyalty of the female shopper, men would follow. Men are very simplistic. If you've got the damn stuff in stock and it's at a good price, and they can get out in hurry, they're happy. They say, 'I've got a golf game this afternoon, so let me go get this done.'

"Women shop. And they shop intelligently. They know the prices of things. They know what's available. They look at magazines. They look at Home and Garden Television. How many men watch decorating shows when a football game is on? Women are different customers, and you have to market to them differently. We needed to create a more invit-ing environment. A store that was lighter and brighter, with bigger aisles and clean floors."

The changes went further.

"The overall ambience of the store is more upscale and we can cover a broader range of customers' wants, needs, and desires. Our customers have told us they want more style and fashion and more choices. Major appliances, which are part of our kitchen business, are an example. We're the fourth-largest retailer of major appliances in the United States, behind Sears, Circuit City, and Best Buy and we are growing faster than they are. We also sell lifestyle furniture, which the X-er generation really likes. We do this because our customer wants it. Our customer wants more home decoration. And you're going to see major brands that you've seen principally in department stores in Lowe's stores in coming years."

What About the Employees?

How do you inspire people in this new environment?

"You have to tie individual goals and rewards to the performance of the company. If the corporation wins everybody wins. You have individual objectives you want to accomplish, and you incentivize people that way. But, overall, we've tied everybody's performance to a team concept. Within the merchandising group, their logisticians, their market research people, their financial planning people, their store design people, are all tied to the performance of how the team achieves its goals and objectives.

"That's one thing you do. A second is you let employees make decisions so that they can say, 'It's my store, or my department.'

"My expectations of every person are far greater than their own personal expectations for themselves. I believe they all can do great things, if they are put in the right environment, and given the right challenges and the right tools.

"So I'm very challenging. I expect a lot from people, but I expect no

Company (Ticker): Lowe's Companies, Inc. (LOW)

Location: North Wilkesboro, North Carolina

Leader: Robert L. Tillman

Description: Lowe's Companies, the second-largest home improvement retailer in the United States (following Home Depot) has over 575 stores in more than 37 states. The company offers everything the do-it-yourself homeowner could want—and given the company's services, they don't even have to do it themselves. Lowe's sells a broad range of building supplies, hardware, home decor and garden products, appliances, lumber, tools, paint, and consumer electronics. Lowe's helps customers design kitchens and even installs many of its products, including doors, flooring, and cabinets. The company continues to expand from its original eastern U.S. stronghold and is adding more stores in the South and Midwest; it acquired Eagle Hardware & Garden as part of its plans for major growth in the western part of the United States, and is looking to expand into Arizona, California, and Nevada by 2002.

1999 Financial Results

—Revenues: $12.2 billion

—Net Income: $482 million

more of them than I expect from myself. I expect strong commit-ments. But also I reward people accordingly. That's how you keep people motivated.

"I think it's also important to recognize that success itself motivates. It's very critical that the CEO crafts plans that lead to successful performance for the corporation. You've got to be so careful about that because you can destroy the attitude of everybody in the company. Nobody wants to be part of a loser. They want to be part of a winner. They've got to see tangi-ble, measurable results that we are winning. It's the CEO's job to make sure that happens."

ALEX TROTMAN
Ford Motor Company

Drive

When Lawrence Taylor joined the New York Giants in the early 1980s, football commentators took to calling him the prototypical linebacker of the future: someone who was real big, real strong, and real fast.

About 15 years later, awed by Mark McGwire's size and strength, people said that the St. Louis Cardinal's record-breaking first baseman had become the prototype of what future generations of home-run hitters would look like.

In the future, we may look back on Alex Trotman, of the Ford Motor Co., as the prototype for future CEOs of large multi-national corporations. Born in England, and raised and educated in Scotland, Trotman recently stepped down as head of the international concern.

Although he spent his entire professional life at Ford—he began as a student trainee in the purchasing department, arriving to work on a double decker bus—Trotman has a wide-ranging perspective on the company, having worked in numerous departments around the globe. When a leader heads a company

CAREER
1993–1998 Chairman and CEO, Ford Motor Company
1992–1993 President, Ford Automotive Group
1989–1992 Executive Vice President–North American Automotive Operations
1984–1988 Chairman, Ford Europe
1983–1984 President, Ford Asia-Pacific
1979–1983 Vice President, of Truck Operations, Ford Europe
1977–1979 Executive Director of Operations Planning, Ford Motor Co.
1975–1977 Chief Car Planning Manager, Car Development Group
1972–1975 Director, Product Planning
1970–1972 Manager, Lincoln-Mercury's Product Planning Department
1967–1969 Director, Ford's European Car Planning Office
1955–1967 Supervisory and planning positions in Ford of Britain

EDUCATION
Boroughmuir School, Edinburgh, Scotland, Higher Learning Certificate, 1951
M.B.A., Michigan State University, 1972

FAMILY
Married, Valerie; four children

Born: Middlesex, England, July 22, 1933

"*I am a businessman, and that's what I brought to the job.*"

that operates on six continents, this kind of experience is ideal.

As more and more companies go global, more and more boards of directors are looking for chief executives like Trotman, men and women who have unique perspectives on world markets, because they have experienced them firsthand.

Interestingly, while Trotman agrees that senior managers today need to have a wide range of experiences, he does not believe that there is one style of management that is right for any particular culture.

IT IS A QUESTION ALEX TROTMAN HAS THOUGHT ABOUT A LOT: ARE American business leaders fundamentally different from executives in other parts of the world?

It is not an academic question. As companies become progressively more global, boards of directors are spending an increasing amount of time thinking about the necessary characteristics the person at the top should have. More frequently than ever before, they are deciding that an international perspective is required.

That is, of course, a major change. For the longest time, if you served on the board of directors of an American-based firm, even one with a global presence, and you were dealing with the question of CEO succession, there was no doubt about one thing. The next CEO would be an American. Of course, there was an occasional exception, such as Roberto Goizueta at Coca-Cola, David Johnson (p. 181) of Campbell Soup, and an occasional Canadian or two might be appointed to run American firms, but these appointments were far from typical. Generally speaking, Americans ran American companies, and this attitude continued right down the line when it came to filling senior positions. Ford Motor Company was typical of companies that used to be managed this way.

"There was a period, certainly up through the 1970s, when management decided that you couldn't trust the natives, and you had to send a good American to every trouble spot around the world," Trotman recalls. "The assumption was that the natives couldn't handle it. You had to put a Yank there. An exception might be found in Australia, or Germany, or Britain. But in many other places—South America, Argentina, Brazil, Mexico—you had Americans all over the place. Even Canada at one time."

So not surprisingly, Trotman, who had to pay his own way to the United States when he told Ford executives he wanted "home office" experience, has thought about whether there is a uniquely American style of managing. Can you look at how an executive handles a situation and say, "He is an American business leader"?

Trotman's conclusion?

No.

"The adjective doesn't belong with the noun. I mean, there is no such thing as an American business leader or a Japanese business leader. There are good ones and mediocre ones and absolutely awful ones. And nationality doesn't matter. I know some very good executives of all shades and colors and backgrounds.

"There are some stereotypes that you can dream up, but they're mostly in the movies. I don't think the phrases American business leader or German business leader mean anything to me at all."

But just because there is no defining national trait to identify the best businesspeople, that does not mean that Trotman thinks that someone who has only worked in one culture should be put in charge of an international company.

"I'd have a problem with that," he says. "You'd have to give me a long and detailed explanation in order to convince me that this person is really going to be a globally effective businessperson if he or she was born and raised in Stuttgart, or in Detroit, and he never worked anywhere else. I think it would be very likely he would have some major holes in the boat from the perspective of maximum effectiveness in a global company."

That's why Ford works so hard on making sure people destined for top management have had a series of international postings.

It is something that employees are made aware of on their first day on the job.

"I make it a point to say to every orientation group that I would bet big money that whoever is the next chief executive of Ford, or next group vice president, will be multi-cultural, and in most cases, multi-lingual.[1] Somebody who's born and raised in Detroit, or New York, or Europe, or Japan is not going to be in one of those positions unless they've hopped around functionally and geographically."

The reason for that is simple, Trotman says.

"They need to be representative of the world that we live in rather than being just a small part of it."

Trotman is committed to making sure that top executives at Ford will have that grounding.

"If you take the top 40 people at Ford, I don't think there's another

---

1. While chairman William Clay Ford is an American, Jacques A. Nasser, formerly Ford's president and now CEO, is an Australian who made his mark running international operations for Ford.

company that would have the mix of cultures and backgrounds that we do, and we have further to go in mixing ourselves up more as we go along. But we're a very multi-national, multi-cultural, multi-experienced group of executives at Ford."

Making sure people have international experience is more than making sure that they have their "ticket punched" he says.

"It's not just moving them around for the sake of moving them around. It's to help them gain the knowledge that they'll need to be able to effectively lead as they get higher and higher up in the company. What we're paying them for is leadership more than anything. We want them to lead a very complicated process that is staffed by a bunch of very different people. And experience as much as skill is required to be able to inspire those diverse people to work together as a effective team and deliver global results in a highly complex organization.

"It is an extremely difficult task. But the likelihood of scoring a 10 on a 10 scale is much enhanced if a talented person—and talent has to be a given—has had the experience of multi-cultures and functions, has worked in marketing, sales, perhaps in manufacturing or product development, and has been around in two or three different countries and is comfortable in the Spanish culture as well as ordering a meal in an English pub. That kind of person is much more likely to be an inspiring leader for a multi-cultural group of people. To me, this is not rocket science. It's very straightforward."

Measuring for Leadership

Since Ford believes international experience is one key aspect of leadership, it tracks executives' overseas experience along with the other traits it believes to be important.

"We have a matrix of all the leadership characteristics that we're interested in, and we measure people on that matrix," Trotman explains. "We're tracking your courage, durability, teamwork, integrity, and commitment to diversity. Do you just talk about it, or do you actually do anything? Let's have a look at all the metrics in your organization. What is your percentage of female executives? Why is it only 2% and the company average is 12%. Is that going to change by next year or not?"

It is not surprising that Trotman put this much emphasis on what it takes to develop successful leaders. Ford is in an industry where total sales are basically flat, margins are declining, and consolidation—as the recent Chrysler–Daimler Benz merger shows—is well under way. In this kind of environment, you want to develop leaders so that you do not fall by the wayside.

"The metrics required to manage a company are easy because you can read those in a book. And if you're disciplined and tough about it, anybody can do accounting. Mastering financial measurements is easy. But how do you get a diverse team of people to want to do great things? And then, how do you inspire them to keep on doing them despite all of the difficulties and the hard work that they'll face? That's leadership and that's hard.

"Look what happened to Brazil in the 1998 World Cup Final. They had the most talented players in the world, but they couldn't get them to work together. And the French did not have the highest level of talent, but they had total cohesion and passion. They said to themselves, 'We are going to win this thing, and we don't care that the other guys are a 10 on the skills scale and we are not on that level. We're going to beat them,' and they did.

"I think results stem from a combination of passion and skill. It's a multiplier."

How do you develop that passion?

"I think it begins with knowing the people. Establishing trust in the key movers and shakers in a company. Getting rid of the people that you don't trust. You can't sit around for years saying I'm going to have to wait until 'X' retires. You've got to move people out of the way if they're not totally dedicated to making whatever it is we want to make work. If there's not total dedication to that, then they've got to go.

"So, first, you've got to get a team. I don't think where you start is all that difficult. You start with a group of people who have all agreed to join hands and are committed to putting their maximum effort into working together and trusting one another. That's first. And until you've got that done, don't waste your time making beautiful strategies and talking about beautiful symphonies, because you won't play them unless all the instruments are totally dedicated to playing together. Do that first. And be totally sure you've got it right.

"Once you've got a team that you trust, and they trust you, you've got to agree, among other things, that mistakes will be made. Many of them. You don't get fired for mistakes. You only get fired for disloyalty or a lack of teamwork. And then, the energy will start to flow. Fear goes out and energy rises, and things get done.

"Then start evolving the major changes that you want to make. I assume you want to make the changes. If you don't want to make a major change, life is much simpler. You can play the incremental game all day and every day. And if you're reasonably disciplined about that, that works too for some companies. But if you're in the mode where you need to make major changes, you need to get the team in place and start doing what needs to be done."

There is no doubt about what Trotman believes needs to be done, when it comes to developing a winning team.

"In my case, I was involved with the careers of maybe 100 people, their development, training, selection or deselection from positions in the company. And it cascades down, so that we—the top 20 or 30 people—collectively probably have our arms around a couple of thousand of the leaders of the company. And it's all very structured. We don't leave it to chance.

"In the old days, you'd say to George or Mary over lunch, 'Oh, by the way, I've got a very promising young executive. Do you think you could give him a couple of years in marketing?' It was ad hoc. Today, we track a person's development. What's his rating on the leadership scale? He's a nine. Good. When is his next transfer? What's the plan?

"We have a leadership process now that we started three years ago, called Capstone. We select 24 of the best leadership people that we have in the company and we put them through hell for about four or five months with specific projects, which, in almost every case since we started, have resulted in real and positive things happening within the Ford Motor Company. Real changes happening to compensation policy, asset utilization policy, customer satisfaction, you name it. We put these people in groups of six and we say, 'Here's an impossible assignment that we can't figure out the answer to. We'll see you in four or five months.' They work on this, in addition to their regular jobs."

What does Trotman look for in these people?

"Well, it depends. It isn't a consistent specification. With someone who has the potential of being the head of Information Technology, I'd be most interested in his or her knowledge. But I'd also be interested in their teamwork ca-

Company (Ticker): Ford Motor Company (F)
Location: Dearborn, Michigan
Leaders: William Clay Ford, Chairman
Jacques A. Nasser, President and CEO
Ford at a glance: Ford Motor Co. is the world's largest truck maker and the number-two manufacturer of cars and trucks combined (behind General Motors). It manufactures and markets vehicles under the Ford, Volvo, Land Rover, Lincoln, Mercury, Jaguar, and Aston Martin brands. The company also owns interests in various non-U.S.-based automakers, including Mazda. Approximately one third of Ford's sales come from outside the United States. Its Ford Motor Credit subsidiary is the United States' number-one auto financier. The company also owns 81% of Hertz, the number-one car rental firm in the United States. Ford has also acquired Kwik-Fit Holdings, the leading car-repair shop chain in Europe. The Ford family owns about 34% of the company's voting stock.

1999 Financial Results
—Revenues: $162.5 billion
—Net Income: $7.2 billion

pability, and their personality. Would they fit in with the team? Could they work across functions? What about their energy level and reliability, with a big 'R'? Is this person going to deliver on time, every time, what he or she says will be delivered? Those kinds of things."

Is passion for the product necessary?

"I think it is important, but not vital. I'm very wary of people who profess to have gasoline in their nostrils and all of that. I'd like them to have shareholder value in their nostrils more than I would a passion for gasoline. I'd rather somebody tell me I'm going to deliver the right return for the shareholder than I'm going to produce the greatest Mustang that ever hit the street.

"So, a controlled passion for the product, I guess, would be best.

"Now, someone who says, 'I hate cars; they're polluting, wasteful, irresponsible,' I don't think they would recommend themselves for a leadership position. But somebody who just wants to come in and be a car buff would most likely not be the person we're looking for."

Ford is looking for leaders. And if a person doesn't have an international background, the company is going to make sure he or she acquires it.

DAN TULLY AND
DAVID KOMANSKY
Merrill Lynch

"There is only one question to ask:
What's best for the customer?"

AN AUTOGRAPHED PHOTO HANGS ON THE OFFICE WALL OF DAVID
Komansky, chairman and chief executive officer of Merrill Lynch and
Company, in the World Financial Center in downtown Manhattan. In it,
he is standing next to five distinguished-looking gentlemen—the five previous chairmen and CEOs of Merrill Lynch.

The picture helps explain what makes Merrill unique.

The identical photo hangs on the wall of Dan Tully's Stamford, Connecticut, office, where one of Merrill's two chairmen emeriti still goes to
work each day. The other chairman emeritus, William A. Schreyer, has a
copy as well, though his office is more than a hundred miles away at Merrill's sprawling corporate campus near Princeton, New Jersey. The transition from Schreyer to Tully to Komansky has been almost seamless.

In 1984, Schreyer took over the reins of a company that was largely a
U.S. retail brokerage firm. Not only did he push Merrill Lynch to become
the leading capital markets firm, he initiated vigorous expansion in Europe and Asia. While the firm had long been known for taking Wall Street
to Main Street, Schreyer's Merrill Lynch took Wall Street to the world.

When Wall Street was afflicted with the insider trading scandals of the
late 1980s, Merrill Lynch and Schreyer were steadfast in defense of
the firm's reputation for integrity, convinced that it was by far the company's most important corporate asset. When the October 1987 stock
market crash sent a shock through the economy, Schreyer immediately
took to the airwaves, assuring the public that the economy remained
sound and that Merrill Lynch remained bullish for the long term.

One of Schreyer's most inspired acts as CEO was his choice of successor, Tully, a tall, enormously affable man with a shock of gray hair and an
instinctive gift for leadership. Schreyer and Tully had worked as a team,
pulling Merrill through the difficult years of the late '80s. Tully's choice of

successor was Komansky—like Schreyer and Tully before him, a man whose professional roots lay in the company's retail operations, but who had also proven himself in leadership roles on the capital markets side of the business. And like his two predecessors, Komansky continued to build the firm through acquisitions and organic growth into a leader on the London and Tokyo Stock Exchanges, creating one of the world's largest active asset managers and becoming a leading banker and advisor to major corporations and sovereign governments the world over. The Internet is the next area Merrill is committed to winning in, although the firm recognizes the lead of some of its rivals.

In no other Wall Street firm—nor in almost any other leading corporation, for that matter—can you find such appreciation and affection for the ongoing chain of leadership. At most companies, it is commonplace for a newly appointed leader to undo the major initiatives of the old, or else to take the firm in a fundamentally different direction—whether by entering new markets, making a significant acquisition, or undertaking an internal reorganization.

That does not happen at Merrill Lynch. The heir apparent is consulted about decisions the incumbent chief executive officer is contemplating, and the retired CEOs do not hesitate to give advice to the current leadership. So it is not surprising that the company is larger than its individual leaders and that it strives to continue down the same path of market leadership, no matter who is in charge.

This makes Merrill unique and also explains why we decided to feature both the company's current leader *and* his predecessor.

We begin with Dan Tully.

IT WAS NOT AN AUSPICIOUS BEGINNING.

Fresh out of the Army in 1955, Dan Tully went looking for a job. A local brokerage firm was impressed enough to offer him $75 a week.

"I came home and said, 'Mom, I've got a job.'

" 'That's great son. With whom?'

" 'Merrill Lynch, Pierce, Fenner and Smith.' "

" 'Oh, that's nice, son. I always knew you'd do well in advertising.'

"She had no idea. Unless you had a pot full of dough, which we didn't, you didn't spend your time reading the *Wall Street Journal*. I didn't sit down and systematically go through all the possibilities out there and say, I'd like to work for an investment banking firm. It was just the luck of the draw. I was looking for a job.

They were hiring. I think I started the next day.

Regardless of how it happened, as everyone at Merrill will attest, it was a perfect fit.

For one thing, while there might have been people who had gone to more prestigious schools than Tully, there was no one who worked harder.

"When I got into sales, I said, "How am I ever going to differentiate myself? I'm not as smart as some of these folks, but if they make 10 sales calls a day, I'll make 12. If they work eight hours, I'll work 14." Nobody can take away effort, and blood, sweat, tears.""

That attitude was important, but even more important was the fact that Tully intuitively understood the principles on which the company—which was primarily focused on selling stocks to individuals back then—had been built.

"When Mr. Merrill started the firm he said something that sounds corny, but is our religion. He said, 'The client's interest must always come first.' If you're really driven by that, you will almost always do the right thing. And if you're willing to adapt, and innovate, and change as your clients change, you are bound to prosper."

The decision to take better care of customers was really the turning point in both Merrill's success—and Tully's career.

"Back when I started, each of our salespeople were all things to all clients. I dealt with 'the widow Jones,' but I also dealt with the largest banks in Connecticut. So, I would go from dealing with someone who had a $40-a-month reinvestment plan to the Stamford Savings Bank, which was buying $100,000 worth of securities.

"At a certain point, we realized that there's no way you can give the client the best you have to offer if you have one person dealing with both retail and institutional accounts. We had to specialize. I was part of that decision, having been director of sales at the time.

"We told our sales force that they would have to choose between retail and institutional clients, and they weren't very happy. They loved the idea they were doing lots of business with the local banks and they would say to me, 'Why are you doing this, Dan? I'm doing $50,000 worth of business with the bank, and I'm not even working very hard.'

"I was convinced that the $50,000

CAREER—Daniel P. Tully
1998–PRESENT Chairman Emeritus, Merrill Lynch and Company
1993–1997 Chairman, CEO, and President
1985–1993 President and COO
1984 President, Consumer Marketing
1982–1984 President, Individual Services Group
1979–1982 Executive Vice President
1971–1979 Vice President
1963–1970 Manager, Stamford, Connecticut, Office
1959–1963 Account Executive
1955–1959 Member Accounting Department
1953–1955 U.S. Army

EDUCATION
Advanced Management Program, Harvard Business School, 1978
B.B.A., St. John's University, 1953

FAMILY
Married, Grace; four children

Born: New York, New York, January 2, 1932

> "What should a CEO do? Try to build upon the successes of the past. In the process, you hope to maintain and expand upon the core values the company has in place."

could be $500,000, if we just specialized, provided the bank with a bit of service, and provided a bit of value-added."

That decision to specialize was driven by this thought: If you want to be in business for a long time, you need to do what's right for your client.

"Most of our competitors just sold what they had. If they were a bond firm, they just pushed bonds. If they were an equity firm, they pushed equities. We made a decision—Don Regan was chairman at the time—that we would no longer be a transactional, product-oriented firm. We would be a relationship-driven organization looking for repeat transactions from our clients."

To underscore this new approach, Merrill (internally) designed an acronym: FAFI. "We wanted to be where clients had Funds Available for Investment. We were no longer going to be just sellers of stocks or bonds. We would be the people who solved the problems for our clients.

"From that point on, I really didn't care whether we sold municipals to one client or equities to another. We became indifferent to the product. We were going to take care of our clients, and if we did they would let us help invest their assets."

Not all of this worked perfectly. Merrill thought that being in the residential real estate business would be a perfect fit. It was not. It proved to be too transactionally oriented. But ideas such as the Cash Management Account, where all of a client's different sources of funds—cash, checking, savings, stocks and bonds—are linked together, became a huge hit.

The new philosophy on the consumer side, coupled with strategic acquisitions on the corporate finance side of the business—such as the purchase of White Weld, a leading investment bank—and Merrill quickly became a major player on Wall Street.

When Tully was promoted to the executive ranks, his charge was to ensure that Merrill stayed there.

"Two of the biggest problems we face are complacency and arrogance. As long as we continue to be focused on the clients, and the challenges that come in taking care of them, we should be okay."

Here's What We Believe

To make sure the company remains focused, Tully had the company's value statement—which dwells on integrity and service—prominently displayed in every Merrill Lynch office around the world. It is the first thing you see as you step off the elevator onto the executive floor of the company's headquarters in lower Manhattan.

"Your beliefs have to be your operating philosophy," Tully says. "You have to live them every day. When someone made $2 million or $3 million a year, and we have a lot of people who do, I'd call them. They thought I was calling to congratulate them. But I was really calling to ask them a few questions. 'How did you make all that money? If the *New York Times* put how you did it on the front page, would you be proud?' I wanted to remind them of the culture of this firm and I wanted to make sure they lived it."

Tully and his team instilled this spirit throughout the ranks.

"We have performance appraisals of our top 200 people every year and we share the results with the board. Senior management is at that meeting and we go down the list and call out a name, say 'Dan Tully.' And whoever was chairing the meeting would say, 'Who knows Dan Tully best?' And the first question we always asked was never, 'How much did Dan produce?' It was always, 'Have you ever known Dan to distort or color the truth in any way?'

"Sometimes we heard, 'You know, I've never known him to not tell me the truth. On the other hand, I suspect sometimes he doesn't volunteer everything.' Some people just don't give you the whole story. They won't lie, but they wouldn't give you the whole picture." That would be something that would be noted as the Merrill Lynch hierarchy went through the evaluations.

"Someone else would ask, 'Does Jim treat his subordinates similar to the way he treats his peers?' And people would say, 'You know, managing up he's a sweetheart, but managing down is another story.' "

And wherever the critique was less than stellar the problem would be addressed immediately.

"We constantly clarify expectations. It emanates from a love of your fellow human being. The reason you fight with your wife and kids is because you love them. You want them to be better. I feel the same way about my fellow employees. I want them to get better. How is that going to happen if I never tell them what I think they're doing wrong?

"You never do it in front of other people. Maybe it's over a cocktail or something like that. You get it out. And you also say, 'By the way, you wouldn't be where you are if you were a stiff. What we are talking about here are subtleties. This is to make you even better than you are.'

"You have to tell it like it is. You must give people honest, candid feedback. You have to do that so they know you are totally sincere, that you really care about their success. You owe it to them so they can reach their full potential, and you owe it to the people in the organization around them, the ones above and below them.

"If the guy in the middle is a stiff, and I let him stay there and destroy the people around him, shame on me. One thing I can do as a manager is make sure that good people surround you. That's what I always try to do. All this seems to me to be basic stuff."

Equally basic, Tully says, is to listen to employees and take advantage of their abilities.

"I used to joke with my colleagues, 'If I have to make all the decisions, why do I need you guys?'

"While I would never let someone do something I was diametrically opposed to, very often I would say, 'Well, what do *you* think?' And I'd listen and let them do it their way. That's the way you grow, by trying things. And that's the way a company grows too. Merrill would never be where we are today without taking the concepts that the younger people brought to us.

"When I managed the little branch office in Stamford [Connecticut], we'd send the new employees down to the Merrill Lynch training school in Princeton, the same as we do today, and they'd return and they'd say: 'Mr. Tully, I'm back. I'm ready to go. What should I do?'

"I'd say, 'Beats the heck out of me. What do you want to do?'

" 'No, come on, Mr. Tully, really. What do you want me to do?'

"I'd say, 'Hey, what do you want to do? If I tell you what to do, you're going to do it my way. I want you to do it your way. I want to see if you can come up with something new and different than the rest of us have been doing around here.'

"And they'd be disappointed that I didn't give them the Holy Grail of doing business. But they'd go out on their own—I monitored them every day, checked on their number of calls and new accounts opened, their prospects, all that stuff—and maybe they'd develop a new approach to going after a savings and loan account that the rest of us in the office never thought of.

"It's amazing what you can accomplish when you don't seek all the credit. I find nothing is really one person's idea. It grows out of a lot of little nuisances and changes that you make as you go along."

But while the approach may change over time, the core values never do.

"You have to live those values, and have them guide you through everything you do. I wasn't running the firm when the market dropped in October of 1997 but I was there in 1987 and 1974 and I could see how we acted. At the seven o'clock meeting I called the morning after the

1987 crash [when the stock market fell more than 20% in one day] I said today's going to be a day when we're going to be remembered for how we act. And I want you folks to get out there. I don't want you to be heroes, but I do want you to be certain you answer the phones, treat your clients with respect, and give them good counsel and advice.

"And we did. Some firms didn't do that, and they hid from their clients. And, ultimately, they lost the clients. I am extremely proud that during the market turmoil of 1998, our current chairman, Dave Komansky, and chief operating officer, Herb Allison, acted the right way."

When asked what has made Merrill Lynch, the company his mother thought was an advertising agency, so successful, Tully has a simple answer.

"The key to the whole thing? We do things right. We treat our clients right and we treat each other with dignity and respect. If you do those things, and are not motivated primarily by profit, you'll make a pot full of profit. However, if you start off trying to make a profit, you will be myopic and bound to fail. Go the other way. Do what's right for people, and all of a sudden you will develop a lot of clients and you will be awash in profits. It never works the other way around."

NOW IT'S KOMANSKY'S TURN

That photograph that hangs on the wall in the offices of Dan Tully, Bill Schreyer, and David Komansky has special meaning for the current chairman and CEO of Merrill Lynch.

"It was taken a few years ago at a global leadership conference. And all six of us were up on the stage and there were 800 people in the audience. The sensation, the wave, of familial cohesiveness was unbelievable. What firm could have six chairmen alive on the same stage, who actually like and talk to one another? That's a very unusual thing. I'm fortunate that I still have Don Regan, Roger Burke, Bill Schreyer, and Dan Tully around. (Mike McCarthy has since passed away.) I talk to them all the time. They have no problem providing me with a lot of input, and I have no problem ignoring it—as they did—when I

CAREER—David H. Komansky
1997–PRESENT Chairman and CEO, Merrill Lynch and Company
1995–1996 President and COO
1993–1995 Executive Vice President, Debt and Equity Markets
1992–1993 Executive Vice President, Debt Market Group
1990–1992 Executive Vice President, Equity Markets Group
1988–1990 Director of National Sales, Private Client Group
1968–1988 Various positions starting as a trainee and moving to account executive and manager

EDUCATION
Attended Miami Dade Junior College and The University of Miami

FAMILY
Married, Phyllis; children: two daughters

Born: Mount Vernon, New York, April 27, 1939

don't think they are right. But it's a very different environment than you'll find in any other financial services firm."

Implicit in that feeling is that you build on the strengths of the past. That is something Komansky works hard to do.

THERE ARE NUMEROUS PARALLELS BETWEEN THE MERRILL LYNCH careers of Dan Tully and David Komansky. For one thing, like Tully's, Komansky's arrival at Merrill was a matter of luck.

"I was kind of at loose ends, kicking around for a number of years down in Florida where we lived. One day, while we were visiting my in-laws in New York, my father-in-law, who was addicted to the stock market, said to me, 'You should go to Wall Street. It's ready-made for you.'

> *"I do not expect any employee to walk down the exact center of the road that we have laid out for our future. I do expect them to be* on *the road. As long as they're going in the right direction, in terms of what we want to accomplish and how, I am happy. Where they are on the road doesn't matter. You must give people the flexibility to be able to make their own decisions and grow."*

"I knew so little about it. Nevertheless, we came back up here on a Friday, and on Monday I started calling for appointments. That week, I interviewed with 10 or 15 firms. We went back to Miami and Merrill Lynch was the first job offer that I got. We put everything we had in storage, got in the car, took the $650 we had, and came up North and moved in with my in-laws, and I went to work for Merrill Lynch. I was just looking to get started with something and that was the first offer I got. Someone had told me if you can get a job with Merrill Lynch, you ought to take it because they have the best training program in the business. Fortunately, they're the ones that called first, and I went to work as a trainee and that was it."

And where Tully's decision to shift from accounting to sales was prompted by a desire to make more money, Komansky's decision to shift from sales to management was prompted by a desire for more control over his career.

"By my second day on the job, I saw what unbridled influence my manager had over my career, and therefore my life. I saw immediately that I was on the wrong side of this equation. It was clear that this was going to be a great job, but I did not enjoy someone having that much control over my life. And so from early on, I decided that management was where I wanted to be."

Komansky excelled in sales, so it was not until six years later—in 1974—that he got his chance to move to the other side of the desk, and quickly worked his way up the ladder. As such, he was a factor—albeit a minor one, he is quick to stress—in Merrill's transition from being simply a large retail broker to becoming a global full-service financial services firm.

Building on the Strengths of the Past

"I think there were three reasons why we were able to make the transition," Komansky says. "One was affordability. We had the financial wherewithal to fund our entire journey. That made us rather unique in the business, where most others have had to sell out or merge to fund their growth.

"Maybe more important than the affordability was the courage of the people who led the firm in those years. And I would say that the entire roster of them, from Regan and Burke to Schreyer and Tully, showed tremendous courage in standing up year after year defending what we were doing against the constant criticism that we were losing money on the way. We did suffer losses for a long time. However, the previous leaders of this firm are not the kind of men who fold in the heat of battle. They have the courage of their convictions.

"Schreyer—who was perfectly friendly with the then head of Goldman Sachs—loves to tell the story of sharing a cab with him one day. As Schreyer tells it, the guy turns to him and says, 'Why are you spending all this money and time and effort to build an investment bank? You have great distribution. Why aren't you happy being the greatest co-manager [of equity offerings] in the world?'

"And the answer was that we simply were not going to be happy being a major player in only a limited number of businesses. He just knew that we could be more. And then Dan just picked up right where Schreyer left off and the firm never wavered.

"Each man built on what the prior CEO had done."

What has Komansky done since taking the leadership baton from Tully? Focused on turning Merrill Lynch into a global financial services powerhouse.

"In the early 1980s, Bill Schreyer was really the first one to start talking about globalization in this firm. He traveled extensively, waving the flag, and encouraging a buildup of our private client business overseas. A lot of people used to kid him about going to Paris or Tokyo for a good time, but what he was really doing was planting the flag.

"When they asked me in 1990 to come from the retail side to run the equity business, one of my predecessors was a brilliant, research-oriented guy named Jack Lavery. He was talking about the world entering an era of 're-equification,' where global corporations were going to deleverage from all the debt they took on in the 1980s by issuing equity.

"As I got into the equity business, this started to make an awful lot of sense to me, especially in light of the fact that we were at the dawn of the era of privatizations around the world.

"So what really motivated me to drive the equity business on a global basis was to take advantage of this period of re-equification, and garner more than our share of the privatization business.

"Two years later, I went from the equity business to the fixed income business, which Roger Vasey had already started moving globally. Then I wound up leading both fixed income and equity, and while I wasn't managing investment banking, they too were building their international capabilities. So across the firm, we were marching aggressively internationally. To me, our globalization has been both the most exciting phenomenon and greatest accomplishment that Merrill has been involved in over the past decade."

A Visit from the Queen

"Here's an example of the progress we made. We went from being a role player in London to a position where our firm dominates the markets today. We account for more than 20% of trading volume in the City of London [the United Kingdom's financial district].

"Perhaps the following is a better way to illustrate how far we have come. In late 1998, the British government wanted to do something to signify the importance of the City of London to the U.K. economy. So they had the Queen agree to visit an investment bank, and they chose Merrill Lynch! Now I've got to tell you, from our point of view, we thought that was quite an honor. However, from our employees' point of view over there—and at least 95% of them are British—they were just beside themselves with glee over this. And the British banks, by the way, were thoroughly ticked off.

"We have gone from having a handful of people in Europe to 8,000 employees on the continent. We are probably the largest single securities firm in Europe today."

It's the People Who Make It Work

The company is expanding globally by both opening new offices and acquiring other firms. Is there one thing that makes an acquisition work for Merrill?

"We consider the compatibility of the people and try really hard to understand them," Komansky responds. "It is absolutely one of our top criteria. Clearly, it is very easy to understand the strategic value of an acquisition, and it's even easier to understand the past financial performance. But to me, the real art of a successful acquisition is accurately assessing the people in the firm you are going to acquire. Do they bring you the talents you think you're going to need? If so, can you retain them, which is obviously key? And will they thrive in your culture and organization?"

Komansky says he will spend months speaking with the principals of companies that Merrill Lynch is considering acquiring before pulling the trigger.

"You have to get to know them. They have to get to know you. You need to know that you are going to be on the same page. We have found that when we spend the time to really understand the people we are dealing with, the deals work. When we don't, there are problems.

"I look at it this way. When we are trying to acquire a company—or even when we are trying to recruit a senior executive—everyone has to be comfortable. The people we are interested in can get a job anywhere. So we shouldn't be talking to them about 'finding a job.' And we shouldn't be talking to them about money, because they are going to make the kind of money they want

Company (Ticker): Merrill Lynch and Company (MER)

Location: New York, New York

Leaders: Daniel P. Tully, Chairman Emeritus

David H. Komansky, Chairman and CEO

Merrill Lynch at a glance: Merrill Lynch is the leading investment banking and brokerage firm in the United States. Merrill Lynch operates in three segments. The Private Client Group covers retail brokerage, life insurance, and cash management. The Corporate and International Group deals in investment banking and capital market services to corporations, institutions, and governments. Merrill also deals in government bonds and derivatives and provides insurance services. Its asset-management arm makes it one of the world's largest mutual fund managers. The company is a market leader in the U.S. mergers and acquisitions market. It also has a large presence internationally. The company's e-business division (ML.com) has become a leader in the market for individual investment services.

1999 Financial Results

—Revenues: $34.8 billion

—Net Income: $2.6 billion

wherever they go. These aren't the issues. To me, the right question is, 'Does Merrill Lynch have the culture and environment where the person can flourish and be happy?' If the answer to that is yes, then this is where they should be. If the answer to that is no, I don't care how much money we're talking about paying, there will be a big mistake."

And once these people—whether they have come through an acquisition or have been recruited—are in place, what are Komansky's secrets to leading them?

"I don't think the principles of leadership change," Komansky says. "I think styles of management change. At different times, different managerial styles are called for. Sometimes you need to be more autocratic, sometimes more democratic. But leadership doesn't change very much."

What are Komansky's principles of leadership?

"I think there are three keys:

"One, don't think you can ever ask anybody to do anything that you are not prepared to do yourself. If you're going to ask somebody to run through a field of fire, you had better be out in front of them, not behind them. I think that's critical.

"Two, it's essential that people know you care about them. That does not mean that you pander to them, or that you don't call their attention to things that go wrong, or that you're afraid to say no. But they have to know that you care about them as individuals.

"Three, you've always got to ask more of yourself and your people than either you or they think can be accomplished. The human psyche is an amazing thing. If you ask someone to climb a four-foot wall, they're going to climb the four-foot wall and feel great. Chances are, if you had asked them to climb an eight-foot wall, they would have climbed that wall just as well, but you never asked them and they didn't think about it.

"I think if you ask people to accomplish great things, you have as good a chance of getting them to do it as you do if you ask them to accomplish average things."

It is clear that Komansky is on his way to accomplishing a lot. Does he think the international expansion will be his legacy?

"This—along with positioning ourselves to thrive on the Internet—is one of our key challenges. If we are successful, I'll want to be judged by it. If not, I'll blame Tully."

He pauses, and then is serious for a moment.

"If I can look back and say, 'I built on what my predecessors accomplished and the organization was better as a result of me being here,' I'll feel good about my time in this job."

MIKE VOLKEMA
Herman Miller

Serious about business, serious about people

IN THE LATE 1980S AND INTO THE EARLY 1990S, THE HERMAN MILLER furniture company was widely regarded as a model of how organizations would be structured and operated during the upcoming millennium. The company's recently retired CEO Max DePree earned a far-flung reputation for his management style and emphasis on the softer side of business issues. DePree's bestselling books, *Leadership Is an Art* and *Leadership Jazz,* became mandatory reading for managers looking for methods to inspire their employees.

In the aftermath of the publication of those books, a number of business executives and journalists flocked to Herman Miller's corporate headquarters in the bucolic West Michigan village of Zeeland. The goal of their pilgrimage: discovering the secrets of creating a thriving organization.

Ironically, just as Herman Miller was achieving broad notice for its enlightened approach to management, the company began to struggle. Although Herman Miller continued to register record sales, expenses were soaring at a faster rate. At a time when the firm broke through the $1 billion mark in sales, expenses reached more than 30% of revenues and the company barely broke even.

CAREER
1995–PRESENT President and CEO, Herman Miller, Inc.
1995 President and COO
1993–1995 President and CEO, Coro, Division of Herman Miller, Inc.
1993 Chairman and CEO, Meridian, Division of Herman Miller, Inc.
1990–1993 President and General Manager, Herman Miller's File and Storage Product Sector
1985–1990 President, Meridian Inc.
1984–1985 Director and General Manager, Meridian, Inc.

EDUCATION
J.D., Wayne State University, 1983
B.A., Western Michigan University, 1980

FAMILY
Married, Valerie; children: Timothy, Tricia, Daniel

Born: Columbus, Ohio, October 15, 1955

In 1995, the Herman Miller Board of Directors decided it was time for new leadership. They turned to Mike Volkema, a quiet-spoken executive who was then only 39 years old. Volkema, who perhaps could be described best as "a reluctant CEO," has built a 12-person Executive Leadership Team that has transformed Herman Miller in the ensuing years into a nearly $2 billion corporation serious about both business and people.

THE MORE VIGOROUSLY MIKE VOLKEMA RESISTED BECOMING AN EXECUTIVE, the more quickly he rose to the top. But then, he's been fighting against type from the very beginning.

> *"Invariably, the mistakes you look back on with regret involve situations where you played it too safe. In our case, we decided for a period of time to follow instead of lead. As a consequence, we fell back into mimicking and reacting to what others were doing instead of deciding that leadership was the way we needed to go."*

"My whole family is made up of attorneys," Volkema says. "It wasn't a matter of whether you were going to law school, it was just a matter of which law school you would attend. But somewhere in the course of earning my law degree, I determined that I was a hugger rather than a slugger. I was more interested in building things than being in the kind of rigorous and routine combat that goes on in the legal community.

"So I ventured out into business and encountered an elderly gentleman who owned a small furniture business that manufactured high-quality metal files and desks. It turned out that the business leader of the company had just had a heart attack, and the owner was in the process of finding a replacement. He asked me to come in and handle some legal work and pitch in while the company was leaderless."

That serendipitous meeting proved decisive at the dawn of his career. Volkema became the de facto leader of Meridian, Inc., then a $5 million–a–year company. Before long, at the age of 27, he was named Meridian's president.

"Fortunately, the industry was pretty robust. We were able to grow at a compounded rate of 25 percent a year, even though there probably were no compelling reasons why the world needed one more small furniture manufacturer."

In time Meridian, based in Spring Lake, Michigan, attracted the attention of Herman Miller, and the two companies entered into a marketing alliance in 1987.

"In 1990, the owner—who was by then in his late 70s and whose children were not involved in running the business—began to wonder what the point was of remaining independent. That led to a series of negotiations with Herman Miller, which acquired the company later that year.

"I came along with the acquisition and agreed verbally to stay on for three years," Volkema continues. "My dreams and interests were directed more toward the entrepreneurial end of the business spectrum. So in 1993, after Herman Miller had allowed me to do a number of different things—such as handling a product category (filing and storage products) on a global scale in addition to being president of Meridian—I was determined to go off on my own. But some executives and board members at Herman Miller came up with an interesting and intriguing wrinkle. They said, 'Why don't you come up with something you want to do that you can do with us?' "

Volkema developed a list of eight proposals after conferring with family, friends, and other trusted advisers. Herman Miller authorized him to draw up business plans for two particularly promising ideas.

"One of the plans led to what today is Herman Miller's facility furniture management business."

The agreement struck between the company and Volkema was that he would run the start-up business, with Herman Miller holding an equity stake in it. But soon thereafter, the organization turned back to Volkema with another offer. Although Herman Miller's sales were growing, profit margins were eroding at an even faster rate.

"The year we crossed over $1 billion in revenues we, for all practical purposes, just broke even. The board decided that it was time for new leadership, and they asked me to come in and help out in an operating officer capacity."

Volkema did not leap at the chance. "I was happy doing what I was doing," he says. "I told them I did not like bureaucracies. They drain creativity and energy. I also was not interested in the politics associated with large corporations. I'm more interested in entrepreneurial energy and action. And that's now one of our themes. We believe, going forward, that leadership needs to be much more entrepreneurial. It also needs to be much more collaborative, with many people contributing their ideas to the enterprise."

In the end, he accepted the challenge to revitalize and transform one of America's most admired companies.

"In 1995, it became clear we had to make some major changes," Volkema recalls. "Just prior to my appointment, the company had let 500

people go, which was about 7 percent of the workforce. People were talking about the possibility of more layoffs. Yet, it was clear that about 80
percent of our costs were tied up in the way we organized the work—not
in the worker. If we failed to understand that, we were bound to go down
the wrong road. Ultimately, the work processes had to be changed."

Before significant change could be accomplished, Volkema set out to
build a leadership team with the capabilities to drive those changes
through the organization. Some senior managers were let go.

"That was the toughest thing I've ever had to do," Volkema says. "I was
accustomed to recruiting and building leadership teams, not tearing them
apart and rebuilding them."

The rebuilding began with a conscious effort "to return to ground zero
and ask what was important to our customers. That was the starting
point. And then we promised the organization that we would, in a very
short period, have a strategy in place to help the business grow and prosper so our employee-owners could grow and prosper."

The strategy that was devised was simple and straightforward: expand
Herman Miller's market beyond its traditional customer base, and develop innovative new products and services for existing clients.

"Our leadership team arrived at a fundamentally different belief about
our business. We don't believe our business is about pushing product anymore. It's about assembling productive and safe work environments for
real people, and determining what it takes to do that.

"The furniture industry traditionally aligned itself around an industrial
age 'product push' mentality. That's where you go out and design something and then try to find customers willing to buy it. We've clearly decided that our mission as an organization is to design solutions based on
customer needs.

"Our industry used to think that one size fits all, and that we could do
business with every customer in exactly the same way. It's our business to
understand the different kinds of work practices and to be able to respond
to them in customized and intelligent ways.

"Our leadership team understands that true value creation is going
to be about taking the fragmented value chains that have been used
to support customers and reinventing them to improve the customer
experience."

The transformation philosophy at Herman Miller ultimately is no more
complex than redirecting the company's perspective through the lens of
its customers and would-be clients.

Some new customers are being served through Herman Miller's virtual
store at www.hmstore.com, an e-commerce site where a growing catalog
of classics and home office and small office furniture can be ordered on-

line. The company also is creating new products for the increasing number of people who are working from their homes.

"Wherever people work today, we have to assemble productive work environments to support them. We have to help them find the right place to work. I have a home office, and I work there often. With the laptop computer, almost anyplace can become an office. We now understand that we need to support knowledge workers in the ways they actually work.

"At the same time, we also need to offer more value and service to the customers we already serve. And the only way we're going to get at that is to better understand what their needs are."

The end result of this shift in thinking is an expansion of the company's target marketplace.

"Now for many companies, that may not sound like a big deal. But in this industry, it is a big deal. We have had to refocus ourselves to a 'customer pull' mentality. That's what we're doing now at Herman Miller. We are identifying customers in the marketplace who have unmet needs that we are well equipped to respond to. Then we have to reinvent and align our capabilities to respond to those identified customer needs. We must do this in order to offer them as close to pure value as possible."

It is also a formula that Herman Miller's leaders believe will help the company grow in the 21st century.

"You can't just try to steal market share from existing players. You've got to create new value in order to attract new customers."

For many of Herman Miller's largest customers, that means offering greater speed, convenience, and reliability—as well as providing an innovative approach to developing products that are exactly what the customers want, when they want it.

"We have a tailored product-development process in which we engage outside creative designers and couple them with a cross-functional internal development team. We can create, literally within six to 10 months, a work-environment solution developed for a single customer."

That's only one way of providing more value. Another is to collaborate with other firms, in order to give customers what they want.

"We grew up in a business environment where you tried to do everything yourself. But the world is getting more and more interconnected and more collaborative. We have to get comfortable with the fact that we don't have to own everything. We have to figure out how to get people connected and how to best create great value for customers—and then capture our share of that value creation. It's all about getting the right players together and becoming seamless in the eyes of the customer. I don't think this approach exists in too many industries. It surely doesn't exist in ours."

How Do You Obtain "Buy In"?

Since the new leadership team came together at Herman Miller, there has been a radical restructuring of the way the company does business.

How do you change a company that has been around for more than 75 years? It's been done by appealing to the values that made the company successful in the first place—and gaining the required understanding and commitment for the changes that needed to be made.

"We have a theory about how to disseminate critical information, which is an important part of the change process. It's called the concentric theory of disseminating information because, as the analogy has it, you drop a pebble in the water and you start with the ripples or the circle closest to the point where the pebble entered the water. You start there, and you get the required understanding and commitment. Then you move out to the next circle, and the next circle, and the next. That's what we did with the strategy and the company's long-standing values.

"It all started with the leadership team. We got all of them to participate in answering the questions 'What is it that we want to become?' and 'What is it that you believe?' and 'What values are important to you?' We started with the first line of leadership, because if the vision and values weren't important to us and we didn't believe in them, it's likely that we would never get them to be accepted or understood throughout the organization. Together, we came up with a new strategic direction and five core values.

"Identifying and framing the strategy may be the job of leadership, but values must be owned by everyone in the organization. So we then went out and brought together small groups of employee-owners all around the company to give us input about whether our statement of values captured who and what we wanted to become."

Through this process, Herman Miller created its Blueprint for Corporate Community, a document that has been disseminated to all 8,000 of its employee-owners, as well as to shareholders, suppliers, and customers.

"The first core value in the Blueprint calls for the company to make 'a meaningful contribution to customers.' We always have sought to give a customer something more than a mere exchange of goods and services for dollars. We have this deep desire in our corporate heritage and culture to know that we've had a positive impact on the lives of the people we serve.

"The second value is cultivating community participation and people development. We believe that the more minds in the game, the better it is for all of us—including our customers. We also believe that each person has been endowed with gifts and talents, and it's important for us to tap into that—and to share those gifts with our communities.

"The third value is creating economic value for shareholders and employee-owners. This ties directly into the belief that we have to be a strong and viable business. We take this obligation very seriously. I recall that Peter Drucker once said that any company that doesn't generate a positive return on its capital is a drain on society. He said that such a company is in effect lowering the standard of living for the people who participated, since that capital could have been used more productively somewhere else. In the past several years, we have substantially exceeded our cost of capital, and we don't plan to be a drain on society going forward.

"Our fourth value calls for us to respond to change through design and innovation. This is a commitment on our part to lead and not follow. We believe that the design process, which is really a problem-solving process, is going to be a more valuable gift as we proceed.

"Our final core value calls for us to live with integrity and to respect the environment—two distinct but related thoughts. Integrity at Herman Miller means that our deeds must match our words. And clearly, we have a strong emphasis on environmental stewardship at Herman Miller. We think this economic prosperity that we enjoy as a business needs to be linked with a sustainable environment. Also, our values really drive us to say that we ought to be able to respect diversity, and the greatest diversity we have is the diversity of thought. That means we must honor the idea generators."

Why Spend All of This Effort on Values?

At first glance, it might appear odd to have devoted such substantial time and effort to developing a values statement at a time when the company was struggling to make a profit.

The leadership team at Herman Miller, however, regarded the exercise as a sound business decision.

Company (Ticker): Herman Miller, Inc. (MLHR)

Headquarters: Zeeland, Michigan

Leader: Michael A. Volkema

Herman Miller at a glance: Herman Miller is the second-largest designer and marketer of office furniture in the United States (after Steelcase). It manufactures its products in the United States, the United Kingdom, and Mexico, and sells globally through subsidiaries in Australia, Canada, France, Germany, Japan, Mexico, The Netherlands, and the United Kingdom. Herman Miller also sells directly to the small office/home office market through its Internet site, hermanmiller.com.

1999 Financial Results
—Revenues: $1.7 billion
—Net Income: $141 million

"Good leaders are required to have a nonnegotiable set of core values that allow them to do the right thing, and make the right decisions, in those moments when it's most difficult to do so."

The core values provided the touchstone for the leadership team to carry with them as they went about the business of restoring Herman Miller to prosperity.

CHARLES WANG
Computer Associates

"You must have a moral compass."

No one has ever accused the *Wall Street Journal*'s editorial coverage of hyperbole. With that in mind, here is how it began a profile of Wang a couple of years ago:

> Through the most aggressive strategy of mergers and acquisitions ever pursued in the software world, Charles B. Wang has built a public company that sold $4.7 billion worth of software in 1997. [It was $5.1 billion in 1998.] That still makes Computer Associates the other software giant, the one that people don't think about when asked to name the world's biggest software company. Microsoft and Bill Gates are household names, and CA and Charles Wang are also household names, if the head of the household happens to be a CIO [Chief Information Officer].

The company the *Journal* is extolling began by supplying software for IBM mainframes, but has expanded into all areas of computing, thanks to those acquisitions the newspaper talked about. Since its creation in 1976, Computer Associates has bought about 70 companies. The total price tag for all those acquisitions? Some $5 billion. The result? Nineteen out of 20 of the Fortune 500 uses at least one of CA's more than 500 software products.

The man responsible for all this was

CAREER
2000–PRESENT Founder, Chairman,
    Computer Associates International, Inc.
1976–2000 Founder, Chairman, and CEO,
    Computer Associates International, Inc.

EDUCATION
B.S., Computer Science, Queens College, 1967

FAMILY
Married: Nanci; three children

Born: Shanghai, China, August 19, 1944

> *"I don't think success is a place or a definition, I think it's a direction. It's very important to look at how you're living your life—and it should be pointed in the right direction."*

born in Shanghai, but his family fled first to Hong Kong, then to New York, following the Communist takeover of China. After college, he chose his career by going through the want ads and seeing that there were two and a half pages of classifieds searching for computer programmers. Wang wasn't exactly sure what a computer programmer did, but it was clear that they were needed and he got himself hired as a trainee.

It wasn't long after he started working that Wang noticed a "huge disconnect" between what technology companies offered and what their business clients wanted. The technology being developed might have been state-of-the-art, but it did not necessarily address a client's need. Wang started Computer Associates to solve that problem.

CHARLES WANG ALWAYS MAKES IT SOUND SIMPLE.

He became a programmer because his college grades as a math and physics major weren't strong enough to get him into graduate school and he needed a job. All those want ads in the *New York Times* convinced him that computer programming was the place to be.

Simple enough.

Similarly, when he was asked about the challenges of running a business, Wang says, "It's not that complicated. I make sure that what comes in exceeds what goes out. The difference is called profit. If it's the other way around I have a thing called loss, and I'm not happy. My shareholders are not happy, my employees are not happy, and my clients are not happy."

Simple.

Not surprisingly, when he thinks about the future, it is in simple terms as well.

"We feel we have just scratched the surface in terms of what we can accomplish," he says. "The industry is still doing the same stupid things it was when we started this company. We're trying to impress each other. All the hardware and software are still not connected. Yes, we're better connected and there are some brighter companies, like Federal Express, that really make use of technology. But many companies have lost their edge, because they went into too many technical things. The industry still doesn't have the mind-set right."

For that, Wang argues, you can usually blame the fact that companies have lost their focus.

"Most businesses start one way. Somebody has a better idea to do something, and becomes wildly successful with it. And then the bureaucrats take over and all they do is try and maintain the status quo and administer it properly. The company loses its edge, and then another company comes along and catches up.

"If you're really a growing company you should be always thinking, what's the next big idea? Where do we want to go? People don't do enough of that."

What's the secret to keep that drive?

"I think you have to be very insecure. With today's communications you don't even know who your competitor is. It's not like the old days, when you had a pretty good idea where he was. He was down the block. Today, you don't know. The guy could be selling the same stuff you're selling on the Net for much less and your market changes.

"The telephone company was completely blindsided, right? Where did those guys come from? AT&T asked. Cable guys are going to get blindsided, too, because maybe their competition is going to come through the satellite, maybe it's going to come through electrical currents. You've got to be always thinking way ahead, asking how could I be differentiating my business.

"I always tell my people the biggest challenge we have is to continue to think like a small company. If we lose that and start thinking like a bureaucracy, then we are in trouble."

Budgets, Wang says, are a case in point. "People always say, we budgeted that amount last year, so we should budget that, plus a little bit more, this year. That's institutional thinking. If you are different, better, and all the wonderful things that we believe we are, maybe you should view yourself differently. I question people constantly about why we are doing certain things. I tell them, let's not measure your success by how big your group is. Let's measure it by what your overall contribution to CA is. Maybe your department needs to be smaller, not bigger.

"A lot of what they teach in business schools becomes 'How do I get ahead?' And it's wonderful, because some of the disciplines they teach are needed in order to manage a company. But a lot of that isn't creating, it's really managing, and that's not necessarily appropriate."

What is needed, Wang says, is a clear overall picture of how your company is organized. Once you have that, stop and think if the organization makes sense.

Wang gives an example.

"Most of the chief information officers report into CFOs. Why? Because of the pedigree of software. Software lets us count faster, more accurately, and everybody thinks, if I had all the numbers I could make decisions. Nobody is taking a look at the technology and saying, 'How can I use it to make our company different?'

"Let's say you're a company that spends 5% of your revenue on IT [information technology]. What if you could use that IT and add 10% to the top line? Who cares if it costs 6% or 7% to do it? You've got a future because your business is growing differently because of your use of IT. Not enough businesses think this way."

The technology people deserve some of the blame, Wang concedes.

"I always use this analogy about why letting technology people make all technological-related decisions is a bad idea," he explains.

"Say you want to go from A to B. I'd tell you to go out and buy a car.

"You ask a technical guy, he'll tell you how to build a car. And by the time he finishes describing this car, it's got jet propellers. And the larger the company, the more car builders you have. That's what these guys do. At the brilliant companies, they say, we have to hire new people. They go into the most wonderful universities and hire the best computer science graduates. But they are often the wrong guys. All those guys want to do is invent cars. It's more than the money that's lost. It's the time lost, the loss of opportunity.

"You have to understand what value you bring to the marketplace and stay focused on that."

And what is the biggest value, Wang—a technology guy if there ever was one—brings to the table?

He says that's a simple question.

The answer? Integrity.

Your Word Has to Be Worth Everything

"I think to be a successful person, and CEOs are often very successful, you have to have integrity. Your word has to be worth everything you've got. You must have a moral compass. That's especially true if you're a leader because you're exposed more. People will get a sense of you, and if you are not true, you may not feel the effect today, this week, this month, this year, but it will get out. They'll get a sense that you're sleazy, and your company will suffer.

"The chance to fail happens all the time, not in big things, in little things. For example, say someone didn't put in all the paperwork for a medical claim. While you could easily defend a decision in court not to pay, you know what the right thing to do is. Pay the claim. We buy a company, there's a contract that's just terrible, but you inherit all the contracts. You can argue that the guy had no authority to sign it, but you knew what happened. Honor the contract.

"You don't only do this for the reputation you have with your clients. Forget clients for the moment. There are more people in the company that know about these situations than there are clients. If you do the wrong thing, everyone in your company will eventually find out.

"People in CA know, 'If Charles says it, that's it.' They've got to be able to take it to the bank."

That integrity must extend to how you interact with employees, Wang adds.

"I think one of the things that leaders forget is that people look to us to tell them the truth in terms of how they're doing. It's almost like, I don't want to tell you're screwing up because it makes me feel bad. It's hard for me to tell you. And then you're worse off because you don't know where you stand.

"As management, we must tell people what we expect. And if they don't meet the expectations we have to tell them, and tell them why, so they can improve. Maybe it's something we can work on together.

"It's so important to be brutally honest with your people. People respect that. I've had people thank me. If managers don't do it, they are not really taking ownership."

This is all part of a broader perspective that Wang has.

"You should be doing some good, making the world better. I tell my people life lasts a long time. Don't think that your only goal is to make $100,000 a year, because you'll make $100,000 probably quicker than you think. So what? Is your life over once you're made $100,000? No. You have to be pointed in the right direction. You're building a career. You're doing something you really enjoy."

Company (Ticker): Computer Associates International, Inc. (CA)
Location: Islandia, New York
Leader: Charles B. Wang, Chairman Sanjay Kumar, President and CEO
Computer Associates at a glance: CA is the world's third-largest independent computer software company after Microsoft and Oracle. (IBM is number two overall.) The company offers more than 500 software products, from data access to systems and network management tools. Its flagship program, Unicenter, gives customers centralized control over their software, hardware, and networks. CA has a history of aggressive growth through spin-offs and acquisitions, shown recently by its acquisition of Sterling Software and its spin-off of iCan-ASP. CA is currently under realignment. This will organize the company into three main businesses: security and storage management; network, event, and performance management; and application development.
1999 Financial Results
—Revenues: $6.7 billion
—Net Income: $696 million

And to have a better world, you should give something back.

"I always tell everybody, give back, give back. Because if you don't give back, this world is not going to get better. And if you're fortunate enough to do really well, give more."

Wang does. One of his biggest causes is the "Smile Train."

"I want to eradicate all cleft palates, hare lips, and other facial deformities. But this isn't about just sending doctors in to operate on kids; it's about training the local doctors so that you can perpetuate what you're doing. All the other programs that people do, they get lots of publicity. They go into a local place with all the fanfare, get the public relations attention, and leave.

"I don't know if you know this, but when you do one operation to correct a facial deformity, there's usually another four to follow. You've got orthodontia work, you've got speech therapy, you've got to place all the teeth back in. It isn't just fixing this hole in the mouth and cosmetically it looks good. Yes, that's a great start, but you can't keep sending people in to take care of those four other operations, you've got to train the local doctors."

Wang funds the "Smile Train" personally. But CA is also very generous.

"The company will match two for one to whatever recognized charity our employees contribute to. If they give one dollar, CA will give two dollars to the same charity. I don't think we give enough, I keep on my people, and it drives them nuts."

You are supposed to live by your moral compass and give something back.

It's simple.

SANDY WEILL
Citigroup

Let's build something together

MANY PEOPLE WERE SURPRISED THAT AT AGE 65—WHEN MOST OF HIS peers were thinking about retirement or had already retired—Sandy Weill engineered the world's largest financial services company. Weill's $78 billion deal that combined Travelers Group—which included Salomon Smith Barney and Travelers Insurance—with Citibank in late 1998 created a true international powerhouse, in what was then the largest corporate merger of all time.

But people who know Weill were far from shocked by the Citibank deal. After all, almost since he went into business, Weill had made it clear that he wanted to create a brand-name, financial services empire. Yet with the Citibank merger, he and co-chairman John Reed have created a firm whose breadth surprised even the most out-of-the-box thinkers. Citigroup, as the combined company is known, has interests that range from banking and life insurance to underwriting, mergers and acquisitions, and stock-brokerage worldwide.

It took a while. Weill, a Brooklyn native, entered the business immediately after graduating college. Through a series of acquisitions, he ended up running a brokerage firm that was known as

CAREER
1998–PRESENT Chairman and CEO,
   Citigroup, Inc. (Co-CEO, 1998–2000)
1986–1998 Chairman, CEO Travelers Group
   (includes Commercial Credit, Primerica,
   Travelers, Shearson, Aetna Property,
   Casualty)
1983–1985 President, American Express
   Company
1984–1985 Chairman, Fireman's Fund
   Insurance Company, American Express
1960–1985 Chairman, CEO, Carter, Berlind,
   Potoma & Weill and successor companies
   (name changed to CBWL-Hayden, Stone, Inc.
   1970, Hayden Stone, Inc. 1972, Shearson
   Hayden Stone 1974, Shearson Loeb Rhodes
   1979, Shearson/American Express 1981,
   and Shearson Lehman Brothers 1983)

EDUCATION
B.A., Cornell University, 1955

FAMILY
Married, Joan Mosher, June 19, 1955; children:
   Marc P., Jessica M.

Born: New York City, March 16, 1933

"The thing I believe in most is the power of people. I believe in letting them know that if they make a mistake it's not the end of the world. What would be the end of the world is making a mistake and hiding it. But if people aren't willing to make mistakes they're never going to make any right decisions. On the other hand, if they make mistakes all the time, *they should go work for a competitor."*

Shearson Loeb Rhodes when it was sold to American Express in 1981.

Blocked from getting the top job at American Express, Weill set off to replicate his past success. And through another string of acquisitions, he did. Even before Citibank came together with Travelers' well-known red umbrella, Weill had built Travelers into a firm that had market capitalization greater than that of American Express.

Weill scores near the top of all American CEOs in adding the most shareholder value, in large part because he is obsessed with increasing the wealth of his shareholders. One reason for that could be that a large portion of his net worth is tied to Citigroup's performance.

He also scores near the top in philanthropy. Weill is chairman of Carnegie Hall, the Medical College of Cornell, and the National Academy Foundation.

SANDY WEILL USES A TELLING EXAMPLE TO EXPLAIN HOW LONG HE HAS been in the financial services business.

"When I went into this business in 1955, the average volume on the New York Stock Exchange was a 1.5 million shares a day. Today, our company stock sells 10 million shares a day. Citigroup alone trades more than six times the volume of the whole stock exchange 44 years ago."

Not surprisingly, when you have been in business this long—and you have watched the kinds of rapid changes that have swept through your industry over the last four decades—you develop a series of principles that help guide you. For Weill they boil down to three:

- First, execute;
- Second, pay everyone like a partner; and
- Third, rely on people smarter or better positioned than yourself to help you succeed.

Weill walks us through these principles one at a time, starting with execution.

It's All About Execution

"In our business, no one has unique products," he says. "Therefore, you have to be a low-cost provider. We're very focused on the bottom line and how efficient we can be in delivering our product. We deliver a product that the consumer really wants, not what we think he wants, at an efficient, profitable price."

The customer only sees the product. He does not see the process that got it to him. It is in these processes, in the details, that Weill's companies have always stood out.

"We have to deliver our products without a lot mistakes," he says. "If we are clearing a trade [the back office transaction that records whether a person has bought or sold stock; who was on the other end of the transaction; what was paid for the stock, and what commissions should be paid to the brokers involved] it is imperative to get it right the first time. It's very costly to correct a mistake. So we've always paid a lot of attention to the quality of our operations and have attracted good people to this area of the business."

When asked what is a good way to attract and keep the technical people who oversee back office transactions, Weill's first response is intriguing.

"I think it's the commitment of senior management to this area. They need to know that senior management cares. There was many a night that I slept on the computer room floor, as they tried to work something out."

Why was Weill there? To show he understood how important the work being done was and to contribute to the problem-solving process.

"If we were not up and running by the next morning, we were out of business. In the securities business, you don't have another day. It's not like in the banking business, or the insurance business, where you can have your computers go down, and you still have time to recover. In the securities business, there's no time to recover. It was important that I showed our people how important they were."

Partnership Pay

Symbolism is important, of course, but so is money, especially in the financial services industry. Weill has always made it a point of paying people for performance.

"We've bought a lot of companies where they didn't really differentiate that much between levels of performance. Employees had a significant part of their compensation tied up in pensions and medical benefits and all that kind of stuff. We've always said, if you want to come here, don't get sick. We really wanted to run a business where the great majority of the person's compensation would be dependent upon how they did, and how the entity that they were a part of did."

And a lot of that pay would be in the form of stock and/or stock options.

"That way if we did a good job together, we would all benefit," Weill says. "And it would really help change one's life. If you give people a little something extra, they spend it and it's not there for the future. I would always tell people, let's not rely on the government and Social Security. Let's not rely on pensions. Let's rely on building something together.

"This was a big challenge with Travelers, where maybe 70% of the compensation was fixed or in benefits and 30% based on performance. And we basically flipped it. I think if you go to Hartford [Connecticut, where Travelers is based] and ask anybody if they want to go back to the old way of getting paid, they wouldn't. They're really proud of what they've accomplished over the last five years and what they've built."

Weill has kept that tradition of paying for performance going at Citigroup.

"Right after the merger, we gave out stock option grants, which we called founders' options because we were all founders of this new organization," Weill explains. "And 32,000 of our people participated in that option grant—it went much deeper down into the organization than Citi had ever done. This way more people can feel ownership in what's going to be accomplished."

Making sure that as many employees as possible can own stock is a powerful management tool, Weill says.

"Many times you'll meet people in a company that has done well, but they feel disenfranchised because they didn't have any of the options. We want people to share in our success."

And "people" includes the company's board of directors. Weill was an early proponent of board members receiving a substantial part of their compensation in stock.

"It makes sense. This way we are all on the same page. The directors are going to be thinking about what's in the best interest of the shareholders because they are all shareholders."

Relying on Smarter People

The discussion of boards brings us to how Weill says that he always tries to draw on the skills of people smarter than himself. He is being modest, of course. But he makes an important point. No CEO, no matter how smart, has the ability today to handle every aspect of a multi-billion-dollar company flawlessly on his own today.

"We have people on our board with an incredible amount of different experiences, and we use them as a sounding board that makes us better."

Drawing on the strengths of others is something that Weill has done from the beginning.

"There are lots of different characteristics that can make somebody a success," he says. "I think it is important as a leader to play to your strengths and not try to be somebody that you're not. My strength is involvement. People know that I am going to be there for them and also know that I am going to be on top of the details. I am also good at listening and learning. I'm fortunate in this combination to have John Reed (his co-CEO) as my partner. John is incredibly bright, and has had unbelievably strong global experience, something that I haven't had. So I have been on a steep learning curve."

Indeed, that is what ultimately led to the Travelers-Citibank merger.

The Making of Citigroup

"We [Travelers] had just announced in September of '97 that we were going to buy Salomon because we felt we had to go global. Our company was mainly domestic and the growth of financial services appeared to be going global with countries privatizing industries, and pension systems, and having their securities trading in the United States. We really weren't participating in any of that. We decided that Salomon Brothers would give us a foothold in that marketplace.

"So we bought Salomon Brothers. And one week later, Thailand defaults, Indonesia goes broke, Korea goes broke. And we said, 'Oh my God, we're global.'

Company (Ticker): Citigroup, Inc. (C)
Location: New York, New York
Leader: Sanford I. Weill, Chairman and CEO
Citigroup at a glance: Citigroup, formed in 1998 through the merger of Citicorp and the Travelers Group, is the largest financial services company in the United States. Its product line, designed to serve the needs of customers ranging from individual consumers to the world's largest corporations and governments, includes credit card, consumer and commercial banking, insurance, and investment services in almost 100 countries. It also offers brokerage services (via its Salomon Smith Barney unit), mutual funds (Primerica Financial), property/casualty insurance (83% owned Travelers Property Casualty), retirement products (Travelers Life & Annuity), and real estate services (Citicorp Real Estate), among other services. The company has retained Travelers' red umbrella logo. Citicorp has focused on expanding into Japan, Europe, and e-commerce.
1999 Financial Results
—Revenues: $82.0 billion
—Net Income: $9.8 billion

And this is pretty scary to me. The volatility, coupled with the liquidity that came out of the market in October and November of '97, was a little nerve-racking.

"When things stabilized, we realized we had about $22 billion of equity and something approaching, on an normalized basis, $3.5 to $4 billion of after-tax earnings. That's not enough if you want to be global, assuming you really want to sleep at night. We liked being global, but we realized we needed to be more diverse and have larger sources of income and equity.

"It was then that we decided to call John Reed [the then-chairman and CEO of Citibank] because they had done the best job of any consumer company in the financial services business on a global basis. They were in 100 countries. Their income was diversified all over the place. They had 70 million customers. And they also had $22 billion of equity to create a $44- or $45-billion equity base. It was the right decision because combining gave us an opportunity to grow faster than we might have on our own."

In other words, team up with someone whose strengths complement your weaknesses.

So, as Weill has demonstrated in a career that has been both long and successful, a formula that works is: Execute, find people who know more than you do, and pay them like partners.

JACK WELCH
General Electric

"I don't think anyone understands the value
of informal."

HE HAS SPENT HIS ENTIRE WORKING LIFE WITH THE COMPANY. HE HAS A
Ph.D. (in chemical engineering). He is a passionate, competitive golfer
who includes among the greatest moments in his life beating professional
Greg Norman by a stroke in what started out to be a purely recreational
outing. ("I had one of those days where God comes down and blesses
you. In fact, I should have shot 66. I missed three putts of less than four
feet in the last seven holes.")

He is John F. Welch, Jr., perhaps the most studied—and emulated—
CEO in America, and arguably the world.

There is a reason that Welch attracts all this attention. GE's performance during his nearly 20-year reign
has been extraordinary. Sales and earnings have steadily increased. Market
share has climbed. And along the way
Welch has developed enough managers
to lead a significant component of the
S&P 500. Everyone from Larry Bossidy
(see p. 61) to John Trani, who is now
CEO of Stanley Works, has spent significant time as one of Welch's lieutenants.
Indeed, GE is one of the first places corporations look if they are searching for a
new chief executive.

In an age when it seems that the last
thing most executives want to do is pre-
side over a conglomerate, Welch has
built a company that would be at home
if it were placed among the corporate

CAREER
1981–PRESENT Chairman and CEO, General
  Electric Company (to retire at the end of
  2001)
1977–1981 Senior Vice President
1973–1977 Vice President
1960–1972 Various staff positions

EDUCATION
Ph.D., University of Illinois, 1960
M.S., University of Illinois, 1958
B.S., University of Massachusetts, 1957

FAMILY
Married; Jane Beasley, April 1989; children:
  Katherine, John, Anne, Mark

Born: Peabody, Massachusetts, November 19,
  1935

> *"We reward failure. I remember some guys came up with a lamp that didn't work, and we gave them all television sets. You have to do it, because otherwise people will be afraid to try things."*

landscape of the 1950s. GE sells everything from power systems to lightbulbs and owns businesses as diverse as television networks (NBC) and financial services companies (GE Capital).

But even given its size (Welch is convinced his company will have revenues of more than $125 billion by the year 2000) and scope, GE responds remarkably quickly to changing economic circumstances.

Seeing that a deflationary environment was developing a couple of years ago, Welch told leaders of each of the company's major divisions to accelerate quality training, put extra emphasis on cost reductions, and reexamine all plant and equipment investments. This wasn't yet another memo from corporate. How well they did in refocusing their divisions to respond to a world where prices would be constantly falling went a long way toward determining their salary and bonus when it came time for their annual review.

Managers everywhere around the world have adopted Welch's ideas. Over and over again, in countless languages, you'll hear executives say, "We need to be number one or two in the fields in which we compete." They talk about "boundarylessness," the need to share information, a concept that breaks down traditional corporate hierarchies and is designed to make sure that ideas flow up as well as down. And even managers who aren't exactly sure what it means talk about Six Sigma, a quality program that is now part of the business landscape everywhere. These are all ideas that Welch has introduced while running GE, and over the years they have become touchstones for the organization.

What people tend to forget, given all the success that Welch has had, is how foreign those ideas once were.

"IT HAS BEEN NEARLY 20 YEARS SINCE WE DECIDED TO FIX THE HARDware, that is, make sure all our divisions were either one or two in the marketplace," Welch recalls. "And it has also been 20 years since we began to de-layer the company to make it faster and smaller.

"When I delivered a speech in 1981 about those ideas, the Wall Street analysts basically ignored it, and left the room disappointed because there were no hard numbers—just a broad vision.

"We took a company that everybody thought was perfect and had a fight with it."

And fight with it he did. Within a couple of years of taking over GE, through divestitures and downsizing, Welch had cut the number of employees from 400,000 to 220,000. In the process he earned the nickname of "Neutron Jack," the man who kept the buildings standing, but eliminated all the people inside. Welch has heard the description, but says the reputation came out of the blue.

"I was never known as a slasher, or a cutter, or any of those things. All I was ever known as was a growth nut. All I did was add employees. I globalized Plastics. In fact, I was in Europe buying so many companies that I was once called back here by the general counsel, who told me, 'You're the steward of these businesses, you don't own them, and you can't go buying all these companies.' I was doing all these crazy things, because Plastics wasn't in the mainstream, and wasn't followed in detail by all the corporate staff. As a result, we were able to keep doing what we thought made sense."

When Welch was named chairman, he kept on doing what he believed was right. But while his strategy didn't change, his tactics did. He believed it was incumbent on GE to be a market leader in fields that played to its strengths.

"Peter Drucker asks a great question," Welch explains. "He asks: 'If you weren't already in this business, would you enter it now?' That's a great question. And [once I became CEO] we began asking it about every business we were in. What we decided was that we would keep a business if it required a high amount of technology, a lot of money to run, and there were reasonable cycle times, that is, it didn't operate on short cycles. These factors were our strengths. We are good at technology. We are willing to make capital investments and it takes us a relatively long time to get to market. We're the fastest elephant at the dance, but we are still an elephant.

"So those became our tests for keeping a business. Our housewares division failed the test. Housewares required no money. A guy in a garage could build a widget. It is a fast-cycle business, and we weren't fast. So we got out, although a lot of people wrote me letters saying we were selling our birthright. This is also why I got out of semiconductors. It required a lot of capital, but the cycles were too fast, and it was too cyclical. We've tried to play to our strengths, like aircraft engines, like materials. Places that require lots of capital investments, and lots of technology."

This Would Have Been Impossible, Without Board Support

The radical transformation that Welch envisioned—and subsequently executed—would not have been possible without the complete support of the GE board. Welch is thankful for that, but he is even more thankful to board members because of the way they treated him.

"I see the board's responsibility as somewhat different than some people do," Welch says. "Like a lot of people, I see their role as being absolutely critical to any transformation a company makes. But I think their primary job is to pick the CEO, and then, as long as the CEO is the CEO, be there in every way to make him feel 10 feet tall. The biggest advantage I had when I was first in the job was that Walter Wriston [the then-chairman and CEO of Citibank, who was on GE's board] was walking around New York saying, 'We hired the smartest guy. We love him.' And when I was causing external controversies by selling off all those divisions, the board would say, 'Great. Keep going.' It was an enormous confidence builder. We get confidence at all levels of our lives. We get it in college, we get it at our mother's knee, we get it in a whole series of steps. But you never need it more than when you first become a CEO, because all of a sudden you're alone. And your board's real role is to pump you up, in the early days, and eventually remove you if you don't deliver."

Not surprisingly, Welch also has strong beliefs about a typical move that boards frequently make.

"The worst thing that ever happens is when the board names a new CEO and then has the former CEO in the background nibbling. I followed the best CEO in the world [Reginald Jones] and he never came in the office once he stepped down. He never came near it. I sold the biggest acquisition he had ever made within 20 months of taking over the job, and he never for a moment caused a problem. He never said anything negative. He never did anything. I always talked to him, always kept him apprised, always worked with him. And never once in my life, in any interview that I did, did I ever fail to say that he was the greatest CEO for the world he lived in."

The support Welch got from the board, in general, and Jones in particular, allowed him the time to get the "hardware right," that is, to make sure he had the right mix of business. The next challenge was to create a company that had the right "feel," that operated in a way that Welch felt was most productive. Here, Welch relied heavily on his experience of running GE's Plastics Division.

"When I was running Plastics, I had one employee in the beginning. Then we got two employees, then five, and I brought them all home, they met my family. So I communicated with them well. It was a garage operation, literally.

"But as I got promoted, I increasingly got into these sorts of very formal, ritualistic parts of the company, where we just couldn't move. There were all these forms and charts. So, once we had the hardware done, I wanted to get back to that informal style we had in Plastics where employees came to the house, where you drank together and had pizza parties and had fun. I wanted to make all of GE feel like that.

"When you have 10 employees you need all 10 playing. Somehow or other when you get 400,000 you don't think you need all 400,000, so you don't try and engage them all. But we desperately wanted to get everybody's mind in the game, which is why I wanted to create that informal feeling.

"If you think about GE, one of its major strengths today is its ability to get ideas from across many different businesses. We operate best when we get ideas moving across boundaries. When I took over, we were like most organizations, very boundary-full. You couldn't change that unless people were open to ideas. So one of the things we did was to change the game. We went from where the inventor was the celebrated person to where the person who took an idea from anywhere, embellished it, and did something with it was the person we made the hero.

"And that became a key element of our culture. And that's where this company is today.

"What counts today is not the number of epaulets on your shoulder, but the quality of your ideas, and the intellect behind it. That's how we ran Plastics when we had 10 guys, and that's what we wanted to get back to. The question I keep asking is, how do we get to be the family grocery store? That's our goal. People now have meetings in GE where they call all levels together and solve problems. They don't realize that 15 years ago you didn't do that. You didn't often see people on a different level.

"We just had a video conference to deal with a product problem we are having in Japan," Welch says by way of example. "We set up a team to deal with it. We had people in Japan, R&D folks from Schenectady, and several of us here [at corporate headquarters in Connecticut] working on it. And the people in Japan were relatively low level. But no one even thought about it. They were the people who could solve the problem.

"I don't think anyone understands the value of making a large organization informal. I think making a company informal is a huge deal in the business world, but no one ever talks about it. The biggest thing we did was to make this company informal. No one would dare act like a pompous boss around here; they'd get shot, or laughed at. It would be silly.

"Being informal gives you speed. It allows fast information flow. It allows you to make decisions by fax, by phone, by e-mail, by anything. We can buy companies, and we can do it quickly. To make this approach work you need to have senior managers who have tons of energy, love to energize others, and want others to win and grow. And they must be really serious about wanting to have an open network of information. Information moves so fast today, and everyone has more information than the CEO does. So the only role of the CEO is to be out there energizing people and turning this information into action."

Going Forward

What will this informal, information-obsessed GE look like in the future? A service company, says Welch. "In 1981, we got 85% of our sales from product and 15% from services. In the year 2000, we will be at $125 billion in sales and 75% of that will be in services, and only 25% will be in product."

That kind of transformation won't be an accident.

"We're spending some $230 million on research and development to beef up our industrial services business," Welch says. "We took our best engineers and put them on it. You have to take the best and move them over because historically no one wanted to be in services. When you said service to them, they thought of people in white overalls and oil cans. Maintenance guys. We had to change the situation, and we've done it by coupling service with technology. Information technology has changed the nature of services.

"Here's how it works. Say we have a product—for example, an aircraft engine—that is sold in an intensively competitive marketplace. What do you do to enhance the competitiveness of what you have to sell? We try to offer services that airlines can't get elsewhere. We now can monitor all our engines in the air. So, today, when a plane lands we've got on-wing service people right there to fix it. The engine can stay on the wing longer. As a result of adding this technology to what was a commodity—the aircraft engine—we've been able to take on multi-year contracts with companies such as USAir, British Airways, and Southwest. These are 10- to 20-year contracts worth billions of dollars.

"You have to be in services in some form today, if you are going to be in the game. Product is dead. The days of just grinding out widgets are long gone. Customers want total solutions. When I sell an engine to an airline, they increasingly don't want to maintain it. They just want to take people from point A to point B. Most don't do food anymore. Most don't want to do engines. They want to get from A to B in the most effective and efficient manner.

"The same focus on their customer is taking place in other major markets—hospitals, railroads, utilities, etc."

The Role of the Leader

Above all else, Welch sees his job as preaching the gospel.

"We've only done three fundamental things in this company in the 20 years I've been in this job. We've changed the hardware; changed how we behave, and changed how we work.

"Within the hardware framework, the most important thing was deciding what businesses we wanted to be in, and we used the 'number one or number two fix, sell, or close the thing' idea to guide the organization's thinking.

"How we behave—this drive for boundarylessness, open idea-sharing—came from several years of town meetings where everyone in the organization was urged to participate.

"Our latest initiative—Six Sigma—defines how we work: We want to have a quality mind-set in everything we do.

"These are the three fundamental things we've done. Within any organization, there are periodic programs to energize the team—sourcing, pricing, sales contests, etc. But sometimes people get confused by these periodic programs. They say, 'What is the hot button next year?' They ask, 'What is the flavor of the year?' That's how organizations get energized. You energize people around these programs, but you don't change the fundamentals. There are three fundamental things in GE—the hardware, how we behave, and how we work—and they don't change.

"Now, what those three things have in common is people. I spend 60% or more of my time on people stuff, and that's the way it should be. I couldn't produce a show on NBC, I couldn't build an engine, I couldn't do any of these things. So my involvement revolves around people. And I constantly repeat our message. I'll say things like 'We grew 6% a year domestically last year

Company (Ticker): General Electric Company (GE)
Location: Fairfield, Connecticut
Leader: John. F. Welch, Jr.
GE at a glance: The fifth-largest U.S. corporation, industrial giant General Electric owns a wide array of businesses, including TV network NBC, power plant parts manufacturing, aircraft engines, transportation equipment such as locomotives, electric appliances such as kitchen and laundry equipment, lighting, electric distribution and control equipment, and materials (plastics, silicones, laminates, and abrasives). The company's GE Capital Services division is one of the largest financial services companies in the United States.
1999 Financial Results
—Revenues: $110.8 billion
—Net Income: $10.7 billion

and 17% globally. So, it isn't a very hard equation to explain why we've got to be global.'

"In leadership you have to exaggerate every statement you make. You've got to repeat it a thousand times and exaggerate it. So, I'll say things like 'No one can get promoted if they're not a Green Belt in Six Sigma.' Such overstatements are needed to move a large organization. And then you must back them up with personnel moves to show people you're serious."

One Regret

Given all the success Welch has had, you would think he wouldn't have any regrets, as he contemplates his retirement, which is scheduled to take place in the year 2000. But he has one major one.

"I think the biggest mistake I made is a fundamental one. I went too slow in everything I did. Yes, I was called every name in the book when I started, but if I had done in two years what took five, we would have been ahead of the curve even more.

"You rarely do things too fast," Welch adds. "If you think about your life and the decisions you've made, you can't come up with too many where you said, 'I wish I took another year to do it.' But you can sure come up with a list where you say, 'I wish I had done a bunch of things six months earlier.'"

AL ZEIEN
Gillette

Focus

THE LEADER OF GILLETTE, THE COMPANY BEST KNOWN FOR ITS SHAVING products, literally bristled. Alfred M. Zeien (pronounced Zane) was having lunch with the editors of one the national leading business magazines when he was asked if he had ever thought about private labeling some of his products.

"Why would we want to do that?" Zeien asked, trying to be polite.

Well, it would absorb excess capacity, open up another line of distribution, and help stave off competition, replied the editor, who thought he knew something about marketing.

"But that would be contrary to everything we stand for," Zeien explained. "We are the premium brand. The best in the marketplace. We should get paid a premium for what we sell."

And they are.

Gillette's relentless product innovation, coupled with an unsurpassed marketing organization, has created a remarkable string of victories, not only in shaving and blades but also among the company's other products.

That "others" list is impressive in its own right. The company makes Braun electrical appliances; toiletries and toothbrushes (Right Guard, Oral-B); statio-

CAREER
1991–1999 Chairman and CEO, The Gillette Company
1990–1991 President
1987–1990 Vice Chairman—International
1981–1987 Vice Chairman—Technical Operations
1978–1981 Senior Vice President
1976–1978 Chairman, Braun (part of Gillette)
1974–1976 Division General Manager, Braun
1973–1974 Group Vice President, Gillette Co.
Prior experience in naval architecture

EDUCATION
M.B.A. and postgraduate, Harvard University
B.S., Webb Institute

FAMILY
Married, Joyce Valerie Lawrence; children: Scott, Grey, Claudia

Born: New York City, February 25, 1930

> *"I preach a lot. I'd say 90% of my time is spent on 'the three P's—people, product, and something I call 'purpose,' but it's really preaching. This is explaining to people all the whys. Why do we have to close this plant up? Or why should we do this? Or why should we do that? That's preaching."*

nery products (Parker, Paper Mate, and Waterman pens and Liquid Paper); and Duracell batteries.

It is an extremely focused strategy. It is also one that works.

It is not very hard to explain what all these brands have in common: They each lead their particular category, are extremely profitable, and depend on technological advances to keep revenues growing.

That is no accident. Zeien, who was trained as a naval architect and engineer, believes in research. The company has 11 research facilities around the globe and once a new product is created, three things happen simultaneously:

1) The company throws huge dollars behind it to introduce it to the world;
2) Gillette's engineers go to work trying to figure out how to make the product as efficiently as possible; and
3) The people working on the product that will replace the one that has just been introduced are pushed to get their idea into the marketplace as soon as possible. Zeien knows that if Gillette doesn't come out with a better product, someone else will.

This three-step approach is replicated around the world. More than 70% of Gillette's sales and profits come from overseas operations in 200 countries. The approach is always the same. The company first establishes shaving goods in a new market, then pours a stream of other Gillette products through the same retail pipeline, steadily reducing distribution costs.

It is an extremely focused strategy. It is also one that works.

MOST COMPANIES HAVE A MISSION STATEMENT. NONE IS LIKE GILLETTE'S.

Most mission statements talk in generalities about a quest for excellence and the need to respect fellow employees, Gillette's lays out a business strategy.

It says the company will divide its business into "core categories" (shaving is one; writing instruments another) and noncore. It then goes on to say that noncore businesses can never account for more than 10% of revenues.

If that is not specific enough, the mission statement goes further. Not only must 90% of business come from the core businesses, but those businesses must either be the world leader in their category or have a plan to get there. First or second in a specific market is not enough.

"When we created that statement in 1991—using 1990 as the base— we were the worldwide leader in 50% of our sales," Zeien says. "But of that 50%, the blade business accounted for 38%. We are now the worldwide leader in about 78% of our sales. The blade business, principally due to the Duracell acquisition, has gone down to about 30%. The nonblade business has gone from what was 12% of our business to about 48%. That means we have quadrupled the categories where we are the world leader."

It is clear, in retrospect, that the goals spelled out in the mission statement were right. However, not everyone saw it that way at first.

"It took about six months for me to sell it. And I mean sell it," Zeien explains. "That's what you have do with this sort of thing. I went around to almost all of our major operating centers with a draft of the statement and asked what we should we change. One of things that helped was that before I got this job I was president of the international business, so I knew all of these people, and that made the conversations easier."

But while Zeien was happy to discuss tweaking the idea, his commitment never wavered.

"It's not hard to figure out what the advantages of worldwide leadership were. But I think what really inspired us was that we decided to do the mission statement at the same time as we were going through a major change in how we did business.

"For most of our history, roughly from the turn of the century to about late 1989 or early 1990, we introduced the same product into different markets at different times. We'd introduce a product first into either the United States, Switzerland, or Sweden, markets that tended to be at the forefront. And then we just kind of cascaded, over a number of years, into market after market around the world.

"We used the production machinery over and over again. We passed it down from country to country. We were so proud of the fact that when we put a piece of machinery into Indonesia it was the fourth country it had been in. This is the way we ran the business for about 90 years.

"But it became apparent we had to change. Communications was changing at a rapid rate. Everybody was seeing the same television programs. *Time* magazine was available everywhere. At least the opinion leaders immediately knew what was selling in the United States even if they were Indonesian.

"And so we went to what we call the one-palette concept. We said we would sell the same palette of products everywhere in the world at the same time. We may sell more A's, B's, and C's in Switzerland and more D's, E's, and F's in India, but the offering will be the same.

"The decision to go to the one-palette concept came about the same time as we were doing the mission statement, so the two really fit together."

The bad news with this approach is that if you guess wrong about demand you are in a lot of trouble. You have made a huge, international mistake. However, if you get it right, the results, as Zeien says, are "fantastically different." You receive a tremendous jump in sales and earnings immediately, instead of having to wait to have them phased in over a period of years.

"The mission statement is a huge help here," Zeien says. "It keeps the company focused on exactly what it is trying to accomplish. It keeps us from dillying around with things that don't meet the mark. It makes us constantly look at the big picture and for places where we can get a substantial amount of volume."

And that focus requires the company to do something else: It forces Gillette to be ruthless when it comes to the introduction of new products. After all, the goal is not to get to the number-one position in the world; it is to stay there once the company does.

"That means we must constantly be cannibalizing our sales," Zeien says. "If we don't, someone else will do it to us. That's the simplest explanation why we must innovate. And since we have relatively restricted lines of business, our most successful new products are going to be in categories where we are already established. And since we have worldwide leadership in those categories, we can't help cannibalizing ourselves."

Zeien gives an example of what he is talking about. "We've said on the launch of the Mach3 (Gillette's new shaver for men) that we expect 75% cannibalization of our existing brand. Therefore, that product has to earn more for us than the 75% that it's replacing. You can't just make it up on the other 25%. We will be making more money with the Mach3 because the replacement cartridges cost more."

It is not the first time that this has happened.

"When we introduced Sensor, the cannibalization was actually somewhat higher," Zeien says. "That's because it ate into our disposable razors. But it was a very profitable conversion, since our profit per user per year out of disposables was less than half."

Because of this constant need to replace existing product, Zeien has developed a simple rule: "We will not launch a major product, until its successor has moved out of the research lab into development. No matter how great the product is, we are going to hold it up until its replacement has been identified."

This discipline imposes disciplines of its own. It puts tremendous pressures on Gillette's research laboratories and it puts pressure on its people. Zeien is proud of both.

"First of all, this is a technologically driven business. A lot of people think we're great marketers. We *are* great marketers, but, fundamentally, we're only as good as our products. And from a research point of view we look more like a pharmaceutical company than someone in the consumer goods business. Our research laboratories do research—period. They do no development. We won't even put research in the same building with development, because once you do, development starts driving the research and we don't want that to happen.

"We define research in a number of ways. Over on the very, very left is what we call pure research. We don't do any of that. Pure researchers are the people who win Nobel Prizes, they discover new phenomena. We don't do work in that category.

"The next category is basic research. That we do. Basic research, in effect, is developing an understanding of how any new technology will impact our business. And, generally, that research ends up with a piece of paper. And that piece of paper says, 'Did you know that if such and such and such and such happened, we'd end up with this kind of product or material?'

"Then we do applied research. And applied research is to demonstrate feasibility. We figure it takes about 15 research projects for every three that go into development. And for every three that go into development, one goes to market.

"People say, 'I can understand the fifteen to three. But I don't understand the three to one. Why would you spend all that money on development and then not launch two out of three products?' The answer is that most of our development projects die on the basis of cost. Until you develop the process, you really don't know what the cost is going to be. We design and build our own equipment. We don't buy from other manufacturers and that gives us a real good handle on our costs.

"Let me give you an example why two out of three die. You come out of research and say, 'This is just a great concept and we could sell a million of these at 10 bucks.' But to do that, we have to make them for two dollars, two-fifty. Then you go into the process development and find out, 'Hey, you can't make them for two-fifty, it's going to cost four dollars.' Therefore, you'd have to sell it for $20 to have a good profitable business. The idea dies.

"But it's better to have that happen than the other way around. Which is, we go with a $20 price and still tell ourselves we can sell a million of them. And then maybe only sell a half a million.

"So our approach is a very disciplining process. But what it means is if we are going to launch 20 projects a year, which we do, we need about 300 projects going on in the research labs at any given time, and we have."

This approach puts a great deal of pressure on Gillette's employees. And as a result, the company has come up with a unique—and yes, disciplined—approach to developing its people.

"We have a rule concerning our management group, which consists of about 800 people," Zeien explains. "It says only 10% of promotions in a given year can be 'vertical.' That's where you get your boss's job. The rest have to be 'diagonal' promotions. A diagonal promotion either changes function, geography, or it changes product line, in addition to giving you more responsibility.

"Why do we do this? Three reasons. First, obviously, you get the rounding of the personality. You're building talent breadth.

"Second, how does someone get a vertical promotion? The boss has 10 people working for him, and he picked Jack. Why? Because he figures Jack is most likely to perpetuate his way of doing things. Because obviously, that's the best way to do them, right? You get very little change when you have a vertical promotion.

"But the third reason is the most important. If you're not going be promoted vertically, you can only get promoted diagonally and that means someone has to ask for you. How did another boss know to ask for Jack? Some of his people have worked with Jack. Given the way promotions work, it didn't take Jack very long to figure out, 'You know, I'm not just working to please my boss. I'm working to please these guys over here who are going to tell everybody what I great guy I am.'

"So by limiting vertical promotions, we break down the artificial walls between departments. It greatly strengthens the organization."

When you put it all together, you get an organization, and a business, which is remarkably disciplined and produces consistently superior results.

Company (Ticker): The Gillette Company (G)

Location: Boston, Massachusetts

Gillette at a glance: Although best known for being the leader in male grooming products with products such as its Sensor, Trac II, and Mach3 razors, Gillette is the world leader in more than a dozen consumer product categories including alkaline batteries (Duracell), dental care (Oral-B), toiletries (Right Guard), writing products (Paper Mate, Parker Pen, Waterman, Liquid Paper), and electric shavers and other small appliances (Braun). A global power, Gillette derives more than 60% of its revenues from outside the United States and manufactures its products in more than 26 countries. Gillette's small appliances and haircare divisions are being sold off after not performing.

1999 Financial Results

—Revenues: $9.8 billion

—Net Income: $1.2 billion

PART III

Lessons Learned

Introduction

OUR HOPE FROM THE START OF RESEARCHING *LESSONS FROM THE TOP* was that by studying the careers and successes of the best business leaders in America, we could find patterns that we could apply to achieve our own dreams and aspirations.

To open this section of the book, we have included a profile of Peter Drucker, an honorary addition to our list of 50 business leaders. Although Dr. Drucker is not a traditional business leader in terms of managing a large organization, through his teachings and ideas, he has been one of the great leaders of business (and society) over the past 50 years. He was one of the leaders most widely cited in both the Gallup survey component of our research and by the business leaders themselves in our interviews. Most of the leaders on our list cited Peter Drucker as an important influence in their careers and thoughts. And so we felt that it was appropriate to include and indeed honor Dr. Drucker and his work in making him our "51st Leader."

The heart of this section of the book, however, synthesizes what we learned about business leadership from the various leaders on our list into a model that we call "doing the right things right." Overwhelmingly, the business leaders on our list followed these mutually reinforcing principles in achieving outstanding corporate performance and it is our hope that this model can serve as a guide for all of us as we strive to excel.

None of the individual leadership principles we have delineated is new. Many are as old, perhaps, as human civilization. But given the widespread shortcomings of business leadership today, perhaps what is needed is not new leadership ideas but rather a guiding set of principles that will serve as a tool to help people manage and lead successfully. We believe that "doing the right things right" offers such a tool. It is an approach that allows individuals to focus on the basics and use them to improve their careers and day-to-day performances.

The last chapter in this section offers our assessment of the common traits displayed by the 50 extraordinarily successful business leaders on our list. Over the history of leadership research, it seems that everything that can be measured has been: parentage, birth order, gender, age, height, weight, health, perception, cognition, interpersonal competence, task competence, charisma, values, power (and its use), and environment. We realized that the world did not need another "scientific" study of leadership. But this chapter is different. It provides a more empirical synthesis, based on our interviews with the 50 leaders profiled in this book, of the traits that have helped make these leaders so successful. Our hope is that we can all adapt and incorporate these traits to one degree or another in our own careers and lives to help us realize our own professional and personal goals.

CHAPTER 1

The 51st Business Leader: Peter Drucker

"Yes, you want to manage for results. But what do you mean by results?"

ONE OF THE QUESTIONS WE ASKED ALL THE BUSINESS LEADERS ON OUR list was: "Tell us about the people and writings that influence you." In retrospect, we could have just as easily put it this way: "Please tell us how Peter Drucker influenced your thinking." For it would be far easier to cite the leaders who did not mention Dr. Drucker during our one-on-one interviews than to list those who did.

Intriguingly, the various business leaders cited different aspects of his work. Some mentioned *The Concept of the Corporation*, Drucker's study of General Motors that was published in 1945. Others quoted later works, notably *Innovation and Entrepreneurship*. Still others had absorbed Drucker's ideas through articles he had written in publications as diverse as *Esquire* and *The Harvard Business Review*. A few had hired Drucker as a consultant and they seemed able to quote what he told them verbatim.

Because Drucker was such a major influence on the thinking of the leaders, and because few scored higher in the Gallup survey we commissioned to identify America's most influential business-

Peter F. Drucker has held a variety of jobs since he started working 70 years ago. He has been everything from a securities analyst to a business consultant (for companies such as GE, Sears, and IBM) to a professor (at Bennington, New York University, and the Claremont Colleges). But when asked to describe his career over the last 70 years, Drucker says, "I write."

Instead of listing every job he has ever had, we decided to highlight some of his works.

As Jack Beatty points out in *The World According to Peter Drucker*, the 30 books Drucker has written fall into three broad categories: social and political analysis, such as *The Future of Industrial Man* and *Age of Discontinuity*; books on management theory, such as *The Practice of Management*; and advice to managers, such as *Managing for Results* and *The Effective Manager*.

EDUCATION
Doctorate in public law and international relations, University of Frankfort

Married.

"The corporation is the 'representative institution' of the era. Only now have we realized that the large mass-production plant is our social reality . . . which has to carry the burden of our dreams.

"Those dreams are the American dreams of equality of opportunity and personal achievement.

"More people can realize more of these dreams in an industrial society than ever before in history. This is primarily because the industrial system requires whole new categories of skilled workers—from managers to technicians—that did not exist a generation before. Industrialism creates its own middle class."[1]

---

1. From Peter F. Drucker's *Concept of the Corporation*, published 1945.

people—particularly on the question of impact on business and society—we decided that we had to go right to the source: Peter Drucker.

Professor Drucker was polite but firm when we approached him insisting repeatedly that he did not belong in this book. It was not false modesty: It was just that he felt he did not fit into the majority of criteria we were using for selection.

"I am not a business leader, and my work has not even been primarily about business, but society, institutions, and organizations in general (including business)." The note was written on an electric typewriter. Drucker has said that he finds working on a word processor makes him too verbose.

Although we told him we agreed that he did not fit the criteria for everyone else, we informed him that at some point in just about every interview we conducted, his name came up. When asked about potential divestitures, for example, Jack Welch said: "Drucker once asked if you weren't already in this business, would you enter it now? That's a great question. And we asked that of every business we are in."

Given the influence he had over so many of those featured in the book—Fred Smith of Federal Express, Dan Tully of Merrill Lynch, and Larry Bossidy of AlliedSignal, as well as Welch, were particularly eloquent on Drucker's influence on them—we told Professor Drucker we would be remiss if we did not include him.

Normally when you try to contact Peter Drucker, as part of a project such as this one, you get back a postcard with the following words printed on the back:

> Mr. Peter F. Drucker
> greatly appreciates your kind interest, but is unable to: contribute articles or forewords; comment on manuscripts or books; take part in panels or symposia; join committees or boards of any kind; answer questionnaires; give interviews; or appear on radio and television.

We are glad he made an exception in our case.

"WHAT GETS MEASURED GETS MANAGED."

There is probably no more quoted business adage than that. And the natural by-product of this approach is that we get executives who manage for results.

There is nothing wrong with that, Drucker says. In fact, he is the man who introduced the concept of managing by objective. But after reaffirming that he still believes in managing for results, he asks a question that probably has never occurred to most performance driven managers.

"What do you mean by results? Results are different for every organization. I have my clients rethink what results are, or should be, every three years or so."

The implication, of course, is that managers may be trying to achieve the wrong thing, or that goals and objectives need to be adapted to changing circumstances.

This is the kind of simple question that Drucker is fond of asking that can force even the savvy executive to stop and reexamine his or her key principles. But asking questions that jar executives out of complacent thinking is nothing new for Peter Drucker. When he asked, decades ago, "What business are you really in?" he got executives to think about what we now call "core competencies." If you answer the question, "We're in the telephone business," you are likely to structure your company one way. If you say, "We're in the communications business" or in "the service business" (as a former chairman of AT&T answered years ago when Drucker asked him), you are quite likely to go in another direction. As a result, the question "What business are you really in?" has profound importance.

Similarly, by wondering out loud what results are worth striving for, Drucker may very well get managers to rethink what the mission of their companies should be.

Not surprisingly, this is one of the key jobs a manager has, Drucker argues.

When we asked him about the "ideal relationship" between a CEO and his board of directors, Drucker was clear, direct, and offered an answer that might make some chief executives, and some boards, uncomfortable.

First and foremost, Drucker told us the board and CEO are "colleagues." But that does not mean that they have the same job or even that they need to be congenial. Drucker sees the role of the board as demanding that management develop strategy for the board's discussion and approval. And that is true of the relationship between any board in any country and any CEO, Drucker contends.

Again, such thinking can force managers to rethink key assumptions.

When we asked Professor Drucker what he was most proud of in his career and his life he answered: "A few people for whom I made a difference."

We are willing to bet the list of people for whom Peter Drucker has made a difference is slightly longer than "a few."

CHAPTER 2

Doing the Right Things Right: A New Definition of Business Success

"As for the best leaders, the people do not notice
their existence. The next best, the people honor and
praise. The next, the people fear, and the next, the
people hate. When the best leader's work is done, the
people say, 'We did it ourselves.'"
—*Lau-Tzu*

GIVEN THE DRAMATIC CHANGES TAKING PLACE IN THE UNITED STATES
and global economy, creative responsible business leadership had never
been more important. Warren Bennis, Distinguished Professor of Business at the University of Southern California and a renowned expert on
leadership, suggests that in today's environment, people in corporations,
not-for-profit institutions, and even countries "are looking toward their
leaders to provide three basic qualities: direction, trust, and hope."

We believe that the profiles in this book demonstrate that the 50 business leaders on our list have provided precisely this kind of leadership to
their organizations.

Why have they been successful?

Our research and analysis indicates that when leaders succeed in doing
the right things—both personally and within their organizations—the
traditional measures of success inevitably follow.

Analyzing the careers of our exceptional business leaders, we found that
their stories were as different as the individuals themselves. What was a
surprise was that we discovered six principles which all of the leaders on
our list, to a greater or lesser degree, shared. As we sought to synthesize
their success into principles of business leadership, we concluded that
these six mutually reinforcing principles help bring about the outstanding
corporate performance these leaders had enjoyed. We call the execution of
these six core principles "doing the right things right." And we discovered

these principles in the stories of the business leaders in this book again and again.

We found that while the men and women running the best companies are substantially different from one another, how they went about achieving their success is remarkably similar. They do the right things right. The six core principles are:

1) Live with Integrity and Lead by Example
2) Develop a Winning Strategy or "Big Idea"
3) Build a Great Management Team
4) Inspire Employees to Achieve Greatness
5) Create a Flexible, Responsive Organization
6) Tie It All Together with Reinforcing Management and Compensation Systems

Perhaps the best image to help keep these principles in mind is a wheel—with each principle naturally leading to the next—creating a con-

DOING THE RIGHT THINGS RIGHT

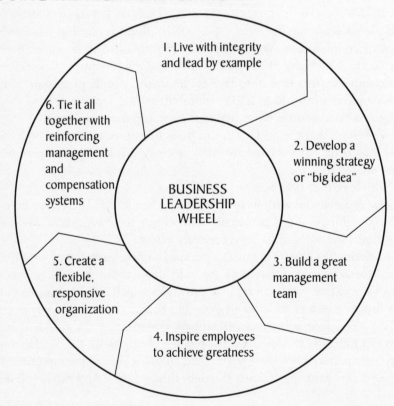

tinuous, forward-moving process. We have called this image the "business leadership wheel."

There is one other notion that underpins these six principles—and keeps the wheel moving steadily ahead. The best-managed companies—led by the most successful business leaders—do not apply these principles in a one-off fashion. They do not make one principle the focus of their attention for a short period of time and then move on to something else. Rather, they apply every one of these principles constantly and consistently. There are no contradictions.

And that is true of them personally, as well as throughout their organizations.

In an individual, this kind of consistency is often described as "walking the talk." Within a company, it is typically called "executing on strategy." The lesson is the same in either case: The greatest success is achieved when a leader of an organization is consistent, when the organization is consistent, and when this consistency is linked to what the company stands for and how it behaves.

One clear example is Bill Marriott and his company, Marriott International.

Bill Marriott is driven by a series of deeply held beliefs and values. They include hard work, providing exceptional service, honesty, financial discipline, and a commitment to family, community, colleagues, guests, and the world at large. Everything he does, every speech that he gives, and every decision that he makes is consistent with these values. He truly walks the talk. And by talking about these values every day, Bill Marriott keeps reinforcing them throughout the organization.

It also happens that these same values are responsible for the sustained success of Marriott, the company.

While successful companies have different strategies, values and beliefs, different strengths and weaknesses, and different organizational approaches, a key to their success is that they are thoroughly consistent with themselves.

Let us examine each of the six principles and try to bring them to life with comments from our interviews with the business leaders on our list.

1. LIVE WITH INTEGRITY AND LEAD BY EXAMPLE

Living with integrity and leading by example is the internal sense of right and wrong that should direct everything a person—certainly a successful person—does. It is also, as Elizabeth Dole reminds us, "the one thing that every person has 100% control over." Integrity builds the trust in senior management that is common among—and critical for—high-performing organizations.

Integrity is the first ingredient that is necessary if someone is to be successful. You can have integrity and still fail, but the opposite is not true.

John Chambers of Cisco Systems puts it this way: "Treating other people like you like to be treated is truly the Golden Rule."

Fred Smith of Federal Express makes the point that integrity and leading by example are the first ingredient of leadership around the world. "I have always been fascinated by the fact," he says, "that if you look at every religion in the world, they all have the identical Golden Rule, almost word for word. It does not make any difference what religion or geography it is. There are universally transferable fundamental truths about how you treat people in both the business world, as well as in the larger scheme of things."

Hank Greenberg of AIG uses the principle of living with integrity and leading by example as a key determinant in deciding whether someone should move up the ranks of his insurance and financial services giant. In promoting people, he looks, of course, at performance, knowledge of the business, and management skills, as well. But, he says, "the primary ingredient is a person's value system, ethics, and commitment to what they are doing."

Greenberg thinks integrity, coupled with the ability to achieve results, is what makes a leader. "People either recognize you're a leader or they don't. They've got to feel comfortable. They've got to feel that the leader knows where he's taking them and feel confident in that direction. They want the people leading them to set an example."

All of our business leaders pointed out that employees spend a lot of time watching what the boss does and that brings us to one of the keys to leading by example. A successful leader needs a strong dose of humility. This is increasingly difficult to do in an era when many business leaders have become media stars. When we invited our business leaders to participate in this book, for example, a large majority of them (or their corporate communications departments) told us of the many book requests they have recently received. If a business leader takes this attention personally, or tries to take all the credit for the company's success, it will undoubtedly have an adverse effect on company morale. People need to feel valued and appreciated. If not, good ideas are hard to come by.

"People's egos are a big problem in running a business," Don Fisher of The Gap told us. "I haven't let my ego get in the way of anybody. I'd just as soon have other people get credit for stuff rather than me. If I were to take credit for all of it, it would be very discouraging to the guy that really did the work."

On the one hand, Fisher says, "Credit should go where it belongs." For an executive, on the other hand, it really doesn't matter who created the breakthrough idea as long as it happens. "If you were the head of the area and had total responsibility for delivering something, I don't care where you get the idea from—as long as you get it. You're going to get credit because you got it, not because you invented it. You may have called up a friend. What difference does it make where you get it, just as long as you get it."

Herb Kelleher of Southwest Airlines takes this concept of a leader sublimating his or her ego a bit further. "The best leaders have to be good followers as well," he says. "You have to be willing to accept other people's ideas, even when they are in conflict with your own. You have to be willing to subjugate your ego to the needs of your business. You have to be selfless and take risks for your people. If you won't fight for your people, then you can count on your people not fighting for you."

These kinds of actions are noticed, commented upon, and eventually internalized by the organization so that it becomes a reflection of the person at the top.

The best leaders know this, so they spend a disproportionate amount of time acting in such a way that makes it clear to everyone what they and their company stand for.

Alcoa's Paul O'Neill, for example, has taken the idea of modeling behavior to the point where you can say that he leads by serving as the exemplar of his company's values. As we saw, he fired the head of a business—a 28-year veteran who had grown his division from $100 million in sales to over $1.5 billion—because the man had hidden from upper management a report that identified an environmental problem. O'Neill also makes sure that the company's overseas plants meet tougher American safety standards.

O'Neill says, "If people can find even trivial examples of deviation, those deviations will become the norm. You really have to be almost religious in making sure that you don't do something somebody can point to in a negative way."

2. DEVELOP A WINNING STRATEGY OR "BIG IDEA"

Today's competitive environment increases the need for winning strategies. As Larry Bossidy of AlliedSignal told us, "I think the most significant challenge that businesses will be facing over the next few years is the acceleration of intensity. Because of that, you need to be in a business where you have a competitive advantage or you are going to get killed. I don't think that any business franchise that I know of is secure. It was only 20 years ago when you could not conceive of IBM or Kodak having any trouble. Today, thinking like that is over. And I think the competitive intensity will continue to increase."

In this environment, a leader must be the source of creating a winning strategy, based on a company's competitive advantages and fundamental customer needs. This demands carefully listening to the customer and keeping a continuous eye on the competition.

Hank Greenberg of AIG argues, "The CEO must be the top strategist of the organization." In AIG's case, that means: "We don't go into unrelated areas where we have no special skills or anything unique to add. We only enter into businesses where there is an unmet need and where we can bring value. For example, we acquired an airline leasing company, for which our triple-A rating helped the entity significantly on their financing costs, and our relationships around the world opened doors for them to lease more aircraft."

Jack Welch has also been GE's chief strategist for nearly 20 years. His decisions to buy NBC, beef up GE Capital, the company's financial services division, and expand aggressively overseas are well known. What is Welch's big idea for the next decade? "Product is dead," he says. As we saw, Welch is now shifting GE's focus to services, where the opportunity for higher margins and recurring revenue streams offer a better chance of creating and capturing value.

Federal Express was founded on Fred Smith's idea of creating a hub-and-spoke distribution network to provide overnight delivery of packages. In the process, scores of new companies and, indeed, industries, including some forms of electronic commerce—such as selling books and computer-related products via of the Internet—have been created.

What are Smith's principles for developing breakthrough strategies? Smith cites Rosabeth Moss Kanter, Harvard Business School professor and former editor of *The Harvard Business Review*, for providing the requisite tool: "kaleidoscope thinking."

"Sometimes you look at a business problem and it's intractable, you just can't solve it," he explains. "You need to keep looking at it and turning the kaleidoscope until you see a different pattern. Sometimes you can develop an idea that's very different and a solution that hasn't been thought of before. The key is to recognize that there is almost always a different way to approach the issue and many times it is not the conventional way you have been doing it in the past."

What would represent a current example for FedEx? Smith responds with an anecdote that is surprising.

"One time I was talking to some of our managers and they asked me, 'If you could just do one thing'—and it had to be achievable—'to improve service levels meaningfully at FedEx, what would you do?' I'm sure they thought that I would say something about purchasing more planes or implementing faster package sorting. But I said the thing that I would do is to go to Washington, D.C., and lobby very hard to change the time zones in the continental U.S. from four to three, because that would give us an additional hour in the day to work. We're constrained by taking off in Los Angeles at 7:15 P.M. in order to arrive in New York by 6 A.M. Adding another time zone (which would give FedEx West Coast customers an extra hour to drop off packages) is an idea that is based on a totally different pattern."

Dennis Kozlowski of Tyco International attributes much of his company's success to an "idea" he developed and implemented at the time he became CEO in 1992: increasing recurring-revenue businesses. During his tenure as chief executive, the company has shifted from 85% cyclical businesses, where transactions occurred one at a time, to 85% recurring-revenue businesses such as disposable medical supplies. This simple but powerful concept has led the company into such businesses as producing health care supplies, monitoring security systems, and maintaining underwater telephone lines.

Coming up with a big idea is one thing. Executing it is quite another. The companies that have been most successful—not surprisingly—focus relentlessly on execution.

DaimlerChrysler is a case in point. With the help of his team, chairman and co-CEO Bob Eaton came up with a strategy that shaped Chrysler's future. As he put it, "The purpose of this company is to produce cars and trucks that people want to buy, will enjoy driving, and will want to buy again."

That, and that alone, is what Chrysler focused on during Eaton's tenure. As a result, divisions devoted to defense, financial services (other than helping customers purchase and enjoy their vehicles), and aerospace systems were sold off.

It was the same story at Pfizer. CEO Bill Steere decided that the company was in the business of "research-based pharmaceutical products." This led the company to divest such diverse businesses as cardiac catheters and talc mines. The resulting numbers speak for themselves. Pfizer's total annualized shareholder returns, and cash flow growth, both lead the pharmaceutical industry.

Not only must leaders come up with a big idea, it must be the right big idea.

Of course, there are many companies (none of whom made our final list) that came up with a big idea that was wrong, or for which the timing was off.

How do you increase your odds for success? A successful leader must go to the company's roots and build on the things the organization truly does best then link this to what matters most to customers (defined by what they will pay for). This will lead you from simply making and selling products (which may or may not lead to success) to developing solutions for customers (a far more likely strategy for achieving success).

3. BUILD A GREAT MANAGEMENT TEAM

The importance of this principle simply cannot be overstated as a core component in the "business leadership wheel." As Michael Dell of Dell Computer says, "One person cannot do anything alone." Adds Steve Case of America Online: 'There is a one-to-one correlation with the quality of the people on a particular project and the quality of the project's leader. Since companies are really a collection of people, results can be tied directly to the quality of the management team."

Pfizer's Bill Steere has a straightforward but powerful rule for building a top management team: Play to people's strengths.

"Everyone has weaknesses," Steere acknowledges. "If you focus on their weaknesses, you're just going to make everybody unhappy. So you manage to people's strengths and work around—not punish—their weaknesses."

Great business leaders have all, to one extent or another, built highly successful management teams. Some of the teams have been centered on complementary business partnerships. Others are created by focusing religiously on hiring and training. And there are some management teams that have been formed by a group of people putting mutual trust above all else.

But in no case is the priority of creating a great management team more important than with entrepreneurs attempting to transform their ventures into successful, sustainable, large corporations.

Consider:

THE GAP. The company did well under its founder Don Fisher from its creation in 1969 until the early 1980s, when rampant price cutting of its core product—Levi's jeans—broke out. Gap vaulted that hurdle and moved on, becoming a recognizable brand name when Fisher brought in Millard "Mickey" Drexler. "At the point Mickey arrived," Fisher says, "we didn't have anybody who was a really good merchant. Mickey and I worked together as a partnership. I focused on the operational side of the business. Mickey was dedicated to the merchandising and marketing side. It's not that we didn't listen to what the other had to say. But we didn't mess around with each other's area. So it worked out really well."

SOUTHWEST AIRLINES. There have been two keys to building a great management team at Southwest; 1) hiring, and 2) training. As Herb Kelleher explains, "We hire for attitude and teach skills if we have to. The one thing you cannot change is attitude." After making sure to hire the right people, the company devotes substantial resources to leadership training. "We give class after class on leadership skills," Kelleher says. "It's long been a saying that the military looks for managers in peacetime and leaders in wartime. Since we're always at war in the airline business, we should always be looking for leaders. We are teaching individuals to lead a diverse group of people that have different personalities and backgrounds to coalesce around a common cause. That's leadership, simply put."

CHARLES SCHWAB. One of the best things entrepreneurial leaders can learn is where their strengths lie and build a great management team that compensates for their weaknesses. Charles Schwab learned early on that he was best at plotting the marketing direction of the firm. He delegated all other tasks to people he hired for their complementary skills. Today he shares the co-CEO title with renowned operating executive David Pottruck.

AMERICA ONLINE. Another of the most successful entrepreneurial leaders in the nation is Steve Case of AOL, who has a somewhat different philosophy about how to build his management team. "Some of the best people we have attracted have come here through rather unorthodox ways," he says. "Some came through traditional recruiting, I'm pleased to say, but many through acquisitions or other means. If you look at our management team, several people with significant responsibilities were presidents or CEOs of their own companies we acquired, including Barry Schuler (president of AOL interactive services), who had been CEO of Medior, Ted Leonsis (president of AOL Studios), who had founded and run Redgate Communications, Miles Gilburne, SVP, Corporate Development, and Bob Pittman (AOL's president and COO), who signed on a year after we recruited him to join the board. These people had demonstrated track records in having built something and possessed the passion, perseverance, and paranoia that we look for."

Conventional wisdom has it that entrepreneurs cannot make the transition to successful corporate leadership. Unfortunately, this is often the case. In fact, we at Spencer Stuart are often hired by boards and venture capitalists to recruit "experienced corporate management" for rapidly growing companies where the management demands apparently exceed the limits of the founder/entrepreneur.

Does this have to be the case? No. Not if an entrepreneur builds a great management team, and ideally, sooner than later. In fact, of the 50 business leaders profiled in this book, a significant number, 11—nearly a quarter of the total—are the founding (or co-founding) entrepreneurs. They are: Steve Case of American Online, Michael Dell of Dell Computer, Bernie Ebbers of MCI WorldCom, Don Fisher of The Gap, Bill

Gates of Microsoft, Andy Grove of Intel, Herb Kelleher of Southwest Airlines, Howard Schultz of Starbucks, Charles Schwab, Fred Smith of Federal Express, and Charles Wang of Computer Associates.

Within these companies, great management teams abound. Bill Gates
hired Steve Ballmer, now Microsoft's president. Howard Schultz hired
Howard Behar as Starbucks' COO; Michael Dell hired Mort Topfer and
Kevin Rollins, who today are both vice chairmen and members of Dell
Computer's Office of the Chairman; Charles Schwab hired David Pottruck, who is now co-CEO; and Don Fisher hired Mickey Drexler, now
Gap's CEO. To become great enduring companies, these entrepreneurs
and the other leaders profiled in this book rounded out their executive
ranks with other strong leaders whose skills and experiences *comple-
mented* their own, but whose passion, attitudes, and values were *one and
the same.*

Perhaps Steve Case explains this point best. "Rather than thinking you
have to do everything as CEO, why don't you assume that there's actually
nothing you have to do and organize things in a way such that there's as
little to do as possible.

"The key to taking this approach is hiring great people that you really
have confidence in and that you can trust. You basically organize things in
a way that the overall company is headed in the right direction with the
right people doing the right things. To me, the perfect week is when there's
nothing that I have to do; so that I can concentrate on strategy development, people development, and customer service. Instead of being the
'do-everything entrepreneur,' I'm basically trying to be the CEO who
does not *have to* do a thing."

What is the key to making the transition from entrepreneur to manager? There are several ways, says Fred Smith of Federal Express. First, you
have to learn how to do it, through reading, studying, and talking to people who have been down that road before. Second, you should "surround
yourself with people within management and on the board who plainly
have a lot of experience."

The principle of building a great management team involves continuous evolution—and pruning when necessary. It also applies to the "extended organization," which includes the company's board of directors.
Gone are the days when the best-performing CEOs stack the board with
insiders or cronies.

Larry Bossidy of AlliedSignal is one of several leaders profiled in
this book who made this point to us. "I think the board is a wonderful
device—if staffed properly. To begin with, you must attract the very best
people you can. When it comes to critical moments, you're much better
fortified by a good, strong board than you are by people who may be loyal
but are not qualified or who haven't been asked to get involved."

Professional development is also a key part of building a great executive team, as the chapter on Andy Grove of Intel demonstrates. Similar to Grove, great business leaders ensure that their companies commit substantial time and resources to developing managers.

4. INSPIRE EMPLOYEES TO ACHIEVE GREATNESS

As we mentioned in Chapter 1 of Part I, there are powerful trends at work in America today that affect the attitudes that people—especially young people—have about their jobs. Employees today seem to look for a deeper meaning from their work. As Professor Bennis wrote in *On Becoming a Leader:*

"You're not going to attract or retain a top-quality workforce under those silly and obsolete forms of bureaucratic or command-and-control leadership. You cannot release the brain power of any organization by using whips and chains. You get the best out of people by empowering them, being supportive, and getting out of their way."

Another way to say this is if business leaders are to be successful, more than ever, they need to tap into employees' deepest motivations and desires.

This is entirely consistent with how the best business leaders lead. "Management is what used to be required to run a company," says Bob Eaton of DaimlerChrysler. "Today it's leadership. A manager basically controls, establishes plans, makes a budget, allocates work, and tracks results. A leader is much more focused on vision and beliefs. He or she inspires people and breaks roadblocks so that people can accomplish more."

Herb Kelleher, one of the business leaders known to have the most inspirational effect on employees, has built his company around the idea that people work better and are much more productive when they enjoy what they are doing.

"You shouldn't have to change your personality when you come to work. At Southwest, we have created an atmosphere where we hire good people, let them be themselves, and pay a great deal of attention to them and their personal lives. In other words, we create an environment where people can really enjoy what they are doing."

Martha Ingram of Ingram Industries concurs, explaining how she added a sense of fun to the workplace when she began leading the company in 1995. "I want people to love to come to work. I want them to have a good time. I think a sense of fun can be good. People become more productive."

For this kind of workplace to endure, Kelleher says, it must be genuine. "People know whether you are doing it for purely economic reasons or whether you really like people and value them. We're not at all loath to talk to people in terms that involve love and idealism. We believe it's important for everybody to realize we're in an enterprise that has some worthwhile meaning."

Kelleher offers a metaphor to drive home his point. "The bricklayer is not just laying bricks. He is building a home for a family. He will probably do a better job if he understands what the ultimate goal is. That home is a very expensive purchase for the family, so you want it to hold up and not be subjected to tremendous maintenance expenses."

For Alcoa's Paul O'Neill, inspiring people is no more complicated than addressing basic human needs, needs that he says are the same worldwide. "People have different levels of desires, but directionally, they want the same kinds of things. They want to be respected and have a sense of being dealt with fairly. At every level, they want to make a contribution and be recognized for it."

Elizabeth Dole speaks publicly a great deal about inspiring people. "I tell young people all the time the influence and accomplishments I've come to respect are united by a single trait of will and character—a sense of mission. Finding a calling that just summons you to selflessness and that you put your heart into gives you the energy and enthusiasm that will inspire others. It becomes contagious; people want to be a part of what you are doing."

What It Takes to Inspire People

No matter how they expressed it, the basic concepts the leaders on our list mentioned when they talked about inspiring people were remarkably consistent: Communicate continuously, listen carefully, genuinely tolerate failure as a learning experience, build on people's desire to make a positive difference, and maintain a commitment to innovation, creativity, diversity, social responsibility, and continuous development. It never hurts for a leader to have the gift of charisma, which is often confused with leadership. However, we have come to conclude that in today's sophisticated workplace environment, actions speak louder than words. The true energy of any organization lies within the people who make up that organization. If those people are only going through the motions, corporate performance will be substandard. One of a leader's primary challenges is to unleash their energy and harness it to the organization's strategy.

5. CREATE A FLEXIBLE, RESPONSIVE ORGANIZATION

Much has been written about Jack Welch. But until now his invocation for organizations to become much more informal has not been discussed outside of GE.

The concept will catch on. It has to.

With today's information technology facilitating instantaneous global communications, the successful business leaders will be those who break down slow, overly formalized hierarchies and decision-making processes. Welch has coined a phrase to capture the concept: He calls it "the power of the informal."

The key, in Welch's words, "is to have the right people solving problems, no matter where they are located geographically or hierarchically."

We heard the phrase "having the right people" many times during the course of our interviews. Like Welch, Don Fisher of The Gap, Al Zeien of Gillette and others have said that 50%—or more—of their jobs leading their companies were focused on human resources. Now that Drexler is CEO of The Gap, Fisher says that "this is true for him as well. Mickey is always talking to me about people. 'What do we do with this person? How do we hire that one? What kind of bonus do we pay her?' These are the things we talk about."

Once you have the right people, they must be able to move quickly. The best leaders have redesigned their organizations to make sure decisions can be made fast. O'Neill of Alcoa points to a reorganization in 1991 he led that created 21 different business units and made the accountability and responsibility clearer than it had ever been before.

Tyco International's Kozlowski cited the company's totally decentralized structure and lean headquarter's staff as keys to outmaneuvering the competition. They, along with Pfizer's Steere, AOL's Case, and Cisco Systems' John Chambers have made speed a top corporate priority. These major companies have to outcompete their traditional rivals, of course. But well-financed, tightly focused, technologically empowered early-stage companies are going after their markets more fiercely and effectively than ever.

"Everything today is speed," Steere says. "Whether it's in finance, research, development, the regulatory process, or marketing, everything is oriented toward speed. For example, all of the things that we used to do sequentially in research, we now do in parallel. This increases the risk—and the expense. But if you win, you win faster and bigger. You know sooner whether you have a winner or a loser." Of course speed cannot be pursued outside of thoughtfulness—and analysis still counts. But companies no longer have the luxury of making decisions after all the facts are in and all the risks are out.

It is no different at DaimlerChrysler, says Bob Eaton. "For product development [an area where the company is widely regarded as a leader], we're organized into platform teams, which can include anywhere from 80 to 1,000 people. They operate under our one-page contract [the "12 Panel Chart" discussed on page 102, which covers all aspects of their business. The team is therefore self-contained and we [management] move out of the way and let them execute. They don't have to come back for additional approvals, providing that they stay within the contract. We've virtually eliminated upper management involvement on a day-to-day basis in product development."

Speed goes hand-in-hand with flexibility. Lowe's Companies, a leader in home-improvement retailing, has based its entire strategy and infrastructure around flexibility. According to CEO Bob Tillman: "We adapt to the way a customer wants to shop. If he wants to produce something and ship it out of a distribution center directly to their home, we'll do it that way. If they want to shop us over the Internet or through electronic catalogues, we have the capability to do that too."

Why all the need for flexibility? Tillman cites the major demographic trends taking place in the American economy. "The business as we know it today [a full line of home-improvement products in a superstore setting] is built off of the boomer generation, which is getting older and much more wealthy. They are probably not going to be traditional do-it-yourself customers much longer. They will be driving their boat around the Caribbean and letting somebody else maintain their house." This will require an increase in services. Tillman continues: "Now all of a sudden, there is a new generation coming along that is extremely technologically literate who distrusts and dislikes store-based shopping. This places additional demands on us as a company. We need to put in place the flexibility so that we do not have to mandate that customers shop us only one way."

The best companies use technology to make sure they stay flexible—and responsive. Cisco's John Chambers credits a combination of information and empowerment with flattening his company's corporate hierarchy, speeding decision making, and improving customer responsiveness.

But this information must be coupled with the ability of people to use it. How does Chambers ensure that people's decisions and actions are consistent with the company's direction and priorities? By linking what each person does to the company's strategy.

"We've reduced our vision down to a mission, with immediate and short-term goals which we've put on cards for everybody." Chambers demonstrated this during our meeting by pulling out his own objectives card that hangs around his belt. He assured us that every single employee has one as well. By giving managers and employees the information they need and the encouragement to make decisions that are consistent with the company's direction, Cisco has become one of the most flexible, responsive, and most valuable companies in America.

Another of the nation's most responsive companies is America Online, which has had to be in order to survive in the lightning-fast Internet industry. CEO Steve Case uses reorganization as a tool in maintaining the company's flexibility. While this approach has been unsettling for some of the company's employees, it has also allowed AOL to overcome the many obstacles that until early 1998 had many industry pundits predicting the company's demise.

"We reorganize this company about every year," Case says. "I sense a reorganization is needed because things start bubbling up and then too many issues start to come up. I know at that time, I have to get involved."

Common Beliefs Let You Move Faster

Having the company's values fully understood by everyone is another method of speeding up decision making, says Southwest's Herb Kelleher.

"It makes everything a lot easier. If someone makes a proposal, we don't spend a lot of time on it if it's contrary to our values. We just say, 'No, we're not going to do that.' Yes, we might be able to make a lot of money, but it doesn't make any difference. It's not what we stand for. We can move quickly and say, 'Okay, what's the next item?' "

6. TIE IT ALL TOGETHER WITH REINFORCING MANAGEMENT AND COMPENSATION SYSTEMS

"Survival of the fittest" goes a long way toward explaining how life on the planet evolved. In our capitalist economic system, the battle up the economic ladder plays a similarly substantial role in driving employee behavior. One of the key principles to successful business leadership is designing and implementing compensation systems that make sense and that are tied to an organization's well-conceived objectives. This also goes for other management systems, including budgeting, information systems, and performance measurement.

To be most effective, management systems such as compensation practices, information systems, and performance measurement must be consistent with and reinforce the values and strategy of the organization.

At Pfizer, where shareholder value has increased at a five-year compound annual rate of 51%, faster than any other pharmaceutical company, CEO Bill Steere says that 85% of his income is performance-based. His long-term incentives are tied to two measures, shareholder return and earnings-per-share growth, compared to the company's peer group.

Jack Welch says employee pay is a key part of reinforcing what the company believes.

"Compensation is a huge component of how you motivate people." But while the absolute levels of compensation are important, they are not sufficient. "Within our culture, differentiation is more important than actual compensation. At GE, it's making sure that you've got big rewards for some, and you flush out the others."

Compensation systems are also one of the main means for retaining key employees. At many of the companies represented in this book, highly valued stock options and restricted stock reach far down into the organization and represent incredible barriers for companies trying to recruit managers away. At GE, for example, there are more than 2,000 employees who hold unexercised stock options worth at least $1 million, plus thousands of others who (after exercising options) are millionaires as a result of the company's compensation programs coupled with the outstanding performance of GE's stock.

At MCI WorldCom, every single employee participates (or will soon participate) in the company's stock options program. CEO Bernie Ebbers explains the impact on the culture. "You can't go through this building without seeing charts revised every day of what options are worth. Our employees are truly motivated by ownership in the company."

(In addition to motivating and retaining employees, of course, MCI WorldCom's outstanding stock price performance, which has grown by approximately 50% annually since it went public, has both given it a currency to acquire other companies [which it has done over 65 times] and made it difficult for others to acquire them in the rapidly consolidating global telecommunications industry.)

One of the most innovative compensation techniques was outlined by The Gap's Don Fisher. "Our approach is to give discounted stock options, which is in the middle between straightforward restricted stock grants and options. You give people twice as many shares as you'd give them if you were to go with straight restricted stock. And unlike normal options, the shares are already half "in the money," representing a real gain."

Here's how it works with The Gap stock at say $66 per share. "Instead of giving someone a thousand shares of restricted shares at no cost to the employee, you give them 2,000 options with a strike price of $33," Fisher says. "The multiple is better and it is more tax advantageous for both the employee and company. To illustrate, if the stock price rises $10 per share, the employee makes $20,000 with discounted options versus $10,000 with restricted stock. And if the stock price stays flat, the employee still makes $33 per share versus normal stock options which would expire worthless. Another key to making a program such as this work is to ensure that vesting periods are long enough so that there is always a substantial amount of wealth at risk should the employee leave the company. This keeps the most valuable employees most locked into the company.

One business leader well regarded for utilizing incentive systems to reinforce his company's values and strategy is Citigroup's Sandy Weill. "We are very focused on the bottom line and how efficient we can be in delivering our product to the consumer. We closely tie our rewards to performance along these two measures. We really want to run a business where the great majority of our people's compensation is dependent on how they perform and how the entity of which they are a part does."

What About the Customer?

At Cisco, both the corporate strategy and culture is focused tightly on servicing the customer. As a result, John Chambers and his team, just like Citigroup's Sandy Weill, measure customer satisfaction in a variety of ways. The company ties compensation to what it finds.

"We have a customer survey once a year," says Chambers. "We also measure the satisfaction of every single customer contact on a scale of one to five. We pay every manager in our company based on that survey and these results."

Another reinforcing management system that is also tightly focused on the customer is how Lowe's utilizes market research.

"I'm a total believer that there are two areas of business that have to be insulated from any politics or adverse influence," says CEO Bob Tillman. "One is audit, because this protects the interests of the shareholders of the company [a common attitude about audit]. And the second is market research, because this really represents the customer [a rather unique attitude about market research]."

"While market research reports to me indirectly, we're thinking about having it report to me directly. I want them to really represent the customer and not be influenced by any other group. This is critical because when retailers fail, it is almost always because of their own personal arrogance in believing that they know what the customer truly wants and are smarter than the customer. We bet our company on the opposite assumption." And market research is a key to acting on this assumption.

Bernie Ebbers is living proof of Drucker's concept, "What gets measured gets managed." He cites his motel background for helping cement this idea into his business practices. "I was a fanatic about being able to measure things. How much soap did customers use per rented room and how much toilet tissue? Today, we develop budgets in a very, very detailed way to make sure that we identify all revenue and expense items that a company has. Over the years, we have compensated our people by their performance against the plan."

Larry Bossidy of AlliedSignal, too, speaks eloquently about the importance of linking management systems to company objectives. "There are so many things you can do in a company," he says, "but if you don't align them with everybody, you're wasting your time. So we spend a lot of time trying to make sure we get the alignment we need to be successful." A long-time student of Peter Drucker, Bossidy follows the professor's advice in changing measures of success to suit the circumstances.

"I usually try to select only three key measures in any one year, depending on the times," Bossidy says. "I don't think you have to measure the same thing all of the time. Our current performance measures are revenue growth, productivity, and cash flow." In other years, he has used net income, customer satisfaction, return on investment, and return on equity, among others.

Bossidy provides an example of how he tailors measures of success to the situation. He suggests using return on investment in periods of disinflation, where capital has to work harder to generate a return than in inflationary environments. When he makes a change such as this in response to the environment, Bossidy makes sure it cascades down the organization.

"We tell the operating people that these are the three measurements that we're going to have this year and make sure that they align their operating plans accordingly. Since the measures are the basis of bonus payouts, we don't have any trouble getting the alignment that is essential to make them successful."

Aside from compensation systems and budgeting processes, another key to successful business management and leadership is to establish information systems that link to and empower a company's most important measures of success. Federal Express was one of the earliest companies to apply this principle to its competitive advantage.

CEO Fred Smith has long said that the information about a package is as important to FedEx and its customers as the transportation of the package itself. "Information allowed our customers to keep near custodial control of their goods and materials in transit for the first time." That decreases their need for warehouses and increases Federal Express's value to them. And the company's various service quality indices represent important parts of employee incentive systems.

It is easy to lose sight of what is important, especially under the relentless time pressure that so many of us feel in today's technology-enabled world. Too often, urgent priorities are put ahead of actions based on the principles for enduring success. We urge you to keep our leadership framework can serve as a handy tool to help you do the right things right. For as this chapter hopefully demonstrates, the leaders that "drive their companies down the road on the business leadership wheel" inevitably create substantial value for their shareholders, customers, and employees alike.

CHAPTER 3

Common Traits: A Prescription for Success in Business

THE 50 BUSINESS LEADERS PROFILED IN THIS BOOK HAVE ACHIEVED extraordinary success. They knew what they wanted, and they accomplished their goals by playing to their strengths, overcoming their limitations, and inspiring others. In other words, they followed the six principles of business success in doing the right things right.

But what is it about these leaders that has allowed them to do this? What traits, if any, do they share? Most importantly, are there lessons we can learn from them that will make us more successful in our own careers? Part of the driving force behind this book since we started our research was the hope that we could identify traits and qualities that the best business leaders in America have in common. What makes these leaders tick, and what we can all learn from them?

While the business leaders profiled here demonstrate as wide a range of personalities and styles as any cross section of the population, we did find as we had hoped, a series of traits—10 to be exact—each of these leaders seemed to hold in common.

Of course people—unlike the movement of a Swiss timepiece or the physical laws of nature—are inherently unpredictable, and uniquely individual. We can't claim that the 10 traits constitute the *last word* in achieving success. Success in business, as in life itself, can be achieved in surprising and unpredictable ways. But there is no doubt that the leaders on our list have benefited from having these traits. Perhaps most importantly, we believe that by developing and improving these characteristics in our own lives, we can improve the odds in achieving our own professional dreams and ambitions.

Here then are the 10 traits that our list of the best business leaders in America share in common:

1) **PASSION.** No trait is more noticeable in the leaders on our list than the passion they share for their people and their companies. Quite simply, they love what they do. In many ways, passion is the counterpart of the principle described in the preceding chapter, *Doing the Right Things Right,* inspiring employees to achieve greatness.

"Having a passion for what you do, a sense of mission that comes from the heart, gives you the energy, drive and enthusiasm that's contagious and essential for leading an organization," says Elizabeth Dole.

Bill Gates echoes Dole: "I have the most fun job in the world, and love coming to work each day. There are always new challenges, new opportunities and new things to learn. If you enjoy your job this much, you never burn out."

When we asked the leaders in our interviews: "What advice would you give to young people as they think about their own careers?" almost to a person, they told us that to be successful, you need to love what you do.

"Passion is probably the most important thing," says DaimlerChrysler's Bob Eaton. "I tell young adults, 'You have to be excited about going to work and trying to have an impact.' "

Perhaps Campbell Soup's David Johnson put it best when he said: "Go out and do what you want to do. Don't wait and don't look for approval. And don't sit around wondering what will happen next. Push the pedal to the metal and make the most of life. Life is not a dress rehearsal. This is our life. This day is dying—'Tick, tick, tick.' What are you doing to make the most of it?"

2) **INTELLIGENCE AND CLARITY OF THINKING.** It probably goes without saying that the most successful business leaders are highly intelligent. Some of their intelligence is clearly the kind of raw intellectual horsepower that is innate. However, equally as important as their native smarts is their ability to make the complex seem simple.

Sitting face-to-face with Michael Dell, for example, it is so easy to understand the enduring benefits of a direct-to-customer business model—from both a customer and company perspective—that you wonder why all computer companies were not set up this way. While Dell's decision to deal directly with consumers—via 800 numbers, a direct sales force, and the Internet—seems obvious today, his gift was the ability to see—and act on—the explosive business opportunity represented by going direct as clearly in 1984. It has taken the rest of the world 15 years to understand fully what he grasped as a college freshman.

We found this kind of clarity of thinking as well in Pfizer's Bill Steere.

When he became CEO in 1991, the pharmaceutical industry was moving toward diversification and offering generic drugs to address the growth of managed health care. It was clear to Steere, however, that Pfizer should go in the opposite direction and focus primarily on the company's core strengths: researching, developing, marketing, and selling proprietary drugs for people and animals. Steere more than tripled research spending, sold off noncore businesses, and developed a number of billion-dollar-plus blockbuster drugs, the most well known, of course, being Viagra.

Again, in retrospect Steere's decision seems obvious, but, it was far from certain to most people at the time.

3) **GREAT COMMUNICATIONS SKILLS.** In many ways, life is all about communicating. Nowhere is it more critical to be a strong communicator than in leading people or organizations. So, not surprisingly, one of the common traits among the 50 business leaders on our list is their ability to communicate well. The best business leaders can effectively explain business fundamentals, strategy, alternatives, and a course of action in ways that tap into employees' sense of meaning.

Audtodesk's Carol Bartz is one of the most effective communicators we interviewed. Bartz uses vivid images to illustrate the management principles she is trying to get across. She advises young people, for example, to seek the broadest possible career experience, in order to climb a "career pyramid rather than career ladder," explaining that a pyramid is much more stable than a ladder and provides people with a more secure base going forward.

Fannie Mae's Frank Raines is another leader with a particular gift for communication. Not only does his baritone voice and clarity of speaking have the rich timbre of a radio announcer, but he articulates the intricacies of his corporation—the world's largest financial services company ranked by assets—so clearly that even a layperson feels like an expert after Raines explains what Fannie Mae does and how it does it.

As Fred Smith of Federal Express told us, "Today, a great CEO must be a great communicator." The ability to communicate clearly also goes hand-in-hand with the previous trait we identified among these highly successful leaders—clarity of thinking.

4) **HIGH ENERGY LEVEL.** Being a CEO has never been more difficult. On average, the business leaders on our list work more than 65 hours a week. And the line between work and private life is becoming ever more blurry.

The physical strain of developing strategy, forging consensus, making decisions, building a management team, dealing with regulators, communicating with Wall Street analysts and institutional investors, lobbying the government, working with and informing the board of directors, serving on outside boards, and traveling extensively both domestically and internationally to meet with both customers and employees around the world requires enormous amounts of stamina.

Jack Welch's energy level, for example, is legendary, but he is not unique. As CEO, Gillette's Al Zeien traveled 250 days a year performing 800 personnel reviews a year. Cisco's John Chambers reviews customer reports 365 days a year. Lowe's Companies' Bob Tillman says that during a three-year period in which he led the company's ambitious change effort (a program that has underpinned the company's financial success and led to him attaining the top job), he did not take a vacation. He says he could not. "If any of the 128 action items didn't all come together, the company may have been history, and I certainly was history."

Elizabeth Dole has a quote from Teddy Roosevelt that hangs on her wall illustrating the energy level required of leaders that applies even more aptly today than when it was first written:

> We're face-to-face with our destiny. And we must meet it with a high and resolute courage, for ours is the life of action, of strenuous performance, of duty. Let us live in the harness of striving mightily. Let us run the risk of wearing out rather than rusting out.

To put in these kind of hours requires commitment, of course, but a good set of genes doesn't hurt. Some people are simply endowed with a higher energy level, and that seems to be the case with the vast majority of the leaders on our list.

Larry Bossidy, who arrives at the office each day at 7 A.M. and stays to about 7 P.M. on days that he does not have a business dinner, says that he finally figured out how to explain his own well-known energy level, drive, and competitiveness. "I recently realized that I'm just wired that way," says Bossidy, who frequently puts time in on weekends as well. "I'm just going to keep going and going and going until I can't go anymore. It's the same in business, on the golf course, and in other parts of my life. It's just the way I am."

5) **EGOS IN CHECK.** When you are the ultimate boss, it is tempting to take credit for the successes of your organization. This tendency is magnified by the increasingly starstruck media culture in which we live. The fact is it is only human nature for employees to lionize CEOs as they do their best to "manage" up.

Despite all of this adulation, we were struck by how *small* the egos of the leaders on our list were. Many were quite humble about what they have accomplished, crediting hard work, good timing, a healthy dose of luck, and the efforts of family members and colleagues for their success.

Scanning the list of leaders profiled in this book, AlliedSignal's Larry Bossidy remarked, "You don't see too many huge egos on the list. There used to be days when the people at the top 'knew everything.' Today, being a CEO is a humbling job. And the more you learn, the more you recognize every reason that you have to be humble, because the competitive environment is so fierce that there's so much more to do all the time. I think this attitude has made companies and executives better today than in the past."

Indeed, Don Fisher of The Gap cited his lack of ego as a primary reason why he and his company have been so successful. For others, avoiding the limelight is a matter of preference. Steve Case of America Online is one such example.

"In my case, it really is about believing that there is work to be done to build a medium [the Internet] that we can be proud of. It's not about so-called power, or visibility, or stature. Those are things that I don't particularly enjoy."

While Bob Tillman of Lowe's Companies agrees that being visible is important both inside and outside the company, in dealing with the financial community and the company's customer base, his first, second, and third reactions are the same: Any attention directed toward him personally is unnecessary embellishment, and he is against it. "You don't build or manage a business with one person," he said. "You have a team that does that. The more you highlight one person, the more it detracts from the whole team."

6) **INNER PEACE.** In reflecting back on all of our meetings with the leaders included in *Lessons from the Top*, another overwhelming conclusion we came to is that the most successful business leaders have a difficult to describe but nonetheless perceptible "solidity" to them. It feels good to be around them. It is no wonder that people—especially employees—are drawn to them and want to follow them.

We are *not* talking about charisma. Whether a person is naturally outgoing, like Southwest Airlines' Herb Kelleher or Campbell's David Johnson, or more naturally reserved, like P&G's John Pepper and Meredith's Bill Kerr, the desire to be around these leaders seems to stem from his or her own inner peace. The most successful leaders appear to be the *least* stressed. They are less frenetic, more self-aware, and more in harmony than the vast majority of people we've met. Having a sense of inner peace may seem counterintuitive, given the demands of the job. However, upon reflection, it makes sense. Scattered thinking wastes energy and saps motivation. It is far easier to focus and achieve what you want when you are calm. By taking time to stop and think each day and focus on the principles for enduring success, we can train ourselves to grow our inner peace.

7) CAPITALIZING ON FORMATIVE EARLY LIFE EXPERIENCES.

We cannot control who our parents are, what order we are born in, or what economic stratum we grow up in. But we can control *what we make* of our early life experiences. Another common trait among our leaders is how they drew upon the early life, family, and career circumstances they experienced.

Four of the leaders on our list grew up on farms and each attributed what they learned there as a partial explanation for their success. Johnson, Bartz, Hank Greenberg, and Caterpillar's Don Fites each cited the self-sufficiency, attention to detail, awareness of cause and effect, and the unwavering persistence required to run a farm successfully as key lessons that prepared them to succeed in business and life.

Several others on our list overcame significant learning disabilities. Both Charles Schwab and Cisco Systems' John Chambers could not properly assimilate information due to undiagnosed cases of dyslexia. However, the help of family and mentors, coupled with their own steely determination, allowed them to not only overcome this problem, but gain the confidence to set and achieve ambitious goals.

Others grew up in dire economic conditions. Ford's Alex Trotman, Starbucks' Howard Schultz, and MCI WorldCom's Bernie Ebbers felt that their work ethic and determination to succeed could be traced directly to growing up on the wrong side of the tracks. Ebbers, who grew up on a mission post on the Navajo Indian reservation, recalled that his most exciting holiday was the Christmas his sister received a deck of "Old Maid" cards, he received a deck of "Animal Rummy" cards, and the family enjoyed some peanut clusters given to them by the local dairy farmers for their Christmas dinner dessert.

Emerson Electric's Chuck Knight spoke about the impact of his father's decision to send him to work in a foundry in Canada when he turned 16 in order to learn about business. Lessons about the physical demands of such labor gave Chuck both a respect for, and fundamental understanding of, manufacturing work. Knight passed this same lesson on to his son, Lester B. Knight III, sending him off to do physical labor in a manufacturing company when he too was a young man. The younger Knight, now in his early forties, is CEO of Allegiance Corporation, a $4 billion medical supply company, and, like his father, is a high-performing business leader.

8) **STRONG FAMILY LIVES.** In America, it is well known that roughly one of every two marriages now ends in divorce. Yet, among the 50 business leaders on our list, there is an overwhelming degree of family stability. No less than 43 of the 50 are married to their original spouse. The vast majority have children and grandchildren.

More important than the mere statistics, however, many of these leaders cite the balancing effect of a strong family life and the quality of objective advice they get from an intelligent spouse as key ingredients in their success. Sandy Weill, for example, relies on his wife's judgments about people, often developed over business dinners, to help make recruiting decisions.

Enron's Ken Lay describes his marriage and his relationships with his children and grandchildren as his most significant accomplishment. Chase Manhattan's Walter Shipley solidified his own belief about playing to people's passions in the way that he supported his son to pursue his own long-held interest: teaching biology. "He is the best biology teacher I can imagine," Shipley says. "His students love him. He would be *miserable* in business. I am very proud of him."

Many leaders described the powerful effect of a parent who believed that they could achieve anything they set their minds to. Jack Welch, for example, cites the influence of his mother, Grace, as one of the key building blocks in his life. "She always felt I could do anything. 'Control your own destiny.' She always had that idea." AT&T's Mike Armstrong can still hear his mother's frequently spoken words—"Go for it"—in his mind as he pursues blockbuster deals to remake the telecommunications giant.

Elizabeth Dole also spoke about the impact her parents had in fueling her drive and giving her the confidence to pursue her dreams—despite the male-dominated conventions of the day when she was growing up in North Carolina. "They were both very conscientious people who felt, 'if it's worth doing, it's worth giving it your very best.'" Her mother, who today is 98, would give her little nudges and encouraging words, such as, "Elizabeth, you finished your homework early today. Have you thought about entering that essay contest?" Her father, who passed away in 1978, was, she says, "simply a man of his word. His word was his bond. It was such a wonderful upbringing to have parents who cared so much and who were always there for me."

Charles Heimbold, CEO of Bristol-Myers Squibb, mentioned his parents to us.

"It is important to me to talk about the strength that I took from my own family, specifically my parents. Both my mother and father are very hardworking, good people. I'd like them to know that I owe an enormous amount of debt to them for anything I've been able to accomplish. I think that there's an awful lot that one can say for the expression 'it takes a village to raise a child, but it truly starts with the family.' " While we cannot go back in time and re-create sage advice given to us by our parents, we can certainly employ this trait of success by urging our own children or other young people to set ambitious goals and put their hearts into accomplishing them.

9) **POSITIVE ATTITUDE.** Another trait we discovered that is shared by many of the business leaders profiled in this book is their positive attitude. As a general rule, the people included on our list tend to look at challenges as opportunities and seek to make the best out of difficult situations. Indeed, they learn from their mistakes and are thankful for the opportunity to try to make a difference.

The most poignant example of this came from Elizabeth Dole, who talked about turning horror into a source of strength and gratitude, during the time she was head of the American Red Cross.

"I saw things with the American Red Cross that will haunt me for the rest of my life. We visited Zaire, which is now the Congo, after a million Rwandans fled during the terrible bloodshed in Rwanda. They went to the worst possible place, Goma, Zaire, which is set upon pure volcanic rock. That's where the refugees stopped. They couldn't dig for latrines, so the cholera and dysentery became rampant. Nor could they dig for graves, so I was stepping over dead bodies. They were lining them up on the sides of the road and twice a day these trucks would carry them off to mass graves. In the midst of this misery, I remember a little boy sitting all by himself on a mound of dirt with thousands of people around, but nobody right there with him. As I looked at that child, nothing was moving except tears. And the tears were just leading a path down this dusty little face. So I sat down and I put an arm around him, just to try to console him. And nothing moved. Not an eyelash, not a muscle, nothing."

How did she deal with such trauma? "I told our people that we have been blessed to be a blessing. We've received that we might give."

MCI WorldCom's Bernie Ebbers, too, expresses deep gratitude for being able to lead his company. "For me, in my lifetime, to have an opportunity to participate in something like MCI WorldCom is unheard of. Every day I think about how fortunate I am to have been given this stewardship responsibility. For many CEOs, it can be easy to forget that it is the people that are working with us that really make us what we are."

Turning mistakes into learning experiences is a corollary of maintaining a positive attitude. Michael Dell said that since he was self-taught in forming and growing a business, he had a lot to learn and did so by experimenting and making mistakes. "One of the first things I learned," he said, "is that there was a relationship between screwing up and learning. The more mistakes I made, the faster I learned." And learn he did.

It is clear from meeting with the leaders on our list that they are individuals who share an astonishing sense of the possible. That attitude underpins the business strategies that they have developed to take advantage of the opportunities they see. Perhaps more importantly, great leaders teach attitude every single day. Their outlooks and commitment to capitalizing on, rather than punishing, mistakes helps give employees a sense of the possible. It also encourages risk taking and problem solving, which in turn leads to success for the organization and the leader.

10) **FOCUS ON "DOING THE RIGHT THINGS RIGHT."** Finally, as we have seen, the 50 leaders in this book all share a commitment to "doing the right things right."

We came into this project with the belief that the most successful leaders focus on the things that create great results, more than on the results themselves. This idea turned out to be more true than we had imagined. The traditional performance measures of financial, market share, or stock price results can be a leaders' primary focus in the short term. But great business leaders, those whose organizations are enduringly successful, achieve their results by focusing on the "right things" day in and day out:

1) Living with integrity and leading by example
2) Developing a winning strategy or "big idea"
3) Building a great management team
4) Inspiring employees to achieve greatness
5) Creating a flexible, responsive organization
6) Tying it all together with reinforcing management and compensation systems

* * *

By now, we hope that we have gone a long way toward answering the question posed by the corporate board member in Chapter 1 of Part I, "What should we be looking for in our next CEO?" More important, by profiling the best business leaders in America and drawing lessons learned, we hope that we have provided some tools and strategies for readers to apply in the ongoing quest for success and satisfaction.

Appendices

Appendix I
(Gallup Survey)

The first step in putting together the list of the 50 best business leaders in America, was to get nominees from their peers. Since we were trying to identify the best managers in America, we turned to the best research firm for help: the Gallup Organization.

The Gallup team interviewed 575 people for us—200 *Fortune 1,000* CEOs; 170 heads of companies on the *Inc. 500* (a ranking of the 500 fastest-growing, privately held companies in America); 88 people who run not-for-profit organizations with more than 100 employees; and, finally, 117 deans and presidents of major universities.

What follows are the survey questions Gallup asked these 575 people, along with the way Gallup presented those questions:

> We are conducting a survey among senior-level executives at corporations, academic institutions, and nonprofit groups in an effort to better understand what characteristics successful leaders among this range of organizations have in common.
>
> As you think about today's leaders of business, industry and organizations in the United States, who first comes to mind for each of the following areas:
> a) Long-term performance
> b) Visionary and strategic skills
> c) Ability to overcome challenges
> d) Organizational and people leadership
> e) Integrity and strength of character
> f) Demonstrable impact on an industry, business, or society

g) Track record of innovation
h) Entrepreneurial or pioneering spirit
i) Commitment to diversity
j) Exemplary customer focus

Finally, as you think of all the individuals you mentioned, which ONE executive comes to mind as most representing successful leaders overall?

What We Came Up With

This process generated a list of nominees from many different fields—business, of course, but also religion, sports, government, and nonprofit organizations.

Here are the nominations in their entirety. Everyone listed below was nominated in at least one of the 10 categories listed above.

CURRENT BUSINESS LEADERS

Paul Allaire, Xerox
Gordon Bethune, Continental Airlines
Larry Bossidy, AlliedSignal
Warren Buffett, Berkshire Hathaway
Ben Cohen, Ben & Jerry's
Stephen Covey, Covey Leadership Institute
Livio DeSimone, 3M
Michael Dell, Dell Computer
Robert Eaton, Daimler Chrysler
Bernie Ebbers, MCI WorldCom
Michael Eisner, Disney
Roger Enrico, Pepsi
George Fisher, Kodak
Steve Forbes, Forbes
Bill Gates, Microsoft
Lou Gerstner, IBM
David Glass, Wal-Mart
Leon Gorman, L.L. Bean
Jerry Greenfield, Ben & Jerry's
Andy Grove, Intel

Wayne Huizenga, Republic Industries
Steve Jobs, Apple Computer + Pixar Industries
Herb Kelleher, Southwest Airlines
Jim Kelly, United Parcel Service
Chuck Knight, Emerson Electric
Phil Knight, Nike
John Kroll, DuPont
Bernard Marcus, Home Depot
Bill Marriott, Marriott International
Hugh McColl, BankAmerica/NationsBank
Scott McNealy, Sun Microsystems
Ross Perot, Perot Systems
Lewis Platt, Hewlett-Packard
John Reed, Citigroup
John Pepper, Procter & Gamble
Howard Schultz, Starbucks
Fred Smith, Federal Express
John Smith, General Motors
Steven Spielberg, Dreamworks SKG
Dave Thomas, Wendy's

Alex Trotman, Ford
Donald Trump, Trump Enterprises
Ted Turner, Time Warner

Ted Waitt, Gateway Computer
Bill Walsh, San Francisco 49ers
Jack Welch, General Electric

RETIRED

Robert Allen, AT&T
Max DePree, Herman Miller
Al Dunlap, Sunbeam

John Galvin, Motorola
J. Whitacre, Nordstrom's

GOVERNMENT

Madeleine Albright, U.S. Secretary
of State
George Bush, Jr., Governor of Texas
George Bush, Sr., former President
of the United States

Bill Clinton, President of the United
States
Alan Greenspan, Chairman, U.S.
Federal Reserve

NONPROFITS

Elizabeth Dole, American Red Cross
Peter F. Drucker
Rev. Billy Graham

Rev. Jesse Jackson
Dave Mercer, YMCA

With this initial nominating list in hand, we set about trying to complement it with a groundbreaking analysis of corporate performance.

To help with that, we turned to Lazard Asset Management, a division of Lazard Frères & Co.

Appendix 2

(Financial Analysis Methodology)

From the very beginning we were committed to making *Lessons from the Top* more than a popularity poll. While the names gathered by the Gallup Organization were a critical part of the process, their results were only the beginning. We needed to establish that the people we ultimately selected had also had a *quantitative* effect on the organizations that they run—that by "doing the right things right," they got great results. In other words, we had to demonstrate that their contributions improved the financial performance of their organizations.

To do that, we turned to one of the best financial and investment managers in the world, Lazard Asset Management, a division of 150-year-old Lazard Frères & Co., a premier investment banking firm. Lazard Asset Management invests more than $62 billion in assets for its clients and employs over 100 research analysts and portfolio managers.

Lazard would need this breadth and depth of experience, given what we asked them to do. We challenged Lazard—specifically, managing director Michael Rome and vice president Jay Genzer, who runs Lazard's Asset Management's Risk Control Group—to determine the best financial measures to look at in order to evaluate a leader's contribution to his firm.

Michael and Jay examined all the existing financial yardsticks—everything from book value and return on equity to earnings per share growth and stock appreciation—looking for the measure that best captured a business leader's impact.

Finally, they concluded that there was not one number we should look at—but two:

1) Total return to shareholders—that is, stock appreciation plus the reinvested dividends that an investor receives
2) Growth in cash flow relative to a company's market value[1]

Their reasoning was intriguing.

The principal number that investors are concerned with is "total return." If an investor puts down $100 to buy a share of stock, and a year later the stock is selling for $115, and has paid $5 in dividends during those 12 months, the investor is pretty happy. He has gotten a 20% total return on his money (the $15 in stock appreciation, coupled with the $5 in dividends).

So why not just use one measure—total return to shareholders—and leave it at that? Because, as Michael and Jay were quick to explain, the number can be misleading.

Frequently, the stock price of a corporation will rise—sometimes dramatically—when a new CEO is named. Wall Street loves to anticipate change, and that anticipation frequently hits a fever pitch when a new CEO is appointed to run a sluggish company. That's great for shareholders, of course, *but it doesn't reflect anything that the manager has done yet*. It just reflects what Wall Street thinks he might do.

That is one reason why just using total return to shareholders can be misleading. Here is a second. The returns are highly dependent on the time period being measure. Lazard, therefore, wanted to add the second measure: Growth in cash flow relative to market value. It would give us another objective measure of performance.

With those two measures in hand, Lazard went about examining the largest 1,000 publicly traded corporations in the United States. Companies were ranked by total return on investment in the most recent five-year period and also on how well they scored when we took their cash flow, or NOPAT, and divided it by their market value, or beginning capi-

---

1. For the students of financial theory, let's explore the second measure—growth in cash flow relative to market value—in a bit more detail.

Lazard defines cash flow as net operating profit after taxes, or NOPAT: NOPAT = Net sales − cost of goods sold − selling and general administrative expenses − total income taxes + deferred income taxes and investment tax credit + depreciation.

NOPAT is the numerator of the equation. The denominator—market value—is the amount of market-weighted capital the corporation had at the beginning of the period under evaluation. Capital is defined as the enterprise value of the company, or shares outstanding × share price + long term debt + short term debt − cash.

Why beginning capital as opposed to average capital over a five-year period, or some other measure? Because the fairest way of judging the impact the manager has had is by looking at where he began and comparing it to where he finished.

APPENDIX 2: TABLE 1 - TOTAL ANNUALIZED SHAREHOLDER RETURNS AND CASH FLOW GROWTH RELATIVE TO MARKET VALUE

COMPANY(1)	INDUSTRY SECTOR	TICKER SYMBOL	ANNUALIZED RETURN (2) 1 year	5 years	CASH FLOW GROWTH (3) Ranking among 1,000
Procter & Gamble	Consumer Products	PG	16%	29%	425
Gillette	Consumer Products	G	−4%	28%	338
Campbell Soup	Consumer Products	CPB	6%	26%	538
Tyco International	Electrical/Diversified	TYC	68%	43%	32
General Electric	Electrical/Diversified	GE	41%	34%	612
AlliedSignal	Electrical/Diversified	ALD	16%	19%	464
Emerson Electric	Electrical/Diversified	EMR	9%	18%	452
Mobil	Energy	MOB	24%	21%	567
Enron	Energy	ENE	40%	17%	496
FPL Group	Energy	FPL	7%	14%	515
Charles Schwab	Financial Services	SCH	101%	65%	173
Chase Manhattan	Financial Services	CMB	32%	33%	300
Fannie Mae	Financial Services	FNM	31%	33%	375
Citigroup	Financial Services	C	7%	33%	23
American International Group	Financial Services	AIG	34%	30%	384
Merrill Lynch	Financial Services	MER	−7%	28%	121
Bear Stearns	Financial Services	BSC	−20%	18%	205
Herman Miller	Industrial	MLHR	−1%	30%	198
Aloca	Industrial	AA	8%	19%	276
Caterpillar	Industrial	CAT	−3%	18%	202
Deere	Industrial	DE	−42%	8%	266
America Online	Leisure/Entertainment	AOL	586%	134%	12
Meredith	Leisure/Entertainment	MDP	7%	32%	265
Marriott International	Leisure/Entertainment	MAR	6%	20%	497
Walt Disney	Leisure/Entertainment	DIS	−8%	17%	157
Ford Motor	Motor Vehicles	F	70%	27%	192
DaimlerChrysler	Motor Vehicles	DCX	35%	18%	272
Pfizer	Pharmaceuticals	PFE	69%	51%	381
Bristol-Myers Squibb	Pharmaceuticals	BMY	43%	40%	472
Merck	Pharmaceuticals	MRK	41%	37%	487
Johnson & Johnson	Pharmaceuticals	JNJ	29%	32%	390
Gap	Retail	GPS	138%	46%	335
Starbucks	Retail	SBUX	46%	38%	140

COMPANY(1)	INDUSTRY SECTOR	TICKER SYMBOL	ANNUALIZED RETURN (2) 1 year 5 years	CASH FLOW GROWTH (3) Ranking among 1,000
Lowe's	Retail	LOW	115% 29%	281
FDX	Service Industries	FDX	46% 20%	190
Dell Computer	Technology	DELL	249% 153%	6
Microsoft	Technology	MSFT	115% 69%	164
Cisco Systems	Technology	CSCO	149% 67%	174
Intel	Technology	INTC	69% 51%	80
IBM	Technology	IBM	77% 47%	726
Computer Associates	Technology	CA	−19% 29%	142
Autodesk	Technology	ADSK	16% 15%	671
MCI WorldCom	Telecommunications	WCOM	137% 43%	21
AT&T	Telecommunications	T	26% 20%	572
Continental Airlines	Transportation	CAL	−30% 27%	38
Southwest Airlines	Transportation	LUV	38% 7%	396
Average of 46 Companies			52% 35%	
S&P 500		SP50	27% 24%	
Nasdaq Index		COMP	40% 23%	
Dow Jones Industrial Average		DJII	16% 22%	

(1) Sorted by industry and five-year returns within industry; excludes private companies (Ingram Industries), subsidiaries (Ogilvy & Mather), and not-for-profit organizations (American Red Cross, Drucker) from list of companies in *Lessons from the Top*.
(2) Total Annualized Shareholder Return ending 12/31/98.
(3) Five-year growth of cash flow (i.e., net operating profit after tax for years 1998 and 1993) divided by 1993 company market value; ranking among largest 1,000 U.S. companies.

tal in the same five-year period.[2] The findings of this analysis are summarized in Table 1 above.

We now had three separate lists to work with: the one resulting from the Gallup survey; the first Lazard list, which ranked 1,000 companies by total return to the shareholders, and the second Lazard list, which ranked companies by cash flow growth relative to market value.

Obviously, we could not use the Lazard research to identify privately held or smaller companies or managers within government or nonprofit organizations. To come up with those names, we would be relying on the Gallup list, and the third part of our research triangle—the industry practice leaders at Spencer Stuart, as explained in Chapter 3 of Part I.

---

2. To make sure there was balance across industries, we divided the universe into 13 industry groups—consumer products, electrical/diversified, energy, financial services, industrial, leisure/entertainment, motor vehicles, pharmaceuticals, retail, service industries, technology, telecommunications, and transportation—and ranked the companies within each segment.

Appendix 3

(Interview Guide)

Soon after we committed to identifying and profiling 50 of America's very best business leaders, we had to determine exactly what we would ask them in our interviews. We needed to design a series of questions that would get these people to reflect, open up, and really explain why they have been so successful.

We spent an enormous amount of time to get the questions right. There were a number of reasons for that.

First, while everyone we interviewed was gracious, all were extremely pressed for time. We were only going to have them for a finite period, so it was imperative that we came away with a thorough understanding of what made these people so successful. As an absolute minimum, we needed to learn:

- How they think about difficult issues
- What is important to them about how they lead
- How all of this has helped their organizations' performance

Second, in many instances we were dealing with people who rarely gave interviews. While Elizabeth Dole and Herb Kelleher may have a better understanding of how to put together a magazine piece than most reporters, many of our leaders—such as David Johnson at Campbell Soup, John Pepper of P&G, and Chuck Knight of Emerson Electric—rarely answer questions from people writing books. We would have to take their reluctance into account, but still make sure we got the information we needed.

Third, the majority of the questions had to be the same for everyone. The basic premise of the book was that there is a series of principles that great business leaders follow that leads to outstanding performance. If that is right—and what you read hopefully proved that it is—then we would expect the answers to our questions to contain common themes. But the only way we could be sure was to ask everyone a common list of questions (adding several tailored to their unique circumstances, of course) and then analyzing and comparing their responses.

We divided up the interview guide into two major categories: leadership questions and questions about business.

Here, then, is the core list of questions in its entirety, followed by the questions unique to certain individuals.

Leadership Questions

1) What are the characteristics that make for a successful CEO today? Have these characteristics changed drastically in the last 10 or 20 years?
2) In looking ahead, what skills and characteristics will be most important for the company's next generation of leadership?
3) What are your most important principles for leadership and inspiring people? Do these principles change during different growth stages of a company?
4) How do you define success?
5) What are you most proud of in your career?
6) Who or what (e.g., mentors, books) have most influenced your thinking and philosophy?
7) What specifically do you look for in hiring or promoting people? Has this changed over time?
8) If you were advising your own children or young people on career strategy, what advice would you give?
9) How did your early family background contribute to your drive and success?

Business Questions

1) What was your vision for the company when you first became CEO? What is it today?
2) What are the two or three most important performance measures you use to manage the company? How do you tie rewards to these measures? Have these measures changed over time?
3) What are the company's most significant challenges over the next three years? What keeps you awake at night worrying? What are you doing about it?

4) Over the past 10 years, what have been the most pivotal points for the company and for you? What were the most important obstacles to overcome?

5) Given your experience and vantage point from competing in an increasingly global industry, how do American business leaders differ from those in other regions?

6) What have been the company's, and/or your, biggest business mistakes? What did you and the organization learn from them?

7) What is the ideal relationship between a CEO and the board of directors? What is the role of the board in developing strategy? Management development? Succession?

Different People Require Different Questions

As we said, we asked those 16 questions of everyone. But we also added several tailored questions for each individual. Here is a representative sampling of the unique questions we posed to our leaders.

MIKE ARMSTRONG, AT&T

- How is AT&T different today from just three years ago?
- How would you define AT&T's competitive positioning?
- What is the logic behind the TCI deal? What will be the key to successful integration?
- When you came in as CEO, you announced that you would neither talk with the press nor to Wall Street for a period of time until you developed your plan. Is this the best way for a new CEO to come into a company from the outside?
- One of the things that AT&T is best known for is its brand. What does the AT&T brand represent? How do you maintain its strength?

GORDON BETHUNE, CONTINENTAL AIRLINES

- What led you to believe that Continental was savable?
- How was the "Go Forward" strategy developed?
- How important were the J. D. Power awards for the marketing of Continental?
- How does running an airline differ from leading companies in other industries?

LARRY BOSSIDY, ALLIEDSIGNAL

- For those who are unfamiliar with the scope of AlliedSignal, could you give a brief overview of the company's lines of business and geographic breadth?
- How is AlliedSignal different today from when you became CEO in 1991?
- How would you define AlliedSignal's competitive positioning?
- What does your success as AlliedSignal's CEO suggest about GE as a training ground for top executive talent?
- What advice would you offer to new CEOs coming into a company from the outside?
- One of the things that AlliedSignal is best known for is its Six Sigma total quality management program. How did this program come into practice? What has the impact been?

STEVE CASE, AMERICA ONLINE

- How did you come to found AOL? What is your most cherished memory of the early stage of the company?
- What was your vision for AOL when the company was formed? What is it today?
- What will "the computer" look like in the year 2010? How will AOL fit into the landscape then?
- How would you describe AOL's culture? How do you make sure that people who the company recruits are good cultural fits?
- What role has "sibling rivalry" played in your success? (Note: Case's older brother Daniel is CEO of San Francisco–based investment banking firm Hambrecht & Quist.)

MICHAEL DELL, DELL COMPUTER

- How did you come to found Dell Computer? What was your vision in Dell's earliest days?
- One of the things that Dell is best known for is changing the game, that is, marketing, selling, and then distributing computers directly to the consumer. How did you develop this strategy?
- What prevents other companies from replicating your approach and threatening your consistently growing market share and healthy margins?
- How have you overcome the common trap of an entrepreneur outgrowing his ability to lead a large enterprise?
- Given that you have created a company and ownership stake of such extraordinary value, what continues to motivate you? Where does "the fire" come from?

ELIZABETH DOLE, AMERICAN RED CROSS

- How did you come to join the American Red Cross? How would you describe the transition from the public sector to leading a large not-for-profit organization?
- What is the mission of the American Red Cross? How have you set up the organization to accomplish this mission?
- How do you lead change in such a large and complex organization?
- In what ways is being an effective leader in government different from being an effective leader of a large not-for-profit? How do you suppose this differs from being an effective leader of a private sector company?
- What are your future plans? (Note: We conducted a follow-up interview on January 6, 1999, the day after Dole announced she was leaving the Red Cross to explore the idea of running for president.)

PETER DRUCKER

- What are the most important performance measures that *you* recommend for business leaders to manage their companies?
- What performance measures are most appropriate for not-for-profit organizations and indeed governments?
- What do you believe are the most important principles for inspiring people? How do these principles contrast between business and nonbusiness organizations?
- Have the characteristics that make for a successful leader changed dramatically in the last 10 or even 50 years? How?
- How would you evaluate U.S. companies' competitiveness in the global economy?

BERNIE EBBERS, MCI WORLDCOM

- What was your original vision for WorldCom? What is it today?
- One of the things that WorldCom is best known for is growing into one of the world's foremost telecommunications companies through its aggressive acquisitions. What has been the key to this success? How have you managed to outnegotiate your industry competitors? What has been the key to successful integration?
- What keeps you awake at night worrying and what are you doing about it? (Obviously, integrating the MCI transaction and upgrading its network have to be up there on the list.)

MICHAEL EISNER, WALT DISNEY

- Over the past 15 years, Disney has created a new entertainment paradigm—creating proprietary content and exploiting it across all conceivable platforms and channels of distribution. Is this the key to keeping Disney's leadership position *in the years ahead*? Can the "creative engine" continue to drive the company, given its current size?
- How would you define Walt Disney's competitive positioning?
- Who are your most formidable competitors?
- How would you describe *your* management style? How does managing and inspiring creative professionals differ from individuals in other businesses or functions?
- Given its influence on the world's children and families, Disney seems to be held to a higher standard. What are the implications—positive and negative—of that?
- What is your vision for how families in the United States and around the world will entertain themselves 10 years from now?

BILL GATES, MICROSOFT

- One of the things that Microsoft is best known for is relentless product development and a culture of innovation. What have been some of the innovations that never became widely known? What, in retrospect, was the craziest idea? What is one of your biggest ideas for the next five years?
- Given that you have created a company of such extraordinary value and have amassed the world's greatest fortune, what continues to motivate you? Where does "the fire" come from?
- For obvious reasons, some people have compared you with John D. Rockefeller. What do you make of this comparison? Which books or historical persons have most influenced your thinking and philosophy?
- Have Callaway golf clubs *really* helped your game? (Note: Gates appeared in a television commercial pitching Big Bertha clubs.)

LOU GERSTNER, IBM

- What are IBM's most significant challenges over the next three years? How is the company capitalizing on the Internet?
- What have been your principal strategies for leading the company in the different phases of your stewardship (e.g., turnaround, reorganization, and growth)? What points in time over the past five years have been *most* pivotal for IBM and for you?

RAY GILMARTIN, MERCK

- What was your process for developing the strategy for Merck after you were named CEO? How did you achieve organizational buy-in?
- How have you approached "filling Roy Vagelos's very large shoes"? (Note: Vagelos was the well-known and beloved CEO immediately prior to Gilmartin.)

ACE GREENBERG, BEAR STEARNS

- Bear Stearns is well known for managing risk. What is the greatest business risk you and the firm have taken? What management and compensation systems have you put in place to manage risk and reinforce desired behavior?

HANK GREENBERG, AIG

- One of the things that you are best known for is managing a decisive, tight, and well-organized enterprise. How have you—and indeed the company—adapted to a more questioning attitude of professionals and workers in today's information society?

CHARLES HEIMBOLD, BRISTOL-MYERS SQUIBB

- Given Bristol-Myers Squibb's international scope (almost half of the company's revenues come from outside the United States), how would you describe how American managers differ from those in other regions? What is the key to a globalization strategy?
- Could you describe some of Bristol-Myers Squibb's more significant new product development and marketing initiatives? What are the similarities and difference in successful new product development across your medicines, beauty care, and nutritional and medical devices businesses?
- How do you get a $16 billion, 50,000-employee company to act quickly?

MARTHA INGRAM, INGRAM INDUSTRIES

- How did you make the transition to CEO after your husband's death in 1996? What was your vision for Ingram Industries when you became CEO? What is it today?
- Given Ingram Book Group's business and having helped put Amazon.com in business, you have a unique perspective on Internet commerce. What do you believe are the keys to success in the new and rapidly changing electronic commerce industries?

- Given Ingram Micro's and Ingram Entertainment's businesses, what are the keys to success in today's electronics and home video industries? What is the key to success in running a distribution company?
- How does success in running a private company contrast from success in running a public company? What can public company CEOs learn from private company CEOs?
- What advice do you have for sustaining family businesses over long periods of time?
- What role did Vassar College play in your intellectual development?

BILL KERR, MEREDITH

- What are Meredith's core values, strengths, and most significant challenges?
- What has been the key to successfully developing new magazine properties?

CHUCK KNIGHT, EMERSON ELECTRIC

- Describe Emerson Electric's famous "management process."
- How important is maintaining the company's record-breaking string of quarterly profit improvements?
- Do you believe that different management styles are required for different organizational situations (e.g., early stage, rapid growth, turnaround)?

RALPH LARSEN, JOHNSON & JOHNSON

- What are the similarities and differences in successful new product development across your consumer products, professional products, and pharmaceutical businesses?
- How did Johnson & Johnson's Credo lay the groundwork for the now well-known crisis-management response to the Tylenol scare? How does it affect how you manage day to day?

KEN LAY, ENRON

- What are some of your most cherished memories from the early stages of your career in the energy business? In the U.S. government?
- Enron is perhaps best known for being "the investment bank" of the energy business. How did this come to be? What are the implications of the approach for the company? For this industry?

SHELLY LAZARUS, OGILVY & MATHER

- What advertising campaigns are the firm's most memorable, in terms of creativity and impact on your clients' business?
- How was the IBM e-business strategy and campaign created? What insights has this process given you and the firm about the nature of electronic commerce?
- One of the things that Ogilvy & Mather and you in particular are best known for is developing global brands (e.g., IBM, Ford). What are the keys to successful global brand development?
- How do you make sure that people who the company recruits are good cultural fits? What interview questions have proved the most helpful in determining fit?
- As a woman CEO, you are by definition serving as a role model for millions of women in business. Do women business leaders differ from men? What advice do you have for women hoping to achieve their aspirations in business?

BILL MARRIOTT, MARRIOTT INTERNATIONAL

- How did Marriott make the transition from a small hotel company into the world's preeminent hospitality and services company?
- Why did Marriott successfully make this transition over the years while many of the other companies faltered?
- Perhaps the thing that Marriott is best known for is customer service. How did this value become so firmly entrenched into the company? How is it reinforced, managed, and rewarded?
- How will Marriott compete in the drastically consolidating hospitality market? How does Marriott's culture and values help *and impede* the company's ability to compete in an industry where deal-making and gaming are so critical for success?

LOU NOTO, MOBIL (NOTE: INTERVIEW WAS CONDUCTED PRIOR TO MOBIL'S ANNOUNCED ACQUISITION BY EXXON)

- Describe the process you used to put in place Mobil's vision after becoming CEO in 1994. How did you get people involved? How critical was this process to Mobil's success?
- Given your own international experience (21 years outside the United States), what is the key to a globalization strategy?
- Could you describe some of Mobil's more significant marketing initiatives and their implications for the company (e.g., bringing back the flying horse logo, Speed Pass)?

- Mobil has long been known for speaking out on controversial issues as a corporate communications strategy. How did this strategy come to be? What has the impact been?

JOHN PEPPER, PROCTER & GAMBLE

- When you joined the company in 1963, what would you have given as the odds for spending your next 35 years with the company?
- One of the things that you are best known for is driving the company internationally. What have been some of the lesser known international initiatives? What, in retrospect, was the craziest idea?

FRANK RAINES, FANNIE MAE

- How did you come to join and *rejoin* Fannie Mae?
- How has the organization managed to strike such a balance between profitability, growth, and public service?
- In what ways is being an effective leader in government different from being an effective corporate leader?
- One of the things that Fannie Mae is most respected for is its commitment to diversity. Given your own almost unique position as an African American leading one of the nation's largest companies, what are your views on diversity? How did your own philosophy on this subject develop? What lessons learned can you offer to other business leaders?

CHARLES SCHWAB, CHARLES SCHWAB

- How did your early family background (including battling dyslexia) contribute to your drive and lay the foundation for your career?
- When you sold the company to Bank of America in 1980, what did you think you were going to do? What would you have given as the odds of buying back the company?
- One of the things that you are best known for is vision and innovation. What's your biggest idea for the next 10 years?
- What role is the Internet having on Schwab's business and on the investment business in general?

WALTER SHIPLEY, CHASE MANHATTAN

- What are Chase's strategies to excel in the globally consolidating financial services marketplace?
- You are well known for successfully integrating many large mergers and

acquisitions (e.g., Texas Commerce Bank, Manufacturers Hanover, and Chemical Bank/Chase Manhattan). What are the keys to making it work?

FRED SMITH, FDX (FEDERAL EXPRESS)

- The story of the founding of Federal Express—based on your senior economics thesis (for which you received a gentleman's C)—is legend. Is the story true?
- You are one of a number of well-known entrepreneurs (including Gates, Dell, and Schwab) who have grown your company from start-up to enduring great company. How did you overcome the common trap of an entrepreneur outgrowing his ability to lead a large enterprise?
- One of the things that FedEx is best known for is changing the game and creating a new industry. What are the *principles* for creating breakthrough strategies (i.e., the right "big idea" for the right time)?
- Given FedEx's business, you have a unique perspective on Internet commerce. What do you believe are the keys to success in the new and rapidly changing electronic commerce industries?

BOB TILLMAN, LOWE'S COMPANIES

- How is Lowe's segmenting the home-improvement market among baby boomers, generation X-ers, and between men and women?
- How are you differentiating yourself from Home Depot and your other competitors?

ALEX TROTMAN, FORD

- How did you first learn about the auto business? As a 43-year veteran of Ford, how have you managed to bring "an outsider's perspective" and lead the company's transformation?
- How does the Daimler-Chrysler merger change the auto industry landscape?
- Given your Scottish citizenship, early experience running Europe, and vantage point from competing globally, how would you describe how American executives differ from those in other regions?

DAN TULLY AND DAVID KOMANSKY, MERRILL LYNCH

- How did Merrill make the transition from retail wire house to fully integrated investment bank? Why did Merrill successfully make this transition while the others have faltered?
- Perhaps the thing that Merrill is best known for is its powerful retail

brokerage network. What has been the key to its success? What initiatives for leveraging this network never became widely known?
- From your perspective, how will Merrill compete in the dramatically consolidating financial services market?

MICHAEL VOLKEMA, HERMAN MILLER

- Every company talks about the importance of values. What is the key to making values more than just talk at Herman Miller?
- What are some examples of how Herman Miller's core beliefs have translated into action?
- How is telecommuting impacting office furniture design and therefore your business?
- How do you make suppliers, dealers, and designers partners in the company's success? What is the most important thing about successfully managing creative/design people?
- Could you describe some of Herman Miller's most interesting, unusual, or surprising new products under development?

SANDY WEILL, CITIGROUP

- What are some of your most cherished memories from the early stages of your career with Burnham & Company and Loeb Rhodes?
- What was the spark that created the idea to merge with Citicorp? How did you act on the idea? Have the reactions of competitors, regulators, stockholders, or other constituent groups surprised you?
- What is your philosophy about compensation systems and tying pay to performance?

JACK WELCH, GENERAL ELECTRIC

- What have been the key points during your tenure? What were the most important obstacles to overcome?
- How do you manage change? What did it take to transition from managing the business through restructuring in the early 1980s to managing for growth in the late 1980s up to the present?
- In looking ahead to your retirement in 2000, what skills and characteristics will be most important for your successor?
- GE is well known for developing among the best managerial and leadership talent in the global economy. How and why has this come about?

AL ZEIEN, GILLETTE

- How do you define the industry in which Gillette competes?
- One of the things that Gillette is best known for is its global branding and management. What is the key to making this work?
- How do you keep in touch with Gillette's far-flung global organization?
- Will you forgive us if we organize our chapters about each business leader alphabetically?

ACKNOWLEDGMENTS

The Making of *Lessons from the Top*

"WRITE THE BOOK YOU WANT TO READ."

This was the advice of Bruce Judson, a friend of Spencer Stuart and author of the bestselling books *Net Marketing* (Wolff, 1996) and *HyperWars* (Scribner, 1999).

We were talking about Bruce's advice in April 1997 when an idea came to us. The book that we would love to read, and therefore write, would be a book that identified and profiled the nation's most successful business leaders. This book would unlock the true nature of these people, and bring them to life so that not only would we learn about them, we would learn what makes them great.

Analytical underpinnings would be key. In order to buy into and learn from the life stories of the business leaders that we wanted to read about, we had to be certain that there was a quantitative, fact-based analysis that justified reading about them in the first place. We had no doubt that the stories would be interesting, but we wanted to make sure that there was a fundamental reason for reading them.

We realized we were in the right place to put together an ambitious book of this kind. Spencer Stuart is in the business of identifying and recruiting outstanding business leaders for our clients every time we undertake an executive search or set off to find the appropriate person to join their board of directors.

What better marriage of our profession—and our budding literary aspirations—than to write the book we were so interested in reading? We were fortunate to have access to substantial resources—our colleagues at

Spencer Stuart and our network of relationships—to help us put all the pieces of the puzzle into place.

The process of writing this book has been a tremendous learning experience for us.

Rather than simply acknowledging the many contributors to this project, we thought it would be more interesting—and perhaps even enlightening to anyone who has ever wondered how a book gets made—to thank them in a way that tells the story of how this book came to be. So what follows, if you will, is *The Making of Lessons from the Top.*

We Get to Work

After fleshing out our initial ideas, we solicited—and received—the enthusiastic support of a wide range of our Spencer Stuart colleagues, whose encouragement we deeply appreciate.

We then contacted our alma mater, McKinsey & Company, where we both had been consultants early in our careers, to get advice on best publishing practices. We are grateful to three of their partners—Bill Mattasoni, Dolf DiBiasio, and Tim Koller—for their advice. Tim, in fact, was an early contributor to the "doing the right things right" concept that is a core part of this book.

One important decision we made during the research process was to develop a survey to solicit nominations for the most successful business leaders. Who better to design and conduct the survey we needed than the Gallup Organization, the world's leading market research and polling firm? We were introduced to Gallup by our friend and client, Mark Wright, founder, chairman, and CEO of @Plan, a leading internet advertising planning service. We would like to thank Cal Martin, Gallup senior vice president; Debra Christenson, Ph.D., research consultant; and Laura Bishop for their help.

Perhaps our deepest acknowledgment goes to Michael Rome, managing director at investment bankers Lazard Frères & Co. Michael oversees Lazard's U.S. asset management business. From the very start, Michael, along with his colleague, Jay Genzer, vice president of Lazard Asset Management's Risk Control Group, were committed to bringing in-depth analysis of corporate performance to this project, so that our book would be more than a popularity poll. Rather than simply providing data, Michael and Jay set about to develop a better model for evaluating corporate performance.

And that's exactly what they did.

They came up with the methodology described in both Chapter 3 of Part I and in Appendix 2 that combines an analysis of management performance with the financial market's recognition of that performance.

When we asked Michael and Jay why they might be willing to invest a couple of man-years into this project, they said that they believed that when used in concert, these two measures of corporate performance could potentially serve as a new and effective investment tool.

The Idea Takes Shape

With our research under way, we drew on the help of many colleagues. We would like to thank Susan Hart, Betty Hudson, Alice Cihon, Karin Pariselli, Joanna Faso, and Jason Baumgarten for their help.

Outside of the Firm, we are grateful to Leanna Landsmann, president of *Time Magazine for Kids*, who introduced us to Byron Reimus. Byron, a communications consultant and student of leadership, worked tirelessly with us over many months, researching the state-of-the-art thinking about business leadership and helping us develop our proposal and early drafts of key sections. As with any outstanding consultant, Byron challenged our thinking, as well as helped drive the project forward.

A key step in any publishing process is securing an agent. But how does one go about finding one, much less a good one? We presented this question to Ann Kirschner, who directs all Internet initiatives for Columbia University, who introduced us to Lorraine Shanley, a principal with Market Partners International, a New York publishing consulting firm. After identifying various agents who might be right for this project, Lorraine narrowed down the list to three finalists and introduced us to Rafe Sagalyn, head of the Sagalyn Literary Agency in Bethesda, Maryland.

While we were impressed by Rafe's track record in representing the authors of *In Search of Excellence, Megatrends,* and *Future Perfect,* and by the fact that he is a successful author in his own right, it was his reputation for adding value along the entire publishing process that really sold us. And Rafe more than lived up to his reputation. He helped shape our proposal, marketed the project, and most significantly introduced us to Roger Scholl and his dedicated team at Currency/Doubleday, who have been our partners ever since.

We also need to offer a special thanks to John A. Byrne, *Business Week's* management editor, who we had met in a different guise. More than anyone, John is responsible for raising the entire profile of the executive recruiting industry. His first book, *The Headhunters,* was the first to truly explain what Spencer Stuart and the other recruiting firms do. John introduced us to Paul B. Brown, author of such bestsellers as *Customers for Life* and *Grow Rich Slowly.* Throughout the project, Paul, who was our writer for this project, showed the ability of translating our thoughts—and the interview transcripts with our leaders—into crisp, clear words and phrases.

The Interview Phase

Arranging and executing 50-plus interviews with some of the most sought-after business leaders in America is a major undertaking in its own right. We received support from a wide range of people that we also want to acknowledge here.

We would like to thank Harold Citrin of Bear-Stearns, who arranged our meeting with Ace Greenberg, and George Sarner also at Bear-Stearns, who introduced us to Merrill Lynch's Dan Tully, who in turn facilitated our meeting with David Komansky; Irwin Ettinger, who helped arrange the Sandy Weill interview; David Silfen, Irwin Russell, and John Dreyer, who helped set up our meeting with Michael Eisner; and Bill Anderson, Ron Penoyer, and Carter Dunkin, all of Fleishman Hillard, St. Louis, and Nancy Wulf, Emerson Electric's director of Investor Relations, who accompanied us to Traverse City, Michigan, to spend the day at the summer home of Chuck Knight.

The others who helped facilitate our meetings and fact checking are the following: Kathy Bushkin at America Online; Joyce Hergenhan at GE; Karen Denne at Enron; Curt Linke of Deere; Kathy Tom-Engle at Autodesk; David Fausch at Gillette; Mark Greenberg at AlliedSignal; Michele Moore and Patty Rowell at Dell Computer; Yvonne Barazi and Stuart Maclarin at the American Red Cross; Mike Morrison at Daimler-Chrysler; Deborah Blackwell and Frank Walter at MCI WorldCom; Sabina Hancher and Laura Satersmoen at The Gap; Dick Stober at Caterpillar; Mark Harris and John Iwata at IBM; John Wooster at AIG; Pam Pollace; Robert Panetta, and Tom Woldrop at Intel; John Skule and Nancy Goldfarb at Bristol-Myers Squibb; Art Slusark at Meredith; Bill Nielsen at Johnson & Johnson; Nora Slattery at Ogilvy & Mather; Charlotte Sterling and Tom Marder at Marriott International; Bob O'Leary at Mobil; Charlotte Otto at Procter & Gamble; Kate Franklin at Fannie Mae; Hugo Quackenbush and Nicole Young at Charles Schwab; Nancy Kent at Starbucks; Lou Clemente at Pfizer; Brian Peace and Jule Schreffler at Lowe's; Charles Snearly at Ford Motor; and Mark Schurman and Bruce Buursma at Herman Miller.

We are also appreciative of Bob Herbold, Microsoft's chief operating officer, and Greg Maffei, chief financial officer, who helped arrange for our interview with Bill Gates. We also worked extensively with Dean Katz, Wendy Geller, and John Pinette to get the Gates interview done. Additionally, we are grateful to Phil Pfeffer for introducing us to Martha Ingram.

Once each interview was completed, we had our tapes transcribed. Over the course of the project, approximately 2,000 pages were typewritten, and we are grateful to Betsy Bowen for her outstanding transcription services. We would also like to thank Gary Mathews for reading the "Lessons Learned" section and offering helpful suggestions. In addition, we would like to acknowledge Yahoo! Finance and Hoover's Online, which provided certain company information and was a model of accuracy and ease of use. We are grateful to Pasquale "Pat" Arbitrio, who updated the company and leader information for the paperback edition.

No one deserves greater recognition, however, than Karen Steinegger of Spencer Stuart's Stamford office. Karen supported all phases of the project as if it were her own, from arranging all the logistics of each meeting, to proofreading and commenting on each chapter as it was drafted, to serving as a liaison with each of the executives' offices, to performing supporting research, to working on a daily basis with Paul and us in the development of the manuscript. We are forever indebted to her contribution, partnership, and friendship.

Of course, none of this would have been possible without the encouragement of our families. Sally Neff and Gail Citrin were both sounding boards and constructive critics of the project as it progressed, making sure that we remained connected to the reader's perspective at all times. They were truly our source of continuous support. The Neffs' five children, David, Mark, Brooke, Bailey, and Scott, were also enthusiastic about the project from their various schools and universities. And from Jim's perspective, there was no greater pleasure than relating stories from the interviews to Teddy (eleven), Oliver (nine), and Lily Citrin (six), who showed a surprising appetite to learn about the book and the great business leaders that we met along the way. So there you have it. This is how the book came to be. *Lessons from the Top* truly has been a collaborative adventure.

Index

ABOUT THE AUTHORS

Thomas J. Neff is Chairman of Spencer Stuart in the United States and has been with the firm since 1976. His consulting practice focuses on chief executive officer recruiting, board of director searches, and succession counseling.

He has worked in a variety of industry sectors, including consumer products, industrial, financial services, telecom, aviation, and life sciences. Neff's notable CEO searches include AT&T, Campbell Soup Company, Delta Air Lines, Dun & Bradstreet, IBM, JCPenney, Levi Strauss, Merck & Company, Prudential Insurance, Quaker Oats Company, *Reader's Digest*, RJR Nabisco, Tenneco, and United Airlines.

Neff, hailed by the *Wall Street Journal* as "The No. 1 Brand Name in CEO Searches," has been the subject of numerous profiles, including cover stories in *Business Week* and the Sunday Business Section of the *New York Times*.

Prior to joining Spencer Stuart, Neff was a Principal in executive search with Booz, Allen & Hamilton. Previously, he was the CEO of an information systems company. He has also held senior marketing positions with TWA and with a firm serving the package goods industry. Earlier, he was a management consultant with McKinsey & Company in the New York and Melbourne, Australia, offices.

Neff serves on the boards of ACE Ltd., Exult, Inc., and the Lord Abbett & Company, and is a Trustee of Lafayette College.

With an M.B.A. from Lehigh University and a B.S. degree in industrial engineering from Lafayette College, he served as an officer and aide-de-camp in the U.S. Army.

He lives in Greenwich, Connecticut, with his wife, Sally, and their five children.

James M. Citrin is Managing Director of Spencer Stuart's Global Internet Practice and a member of the firm's worldwide Board of Directors. In addition to specializing in searches for CEOs of Internet companies, Citrin has recruited over 150 top executives to entertainment, publishing, and hospitality companies. Major placements include the CEOs and top executives of *Reader's Digest*, Primedia, Forbes.com, Barnesandnoble.com, Penguin Group, Discovery Communications, The Motley Fool, Scholastic, RSL Communications, ClubMom, Eastman Kodak, Holiday Inn Worldwide, Starwood Hotels & Resorts Worldwide, Inc., and the John and Mary Markle Foundation.

Citrin has published articles on leadership and corporate governance in the *New York Times, Strategy & Business, Directors and Boards Magazine*, and other publications. He has been widely interviewed on these topics on NBC, CNBC, CNN, National Public Radio, USA Radio Network, and Voice of America, among others.

Prior to joining Spencer Stuart in January 1994, Citrin was Director of Corporate Planning at *Reader's Digest* and before that was a Senior Engagement Manager with McKinsey & Company in the United States and France. Earlier, he was an Associate with Goldman, Sachs & Company, and before attending graduate business school, a Financial Analyst with Morgan, Stanley & Co., Inc. A graduate and member of the Board of Trustees of Vassar College, Phi Beta Kappa, with a B.A. degree in economics (1981), Citrin obtained an M.B.A. from Harvard Business School (1986), where he graduated with distinction. He is a member of the Board of the Harvard Business School Club of New York and is a Senior Advisor with Maveron Equity Partners and ClubMom.

Citrin lives in New Canaan, Connecticut, with his wife, Gail, and their three children, Teddy, Oliver, and Lily.

A former writer and editor for *Business Week, Forbes, Financial World* and *Inc., Paul B. Brown* is the author of several business bestsellers, including *Customers for Life* (written with Carl Sewell, Doubleday/Currency), which has been translated into fifteen languages and has sold more than 800,000 copies worldwide. Brown lives with his son and daughter on Cape Cod Bay.

October 10, 2000